Buddhism and Ireland

Buddhism and Ireland
From the Celts to the
Counter-Culture and Beyond

Laurence Cox

SHEFFIELD UK   BRISTOL CT

Published by Equinox Publishing Ltd
UK: Unit S3, Kelham House, 3 Lancaster Street, Sheffield S3 8AF
USA: ISD, 70 Enterprise Drive, Bristol, CT 06010

www.equinoxpub.com

First published 2013

British Library Cataloguing-in-Publication Data

A catalogue record for this book is available from the British Library.

Library of Congress Cataloging-in-Publication Data

Cox, Laurence.
Buddhism and Ireland: from the Celts to the counter-culture and beyond /
Laurence Cox.
    pages cm
Includes bibliographical references and index.
ISBN 978-1-908049-29-2 (hb) — ISBN 978-1-908049-30-8 (pb)
1. Buddhism — Ireland — History. I. Title.
BQ709.I732C69 2013
294.309415 — dc23
                    2012046464

Typeset by S.J.I. Services, New Delhi
Printed and bound by Charlesworth Press, Wakefield, West Yorkshire, UK

Contents

Illustrations

Acknowledgements

This book would not have been possible without the generous help of many individuals and groups. Particular thanks go to my research assistant and co-author of earlier pieces, Maria Griffin, for the initial research and conversations which made a history of Buddhism and Ireland possible in the first place. Special thanks are due to Brian Bocking, who has contributed hugely to this project in very many ways.

One of the pleasures of the scholar's quest is the encounter with others who can offer insight in an unfamiliar area, and their generosity in doing so. Thanks are due to Philip Almond, Martin Baumann, Mary Cahill, Frances Comerford, Richard Cox, Wendy Cox, John L. Crow, Paddy Dooher, Terry Fagan, Fergal Finnegan, Fiona Fitzsimons, Brian Gurrin, Michael Holland, Michelle Hubert, Wendy Jermyn, David Landy, Joseph Lennon, Shane McCausland, John L. Murphy, Sandra Noel, David Oakley, Thomas O'Connor, Rachel Pisani, Hilary Richardson, Cristina Rocha, Elizabeth Rowen, Oliver Scharbrodt, Gaynor Sekimori, Yoshinaga Shin'ichi, Mihirini Sirisena, Andrew Skilton, Andrew Slibney, Alicia Turner, Thomas Tweed, Mike Tyldesley, Eilis Ward, Sinéad Ward, Audrey Whitty, Joe Wilson and Hans-Bernd Zöllner, as well as to three anonymous reviewers.

Among Buddhists, thanks are due to: Akshobin of the Dublin Buddhist Centre; Bill Burns of the Celtic Buddhism lineage; Julian Campbell; Iain Foster of the Samatha Association; James Moynes of the Irish Zen Group; Eugene Kelly of the Insight Meditation Group; Lalitavira of the Dublin Buddhist Centre; Sinéad Lynch of Soka Gakai; Louise Marchant of the Buddhist Society, London; Anna Mazzoldi; Bernard Murphy; Nyanatusita of the Buddhist Publication Society; John O'Neill of Kagyu Samye Dzong; Marjo Oosterhoff of Passaddhi Meditation Centre; Matt Padwick of Rigpa Ireland; Pavara of the Dublin Buddhist Centre; Andrew Peers of the

Order of the Longing Look; Seonaidh Perks of the Celtic Buddhism lineage; Sanghapala of the Dublin Meditation Centre; John Sharkey; Rachel Stanley; Ani Tsondru of Kagyu Samye Dzong; Órfhlaith Tuohy; and Chris Whiteside of Dzogchen Beara, all of whom gave generously of their time and knowledge. I hope they find the result worthwhile. Thanks also to Arthur Leahy of Cork's Quay Co-op and Ciaron O'Reilly of Dublin Catholic Worker.

Thanks are due to Bernie Gardiner and many other staff at the Library, NUI Maynooth, the staff of Drumcondra Public Library and TCD librarian Sandra Watkins. Seán Ó Riain and Jane Gray at NUIM Department of Sociology gave valuable practical assistance to the project. Thanks also to Catherine Friedrich. Janet Joyce, Valerie Hall, Norma Beavers and Tristan Palmer at Equinox were very helpful in the book's production. Many thanks are due to everyone who helped with sourcing images, particularly where I have not been able to use the results for various reasons.

This book was first drafted in the late Springhall Waldorf kindergarten in Jobstown, west Dublin, and thanks are due to Mary, Leslie, Kerstin and Mathia. At the time I was heavily involved in setting up another Waldorf kindergarten in the Seomra Spraoi social centre. These experiences underlined the practical and interpersonal realities of organising alternative institutions in Ireland, and the worlds of ideas and life choices through which participants in such movements operate. I hope the reader will find that the book has been enriched by these insights.

Lastly, my thanks and apologies to anyone I have overlooked.

Dedication

The joy and heartbreak of writing about a new (if minor) field are one and the same: the laborious piecing-together of material of different kinds, and the emotionally exhausting work of attempting to process, organise, assimilate and ultimately make sense of that material. Chapter two mentions Samuel Purchas' seventeenth-century compilation of all known travellers' tales: at four and a quarter million words, he assembled so much material that it was a quarter of a millennium before anyone republished it. At times I have felt like Purchas.

I hope, though, that the final result is illuminating in its framework and enjoyable in its stories – as well, perhaps, as inspiring in the possibilities it suggests. It has been a privilege to share the past five years with such remarkable Irish people, even if in spirit only, and to reach back and take U Dhammaloka, Maurice Collis, Vivian Butler-Burke or Lobzang Jivaka by the hand.

This book was made possible by the unwilling absence of my daughter, Alannah, and the support of her mother Órfhlaith. It has also benefitted greatly from discussions with my own father, Richard Cox, as he traced his own father's history and reflected on the impossibility of recovering past experience *wie es eigentlich gewesen* (R. Cox 2009).

It is conventional to dedicate Buddhist books to the happiness of all beings. As a father, however, I have a particular responsibility for the happiness of one being. This book is dedicated to Alannah Pema, who at age three was worried that too much meditation might turn her mother into a Buddha statue. I hope that in future years she may find this book some compensation for her father's absences. May she inherit a better Ireland.

Laurence Cox
Dublin, July 2013

Chapter One

Buddhism in Ireland: An Introduction to the Problem

The history of Buddhism and Ireland is at times tenuous, but it is not short. From the seventh century if not the sixth, accounts of Buddhism by Europeans circulated in Ireland and the broader Irish world continuously, though often with a considerable time lag. The distribution and quality of this information expanded greatly from the mid-thirteenth century, and again from the sixteenth century. In the nineteenth century in particular, Irish people became part of the process of *producing* knowledge about Buddhist Asia via the British Empire, missionary work and Orientalist scholarship.

Between the 1860s and the 1950s, a number of individual Irish people 'went native' in Buddhist Asia or privately identified as Buddhist in Ireland. The first known (anonymous) Buddhists in Ireland appear in the 1871 census; the first (named) Irish Buddhists arrived in Japan in the 1860s and Ceylon in 1889; the first ordination, in Burma, came in 1900. The first talk by a Buddhist in Ireland was in 1889; the first visit by ordained (Asian) Buddhists in 1925 and the first explicitly Buddhist event in 1929.

Popular myth assumes that 'real' Irish people are always Christian and other religious affiliations are recent or foreign. Reality is more complex. Throughout the formative period of contemporary Irish culture – the years of Land War and independence, of Catholic revival and Celtic Renaissance – a handful of Irish people were exploring alternative paths to either the defence of Protestant Ascendancy or Catholic nationalism; paths which, at the start of the twenty-first century, may perhaps seem more like missed opportunities than historical mistakes.

After a hiatus, the 1960s and 1970s saw a developing counter-cultural interest, which led to formal Buddhist institutions from the late 1970s on. Buddhist teachers trained abroad arrived from the 1990s on, founding a second wave of institutions. From the later 1990s in particular, new immigrant groups brought their own

Buddhisms. By the early twenty-first century, Buddhism is relatively established as part of Irish society: the third-largest world religion in the 2006 census, Buddhists make up 0.2% of the population of the Republic, roughly in line with other European countries.

This book outlines and analyses this history. In the process, it highlights some features of Irish culture and society which are particularly significant for the development of Buddhism; it also raises broader theoretical and methodological issues for the study of Buddhism in the west.

The academic study of religion involves problematising what is usually taken for granted, and this chapter touches on a series of such questions. Readers unfamiliar with these sometimes complex issues may find it more rewarding to turn straight to the historical analysis of Buddhism and Ireland from chapter two on.

A Bird's-eye View of Buddhism and Ireland

While this book contains much 'what' and 'why', in the form of empirical data and theoretical analysis, there is less of the conventional 'how', in the sense of analysing what people have *meant* by Buddhism in Ireland. The major reason for this is that Irish peripherality has meant that there has never been a single, central discourse (or debate) about Buddhism located within Ireland. Rather, the various 'Buddhisms' within Ireland have mostly related outwards, to a range of different processes whose centres were located elsewhere. Irish Buddhism, in that sense, is a window on a much wider world: Buddhist Asia, western social movements, and global processes of exchange.

Some Buddhists may be disappointed that I do not say more about the practice and experience of the people involved. This is for the very good reason that in the early period there is simply not enough information, while for the present there is not only too much, but most participants are still alive. However, in various schools Irish practitioners have been given traditional forms of recognition, and I have indicated this where possible.

This is a good moment to tell this history, in that Buddhism in Ireland has transformed qualitatively and quantitatively over the last fifteen years or so; twenty-five years ago it would have been impossible to imagine it as becoming so large or so mainstream. In this context, what went before can shed much light on the new period, whether in terms of long-standing continuities or of sharp breaks, and perhaps frame some of the questions Buddhists ask themselves as they practise, communicate the Dharma and develop communities and organisations.

The text draws on humanist Marxism, social movement studies, the literature on western Buddhism and the sociology of new religious movements, but also on the engaged Buddhism developed in Buddhist Asia during the latter part of this period, seeking not just to analyse from outside but also to point out possibilities for greater development within Irish Buddhism. In so doing, it makes arguments which may be relevant beyond Ireland, and beyond Buddhism. They are also, necessarily, critical and potentially controversial.

What is 'Ireland'?

In Buddhist terms Ireland is a 'border region', or in world-systems language semi-peripheral (Cox and Griffin 2009). The leading accounts of western Buddhist history (Almond 1988, Tweed 2000) present a story of the appropriation of Asian Buddhism into the powerful cultures of core states (Britain and the USA respectively). Yet this single-country approach breaks down in relation to Ireland: Almond includes Irish material with no mention of Ireland's role in the religious conflicts that broke up the British state in 1922; Tweed treats the migrant Irishman Lafcadio Hearn as just another Victorian American. Even these 'core countries' are less homogenous, in other words, than we might assume. Yet even when 'western Buddhism' does not simply mean 'in the USA' (Koné 2001: 155, fn1), it is normally written as national history (e.g. Baumann 2002).

Unlike these metropoles, peripheral countries cannot remake Buddhism in their 'own', intensely contested image.[1] Dependency theory sees peripherality as defined by a situation where most economic and other linkages are external (Gunder Frank 1971); world-systems theory has argued that the unit of analysis should

---

1. For example, there are only two known encounters between the early Irish Buddhists discussed in chapter five. In 1889 Capt. Pfoundes and John Bowles Daly both chaired spiritualist meeting in London. Pfoundes was unable to give a promised talk to Daly's group and Daly lectured on Buddhism instead. In the late 1950s, Michael Dillon was briefly patron and student of Lobsang Rampa in Dublin. While Irish Buddhists were sometimes busy public actors, 'Irish Buddhism' was not a collective actor.

be whatever global order actually integrates economic, political and cultural activities (Wallerstein 1988).

To discuss 'Buddhism and Ireland', then, is not to discuss 'Irish culture' but rather to situate Irish *society* within the broader world-system, most importantly its peripheral, internally colonised, diasporic situation. The nearest Irish parallel to Tweed or Almond is Lennon's *Irish Orientalism* (2004), which shows Irish people drawing parallels to colonised societies in Asia as a way of speaking about their own situation.

This book follows this argument and Tweed's more recent (2006, 2011) 'translocative' analysis to study Buddhism and Ireland – not Buddhism in Ireland or Irish Buddhism – as a way into fundamentally global relationships. From the first Irish writer on the subject – a monk in ninth-century France – via the Irish soldiers who looted Buddhist treasures from Burma or Tibet to early Irish Buddhists living in Japan, Ceylon, Burma, Ladakh or Monte Carlo, the Irish encounter with Buddhism has taken place off the island as much as on. Conversely, Buddhists in Ireland are often not Irish by birth, whether they are Asian immigrants or learned their Buddhism in British or continental counter-cultures.

As with other colonised and post-colonial societies, emigration and immigration are constitutive features of the Irish experience, and Buddhism finds its place in these contexts. In the Middle Ages, monks migrated while invaders brought new languages with which to read about Buddhism; later, the Wars of Religion and Irish plantation created a refugee diaspora and new Protestant populations in Ireland. In the nineteenth and early twentieth century, Irish people were involved in the mobility networks of the British Empire, the use of religious vocations as solutions to the problem of surplus population, and escape from an increasingly sectarian society. More recently, Irish people's first encounter with Buddhism has often been abroad, in Asia or other western countries, where most Irish Buddhist teachers are to be found rather than in Ireland.

The language and publishing situation mirrors this. Since the start of our period, Ireland has been a multilingual space, whose languages have also been spoken elsewhere. It has shared publishing and reading spaces with Britain, and often France, wider Catholic Europe or North America. If present-day Irish Buddhists can rely on the Internet for books and podcasts, the early twentieth century saw Irish members of London-based Buddhist societies and subscribers to British and American journals. Further back still, in the eighteenth century, those interested in Jesuit accounts of Buddhist Asia could order them in French from a foreign-language bookshop on Dublin's College Green.

Finally, throughout the crucial period of the nineteenth and twentieth century, ethnic identification and state boundaries have been subjects of intense controversy and violent conflict. Part of nineteenth-century Ireland has become a separate state within living memory, and one whose boundaries – cultural and political – remain contested; it shares this history with many if not most states around the world. In Ireland as in Asia, these boundary struggles have often been bound up with religion.

The Limits of Irish Buddhism

This peripheral situation is connected to the pressures restricting Buddhism on this island. If Ireland lacked the Asian migrant labour which brought Buddhism to the US, Canada, Brazil, Australia and New Zealand in the later nineteenth century (Seager 2002, Matthews 2002, Rocha 2006, Spuler 2002, Kemp 2007) and the later post-colonial migrations that brought it to European countries, Irish-born people were as well-informed about Buddhism as their British or American counterparts, took part in the same colonial and scholarly enterprises, explored Theosophy and developed comparable counter-cultures in the 1890s and 1960s.

Yet while these processes led to early convert Buddhism in Germany, Britain and the United States and the foundation of societies (Baumann 2002: 87–90), public Buddhism barely appeared in Ireland before 1971: to be Irish and *openly* Buddhist, for over a hundred years, was to be in Asia. This makes insular Buddhism a particularly interesting case when trying to understand Buddhism in the west more generally: while the necessary conditions for its development were present, some sufficient conditions were clearly lacking, and the contrast – both with Irish Buddhists abroad and with the development of Buddhism elsewhere in Europe – is significant.

The Politics of Buddhism in Ireland

In a broader perspective, Irish Buddhism's inherently global character, and the sharp discontinuities of its history – tied to anti-colonialism and the formation of new states in Ireland and Asia, to the anti-systemic movements of 1968 and the reshaping of the world in the neo-liberal era – shed light on issues which are not Irish alone.

Most writing on Buddhism in western countries takes the established social and political order for granted, or at best explores how Buddhists negotiated the 'limits of dissent' (Tweed 2002) within their own countries and times, and focuses on explanatory questions within this. This book locates Irish Buddhism in relation to the British Empire in Ireland and Buddhist Asia, post-independence Ireland and the Celtic Tiger. In exploring this, it necessarily explores the politics of race in Asia and ethnicity in Ireland and the questions of family and gender which are central to the solidarity of ruling formations.

It suggests that Buddhism was tied to class desertion from the Anglo-Irish imperial service class, and later from the new Catholic nationalist service class; in one case in alliance with Asian anti-colonial movements, in the other in alliance with counter-cultural migrants from other western societies. In so doing it spoke for 'good sense' against 'common sense' (Gramsci 1991), and resisted the hegemonic formations of various periods, while simultaneously having important limitations of its own. Irish Buddhists were part and parcel both of counter-cultural developments in the 1890s and 1960s, and of broader social movements, but arguably remained more acted upon than acting in these contexts.

Rethinking Western Buddhist Studies

Like Rocha's (2006) study of Brazilian Zen, which links Japanese labour migration, Brazilian interest in Japan as a non-western success story and the search for cosmopolitan cultural capital, this book uses 'Buddhism and Ireland' as a partial approach to a global history. In this perspective, the apparent boundedness of *metropolitan* societies as much as peripheral ones is questioned, paying greater attention to the internal contestation of dominant cultures, anti-colonial solidarity, processes of 'going native' abroad and of immigration from Buddhist countries.

More broadly, a world-systems approach locates the development of western Buddhism firmly within the history of the capitalist world-system, in terms of the changing relationships between states, institutions and classes, the conflicting pressures these relationships place on peripheral societies and the routine mobility of Buddhists from and within those societies.

This highlights *both* the processes of trade and exploration, missionary work, colonisation and control that underpin the formation of the capitalist world-system, *and* the history of anti-colonial movements and anti-modernist cultural critiques as contexts for the changing relationship of Buddhism and Ireland. Contemporary Buddhist modernism was created in the anti-colonial Asian revival before it appeared as western dharma centres; and as we shall see Irish people were closely involved in this process.

As Said (2003) powerfully demonstrated, much 'Orientalism', including apparently rigorous scholarship, is best understood as knowledge as power, representations for the purposes of imperial control, and it is important to be conscious of this when reading the works of imperial academics – or Catholic theologians seeking a 'spiritual empire'.

However, not all Irish people shared those purposes, and this was particularly true for those who crossed the lines of race and ethnicity to become Buddhist. Hence this text follows Lennon (2004) in highlighting solidarity and mutual identification between colonial situations in Ireland and Asia. Specifically, with Clarke (1997) it highlights the strategic use of Asian religions for *western* cultural dissent. The typical Irish Buddhist, between 1890 and 1960, was not a university mandarin but a member of an Asian-led organisation opposing missionary Christianity. Recent immigration brings this history back home in a new way, even if the shared past is rarely recognised.

Class, Race, Gender – and Religion

A key period was that of direct European colonial intervention into Buddhist Asia (beyond coastal Ceylon,[2] long a European colony) in the later nineteenth and early twentieth centuries – which was also

2. I follow historiographical convention in using place names of the period except where, as with medieval European names for Chinese cities, this would now render them unrecognisable.

the period of greatest Irish involvement in empire and of nationalist movements in Ireland. Imperial rule in this context was geared towards a capitalist world-system, but its day-to-day operation was organised as a matter of ethnicity (in Ireland) or race (in Asia) – in both cases increasingly also defined in religious terms, opposing Protestant to Catholic, or missionary Christianity to Buddhist revival.

The concept of hegemony, best expressed in Gramsci's *On the southern question* (1978) is that a given economic regime needs to be held together and given direction by a leading group which involves *both* the formation of alliances between elites (fractions of capital, political parties, churches etc.,) *and* the construction of everyday popular consent to given ways of life, by 'traditional intellectuals' such as priests, doctors or lawyers and the 'organic intellectuals' of rising social classes such as managers or engineers.

In the imperial context, the service classes who managed the languages and routines of daily hegemony were structured in religious and ethnic terms – and through marriage, family, sexuality and gender. This is as apparent in family relationships among the Anglo-Irish (or, sixty years later, the new Catholic service class) as for missionaries, soldiers and civil servants abroad. In-marriage in particular was central to career, respectability, family alliances, elite formation and the maintenance of group power.

This caste solidarity, enabling the 'natural' operation of everyday power (Connell 2001), was upset in Ireland by massive social movements: two waves of women's movements challenging gender relations, an unusually successful land struggle, an early national independence movement and the defeat of the state's nuclear power project. In Asia, Irish people 'went native' as part of equally powerful anti-colonial movements. These conflicts were fought out in individual lives as personal crisis.

Religious conversion – whether to Buddhism, Theosophy or paganism – was part of a broader contestation of everyday allegiances to ethnicity and race, family and gender, and beyond these the wider capitalist world-system and the relationships constructed to external colonies in Buddhist Asia and 'internal colonies' in Ireland (Hechter 1975).

Taylor, studying rural Irish Catholicism, describes religion as

> a powerful organization of meaning, and a meaningful organization of power … The adjective "religious", in this sense, describes an idiom

of thought, speech, and action through which individuals, groups, and even whole nations make themselves. (1995: 242)

This is particularly appropriate to *dominant* religions. The earlier history of Buddhism in Ireland, however, explores individuals resisting this process, in sectarian or hegemonically Catholic contexts which shape attempts at alternatives. Early Irish Buddhists abroad, for their part, were caught up in the Asian construction of *alternative* organizations of meaning and power to the colonial, missionary ones.

Today, most convert Buddhists have been brought up within the Catholic church, which still dominates the Republic's religious field, and conversion marks a break with its still-powerful routines in many family and community contexts. The organising capacity of Buddhism in Ireland is small and fragmentary; and this is part of its attractiveness to the many converts and sympathisers who are wary of 'labels', orthodoxies and hierarchies.

There is power and power, then: the Marxist analysis adopted in this book distinguishes between the routine operation of power by dominant groups and the struggle of subalterns to assert independent organising capacity. This means looking beneath the surface and seeing the difference between Buddhism as a religion of power in Sri Lanka, as a religion of identity in Tibet, and as an alternative religion in Ireland. Resisting the rhetoric which sees a universal spirituality refracted in slightly different ways by different religions – a mode shaped by US history in particular (Sharf 1995) – Marxist theory of religion returns us to the question of how rhetorics of experience are used to make or undermine claims for power (Cohen 2006).

The Politics of Cultural Radicalism

Large-scale power relationships are abstract, but must work themselves out in individual lives to be effective. This book studies people who did not simply accept the lives that were laid out for them, but remade themselves against these pressures, countering power relationships, often as part of larger movements which reshaped the world. The first flowering of Irish Buddhism, in the context of Land War and Home Rule agitation, represents in part the defection of people born into an imperial service class, across the lines of race and power which made an empire. Its second flowering, with war in Vietnam and the North, the rise of second-wave feminism and anti-nuclear struggles, represents in part a rejection by children of the Catholic service class of 'business as usual', a stepping outside of the boundaries of tribe and career. All this took place within wider networks of cultural and political opposition illuminated by the more specific histories of Buddhism. Such networks were not defending a declining social order nor part of the new elites, although they often provided a cutting edge for dismantling the old order. They proposed a different direction for development – successfully or not.

One limitation of Irish social movements has been the avoidance of too much cultural critique by political radicals who put their case within a culture not of their own making – from the subordination of the labour movement to conservative religious nationalism to the subordination of the movements of the 1970s and 1980s to a state-led modernisation which did not produce the world they had hoped for. Similarly, the avoidance of too much political critique by cultural radicals was also debilitating: over time, radical needs in counter-cultural garb were rewritten as a new gentility or a source of cultural capital. This is not to say that overthrowing the British Empire or the church's control of women's bodies were trivial or unnecessary; it is to say that the attempt to ally with (some) powerful groups against others is in important ways self-defeating, and ultimately means fighting their battles for them.

Defection from hegemony, at any level, implies a sense of a potential other, best understood in terms of some sense of human nature (Geras 1983) and needs that go beyond how matters are organised in a particular regime. The line often runs within the human heart, as hegemonic processes offer to satisfy *some* needs at the expense of others.[3] The 'hidden transcripts' of the poor (Scott 1990, Mulholland 2006) may be less visible than the defections of the privileged, but express the same process: a refusal to be cowed or bought-off, and an assertion of unmet needs.

The development of effective counter-cultures and social movements, and the transformation of the social order, is rarely thinkable without some degree of halting communication and fumbling cooperation between these two groups who have

---

3. Buddhist ethical theory discusses these same challenges in terms of choosing between different intentions and motivations.

historically been separated from each other. This is why an apolitical counter-culture, or a culturally conservative left, are problematic: by fixing either the political and social order (and thus coercion) or the cultural order (and thus consent) they put barriers in the way of this alliance-building.

Another way of putting this (Cox 2011) is to say that social movements, alternative religions or counter cultures are in the first instance articulations of needs against the economic, political and cultural order; secondly, they develop alternative 'political economies of labour' (Lebowitz 1991) – institutions geared to meeting these needs directly or indirectly; and they articulate 'tacit knowledge' (Wainwright 1994) about how things are, what we need, and how we can realise that.

Imported ideas – Buddhist or Marxist, liberation theology or Zapatista – have to be seen in terms of how the people who import them, respond to them and build organisations around them, are trying to articulate and express all of this. It is not that ideas produce people, but rather that a shapeless discontent with religious orthodoxy looks elsewhere for practices that seem to hold out alternative possibilities, just as working-class struggles reach for particular languages and tactics. The new forms can then be evaluated in practice – by those who try out a particular new religious movement, feminist, republican or left tradition before abandoning it, and by those who stay with the movement and try to make it more adequate to the needs of others and their ultimate purposes (and, in eternally-sectarian Dublin, criticise the failures of rival groups).

Thus interpretation should not take the world as given and unchangeable. We need to ask how adequate the practical solutions people adopted were to their needs; how far they developed solidarity with others suffering similar problems; how well they built organisations that challenged this; and so on. As against much textual criticism of a 'radical' kind, we need to ask 'did it work?' and 'what can we learn from this?' Otherwise we run the risk, as Marx (1977) observed, of proceeding no further in our minds than the people we 'represent' did in their lives – and thus being theoretically driven to the same solutions which the latter were driven to practically. A minimal meaning of 'praxis', then, is to have a conversation – with the people we study and those who read us – about what we should do, what worked and what didn't, what happens when you try certain things, how social relations have been transformed in the past and what might work in the future.

World-systems and Inner Lives

One way in which people 'do' religion is to sanctify the taken-for-granted: in this mode, asking too many questions – about history, social difference, global contrasts or whatever – threatens a rather fragile sense of the sacred. Nevertheless, seriously understanding 'Buddhism in Ireland' involves some dizzying changes of perspectives. This book explores changing global relationships, from the slowness of medieval knowledge circuits to a capitalist modernity where 'all that is solid melts into air' (Berman 1982) – and asks about the meaning of these relationships for the transmission and reception of Buddhism in Ireland. It also explores the inner lives of people whose family lives were often broken, who crossed the globe and became active members of a radically different culture – and asks how this affected their response to Asian Buddhism.

Early Irish Buddhists, however, *related the two:* one became an enthusiastic preserver of 'old Japan' against Meiji modernism; another a novice monk rejecting race, class and age privilege; a third wielded Tom Paine against the polite elites of the colonial world. They made these leaps in their own lives, and found in Buddhism a language that made sense of these changes. Academic analysis reconstructs this in ways that are more distinct and abstract than they seemed in the lives of people who were struggling with power, race, class, identity and gender in their own lives and making the enormous effort of relating one of the most developed systems of thought and practice available in their day to their understanding of history, psychology or politics in constructing their own perspectives. It does not substitute for their own writings, but it can help to illuminate them.

A Western Marxist Analysis of Western Buddhism?

This book adopts a western Marxist approach to western Buddhism, which sees popular religion as collective agency that can be analysed in terms of the needs it expresses, the visions it articulates and the limits it sets to action. Žižek (2001) famously opposed western Marxism and western Buddhism. Rather badly informed

(Møllgaard 2008), he recycled critiques of Orientalism familiar to Buddhologists (e.g. Lopéz 2000) to arrive at the supposedly new discovery that although

> "European" technology and capitalism are triumphing worldwide at the level of the "economic infrastructure", the Judeo-Christian legacy is threatened at the level of "ideological superstructure" in the European space itself by New Age "Asiatic" thought, which ... is establishing itself as the hegemonic ideology of global capitalism. (Žižek 2001: 1)

Minus the last clause, something similar could have been written any time in the last century; it parallels the *Dublin Review*'s 'Modern society and the Sacred Heart' (Barry 1875), which argued for the superiority of Christianity to a 'modern idea' which held analogies to Buddhism.

Between Barry's time and Žižek's, Buddhism and Marxism met in Asia. The postwar period saw an extensive reflection on the two by South and East Asian intellectuals such as Ambedkar or Buddhadasa in the context of anti-colonial movements, the creation of nation-states and the rise of Communist parties. More immediate political questions came to the fore: could Buddhism develop a 'third way' between Soviet and US power, were Marxists right to see Buddhism as feudal, etc.? (Ling 1966, Queen and King 1996, Lopéz 2002.)

Buddhists also found themselves in the front line of Cold War: under attack by Diem's Catholic regime in South Vietnam, targets of the Chinese invasion of Tibet, anti-communist missionaries in Malaysia. The CIA funded anthropologists to discover whether Buddhist countries were particularly receptive to communism. 'Engaged Buddhism', like 'liberation theology' in Latin America, took the Marxist critique of past oppression on board while trying to sketch out local, post-colonial and non-capitalist modes of development in what little space the superpowers left. What casual critique like Žižek's lacks, then, is history, agency and struggle.

In the 1950s, two perceptions were common among thoughtful western intellectuals. One was that Buddhism was the world's largest religion, one of its oldest, and one spanning 'Asian societies'. In comparative religious studies it was 'Christianity's Other': Theravada in particular was contrasted with theistic and belief-oriented religion. Marxism, for its part, was seen as the Other of capitalism, and indeed of academic social theory. Sixty years on, what might these two 'Others' have to say to each other?

Theoretical Positions

Western Marxists (Kolakowski 1978, Gottlieb 1989) have long been interested in religion (Gramsci 1997, Hill 1975, Thompson 1993, Davies 1998, Holstun 2002 etc.,) and culture more broadly (Williams 1982 etc.) Their engagements in social movements and adult education (Mayo 1999) led them to see religion as a contested and contradictory part of 'common sense', a space where people 'become conscious of ... conflict and fight it out' (Marx 1859). Thus we need to locate what people say within the broader question of *who* they are, *when* and *where:* a situated analysis geared to building progressive alliances.

Not all readers will agree with the particular analyses made in this book: both religion and politics are inherently contested. However, analysis is inherent to categorisation and writing (as Buddhist philosophers no less than sociological researchers know). I have, however, tried to present sufficient information that readers can see for themselves whether there are alternative ways of making sense of the material.

Buddhism and Marxism have important structural similarities: they are transcendent in that they point out of the here-and-now, but the best of their thought is consistently geared to practice in the present, and to relating the given situation and the long-term goal in ways which make the latter achievable starting from the former.

Thus in writing this book multiple perspectives matter. One is the discourse of ultimate aims: a radically different way of being which the people I discuss have usually taken very seriously. Second is the day-to-day practice of building a better world in microcosm, among ourselves and in relationship with wider movements and counter-cultures. A third is how the choices we make in our own lives resonate, in large or small ways, with the lives of others 'throughout time and space' – as global empires, moral monopolies and Celtic Tigers rise and fall.

E.P. Thompson (1978) observed that the question is not whether we are on Marx's side but whether he is on ours. This book uses a similar yardstick, asking whether particular choices and actions mark a step forward in relation to people's previous situation and in the direction of greater personal clarity, interpersonal solidarity and capacity for transformation.

Marxism and Religion

There are two or three positions on religion in Marx. The first settles accounts with the intellectual world of his youth, a kind of counter-theology describing what religion 'essentially' is. In his last years, anthropological reading enabled him to think religion beyond his Judeo-Christian starting points. This was something of an empirical confirmation of his mature period where, rejecting idealism, he also rejected separate histories of ideas, and focused on the *use* specific groups made of ideas, practices and institutions:

> Morality, religion, metaphysics and all the rest of ideology as well as the forms corresponding to these, thus no longer retain the semblance of independence. They have no history, no development; but human beings, developing their material production and their material intercourse, alter along with this their actual world, also their thinking and the products of their thinking. (Marx and Engels 1970: 36–7)

Hence the radical differences between Irish Buddhism in 1912 and 2012 reflect not some essence of Buddhism (or Ireland) but rather the wider histories of human beings in changing world-systemic relations. This, however, states a problem rather than resolving it; and there are different 'western Marxist' approaches within this.

Exploring established religions of power, the Sardinian Gramsci (Nairn 1982) was concerned with how urban, secular Northern workers could ally with the religious peasants of Italy's 'South and islands'. Analysing the power/knowledge relations of peasant life, he focused on how 'traditional intellectuals' such as the village priest, doctor or lawyer drew on their training to organise people's daily lives (and structure their attempts to change them, as when peasants ask the priest to petition the landlord). Here daily religion is part of the machinery of local power relations, and the goal is to support *independent* peasant leadership.

British Marxists, by contrast, have highlighted oppositional religion from below, sometimes seen as the transmutation of secular political logic, the escape into a rhetorical or mystical way of preserving once-political ideals:

> The defeat of the Leveller soldiers at Burford in 1649 [who mutinied over the war in Ireland among other issues] served as a sharp check to the temporal political hopes of the more advanced democrats … For a moment the revolutionary spirit, which had met a set-back in realistic political objectives, leapt to even more outrageous heights of utopian ideals and visionary teachings.
>
> The hopes which were dashed in this world were projected into an inner world of the spirit. Here the old rhetoric lived on, but the stance of the sect towards all temporal things might now be quietist. (Thompson 1993: 23, 52)

Another perspective notes that this assumes a *separation* between 'religious' and 'political' as clearly differentiated institutional spheres when it is in fact the *product* of some of these struggles. In seventeenth-century England, religion was the main form of regular popular assembly and organising – whether a 'priestly hierarchy' controlling all those living in a parish or gathered churches organising independently; it was also the shared language within which conflicts over the nature and direction of society were expressed. Here, religion does not substitute for politics but is a language used to think and speak politics (Hill 1975).

These accounts are not always in contradiction: if, for example, the movements of the English 1640s created a moderately secular public space, and radicals after 1649 were forced back into religious modes of speaking and organising, the earlier space was a real historical achievement.

In Ireland the separation came later (if at all); religion was *increasingly,* from 1798 to the 1920s if not the 1950s or 1970s, a mark of ethnicity and political alignment. In colonial Ireland – from Protestant plantation, land grab and penal laws; the formation of 'Catholic, Protestant [Anglican] and Dissenter' as distinct and opposed communities; struggles over Emancipation, education and power – and the post-colonial period – from Catholic counter-revolution, Northern Protestant power and Southern struggles over 'social issues' in the 1970s and 1980s – religion marks ethnic affiliation and political project, and much politics was about the relationship between the two.

It is not that there have been no other political issues, but that (as one analysis has it) ethno-religious identification gets in the way of 'real politics'. Or, put another way, an effect if not a purpose of sectarianism was to keep other, political-but-not-religious issues off the agenda (Coulter 1999b). Thus for much of Irish history religion *is* politics.

Secular liberalism has diluted but not dissolved this relationship. In tandem with feminism and gay liberation it has undermined many social control aspects of established religion. New religions in Ireland (Cosgrove et al., 2011) have been part and parcel of this process, which is still ongoing, as with church control of education and hospitals; ethnic identification, however, remains structured by religious affiliation.

Religious Practice and Social Change

Western European discussions of religion often privilege questions of doctrine and hierarchy: established Christianity historically marginalised mystical practice, with 'enthusiasm' either repressed or co-opted; while wars of religion and conflicts over the relations between church and state have shaped institutional self-definitions. The priority of theological and organisational debates has had its roots in the power both express.

Buddhism, with other non-mainstream religions, has sometimes been attractive precisely as a way out of this. Meditation, visions, dreams and so on offer a chance to say something closer to the experience of the less powerful (Davies 1998), a way of articulating 'good sense' or 'tacit knowledge' against official versions of reality.

This becomes clear while teaching meditation and Buddhism in Ireland. Students are interested in a religion which does not have a father-figure God, in losing a sense of guilt around approved behaviour, in taking one's own unvoiced thoughts seriously, in more fully inhabiting one's body (particularly for older generations), in taking control of one's time for oneself (particularly for women) and in creating a meditative space to explore previously repressed or controlled feelings. Like antinomianism, meditation too is 'not a place at all, but a way of breaking out from received wisdom and moralism, and entering upon new possibilities' (Thompson 1993: 20).

Mulholland (2006) has similarly argued that new religious movements in Ireland make public hidden transcripts that working-class participants in the New Age – because of childhood coercion as part of social control ('civilising processes') – cannot seek a source of healing and kindness in the church which was partly responsible.

Not all alternative religions have the same meaning, however. Barrow (1986) shows how spiritualism could be used in plebeian hands as a form of democratic epistemology, in contrast to official religion and often in contestation with spiritualism's elite leadership.

Buddhism, too, can be 'read' (or rather practised) in different ways. The foundational proposition that the way to enlightenment can be taught creates a tendency towards an educational hierarchy which can easily solidify. The more participants know about Asian Buddhism, the less scope is available for individual creativity. Conversely, the focus on individual spiritual practice means that in some ways its normatively central activity is an internal one, which can legitimate individual creativity. Different practitioners have different focuses of interest, and this too privileges particular approaches. Thus this book avoids discussion of what practitioners 'necessarily were' as followers of particular traditions and rather asks *who* they were, and what they were trying to *do* with Buddhism.

'Actually-existing Christianity'

This book is not always complimentary towards Irish, or missionary, Christianity. I hope it is clear by now that I am not discussing what Christianity (or Buddhism) 'essentially is', so much as what Irish people have *done* with both. In this context Christianity appears as a religion of power, a way in which various groups within Ireland and empire have attempted to civilise 'natives', organise ethnic solidarity, seek state power or control gender relations. Buddhists, members of a new religion in Ireland and anti-colonial movements in Asia, have therefore encountered Christians in this guise – bearing, as the characteristically blunt Dhammaloka observed in Burma, the Bible, the Gatling gun (of the British Army) and the bottle (of the whiskey trader).

Secondly, Christianity appears as the religion into which most Irish Buddhists were socialised; hence this book sees Irish Christianity from the viewpoints of those whose upbringing was oppressive or unsatisfying and who as adults had to negotiate their existence in a world dominated by Christianity – at costs which were so high until recently that most Irish Buddhists left the country. This book largely discusses people who resisted Christian socialisation; it would be incomprehensible if it did not discuss the reasons why.

There are particular problems in talking about this in a country where religion has been such a controversial subject – central to the struggle for political power until the 1920s in the Republic and until the present in the North; crucial in struggles over gender and sexuality from the 1960s on; and complicit in a massive institutional complex of physical and sexual abuse whose last institutions only closed in the 1990s.

Ethnicity pushes many Irish Christians *both* to identify with 'their' particular church *and* to disavow its most unpalatable aspects. This generates hostility to reminders of what religion has meant within very recent memory. 'We have moved on' – with the assumption that everyone is still part of that 'we'. Yet the past history needs to be named, and seen for what it was. Institutions, including religious ones, have responsibilities, as do their members. This is no less true for the handful of surviving members of orthodox Stalinist parties than it is for the 1930s and 1940s collusion of Zen in Japanese militarism (Victoria 2006), the horrors of Sinhala or Burmese nationalism today – or for members of Irish Christian churches. Religious believers have no special exemption from ethical responsibility for the consequences of their own organisations' actions.

The Meaning of Conversion in Buddhism

This brings us to the question of what conversion is. Buddhist Studies often presents conversion as a predictable outcome of knowledge and interest. However, as this book shows, knowledge about Buddhism was arguably more detailed and widespread in the Ireland of the 1760s or 1860s than it was in the 1960s; while for comparable levels of information Britain and the US showed far greater levels of participation than did Ireland. More recently, rates of Buddhist identification have been far lower in Northern Ireland than in the Republic.

Thus apparently individual decisions have to be seen in social and historical context. This also means treating the question of why people did *not* convert to Buddhism as seriously as the question of why others *did*; or why some became Theosophists and others Buddhists. Chapters three to five explore this issue in some detail.

The Christian implications of the term 'conversion' are misleading (Kemp 2007: 120), notably its implications of a sudden drastic change, followed by decisive affiliation to a specific church.

In western Buddhism, processes of creolization and syncretism (for example, the adoption of Buddhist meditation techniques within Catholic contexts) are important (Tweed 2006, Rocha 2006); and there is a wide spectrum from sympathiser to individual practitioner to organisational adherent (Tweed 2000).

In Ireland, one key meaning of 'Buddhism' in particular has been stepping *outside* the Irish meaning of religion as a quasi-ethnic identification with religious institutions. Thus a major influence is in those who reject 'labels' and religious exclusivity, who identify with 'spirituality' against (organised) 'religion', who think of 'philosophy as a way of life' (Hadot 1995) or a personal quest for meaning (Heelas 1996, 2008) as against institutional affiliation. This ties to Viswanathan's argument that

> conversion can be interpreted culturally as a means of expressing dissent from the secularized narratives of state. [Viswanathan's research disputes] the 'privileged place' that spiritual autobiographies occupy in Western cultural history as stabilizing narratives, in which the progression of the convert from fractured self to spiritual wholeness is charted without reference to the tensions between civil society, religious and political authority from which such conversions spring (Guinness 2003).

If, as Gordon-Finlayson and Daniels (2008) suggest, western Buddhist converts experience themselves as 'coming home' to a religion which 'fits' their personal spiritual quest, that conversion is only partly shaped by what Buddhism essentially 'is'; it is equally shaped by the direction of their dissent.

What is 'being Buddhist'?

In traditional Asian Buddhism, the insider view is more complex than might be assumed,[4] and Buddhists are often *not* 'Buddhist' in the way Christians are 'Christian'. This is of course one reason why Buddhism is attractive to some westerners. (Most forms of) Buddhism differ from (most forms of) Christianity in the degree of soteriological significance given to membership: doctrinally, what is crucial is usually the degree of spiritual realisation. Sharp distinctions between monastics and laity mean that often monastics were seen as the 'real Buddhists' (depending on country

---

4. This section summarises an extremely complex situation only to the level needed to indicate the problem.

and period). Beyond this, religious multilingualism has historically been the rule, not only in East Asia but also in Southeast
Asia (Gombrich 1971), where Buddhism co-exists with spirit cults,
astrology and so on.

The late nineteenth and early twentieth-century Buddhist Revival
often saw sharper boundaries develop, as a form of national cultural
identity in response to imperial Christianity, and in the revaluation
of lay practice. When these modernist Buddhisms were transported
to western countries, new kinds of structures again developed, often
separating off meditation as something which could be taught to
non-Buddhists from forms of Buddhist identity and ritual available
to more committed or experienced participants.

Difficulties in recruiting and retaining traditionally qualified
(especially monastic) teachers mean that many western groups have
introduced new, lay or unofficial categories of de facto teachers
(Wetzel 2002). From the late nineteenth century, too, Buddhist
writers and celebrities have increasingly created their own status,
separate from formal institutional processes. All of this means that
what it means to 'be Buddhist' is very problematic.

Hybridity as Normal?

Tweed (2002) argues for a more complex notion of religious identity.
Noting that religions can be functionally compartmentalised and
that people can consciously draw on multiple traditions, he observes
that people do this unofficially, particularly in conversion:

> There is hybridity all the way down. In this sense, religious identity is
> usually complex. Ambivalence is the norm. (2002: 19)

He deploys categories such as adherent and lukewarm adherent,
seekers or 'Dharma-hoppers' who move between groups or
religions, and sympathisers or 'night-stand Buddhists. Where there
are high social costs of conversion, many of those converted may
not publicise the fact:

> Some celebrate conversion: others conceal it. (2002: 19)[5]

In Ireland, where these costs are particularly high and religion
is tightly bound up with ethnic membership, such hybridity is

5. One reader strongly advised me against 'outing' anyone as Buddhist for this
reason.

important. Many contemporary Irish Christians do not adhere to orthodox belief or practice; while from yoga and meditation to pagan identifications and New Age universalism it is common to remain in the church of one's birth while being thoroughly at odds with official positions (Cosgrove et al., 2011).

Robbins' (1988: 64) distinction between inner conversion and organisational recruitment points in a similar direction. He notes that in the Roman Empire

> One was thus *converted* to the intolerant faiths of Judaism and Christianity while one merely *adhered* to the cults of Isis, Orpheus or Mithra. Participation in a particular "mystery cult" was not incompatible with involvement in another mystery religion or with Roman civic piety. (1988: 65)

It is not that there are no exclusivist Buddhist organisations, or individuals who understand themselves as exclusively Buddhist. Rather, that many Buddhist groups, of necessity or choice, do not require participants to abandon other allegiances; and many participants seek a multiplicity absent from their previous religious experience.

In my own experience of teaching Buddhist meditation, it is important to stress at the outset that meditation techniques can be beneficially used by everyone irrespective of their religious beliefs or lack of them. Similar statements are common in many Buddhist contexts, and even in more exclusivist settings people often ignore official positions.

This also means that Buddhism in particular has an impact far beyond those who are members in the narrowest sense. If it is easiest to research committed, self-identified Buddhists affiliated to public organisations, they are nevertheless a minority among converts (if not among Asian Buddhists). They are significant in that their norms matter to those whose involvement or commitment is less, and they maintain the organisations which mediate many people's access to meditation teaching, ritual, and exploration of Buddhist identity. Such groups, however, are the tip of the iceberg, by comparison with the less easily-researched groups of Asian Buddhists, sympathisers, creolising Christians and so on.

Other, historical categories are important: one for the unknown and unknowable readers of texts in contexts where religious disloyalty was formally punishable by death until the seventeenth century, by dispossession until the eighteenth and by imprisonment until the twentieth; another for the (partly known) reception of Buddhist texts within a context of intra-Christian sectarianism and high *social* costs for disloyalty (perhaps from the mid-nineteenth century to the 1960s); a third set of categories for the founding generations of Irish Buddhists from the 1970s on, where some degree of contact with Buddhist teachers and institutions became possible within Ireland; and a final set of categories for the present period where Buddhism has become partly 'normalised' and far larger numbers of immigrant Buddhists are present.

All of this is to say that this book necessarily operates with shades of grey in relation to what 'Buddhist' means. To do otherwise would be to misrepresent the complexity of the situation, and to miss the point that the significance and impact of Buddhism in Ireland is all about relationality. From a Buddhist perspective, generosity and ethical behaviour are not specifically Buddhist, nor does basic meditation transform one's spiritual situation. Only enlightenment, in its various shades, might be specifically Buddhist, and few traditions see most of their participants as being fully awakened.

Conversion and New Religious Movements

Buddhism is 'new' not in absolute terms but rather in terms of its public availability in Ireland. 'New religious movements' are such

> not as a group of religions that share particular attributes, but as a set of religions that have been assigned an outsider status by the dominant religious culture and then by elements within the secular culture (Melton 2004: 30)

This outsider status is something which Buddhists routinely try to escape in pursuit of social or academic respectability; but as an outsider religion, conversion to Buddhism is what Taylor calls 'awkward' conversion, a conversion 'that may never be called "conversion"' (1999: 35).

If in 1991 fewer than 400 people of Irish or other European Union citizenship identified as Buddhist, in 2009 (when those born in 1991 were reaching 18) the large majority of non-Asian Buddhists, some 3,000 in 2006, were first-generation converts. Thus the sociology of 'becoming Buddhist' in Ireland is more akin to that of becoming pagan, Hare Krishna or a shaman than it is to the sociology of becoming a Catholic, a Methodist or a Muslim, most of whose members were born into the religion.

Rambo and Farhadian's (1999) model of conversion starts with historical or family preconditions, followed by a personal or social crisis. For Irish Buddhists until recently, this has typically meant a combination of imperial relations, socio-political upheaval in Ireland and (often) personally fractured lives. The model then highlights a quest for salvation and a process of encounter, historically represented by purposeful reading, participation in countercultural milieux and travel to Buddhist Asia. Then comes creating new religious identities and formal commitment – the latter until recently as often marked by *publishing* as a Buddhist as through any traditional ceremony. Lastly come the different personal and social consequences of conversion. This model perhaps works best for groups which involve a radical transformation of converts' social roles (Robbins 1988: 83) – and so may be less useful for 'Celtic Tiger' Buddhists, who face somewhat less stigma and are less likely to make radical life changes than previous generations.

Alternatively, Lofland and Skonovd (1981) distinguish between *types* of conversion: an intellectual pattern of personal exploration marked by a sense of illumination; mystical conversion preceded by personal crisis and characterised by ecstasies; experimental conversion based on provisional participation; affectional conversion based on interpersonal bonds; revivalist conversion grounded in collective ecstatic arousals; and coercive conversion, possible only where there is massive institutional control (Robbins 1986: 67–71). Buddhist converts in Ireland certainly follow intellectual and mystical and the lower-key provisional and affectional models; it is less clear where a group like Falun Gong would fit (Chang 2004).

Conversion and Coercion in Ireland

The study of conversion in Ireland (Brown et al., 2005) is also illuminating as it highlights in particular the role of coercion in Irish religion (McGrath 2005). Studies of paganism routinely mention the decriminalisation of witchcraft and US scholars have noted the impact of 'yellow peril' racism on migrant Buddhism, but in the European context the identification between Christianities and the state, and the legal or extra-judicial targeting of pagans, Jews, heretics, Muslims and freethinkers in different periods have yet to be considered in the history of Buddhism and other Asian religions.

Intra-Christian conflict itself, the 'war of souls that took place between the confessions of early modern Ireland' (Brown 2005: 18), has focused religious choice on the small differences – and in stigmatising conversion. Since religious affiliation has primarily meant ethnic and political identity, many people kept their doubts to themselves rather than incur the costs of perceived betrayal. It is only in the Republic, and recently, that these pressures have partially eased for substantial numbers of people who would previously have been 'lapsed Catholics', anti-clerical (but still Catholic), liberal or socialist (but still buried in church) and so on.

Conflict also meant the organisation of much of daily life in competing institutional blocs, so that even once conversion from Christianity became *de facto* legal it nevertheless entailed (and sometimes still does) exclusion from a range of institutions. As O'Toole notes of the Republic,

> An Irish person was, and is, likely to be born in a Catholic hospital, educated at Catholic schools, married in a Catholic church, have children named by a priest, be counselled by Catholic marriage advisers if the marriage runs into trouble, be dried out in Catholic clinics for the treatment of alcoholism if he or she develops a drink problem, be operated on in Catholic hospitals, and be buried by Catholic rites. (1998: 67)

For 150 years, control of education and health in Ireland has been substantially devolved to the churches (Nic Ghiolla Phádraig 1995), a situation which has been a long-standing cause of concern for liberals on issues ranging from different kinds of reproductive issues to access to education. It also impacts many workplaces: the vast majority of schools, and some colleges, are explicitly religious, as are teacher training colleges, and Supreme Court rulings hold that mass attendance can legitimately be used to assess the suitability of a teacher. As late as 2002 a principal was sacked for seeking to move religious education outside of class time.

Less formally, O'Toole's list makes clear how much of ordinary social life takes place within a religious setting. The psychological and practical costs of stepping outside these remain considerable, particularly where children are concerned. Cosgrove (2012) demonstrates the continued prevalence of 'institutional religionism', with implicit expectations as to religious beliefs and practices leading to fear of discrimination against members of new religious groups, widespread 'passing' as Catholic, and high levels of actual discrimination around work, health, education, financial services and participation in local 'civil society'.

The Unknown Dimension: Disaffiliation

Most new religious organisations are a 'revolving door' in terms of membership, with the large majority of those who become involved sooner or later leaving.[6] Most famously, Barker found that of those who visit a Unification Church [UC, 'Moonie'] centre, 'a generous estimate is that no more than 0.005 percent will be associated with the movement two years later' (1984: 147).

Perhaps because of the consistent growth in Buddhist numbers, little if any research in this area exists: a reasonable assumption is that retention might be an order of magnitude better: in the 1980s the UC was considerably more aggressive in its proselytising than almost any Buddhist group, and Western Buddhist recruitment methods are typically more passive (advertising classes) and overt (identifying the organisation), so that people's arrival in Buddhist centres is usually more self-directed.

The UC is also an organisation with little middle ground between 'in' or 'out'. By contrast, someone not satisfied with a particular Buddhist group can easily find another one, practise on their own or bring Buddhist elements into another religion. We should perhaps expect to find that *organisational* disaffiliation is a particularly important category – or, once again, that formal membership of Buddhist organisations is the 'smallest circle' of western Buddhism.

The literature on disaffiliation from new religious movements has as yet little conceptual space for leaving a specific organisation but remaining committed to the same general religion or within the wider 'cultic milieu' (see Bromley 2004 and Robbins 1988: 88–99). By contrast, social movement studies are clear that one of the largest categories of disaffiliation is leaving an organisation but remaining within the wider movement, or changing movements while remaining activists (Cox 2009a). Similarly, in paganism it is common to start within a widely organised tradition (such as

6. Only a small minority of these go on to become the conscious and public 'apostates' who are important in anti-cult controversies.

Wicca) before committing to a different tradition (such as feminist witchcraft), joining an informal group or practising in isolation.

Since only some Buddhist traditions theorise *extra ecclesia nulla salus*, and many are happy to present their teachings and practice as in part independent of Buddhism, someone who leaves an organisation is not as far 'beyond the pale' as in Christianity. Depending on the tradition, it may be entirely possible to practise within it but have no formal membership or links to a particular centre.

The Changing Meanings of Being Buddhist in Ireland

Thus what it means to say someone is Buddhist is vexed; once-and-for-all exclusive conversions are not the norm; identification can play different roles at different times in a life; Buddhism is routinely combined with other philosophies and practices, and is has often not been publicly acknowledged.

Nonetheless, as Richard Cox and Joseph Lennon have asked (pers. comms.), we have to say something about what people *did* mean by Buddhism. The question is central to the transmission of Buddhism from Asia to the west: what should be discarded and what retained. These questions are important for migrant groups too, as they experience their identity in new ways, negotiate the interaction between religion and daily life in non-Buddhist societies and compromise with each other and converts on practical questions. Here I attempt a rough periodisation.

Medieval and Early Modern Ireland

In this period all known texts available to Irish people presented Buddhism at second hand, as the activities of other people. Somewhere else in the world, people worshipped (as it was put) the Buddha, engaged in practices such as asceticism or chanting, told stories such as the biography of the Buddha, had particular kinds of specialist such as monks, and (perhaps) had particular kinds of ideas. This ethnographic perspective (Offermans 2005) presented Buddhism as practices in context, with no sense of the possibility of transmission.

Hutton (1995, 2001) has reconstructed more recent processes through which westerners have drawn on texts to reinvent themselves as pagans or shamans; similar processes exist in relation to Native American religion (Welch 2007). Here, however, extensive mythologies, detailed accounts of rituals and creative religious figures (such as Gerald Gardner, Michael Harner or Carlos Castañeda) have been available. Modern western Buddhism has involved the recovery and translation of texts, the training of teachers directly or indirectly from Asian lineages, the organising of missionary visits and the construction of suitable organisations. Without this effort (much of which would have fallen foul of religious or state authorities) a medieval or early modern reader of western ethnographic accounts of Buddhism was limited in their options.

They could and did, however, respond to the life story of the Buddha, which fitted within a popular genre of holy biography; and they did so from Marco Polo to *The Light of Asia*, not forgetting the misrecognised biography in *Barlaam and Josaphat*. They could also, as with *Alexander and Dindimus*, read accounts of Buddhist asceticism through the prism of popular respect for religious simplicity, as a critique of social inequality and violence and perhaps a defence of animal rights (Wilson 2009). In order to do all this, as chapter two shows, European authors were conscious of taking risks, and had to plead that their purposes were compatible with Christianity.

Nineteenth and Early Twentieth Centuries

In the second half of the nineteenth and the first half of the twentieth century, Irish people in both Asia and Ireland came to identify as Buddhists. It was only in this period that *Asian* reformers developed forms of Buddhist practice for an educated and committed laity, so Irish Buddhists who wished to 'be Buddhist' on Asian terms were pioneers. A number were ordained and 'went native' fully – most obviously U Dhammaloka in Burma and Lobzang Jivaka in Ladakh. Others negotiated different dimensions: John Bowles Daly in Ceylon took the lay refuges and precepts and was involved in the modernising Buddhist Theosophical Society; Capt. Pfoundes in Japan combined ordination in various sects with conventional Orientalist scholarship; and Lafcadio Hearn did his best to go native, identifying emotionally with Buddhism at various periods while struggling with questions of belief and leaving what we would now call practice aside.

Only Jivaka, at the very end of the period, is known to have had what is now the defining feature of a western Buddhist: a meditation practice. Others may have done so: the original texts were increasingly available, Theosophists and others could see meditation as a form of esoteric practice, and authors such as the Buddhist Society's Christmas Humphreys eventually published manuals. However, meditation is notoriously hard to learn from books alone, and there were no teachers in Ireland (and precious few in Europe) in this period.

Equally or more powerful in this period was an interpretation of Buddhism as a philosophy and way of life, which fitted with *non-religious* European models. Tweed (2000) distinguishes the rationalist interpretation of Buddhism as a set of ideas, the romantic reception of Buddhism as an aesthetic and lifestyle, and the esoteric interpretation of Buddhism as a kind of magical ritual (cf Sharf 1995). In some ways all of these fit together under the category of 'Buddhism as a way of life' (reworking Hadot 1995), the selective importation into a certain kind of Irish life of particular elements of Buddhism.

This way of life is exemplified by a figure like Terence Gray (Wei Wu Wei), for whom 'being Buddhist' was on a par with 'being a Stoic' – a vision of human existence from which followed a way of being in daily life. This was of particular concern to those who had most freedom in everyday activities, whether as members of the gentry or as artists. At another level, however, the popular response to *The Light of Asia*, a life story of the Buddha stressing above all the ethical dimension, fit into the concerns of a respectable working class for whom political concerns (eg opposition to militarism) and personal ethics were all of a piece, in a world of self-education and self-organisation.

This was often a response to the increasing intellectual problems of orthodox Christian theology in the late nineteenth-century. The Gothic conservative Hearn, the working-class freethinker Dhammaloka and the aristocratic moralist Dillon all shared an interest in 'spiritual evolution': how to marry the new science (and hence cognitive credibility) and the experience of rapid social change with their own need for personal transformation and a broader philosophical ratification of that need.[7] Unlike their American

---

7. As Barrow (1986) notes, issues of supernatural powers, communication with the dead and reincarnation were often *not* seen as religious but could be seriously pursued by those who understood themselves as rational and atheist.

counterparts, Irish Buddhists in this period were less worried about the absence of God or the soul from Buddhism and more concerned about how to step outside the *Irish* religious problematic – of authoritarian orthodoxy, tribal allegiance and violent intolerance.

The Late Twentieth and Twenty-first Centuries

The contrast to the 1960s and 1970s, with Buddhist teachers and organisations increasingly available and growing numbers of Buddhist immigrants, is sharp. Irish Buddhists still appropriate selectively, but they are appropriating from an increasingly known 'other', and one which is increasingly understood as religious.

While some earlier converts saw it as a religion, the proportion understanding it in this way has grown, as the meaning of 'religion' has shifted in recent decades. Liberal Protestantism has changed theological elements, while membership of the Catholic church has increasingly been separated from participants' views on official doctrine and practice. The net effect is a response to the 'crisis of faith' which no longer demands emotional commitment to orthodoxy.

In this context, Buddhism has routinely been attractive for offering something more, specifically meditation techniques. With the exception of Jesuits and natural mystics, practical meditation teaching has historically been unavailable in Ireland. The Asian Buddhist revival developed new teaching approaches for the urban laity (short courses, brief retreats etc.) From the 1970s, these has become increasingly available in Ireland, in Buddhist, Christian and secular contexts.

New religions often publicise themselves through techniques: something that practitioners (literally) can *do*, with doctrine and identity taking secondary place. This is as true for yoga and tai-chi as it is for shamanism or paganism; in Buddhism, meditation takes this role, and in most traditions in Ireland people are meditators first (whether continuously or only on retreats and during courses) and Buddhists later, if at all.

Methodological Notes

This book adopts cultural materialism in Williams' (1982) sense: to see culture in concrete practices such as writing for Victorian periodicals, translating medieval texts, the distribution of magazines, the practice of meditation, building Buddhist centres, the reception of Theosophical ideas and so on. It involves constantly connecting what was known (the facts of Asian Buddhism), the various frames through which they were experienced (religious, journalistic, plebeian, military and so on) and the concrete processes of distribution and reception which determined who in Ireland, or which Irish people abroad, could have access to this experience and what they could do with it.

Drawing on so many periods, it inevitably uses a wide range of research methods. Initial research, with Maria Griffin's collaboration, involved contact with academic specialists, librarians and museum curators. A brief email survey of contemporary Irish Buddhists and letters to the newspapers produced a series of interesting exchanges with Irish Buddhists and family historians. On the basis of this Maria carried out a number of in-depth interviews, while census officials kindly provided cross-tabulations of relevant data. This enabled us to generate a rough timeframe for understanding the relationship between Buddhism and Ireland.

From this point much of the work was library-based (including online databases and digitisations): searching for references to Ireland in studies of western Buddhism; biographical approaches; newspaper databases; and the catalogues of Trinity and Maynooth libraries, representing the best-established Protestant and Catholic academic institutions. Much 'grey literature' is now available online, relating to early Theosophy in particular.

Recently I have collaborated with Prof. Brian Bocking in University College Cork and Prof. Alicia Turner in York University, Toronto, on the life of U Dhammaloka, the subject of various publications and ongoing research. This has immensely deepened my understanding of the Irish-Buddhist encounter, and brought many new research contacts. Co-organising the Maynooth conference on new religions in Ireland and publishing the proceedings (Cosgrove et al., 2011) has been equally illuminating in terms of the Irish experience.

Nevertheless, the topic is vast, and much remains to be done. The significance of repression of non-Christian religion in Europe deserves greater attention in the study of religious change in general. The Buddhist-related contents of *non*-Jesuit early modern travel narratives (Offermans 2005) formed the foundation of most *popular* understandings of Asian religion until the later nineteenth century and have not yet been studied. Other key sites of the public reception of Buddhism, such as eighteenth- and nineteenth-century magazines and scientific journals (Hayley 1987), the hedge school literature (McManus 2002) and the missionary literature (Hogan 1990) have yet to be explored.

With the exception of Hearn (Rexroth 1977, Tweed 2000), the extensive and scattered writings of the other early Irish Buddhists all deserve greater exploration than chapter five has been able to give them. The study of 'going native' in Buddhist Asia is in a state of infancy (Turner et al., 2011, Cox 2013), while Irish missionary history has as yet little to say about the encounter with Asian cultures (Collins 2009).

Family history approaches to early Buddhist sympathisers in Ireland may become possible in the near future, while oral history of recent decades should now be feasible. Anthropological research on immigrant Buddhism in Ireland is in its infancy (Maguire 2004 and O'Leary and Li 2007 have brief mentions). Northern Ireland, with its ongoing Buddhist emigration and the continued rhetoric of Buddhism as response to sectarianism, deserves study in itself. Finally, here as elsewhere in the west the *sociological* relationship between western Buddhism and feminism, beneath the level of women teachers, has far to go. Pressure of time or lack of resources have made it impossible to pursue these quests; hopefully others will go further.

The Challenge of Reception

Some specific methodological comments are in order. The proposition that western Buddhists simply remade Buddhism 'in their own image' takes account neither of conflicts within western societies nor of their engagement with larger world-systems. The relationship between Irish Buddhists and texts on Buddhism varied widely: medieval and early modern Irish people were fundamentally consumers of texts about Buddhism; later Irish Oriental scholars, and Buddhists abroad, contributed to English-language discourses on Buddhism; Irish Buddhists at home were once again primarily consumers.

But 'Buddhism' is a formidable body of knowledge, history and practice. It has been a major religion in some of the world's oldest civilisations for one or two millennia; it has developed vast bodies of scripture and technical prescription; it is extremely complex institutionally; and so on. Any serious encounter rapidly finds that 'Buddhists-as-wished-for' are simply not as easy to construct to one's own measure as Druids-as-wished-for (Piggott 1968), shamans-as-wished-for (Hutton 2001), 'energies'-as-wished-for (Mulholland 2006) or come to that ghosts-as-wished-for (Barrow 1986).

There are many benefits to this: most major sutras are available in translation, often free and online, with a wide range of well-established meditation trainings and a multiplicity of institutions. However, all of this makes it harder for researchers to hear the *needs* which bring people to Buddhism, the problems they are grappling with in their own lives or the hegemonies they are attempting to dismantle. Instead, well-developed organisations are able to a large extent to impose their own interpretation and articulation of these needs. To quote one of the founding figures of Irish Buddhism:

> Maybe in the 60s and 70s it was a bit more woolly, because it wasn't that clear what Buddhism was. People could imagine it to be anything they liked. But now it's more clear. And that's not what everyone wants either, but it's more clear that Buddhism, for example, has a very strong system of ethics. This wouldn't have been exercised very much in the 60s and 70s. It was more getting spaced out and having some kind of unusual experience, see where meditation would take you ... (Interview C)[8]

To understand what Irish people *mean* by their Buddhism, then, we cannot take accounts formulated within this language at face value – *contra* both the guardians of Buddhist orthodoxy and the left or feminist critique of 'religion' per se – and we need to attend more closely to practice as a pointer to needs.

Texts and Context

Conventional accounts of western Buddhism present the arrival or 'discovery' of Buddhism as a 'textual object' (Baumann 2001: 7), and this book would be impossible without authors such as Lennon (2004), or Franklin (2008). At the same time, the 'textual reification' (Almond 1988) of Buddhism was far more significant when Irish people knew it only through the comments of Church Fathers or seventeenth-century Jesuits than in the nineteenth or twentieth

8. This and similarly designated interviews were carried out by Maria Griffin in summer 2008 with individuals who had been Buddhists in the 1960s and 1970s.

century.[9] In the latter period, as Franklin (2008) puts it, Buddhism was everywhere – and in many different forms: as backdrop for travellers' tales or missionary society advertising, as objects in museums, named or uncatalogued; as translations of canonical texts, as the target of Christian polemic – but above all in the first-hand encounters in Asia by Irish soldiers, sailors, civil servants, missionaries and others.

While some later contributed to the literature on Buddhism, few (other than civil servants) arrived in Asia with any particular western literature as a framework. Most of what they knew they discovered on the spot, by watching and talking to people; like Maurice Collis (chapter three) they often changed their mind. Few could read Asian languages; and access to European literature while in Asia will have been, then as now, patchy and unpredictable.

As Cohen (2006: 26–30) observes, we need to find a middle way which avoids the strong constructivism of an author like Almond, who stresses how British Victorian accounts of 'Buddhism' were driven by local purposes to construct 'Buddhism' as discursive object – but brackets the question of the Asian realities more or less well represented by this object. Conversely, a naïve approach which assumes the natural existence of Buddhism as a readily-known thing-in-itself will clearly not work either.

Orientalist scholarship certainly produced 'Buddhism' as a textual object within some western discourses; but the power of this particular object was restricted to educated elites in imperial states. In this book, it appears most powerfully in late nineteenth and early twentieth-century Catholic discourses, as the attempt was made to construct a 'spiritual empire' in Asia.

Other western actors, such as plebeian Theosophists, encountered Buddhism very differently, for example (Tweed 2000), while front-line imperial actors (from policemen to judges) encountered Buddhism as ethnographic and political reality. In particular, the 'first Irish Buddhists' were rarely European consumers of texts; they were migrants who 'went native' and encountered Buddhism as monastic practices, local folklore or political movements.

---

9. As we shall see in chapter two, even in this earlier period texts were physical objects, constrained by language and circulation; and they did not always remain fixed from one version to the next.

Thus it is important *not* to take the literature of 'Buddhism and Ireland' at face value, but to read it critically as historical documents, to find what political agendas, interpersonal rivalries, display of Buddhist credentials, ethical practice private or public, meditative experiences real or asserted, intercultural uncertainties, half-articulated needs and commercial strategies lie behind what we read; we have to relocate texts in relation to practice (Schopen 1997).

Irish Flavours and Transformative Purposes

In Ireland particularly, religion (from the nineteenth to the twenty-first century) has not been mostly about ideas, but about power and ethnicity. Modern Irish religion is noted for its hold on the population, intensity of practice, obsession with sexuality, its institutional extent – but not for its emphasis on theological creativity.[10] By comparison with European elites, Irish clerics were poorly trained to think about these aspects of religion.

This is also true for Buddhism: the *theological* texts discussed in this book were typically produced elsewhere, and Irish Buddhists are not famous as Buddhologists or doctrinal specialists. However, creative thinkers of other kinds, in particular literary figures and polemicists, who *have* been central to the modern Irish intelligentsia, abound. Thus we should be true to the concerns of the time, rather than taking *our* specialities as defining the concerns of past generations (or of non-academics). When the language of doctrine is spoken in this book, it is typically to make statements about cultural identity, politics, sectarian polemic or aesthetic judgement – all Irish specialities.

Hence to compare texts in an attempt to articulate 'the Irish discourse on Buddhism' would be about as useful as analysing the Soviet Communist Party of the 1930s on the basis of party doctrine. Religion, in these Irish contexts, was about ethnic identity; it was about building institutions; it was about the appropriate practice of rituals. Theology reflected, and served, these realities more than generating them; and this is as true for Irish Buddhists as for Irish Catholics or Anglicans.

From a Buddhist (and Marxist) perspective, however, there is something else to say. There is much truth in those critiques that

10. The golden age of Irish theology lies firmly in the Middle Ages.

show how Victorians always remained Victorian, westerners in Asia remained westerners, Irish Catholics were stuck as Irish Catholics, and so on. Such analyses help to understand the *dominant* discourses on Buddhism in these contexts. Yet for many, the *point* of becoming Buddhist was to change: as with Lobzang Jivaka who went from woman to man, from Anglican to Buddhist, and from aristocrat to kitchen cleaner.

Participant Understanding

Researchers on religion are often also participants (Prebish 2002), and orthodox Buddhists should be able to see 'actually-existing Buddhism' as the product of historical conditions. Among other things, this means that where published work is limited personal experience should be useable as raw material, once it is treated critically, and simply as one participant's experience.

My own understanding of the Irish engagement with Buddhism is shaped by coming to Buddhism with a prior family and personal involvement with social movements. Over the last two decades, I have noted Buddhist opposition to war in Afghanistan and Iraq or the military junta in Burma; responds to the criminalisation of blasphemy; relationships to Ambedkarite *dalits* in India or Tibetan resistance; solidarity with Asian immigrants in Dublin; the complex engagement between Buddhism, feminism and gay liberation; the relationship between Buddhist centres and the working-class communities they are often located in; collaborations around addiction recovery, chronic disease etc.; engagement with the state around education, health, death and dying; Buddhist relationships to radical ecology and 'green consumption'; conversations about politics and protests; responses to radical education projects; and so on.

My engagement is also shaped by the peculiarities of my own (Triratna) Buddhist group, which like most in Ireland is an 'export group' founded by converts based in other western countries. Participation provides informal knowledge of various kinds, which is used here where it is likely to be more widely representative: for example, the practicalities of what happens when setting up a meditation group in a small town. Similarly, my experience of what can and cannot easily be said, what will be understood or provoke hostility, what may be acceptable to leaders or ordinary participants, what activities may gain support and which are best pursued separately is drawn on in this text. As a political activist I have also experienced how other political and cultural movements perceive Buddhism and Buddhists, where they are interested in engaging and where they feel no practical cooperation is worthwhile. All of this suggests what kinds of counter-hegemonic alliances are possible, and what limits exist; what can be done and what cannot and – crucially – how these limits and possibilities might be transformed.

The small group context is not the only one; and as with other social movements change often develops outside and beyond groups, which in turn represent relative stabilisations, for longer or shorter periods, of longer historical processes. But as with Thompson (1993), the microcosm of small-group life and politics can provide a good intellectual check against taking more official discourses at face value.

'The universal *is* the particular': we always know from a particular time and place, and a particular situation within that, and we need to be transparent about this while trying to see what that particular experience may shed light on. The experience of western Buddhism illuminates broader features of western cultural radicalism from the late nineteenth century; its Irish manifestations highlight broader features of world-systemic place and change; and the questions raised by a western Marxist analysis of western Buddhism are broader ones about how popular needs and agency are articulated in worlds which we do not control but which we sometimes change, as with the collapse of the British Empire in Ireland and Asia or the collapse of Catholic power and cultural conservatism in the later twentieth century.

Evaluating Other People's Praxis

The academic's power of interpretation is often neither challenged nor justified, despite the gulf in experience and situation between their situations and those of their subjects. Thompson writes that:

> In this [plebeian, alternative] tradition experience is laid directly alongside learning, and the two test each other. There is nothing of our present academic specialisation: thought may be borrowed, like imagery, from any source available ... (1993: xiii–xv)

This is closer to the subjects of our research than a reading of them as if they were like us. Yeats, who asked of classicists 'what would they say/Did their Catullus walk that way?' refused to take up his college place, while AE denied his formal education any credit for his achievements. Most of those discussed in this book are informal intellectuals or creative thinkers; and they offered their allegiance to other systems of evaluation – adherence to the monastic code, fidelity to their own spiritual development, the laborious acquisition of Buddhist intellectual training, the development of a Buddhism suitable for the modern world, solidarity with their fellow-Buddhists.

In the case of early Irish Buddhists, when studied in detail there are all sorts of things in their writings and recorded comments that might lead us to look at them with suspicion: for example, they use the language of 'race' and 'nation' freely. But we might note something else: for example, that Jivaka wrote more for the Maha Bodhi Society than he did for London publishers.[11] Most of the main early figures not only wrote, but worked for, Asian-led organisations (monasteries, lay Buddhist organisations, educational institutions).

We can ask other kinds of questions of their texts. For example, when Bowles Daly visited thirteen hundred Sri Lankan monasteries, could he talk to the monks without an interpreter? Could he read Pali? If Hearn could read Japanese but struggled to speak it (Murray 1993), how did this affect his daily life? When Dhammaloka's Buddhist Tract Society translated Tom Paine into Burmese, was this his own work, and how comprehensible were the results?

If we are serious about evaluating someone's relationship to a foreign society, these basic material questions – about how they communicated with people locally – are in many ways more important than analysing how their tropes related to those of commercial London publishers; yet they are systematically bypassed in academic commentary. When Jivaka (1962) worked hard to learn Ladakhi and drew on standard Tibetan as a point of reference, he showed all the signs of an excellent language learner through his insistence on being in a natural environment and his motivation to explore the Tibetan scriptures. Language is not just metaphor (as often in academia); it is a practical material reality.

---

11. Harris (2007) is a model of how to replace British observers of Sinhala Buddhism in their *Asian* context, not merely their British and Anglophone one.

'Experience breaks through'

Accounts of western Buddhism – and this one is no exception – tend to focus on those who control and controlled the 'means of intellectual production': those with access to publishing, particularly English-language publishing (which has survived better than Asian-language grey literature and is more likely to be digitised) and more recently those who control meditation centres, temples, etc.

The *systematic* production and distribution of knowledge is itself more concentrated in metropolitan societies than peripheral ones. There are few Irish figures of any period who offer systematic accounts of what it means to be Buddhist (with the exception of Wei Wu Wei, whose theme is that systematic accounts of anything are to be distrusted).

Authors did not hold single, fixed positions; as they travelled from East to West (the returning missionary's daughter, Helen Waddell, shifted from relying on childhood memory to drawing more on Lafcadio Hearn) or from West to East (as Jivaka moved from relying on Lobsang Rampa's fantasies to immersion in Tibetan monastic life). On a larger scale, just as the British Empire was engulfing Burma in the 1880s and drawing Tibet within its orbit (1903–4), it was simultaneously in crisis in Ireland in the face of Land War and Home Rule agitation; the imperial high noon was more of an Indian summer which did not remain stable even over an individual adulthood.

Researching these authors highlights how, as Thompson puts it, experience breaks through – experience of different cultures, of training within particular organisations, no doubt in some cases also meditative experiences of various kinds, and the conflicts involved in 'going native' within empire or converting within Ireland. Again and again, experience breaks up the smooth flow of discourse.

Moreover, what can be described most clearly are not fixed positions but social relationships which structure who authors are arguing with, for or against, and around which they negotiate their own lives in the massively complex structures that brought the two ends of Eurasia together. The history of 'Ireland and Buddhism' is above all a history of people in relationships, rather than a history of ideas; it is a history of empire not so much as ideology but as lived practice; and it is a history of social change as anti-colonial struggle and counter-cultural transformation.

Limitations of This Book

I did not start out to write a book on Irish Buddhism. I had agreed to write a short piece on contemporary Buddhist communities in Ireland, and realised that nothing was known about their origins. Assuming that the answer lay in the 1960s or 1970s, I secured some funding from my department to employ Maria Griffin as research assistant. What we found in two months was fascinating, and increasingly took over from other plans; a contemporary Buddhist might say that I listened to my heart in turning my energies to this work. Maria, not a Buddhist herself, remained involved and supportive far beyond her formal employment.

As it became clear that this was a book, and not simply an article (Cox and Griffin 2009), the limitations of my own expertise have become painfully clear. I am not a specialist in early Irish manuscripts, world-systems theory, literary criticism, Theosophy or many of the other areas thrown up by this research; I have pursued numerous red herrings and abandoned several questions which exceeded my own capabilities.

This work is necessarily interdisciplinary, and specialists will see my weaknesses and misunderstandings all too clearly. The alternative would have been to construct a narrowly-bounded account which would have missed the larger picture and the inter-connections and contrasts. I have attempted to alternate between writing *within* the language of specific disciplines or fields and commenting critically on them.

In attempting to answer the questions raised by this research I have consulted many specialists, and have been comforted by the reflection that no single individual could be expert in all the areas touched on here. I am all too aware of the gaps and limitations in this account, and hope it will be a spur to future research. A particular gap is the history of *Asian* Buddhists in Ireland. Mostly very recent arrivals, scattered in many small communities, with Buddhist practice largely private and operating through their own languages, to research these groups adequately would require substantial funding and a team of native-language ethnographers.

Failing this, chapter seven does its best with publicly-available English-language sources.

I have also been unable to delve too deep in the world of *unacknowledged* or closet adoption of Buddhist practices and ideas by those who see themselves as Catholic – a necessary reticence for many in a period of Church hostility to 'syncretism' and a significant challenge for researchers. Again, extensive ethnography would be required, but I have had to rely on those who are more open and public about their explorations.

In some areas this book breaks new ground, and this asks for particular indulgence from the reader, who cannot rely on many authorities. In particular, as an *Irish* account, there are few other texts which relate directly to the problem; some areas have been obsessively researched and others barely scratched.

Inevitably too, some of what is said is stated as general knowledge (to students of Buddhism, or Ireland), or as the considered opinion of someone who has been involved in the issues concerned. These are cases where it would often be hard, or pointless, to extend a bibliography which is already longer than many journal articles. The reader will have no difficulty following these up, but it would be impossible to identify everything which might be new to any individual.

In particular, the interlinked spaces of religion, ethnicity, and politics are 'essentially contested' in Ireland as elsewhere. Some statements, too, are 'essentially contested', and a book could be written to defend them without necessarily adding to what some people will already accept and others will reject. Where possible, I have tried to argue these statements directly, or to highlight their controversial nature. How successful the final result is must be the reader's own judgement.

Structure

The body of this book is organised in three sections.

Part I consists of a reception history of Buddhism in Ireland up to the mid-nineteenth century (chapter two). The cross-cultural exchange between the two ends of Eurasia relied on economic, political and cultural mechanisms which changed drastically from one period of encounter to the next, and this is traced with respect to Buddhism. This section demonstrates, among other things, that knowledge of Buddhism is a necessary but not a sufficient condition for its development in a new country; what counts are actors' purposes, a theme developed in subsequent chapters.

Part II explores the second half of the nineteenth century and the first half of the twentieth, when some Irish people first became Buddhists and a period in which religion was above all about *ethnicity*. This period is marked by the decline of the old Anglo-Irish imperial service class, and the rise of the new Catholic national service class (chapter three). Defectors from the former often looked to Theosophy as a way of securing their future in the new world of national politics (chapter four); the Irish Theosophists serve as an important contrast for those Irish people who became Buddhist, usually 'going native' on the edges of empire (chapter five). This section draws critically on Buddhist Studies and post-colonial writing to explore Theosophy and Buddhism as alternative religious politics in a contested world-system.

Part III discusses the development of Buddhism *within* Ireland, from the foundational period of the late 1960s and early 1970s (chapter six) to its situation as Ireland's third-largest religion in 2006 (chapter seven). It draws on the sociology of religion, Buddhist studies and research on Irish social movements and counter-cultures to map this new Buddhist period, highlighting the choices now available between conservative respectability and a Buddhism which remains an agent of critical social change.

Part I

Thinking 'Buddhism and Ireland' in World-systems Context (500–1850)

Chapter Two

Bog Buddhas and Travellers' Tales:
How Knowledge Crossed Eurasia

How Did the Dharma Come West?
World-systems and Reception Processes

In 1886, a labourer in Baltrasna, Co. Meath found a foot-high bronze statue of the Buddha buried 'very deep down in the bog ... two miles from the nearest road'.[1] The landowner, Robert Weld-O'Connor, was a prominent Unionist and a bad enough landlord to get threatening letters at the height of the Land War,[2] but enough of an antiquary to have it included on a Royal Society of Antiquaries field trip in 1892.[3] The piece then passed to a relative, Agnes Weld, who realised its significance: daughter of the Royal Society's librarian, niece of Alfred Tennyson and a travel writer in her own right, she is best remembered as the child Lewis Carroll photographed as Alice.

Weld exhibited it at the British Association's 1898 meeting in Bristol, where eminent archaeologists like the British Museum's CH Read and Sir John Evans, father of the discoverer of Knossos, accepted her identification of it:[4]

> She proved that by its erect "preaching" attitude with upraised right hand, and its crisply curled woolly hair, surmounted by a headdress composed of five lotus petals and its long, pendulous ears, this image of Buddha belonged to the earliest Singhalese type of the first centuries of the Christian era.[5]

---

1. *The Times*, Sept 13 1898: 8–9. I am indebted to Brian Bocking for discovering the statue's story.
2. The letters formed the basis of the 1885 Barbavilla trials.
3. *Journal of the Royal Society of Antiquaries of Ireland*, Oct 1892 (fifth series, vol. 2/3: 314).
4. *Nature*, 1899 (vol. 59): 163.
5. *The Times*, Sept 13 1898: 8–9.

Most of the discussion, in fact, revolved not around its authenticity but around how it got there. The 'Chinese seals', salted around Ireland to prove early links, were fresh in people's memory (Galambos 2008); or it might have been stolen property. However no-one came forward to claim it – or attempted to use it to demonstrated Asokan missions to Ireland. It would in any case have been a rare and valuable piece for such an enterprise.

Though the intellectual tide was then turning against the wilder antiquarian claims of Celtic-Asian links (Lennon 2004), the simplest explanation is that the statue was what it appeared to be, brought through well-attested trading chains from Sri Lanka via the Roman Empire. There is unchallenged, though limited, evidence of Roman and Romano-British presence in Ireland (Raftery 1994: 200–219), and goods could travel a long way: in nearby Wales a coin of the Bactrian Menander I, the straight man of the Theravadin *Milindapanha*, appears in a second-century CE[6] site at Tenby (Murphy 2009). Whether transported as a gift, a religious item or exotic art, such a find is remarkable but not unique.[7] The statue's current whereabouts are unknown; it is probably still in private hands.[8]

The Rise and Fall of World-systems

Ireland is a small and usually sparsely inhabited island off the north-western end of Eurasia. Buddhism's homelands, vast territories including some of the planet's most heavily populated areas, lie five thousand kilometers east. Until the thirteenth century, Irish people understood the distance as further still, and India was the far end of the known world. The ninth-century geographer Dicuil wrote:

> [This] part of our earth ... has its longest dimension running from east to west, that is from India to the columns of Hercules consecrated at Cadiz, six thousand six hundred and thirty miles. (v. 1; see also v. 3; Tierney 1967: 57, 25)

For knowledge of Buddhism to cross this daunting space, filled with dangers real and imaginary, implied (then as now) the wider

6. I follow the religious studies convention of CE (common era) and BCE (before common era).

7. Famously, the skeleton of a Barbary ape was found in the Iron Age site at Navan Fort in Armagh.

8. Thanks to Audrey Whitty and Mary Cahill of the National Museum for assistance with this.

economic, cultural and political processes which link the two: what world-systems theory calls world-empires (such as the Roman or Chinese) and world-economies (such as contemporary capitalism). Such systems are constituted by bulk goods trade but also by

> three other types of system exchange, and, consequently, boundaries: political/military exchanges; luxury, preciosity, or prestige goods exchanges; and information exchanges. Each of these three boundaries is successively larger, and all are larger than the bulk goods exchange network. (Hall 2000: 11)

A world-system necessarily has a dominant mode of accumulation but can encompass or engage with multiple modes of production: ancient Ireland's kin-based system on the edge of the Roman tributary system, or Elizabethan Ireland's tributary system as part of the new colonial capitalist order.

Until the East India Company's Irish soldiers, Ireland stood outside the *political/military* exchanges with Buddhist Asia which, from Alexander on, enabled knowledge exchanges between the classical Mediterranean world and greater India. As world-systems grew and contracted, Ireland lay on the margins of *prestige goods* exchanges (such as bronze statues) with the Buddhist world, until nineteenth century empire made tea popular with the Irish poor (Clarkson and Crawford 2001). From the fifth century on, however, Ireland often fell within the widest category, *information exchange*. As Hall puts it,

> all of Afroeurasia (in conventional terms Asia, Europe, northern Africa) has been linked, at least at the information and luxury goods exchange levels, for over two millennia. Hence, one *cannot* explain events and processes in Europe by only examining European processes. (2000: 12)

In fact, Bronze Age Ireland had already been involved in long-distance luxury goods exchange networks across Europe in gold (exported) and amber (imported) (Hawkes 1973: 324). The Greeks were aware of Ireland from the earliest Buddhist period: the island is mentioned in the sixth century BCE Marseilles periplus and by the great traveller Pytheas in the fourth century BCE (Cunliffe 2002). Caesar and Tacitus in the first century CE, and Ptolemy in the second, drew on traders' knowledge of the island. These same links brought the statue to one end of Europe and made the 'Silk Road' possible at the other – and, in northern India, brought about the social changes within which the Buddha's *sramana* milieu flourished (Carrithers 1983).

As one world-system broke down and another developed, new circuits of exchange developed in which Ireland took various roles. There is no single, continuous history but rather a series of different circuits of knowledge which need to be treated differently. What this history does demonstrate, however, is that the conventional assumption that knowledge about Buddhism was absent in Ireland until very recently is simply wrong. It also, of course, highlights the point that such knowledge does not automatically lead to conversions, as naive accounts often suggest: over a millennium elapsed between the first definite knowledge of Buddhism in Ireland and the first known Irish Buddhists.

Non-textual Means of Transmission

Zen's origin myth speaks of a transmission outside the scriptures exemplified by Mahakasyapa's smiling when the Buddha held up a flower. More recently, Schopen (1997) has argued for decentring textual analysis in our understanding of Buddhism and integrating what is known from archaeology and inscriptions – in this paralleling more general interdisciplinary approaches to the past. Even today, Buddhism is arguably far more successfully transmitted to Ireland as images, trinkets, incense, chanting or meditation than as doctrine or texts.

Most national myths of Buddhism's arrival, however, are accounts of bringing and translating texts and teachings (and their use in periodical reformations). Texts are the main focus of this chapter, too – not least because for much of the period, between the end of the Roman Empire and the rise of the British, Ireland lay at the fringes of actual goods exchange with the Buddhist world.

Some links nevertheless existed. The age of migrations which ended the Roman connection saw the emigration of monks such as Dicuil throughout western Europe. If the Viking period put an end to this migration, it created new prestige goods exchanges between the two ends of Eurasia. The ninth- to twelfth-century Hiberno-Norse cities excavated in Dublin and Waterford contained a substantial amount of silk in caps, scarves, ribbons and hairnets (Heckett 1997; Curriculum Development Unit 1978); Chinese or Central Asian silk was also found in thirteenth-century Cork (Edwards 1990: 188).

Viking trade with the lower Volga also turned an eighth or ninth-century Buddha figure from Swat or Kashmir into an amulet or necklace (with leather strap) buried in a Swedish grave. As with the bog Buddha, it is not clear how such prestige goods were understood – an issue which (as later chapters show) is equally relevant for 1907 Cork or, come to that, 2013 Dublin: loot, art, religious artefact, memento, charm?

Church Fathers and Alexander Legends: Time Lags and Mentalités

It is only with the fifth-century arrival of Christianity, bringing with it written books and the institutions of the western Church, that communication from the far side of Eurasia becomes certain and we can start to interpret it.

In the fourth century BCE, after the time of the Buddha, Alexander of Macedonia's army reached the Indus, briefly bringing 'East' and 'West' within a single political-military world-system. Longer-lasting than Alexander's conquests were the ensuing trade and knowledge connections between India and the eastern Mediterranean, mediated through the Bactrian Greek kingdoms in western Asia, the rise of Asoka's pro-Buddhist empire in India and the city of Alexandria.

The early Christian church in turn inherited what the Greeks knew of Asian Buddhism, and this arrived to Ireland in the texts of church fathers such as Clement of Alexandria and Jerome. In the sixth and seventh centuries, Irish scholars were familiar with patristic commentaries; the seventh-century bishop Cummian could quote Jerome in a pastoral letter (Ó Cróinín 2005: 382, 377). Irish exegesis depended on the Alexandrian school (Hughes 2005: 327), while Jerome was another favourite in early centuries (Herren 2005: 40); so that by the seventh century at least we can assume a widespread knowledge among the *literati* of these authors' accounts of Buddhism.

Clement (c. 150–215) thought that Greek philosophy was 'in large part derived from the barbarians':

> First in its ranks were the prophets of the Egyptians; and the Chaldeans among the Assyrians; and the Druids among the Gauls; and the Samanaeans [*sramanas*] among the Bactrians; and the philosophers of the Celts; and the Magi of the Persians, who foretold the Saviour's birth, and came into the land of Judaea guided by a star.

> The Indian gymnosophists are also in the number, and the other
> barbarian philosophers. And of these there are two classes, some of
> them called Sarmanae [*sramanas*], and others Brahmins. And those of
> the Sarmanae who are called Hylobii neither inhabit cities, nor have
> roofs over them, but are clothed in the bark of trees, feed on nuts, and
> drink water in their hands ... they know not marriage nor begetting
> of children.
>
>   Some, too, of the Indians obey the precepts of Buddha; whom,
> on account of his extraordinary sanctity, they have raised to divine
> honours. (Roberts and Donaldson 1869)

This account repeats the commonplace Indian distinction between
brahmanas (Vedic ritual specialists) and *sramanas* (wanderers
including Buddhist monks and nuns), noting the existence of
asceticism and a cult of the Buddha – while failing to identify the
Bactrian and Indian *sramanas* and leaving open the relationship
between Buddhists and *sramanas*. Jerome (347–420), however, was
in no doubt:

> To come to the Gymnosophists of India, the opinion is authoritatively
> handed down that Buddha, the founder of their religion, had his birth
> through the side of a virgin. (Fremantle et al., 1997; orig. 1892: 815)

Irish monks could hardly have ignored these references to Druids
and Celts, although these were presumably more a continuation of
Clement's 'Noble Savage' image of barbarian philosophers (Piggott
1968) than Sutin's modernist suggestion of 'a shared vision of an
underlying spiritual unity to existence'.

We should note at this point a comment which Clement's pupil
Origen is supposed to have made about Britain:

> The island has long been predisposed to [Christianity] through the
> doctrines of the Druids and the Buddhists, who had already inculcated
> the doctrine of the unity of the Godhead. (Mackenzie 1928: 42)

Widely repeated and republished, the reference to Buddhists has
recently been recognised as a piece of modern myth-making, interpolated in 1884 in Thomas Wise's *History of paganism in Caledonia*.[9]

Leaving this aside, a scholarly seventh-century monk could have
a sense of Buddhism as located in India, revolving around a saintly
biography, associated with serious philosophy, and – perhaps

---

9. See the excellent discussion at http://www.roger-pearse.com/weblog/?p=2927.
My thanks to Anna Mazzoldi for drawing my attention to this.

separately – of Indian religion as involving asceticism. This fit easily within a wider picture of non-Christian philosophers who could nevertheless be taken seriously; a category produced by the Church's selective appropriation of classical philosophy (Hadot 1995) and the concept of the virtuous pagan. The ensuing tension between sympathy towards Buddhism as philosophy or doctrine, and hostility towards Buddhism as religion or practice, continued to the modern period in Victorian debates which counterposed the Buddha's exemplary life to shocking concepts such as the lack of a soul, and contemporary Catholic positions which acknowledge Buddhism's ethical strengths while denying its salvific value.

Reception History, National Myths and Timelags

Most accounts of the western encounter with Buddhism summarise a history starting with Greek encounters, moving through Marco Polo and early modern Jesuits up to the 'real' purpose of discussing the birth of Buddhist Studies and the first openly Buddhist westerners. It is sometimes assumed (as with Beinorius 2005: 8–11) that anything which was ever known west of the Buddhist heartland was the common property of 'Europe'; or conversely (as with Sutin 2006) that nobody in the later Middle Ages read anything other than Marco Polo. Both miss the rather more interesting question of how, across periods of ten or fifteen centuries, this knowledge actually circulated.

This chapter asks *what texts* were available, *when, where,* and in what *languages*: a material analysis of the reception of texts as artefacts and stories. It asks how encounters between Europeans and Buddhists were written up, interpreted, translated and plagiarised; how they entered into theology, popular literature and guides for merchants; who could read them, under what circumstances and in what languages, in an attempt to understand what happened at the European end of these stories.

We now think in terms of nation-states ('Ireland', 'India') as natural units of analysis; but both were constructed recently, with partitions and conflicts expressing their more complex pasts; globally, most states were constructed within living memory. Purely national categories of analysis will not help much for these early encounters. The first knowledge of Buddhism in Ireland came through the post-imperial church; the first relevant Irish author wrote in a French monastery; and the first Irish person to encounter Buddhists lived in north-east Italy.

Ireland's encounter with Buddhism has been shaped by an international church, the British Empire and 'blow-ins' from more powerful western societies; circles of emigration and immigration have always characterised the encounter. The languages spoken on the island were also spoken elsewhere; and Ireland variously shared common reading and publishing spaces with Britain, France and (later) the US.

Buddhism, too, was not neatly bounded. First formed as traditional societies were reshaped by trans-Eurasian trade and royal states were built on the ruins of tribal republics, the later Buddhism of the long Asian Middle Ages saw established monastic sanghas tied to monarchical power. This now-'traditional' Buddhism was in turn replaced by forms of modernist Buddhism formed in anti-colonial contexts. The relationships between 'Buddhism' and 'Ireland' are structured by interactions within world-systems, and changes from one kind of world-system to another.

This complexity is underlined by the time lags in the transmission of knowledge. Information from Alexander's fourth century BCE exploits became available in Ireland between the sixth and eleventh centuries CE, up to *fifteen centuries* later. During this period, the age of migrations, from the Franks and Saxons to the Vikings, repeatedly disrupted the transmission of knowledge within Europe. Trade routes East were in turn disrupted by the rise of Islam, so that until the thirteenth century the latest Irish knowledge of Buddhist Asia dated from the second and third centuries CE.

After this period, new routes East were developed and the time lag between what traders and missionaries saw and what was read in Ireland diminished, with time lags of 50 to 300 years between manuscripts arriving in Italy and their availability in Britain and Ireland. By this point, too, Asian Buddhisms had changed dramatically from what the Greeks had encountered.

The Shifting Shapes of Secular Texts

The church route was not the only source of classical knowledge of India. This section discusses the fate of eyewitness accounts from Alexander's expedition, the knowledge of classical geographers, the transmission of Buddhist folk stories and non-textual forms of transmission. 'Secular' is a problematic term in medieval Europe, where most written material was transmitted by clerics; nevertheless the distinction is useful.

Most notably, the writings of church fathers typically arrived in Latin (or occasionally Greek) and remained relatively fixed, so we can have some confidence in *what* was known to the literati. Secular texts changed far more, with complex textual histories. Moreover, there is a huge problem of language. During the medieval period, Old and Middle Irish, Old and Middle English, Middle Welsh, Old Norse, Norman French and Latin were all spoken in Ireland at various times; Irish was an immigrant language in Scotland and Wales and the native tongue of monks much further afield.[10]

Hence we do not know, from the language of a particular manuscript, who read it. At best we can say that *Barlaam and Josaphat* was translated into Middle Irish, or that the *Alexander Romance* existed in several Middle English and Middle Scots versions – and deduce that they were probably known in Ireland, or to Irish people. Languages did not obey porous state boundaries. Immigration, emigration, raiding, slave-trading and conquest meant that multilingualism was part not only of the educated elite's world but also of others who travelled, willingly or otherwise. Such problems of method underlie the non-national complexity of the medieval world.

As travel became easier and printing developed, some of these problems become less visible, meaning that it is easier to fall for the fiction of neatly bounded nation-states, in exclusive possession of a single language – which was no more true in the thirteenth or eighteenth centuries than in the twenty-first.

Dicuil: Living On a Breath

This is underlined by the ninth-century Dicuil. Since the sixth century, *Scotti peregrinantes* (wandering Irishmen) had emigrated to western Europe, founding monasteries, preaching and teaching. The Carolingian period saw a great influx of Irish teachers and scholars with the foundation of a palace school and the development of *scriptoria* (Tierney 1967: 4–7). In 825, Dicuil – probably a teacher at the school – published one of at least five books, *De mensura orbis terrae*, a discussion of the measurement of the known earth.

10. Ó Ciosáin (2010: 182) notes the bias in discussions of literacy towards the 'official' language.

Drawing indirectly on the Roman historian and geographer Pliny the Elder (23–79) and the compiler Solinus (date uncertain), Dicuil discussed the geography of India and Ceylon, before adding this:

> The same author [Solinus] wrote something else which is incredible: That the men who live at the source of the Ganges have no need of any food, but live solely on the odour of wild apples, and when going on a long journey they bring the same with them as a stand-by to sustain themselves on the odour; but if perchance they draw a breath less sweet, they indubitably die. (vii.36; Tierney 1967 :83)

For Dicuil, this is a wonder-tale on a par with accounts of the stars to be seen in the Indian ocean or the fauna of Ceylon. It fits, however, with the broader European consensus expressed by Clement's nut-eating *sramanas*, which saw Indians as ascetic philosophers (Satlow 2008). Such stories were transmitted because they fit with European conceptions; but it is also true that *sramanas* of any kind were ascetic by Greek and Roman standards. Similar points can be made of the Alexander legend.

From Taxila to Ballymote: What Alexander Saw

Tales of Alexander's conquests were immensely popular in medieval Europe, and took various forms. The Middle Irish version, *Scela Alexandir*, exists in two fifteenth-century manuscripts: complete in the Book of Ballymote, and a fragment in the *Leabhar Breac*, the Speckled Book, written in Clonsast, Co. Offaly. The latter claims a seventh-century original, but modern scholars prefer the tenth or eleventh century (Welch and Stewart 1996: 509; Cary 1956: 69–70). This time lag of perhaps fifteen hundred years is a record of sorts, and an indication of how information circulated between and across world-systems.

Unlike some medieval Alexander tales, the *Scela* is based mainly on historical sources, in particular Orosius' fifth-century *Historia*. This text, relying in turn on Roman historians and Eusebius, was also studied in medieval Ireland (Meyer 1949: 3). In England, King Alfred (849–99) deemed it one of 'those books that are most necessary for all men to know', and had it translated into Anglo-Saxon (Bately 1970).[11]

---

11. TCD holds a copy of the Middle English *Wars of Alexander*, itself largely a translation of Orosius.

Orosius stressed politics and military history, but the *Scela* also draws on Onesicritus, who had been on Alexander's expedition. Two sections also circulated independently – a *Letter to Aristotle*, supposedly written by Alexander, on the wonders of India,[12] and the *Correspondence between Alexander and Dindimus*. Both draw on Onesicritus and Palladius' *On the brahmans* to present readers with a sustained encounter with 'naked philosophers'. The *Correspondence* is the livelier source for what Irish people heard about Indian religion.

Alexander and Dindimus

Dindimus is represented as the 'kyng of the Bragmayns' – in other words, the chief philosopher (Westlake 1911: 77). Alexander writes to him seeking wisdom, and Dindimus initially demurs:

> For our way of life is very distant and different from yours ... And if I write you anything about our way of living, you will have no joy in it, because you are busily occupied with feats of arms.[13]

Then he gets down to business, at length, saying that his people

> lead a simple life and a clean one, and we avoid worshipping many gods ... We put up with everything and that, we say, is enough ...

They do not farm, fish or hunt but depend on 'what the earth, mother of us all, brings forth without man's labour'. They do not worry about heat or cold, do not wear clothes and 'never fulfil the desires of our body'. Moreover,

> Through patience we tolerate everything. We slay all our inward enemies, so that we are not afraid of any outer ones ... We do not speak much, but when we are asked to speak we say nothing but the truth ... We live in caves or crevices of crags ... We sleep on the earth.

Dindimus' people avoid philosophers 'whose teaching is always contradictory and uncertain' and frequent those 'where we learn to live virtuously and that teach us to do no harm to any man'. Having praised the beauties of nature, he goes on to deliver a lengthy critique of Western rulers:

12. An Anglo-Saxon translation was made in the ninth or tenth century (Lapidge 2001: 27).
13. This and subsequent selections are my own translations from Westlake's (1911) edition of the Middle English text. This shares the *Correspondence* with the Irish text, which is similar in substance.

> You eat all manner of things that come to hand, and your faces seem as though you were fasting and hungry … You will not allow men to live in their own freedom, but you make them your thralls and their subjects … You have all your wit in your tongue, and all your wisdom is in your mouth. You love gold and silver and gather them together and desire to have large, tall houses with a great number of servants … You want to keep your riches for ever, and everything that you can get; but in the end everything will leave you.

Dindimus finishes his first letter with a (Christian) critique of pagan worship. Alexander in turn, 'wonder wrathe, because of iniury of his goddes', charges Dindimus with making a virtue out of poverty and living like animals. A similar exchange is repeated, and matters finish with Alexander's threat:

> If I could come to you with an army, I would make you leave your wretched life, and become men of arms, as many of you as were able.

The dramatic action operates within the conventions of classical Noble Savagery and Christian critiques of pagan vice. Yet it is not simply an imposition of power/knowledge on a passive Orient (then unaffected by Irish readers' opinion). It is a safe mouthpiece for bitter critiques of the powerful and wealthy within a framework of Christian denunciation of paganism, and more broadly a challenge to the taken-for-granted (Clarke 1997).

From a critical perspective, the 'Indian philosopher', then as now, attracts attention because they are *different* from one's own rulers. This image can denounce the existing state of affairs, or subtly ratify it by setting the bar of righteous living too high. Readers, perhaps, could choose between these possibilities.

Legendary Alexanders

Many *Alexanders* circulated in medieval Europe (see Huber n.d. for a list of those in Britain). Other 'historical' ones include a twelfth-century Latin poem and its thirteenth-century prose translation into Old Icelandic. Most others are 'legendary' ones, deriving from a tenth-century Latin text which was translated into French in the twelfth and English and Scots in the thirteenth. Immensely popular, with five Middle English and two Middle Scots versions, it was probably also known in Ireland. Here the gymnosophists

> never fight or engage in conflict. They always go naked, and they have neither towns nor cities, but live in huts and caves.

Their (unnamed) king writes to Alexander asking why he is making war on them, saying that they have nothing he can take; Alexander promises to come peacefully. Observing their simple life, he offers them a boon and they ask for immortality. He replies –

> I am deadly myself; how then may I give you immortality?

This is perhaps a more fantastic and less hard-hitting encounter than the brutality of *Alexander and Dindimus*, expressing a simpler wish for otherness.

To the availability of all these stories, finally, we must add the massively successful plagiarisation of *Alexander and Dindimus* in *Mandeville's Travels*, translated into Irish in the fifteenth century and discussed below. By the standards of the day, this tale was well distributed.

Buddhism through Greek Eyes

If medieval Christians fitted what they heard into their own categories, what of their Greek sources? What – if any – 'knowledge' was transmitted in the thirteen or fourteen centuries that passed between Onesicritus at Taxila in the 320s BCE and the tenth or eleventh-century composition of *Scela Alaxandir*?

Early Greek writers' concept of *genos* could mean either 'people' or 'caste' (Satlow 2008: 5). Indian philosophers were seen both as an independent people and as separate castes – as in Clement, who envisioned multiple groups of philosophers in a single country. The Greeks were also capable of turning Indian castes into geographical populations (Stoneman 1995: 100–1).

The mark of philosophers was a consciously ascetic lifestyle and a role advising kings. Given the difficulty of interpreting beliefs, the 'actual content of Indian "philosophy" [was] rather secondary to their identification as philosophers' (Satlow 2008: 8). Indians of the period distinguished established *brahmana* priests from ascetic *sramanas*, but *Alexander and Dindimus* turn *brahmana*s into a people and – because they are philosophers – confer on them the ascetic attributes which Indians associated with their religious opposites, the Buddhists, Jains and other *sramanas*.

We observe other cultures through the lenses of our own, and through multiple languages. As the gymnosophist Mandanis is supposed to have said,

> It is impossible to explain philosophical doctrine through the medium
> of three interpreters who understand nothing we say any more than
> the vulgar; it is like asking water to flow through mud. (quoted in
> Sutin 2006: 8)

What came to Ireland was translated on the spot from perhaps a
spoken Prakrit to Sanskrit to Persian and then to Greek (hence three
interpreters: Stoneman 1995) and later via Latin to Middle Irish,
Middle English, and so on.

Like Water through Mud?

Stoneman (1995) nonetheless makes a good case that the basic
content is historical. The Greek geographer, Strabo, summarised
Megasthenes, Seleucid ambassador to Chandragupta's court, who
distinguished *brahmanas* from *sramanas* ('Garmanas'). The latter in
turn were divided between Clement's 'hylobii' (forest hermits) and
'physicians' who

> apply philosophy to the study of the nature of man. They are of frugal
> habits and ... subsist upon rice and meal, which everyone gives when
> asked. (Strabo XV, I, 60)

Strabo also noted that Aristobulus met two sophists and their
followers at Taxila, one with a shaven head and one with long hair.
This led into Onesicritus' account of meeting two naked 'sophists'
sitting before Taxila, one of whom stated that

> The best teaching is that which removes pleasure and pain from the
> soul. (Stoneman 1995: 103)

Stoneman counters the common assumption that these were
merely straw men for an exposition of Onesicritus' own Cynic
teaching by exploring the anthropological information in Strabo.
Megasthenes' philosophers

> tarry in a grove in front of the city in an enclosure merely commen-
> surate with their needs, leading a frugal life, abstaining from animal
> food and the delights of love, and hearkening only to earnest words,
> and communicating also with anyone who wishes to hear them.
> (Stoneman 1995: 105)

As Stoneman notes, this is fully compatible with Indian asceticism
(such groves are frequent in the Pali canon). Megasthenes' description
of their view of life as 'a dream-like illusion' cannot easily be ascribed

Bog Buddhas and Travellers' Tales   59

to brahmanic philosophy of the period,[14] but is a familiar western interpretation of Buddhist and Upanishadic thought. As with the Church fathers, the Greeks were confused as to the Indian schools, and it is not clear whether the philosophers they met were Jains, Buddhists, Upanishadic or other sramanas. The naked philosophers perhaps belonged to more than one kind of *sramana* group (as the contrast between shaven and unshaven suggests).

Nevertheless it is plausible that across this great distance, centuries and languages, these stories transmitted an awareness of the Indian sramana milieu as embodying the philosophical life, particularly in its asceticism. 'Indian philosophers' were seen as highly ethical, limiting their needs to an absolute minimum, opposed to violence and seeking only to 'slay all our inward enemies'. Then as now, lay donors were typically concerned with the virtue of the *sramanas* they supported. It is unsurprising if the Greeks registered this – or if some Irish people used this virtue to criticise their own overlords.

Travelling Folktales

'Aesop's fables' have a complex history. They were known to Bede (672–735); popular in Latin across western Europe by the tenth century (Gibbs 2002: xxvi), eleventh-century English texts are known (Klein and Swan 2004), while Marie de France produced an Anglo-Norman collection in the late twelfth or early thirteenth century. Caxton's 1484 English translation was the first of many print editions; and we can be fairly certain that this was known in Ireland, as earlier ones may have been.

What was not known was that the collection shared much with the Buddhist *Jataka* stories and the Hindu Panchatantra. Best known from the Theravadin Pali Canon, the *Jataka*s tell of the Buddha's past lives, as human or animal. In each he carries out meritorious acts, rewarded in future lives, so that the frame is moralistic; the characters are identified with figures from the Buddha's life. This frame is lacking in the Aesop stories. In the *Jambu-khadaka-jataka* (no. 294), for example, a jackal sees a crow eating an apple on a branch. The jackal flatters the crow's voice, and in turn the crow praises the jackal and shakes the branch so food drops. The spirit of the tree – the future Buddha – comments,

14. Stoneman also projects the post-Buddhist Laws of Manu back to this period, in which *brahmanas* were householders, contrasted with wandering *sramanas*.

Liars foregather, I very well know.
Here, for example, a carrion Crow,
And corpse-eating Jackal, with puerile clatter
Proceed one another to flatter!

In Aesop's fable of the Fox and the Crow, however, the fox's
flattery inspires the crow to sing, whereupon she drops the flesh
she has stolen, and the fox picks it up. The moral is

He who listens to flattery is not wise, for it has no good purpose.
(Aesop 1881: 81–2)

This is a form of worldly wisdom, while the Jataka tale condemns
both crow and jackal for their lack of morality. The frame is different
but the story is the same.

Aesop's fables remained popular as chapbooks in Ireland,
being among the most-loved books in late eighteenth and early
nineteenth-century schools (Loeber and Stouthamer-Loeber 1999:
136–7), transporting Indian stories to the 'hedge schools' of rural
Ireland (McManus 2002), though without awareness of this fact.[15]

Buddhist-Christian Links

The substantial overlap of Aesop, *Jataka*s and Panchatantra can be
explained in various ways. The great folklorist Joseph Jacobs argued
for straightforward transmission (1901–6); another approach might
argue for multiple traditions of a shared Eurasian corpus of folktales;
yet another might propose the inherent logics of story.

These explanations became matters of more than academic
interest when westerners realised the extent of the parallels between
Buddhism and Christianity.[16] Initially used as fuel for Protestant-
Catholic rivalries,[17] the proposition that Christianity was not
unique, underlined by comparative religious studies, contributed

15. By way of contemporary parallel, few Dublin or Northern Irish children who
watched the Japanese TV series *Monkey* on BBC TV in 1978–80 would have known
that its original basis was the Buddhist monk Xuanzang's journey from seventh-
century China to India (chapter three); I took another two decades to make the
connection.

16. My thanks are due to Joseph Wilson for generous commentary and discussion
of the current state of scholarly thinking on these matters.

17. The visual and ritual similarities between Catholicism and Tibetan
Buddhism lent themselves to this, to the delight of Protestants and the concern
of Catholics.

to the late nineteenth-century crisis of faith. Buddhism was (rightly) understood to be older than Christianity and (wrongly) understood to have more adherents; both were disturbing thoughts.

Between 1879 and 1907 there was intense debate about Buddhist influence on Christianity (Tweed 2000: 115-6), prompted by geography and chronology, classical references to Buddhism and knowledge of the Asokan missions of the third century BCE, and many parallels – rosary beads (Miller 2002: 88), monasticism, tonsure or indeed the founders' life stories: the prophecies by Asita and Simeon, the temptation and offer of world dominion, etc. (Garbe 1914).

Albert Schweitzer famously claimed that direct influence of Buddhism on the teachings of Jesus was 'unproved [and] unprovable'. This still seems sustainable, whether or not it is 'unthinkable' (Pettipiece 2009: 133-4, Wilson 2009: 170 fn 2). Certainly there is no obvious way of deciding between direct influence, a shared cultural matrix, and the inherent logic of revealed religion, whether in the 'Axial Age' version (Carrithers 1983) or Weber's (1922) 'charismatic authority' argument.

It is often the case that new ideas have to be presented within the language of the culture they are entering – and lose much of their history – to become acceptable. Even where, as with contemporary Buddhist teachers in the west, external origins are welcome, only a minority of western Buddhists know much of their teachers' relation to Buddhism in their home country; Irish Catholics borrowing meditation techniques often present them so as to make them appear legitimately Catholic, or Celtic. Tracing influences between religions is never likely to be easy.

In terms of actual evidence, the key breakthroughs were the late nineteenth-century development of historical criticism of the Bible and of comparative religion. While there is still much to do, it is only the occasional discovery of new texts that adds anything major – hence twentieth-century interest in possible Buddhist-Essene (Dead Sea Scrolls) or Gnostic (Nag Hammadi) links. Study of the far larger corpus of Buddhist texts lags behind, but it is unlikely that it will definitively settle the question – one major reason why scholars have largely abandoned it (Thundy 1993: 6).

A Transmission Outside the Scriptures

One of the more interesting candidates for a transmission that might reach to Ireland is the development of Christian monasticism. Eusebius of Caesarea ascribed its origins to the Therapeutae, described in the first century CE in Philo of Alexandria's *On the Contemplative Life* as widely distributed throughout the Greek and barbarian worlds but centred on the Mareotis lake near Alexandria.[18] The Therapeutae, with their temperance, asceticism, solitude and spiritual practices, have sometimes been identified as Buddhist monks.[19]

Many centuries later, the Rev. James Hannay, Canon of St Patrick's Cathedral, found himself defending Christianity against claims of Buddhist influence:

> The casual references to monasticism as a realisation in Christianity of Buddhist conceptions, which are made, very light-heartedly, by preachers and essayists, do not seem to be based on any historical study whatsoever. (Hannay 1903: 264)

Unfortunately for this claim to erudition, Hannay wrote interchangeably of Buddhism and Brahmanism (1903: 265) before identifying Manicheanism as a mixture of 'Brahmanism and Christianity'. Nevertheless, no amount of actual research could conclusively answer the question, which remains attractive to Irish Buddhists. It is easy, visiting early Christian monastic cells on Irish hillsides and islands, to think of Himalayan caves, or to link the nature poetry of early Irish monks to that of Chinese and Japanese monks.

In the alternative history mode analysed by Lennon (2004), the conservative proposition that Irish monks 'saved civilisation' can be transformed into the idea that they were, unwittingly, Buddhist at some level – and so, in transcribing the church fathers, transmitting the story of their own origins. Yeats' valedictory 'Under Ben Bulben' opens in similar vein:

> Swear by what the sages spoke
> Round the Mareotic Lake

18. Unfortunately for present-day theories of Buddhist-Essene links, Philo's point is to distinguish the Essenes' active life from the contemplative one of the Therapeutae.
19. Eusebius mistakenly believed Philo, and hence the Therapeutae, to have been Christian.

That the Witch of Atlas knew
Spoke and set the cocks a-crow ...

He goes on to call for celebration of the 'indomitable Irishry', linking the Therapeutae with his own projected alternative Ireland.[20] It may be best to leave origin relations between Christianity and Buddhism at this level: as myth-making whose value is not as historical propositions but rather, like Graves' *The White Goddess* (1961), poetic myths, statements about the imagination.

The Buddha Becomes a Saint

Nonetheless, one relationship is definite. Marco Polo wrote of the Buddha that if he had been Christian he would have been a great saint. As Madame Blavatsky later joked (1877: 581), Polo failed to realise that this had already happened: the medieval St Josaphat had once been the Buddha-to-be, the Bodhisattva.

An early biography of the Buddha had made its way slowly westwards – via Manicheans and Muslims, into Georgian and then Greek as the legend of Barlaam and Josaphat around the year 1000. From Latin, it spread into many European languages, including three thirteenth-century French authors, a thirteenth-century Norse version, a fourteenth-century Middle English version, excerpts in an early sixteenth-century Scots Gaelic text and an Irish version by 1600.

It was also included in the massively popular thirteenth-century Latin *Golden Legend* (900 surviving manuscripts). With the invention of printing translations of this proliferated, notably Caxton's 1483 English version: between 1470 and 1530 it was Europe's most frequently printed book, and in the sixteenth century these popular figures had November 27th assigned as their feast day. Buddhist parallels were recognised as early as 1612, but an accurate study was only published in 1859 (Beinorius 2005: 11fn9).[21]

In Caxton's version (Ellis 1900, vol. 7: 42–50), the Indian king Avennir is persecuting Christianity and is upset by a prophecy that his son will become a Christian. To avoid this,

---

20. By 1939, the Therapeutae were known to be non-Christian, but the theory that they were Buddhist had not yet been proposed.

21. In a period of increasing Irish missionary activity in Buddhist Asia, the Dean of Kerry bought EA Wallis Budge's 1923 *Baralam and Yewasef*.

he did do make without the city a right noble palace, and therein set
he his son for to dwell and abide, and set there right fair younglings,
and commanded them that they should not speak to him of death ne
of old age, ne of sickness, ne of poverty, ne of no thing that may give
him cause of heaviness, but say to him all things that be joyous, so that
his mind may be esprised with gladness, and that he think on nothing
to come.

But of course the young man demands to leave the palace:

And on a time thus as the king's son went, he met a mesel [leper] and
a blind man, and when he saw them he was abashed, and enquired
what them ailed, and his servants said: These be passions [sufferings]
that come to men. And he demanded if those passions come to all
men, and they said: Nay. Then said he: Be they known which men
shall suffer these passions without definition? And they answered:
Who is he that may know the adventures of men?

Meeting an old man and learning of death, he encounters the
monk Barlaam who preaches to him and baptises him. The king tries
and fails to regain his son's allegiance, and is eventually converted
to Christianity. In due course the king dies and Josaphat succeeds
him; he eventually leaves the palace, rediscovers Barlaam and lives
as a hermit for 35 years. As with the Greek encounter with Indian
religion, the story has survived its vicissitudes in a remarkably
recognisable form. Here at least, the question 'transmission, shared
origin or structural causes?' can be resolved.[22]

Travellers' Tales

James of Ireland Goes to Beijing

Around 1317, the Franciscan Odoric of Pordenone left northern Italy
to visit the archdiocese of Khanbaliq (present-day Beijing), travelling
from Venice via India, Sri Lanka, Sumatra, Java and Indochina and
spending three years in China before returning home, apparently
via Tibet. This remarkable journey, through some of Asia's most
sophisticated civilizations, took him until 1330 to complete and
brought him into direct contact with Buddhism. In Quanzhou he
found

22. At the same popular level, Wilson (2009) has argued for Indian influence on
medieval asceticism and popular belief in terms of the ethical treatment of animals.

many monasteries of religious persons, all of which worship idols. I myself was in one of those monasteries, and it was told me that there were in it three thousand religious men, having eleven thousand idols; and one of these idols, which seemed to me but little in regard of the rest, was as big as our Christopher. (Komroff 1929: 237)

He describes offerings of food in a recognisable Buddhist monastery. Later, in Hangzhou, he saw a monk ceremonially feeding animals, who told him that they were

the souls of noble men which we do here feed ... as a man was honourable or noble in this life, so his soul after death, enters into the body of some excellent beast or other (1929: 240).

Returning overland, he visited Tibet or, perhaps more plausibly touched at its northeastern corner on the Silk Road.[23] Here he heard tales of a great city, perhaps a major monastery:[24]

In this city none dare shed the blood of a man, or of any beast, for the reverence they bear a certain idol. In this city their Abassi, that is to say, their Pope, is resident, being the head and prince of all idolaters, upon whom he bestows and distributes gifts after his manner, even as our Pope of Rome accounts himself to be the head of all Christians. (1929: 249)

Odoric was accompanied on his epic journey by *frater Jacobus de Ibernia*, brother James of Ireland. It seems from Odoric's *Journal* that James was the brains of the party: Odoric combined extreme gullibility with a terminal cluelessness about the geography and sequence of his own travels – contrasting sharply with his predecessor William of Rubruck and not conducive to surviving this marathon journey.

James evidently made the most of his situation: when Odoric died the year after his return, his home commune of Udine voted James two Aquila marks. An eighteenth century story records a Venetian friar suffering from a fistula in the throat who approached James for a letter of introduction to the (deceased) Odoric; after a night

23. It would have been hard until the late twentieth century to travel through Tibet and claim that "all the highways in this country are exceedingly well paved"; travelling west from Beijing he would have been more likely to travel via Xi'an along the Silk Road, through Lanzhou on the fringes of Tibetan Amdo.
24. This city is sometimes identified as Lhasa, although Gelugpa supremacy and Dalai Lamas were still some centuries away.

at the tomb he was healed. This sounds like a profitable sideline (Fitzmaurice and Little 1920: 131–2).

Odoric was hugely popular locally, and his account – filled with marvels many of which were true – was a great success. Seventy-three manuscripts exist in Latin, French and Italian, mostly from the fourteenth century, and the story was plagiarised in the immensely successful *Mandeville's Travels*. This distribution makes it possible to establish the continuity of its Irish reception: in the fourteenth century, beyond James himself the tale was probably known in Ireland via the English and Latin *Mandevilles*. In the fifteenth century, a Latin *Odoric* was transcribed in 1422, probably in an Irish Franciscan house (and transferred from Ireland to Regensburg in 1529: Fitzmaurice and Little 1920: 131–2), and the Irish *Mandeville* was available by mid-century. In the sixteenth century, Richard Hakluyt included the story in his 1599 *Navigations*, while in the seventeenth century the Franciscan historian Luke Wadding, founder of the Irish college in Rome, summarised it in his *Annales Minorum* (1625–54), which were re-edited in the eighteenth century. Lastly, James Tennent from Fermanagh discussed it in his best-selling 1859 *History of Ceylon*.

Thus, unusually given the fragmentary nature of our information, we can demonstrate continuous knowledge in the Irish world of this particular encounter in each century from the fourteenth to the nineteenth (and subsequently), along both Franciscan and secular lines.

It would be unwise to assume that no other medieval travellers' tales were equally widely available. Ó Ciosáin (2010: 86) suggests that they entered the bardic repertoire in noble households in the fifteenth century and continued there until the destruction of the Gaelic aristocracy in the seventeenth; after which, as we shall see, they entered other circuits again.

New Relationships and Agendas

In the centuries since the Greek encounter, information exchange between northwest Europe and the Buddhist world had become very restricted, although as we have seen stories circulated as well as prestige goods. The rise of Islam, the demise of Buddhism in India and the T'ang persecutions all affected these connections. In the thirteenth century, however, the rise of the religiously tolerant Mongol world empire cleared the way for new, and considerably faster, communication between the Buddhist world and Ireland. By this point, some nine centuries had passed since the last information filtered west, and much had changed (as the contrasting accounts of monks show).

The purpose of communication had also shifted: Mongol conquest had made the Khanates a power to be traded and, perhaps, allied with against the Muslim world in the context of the Crusades. Religion – the possibility of converting the Mongols to Christianity, or preventing their eventual conversion to Islam – had immediate political implications; and most of the travellers who left records of their journeys were religious diplomats on a mission to the various Khanates.

Pope Innocent IV sent at least four emissaries, the Franciscan Giovanni da Pian del Carpine (1245-7), the Dominicans Ascelin of Lombardy and Simon of St Quentin (1245-8) and the Dominican André de Longjumeau (1245-7). Louis IX of France sent André again (1249-51) and the Franciscan William of Rubruck (1253-5). The journey of Niccolò and Maffeo Polo to Khubilai Khan as merchants, returning as his emissaries (1260-9), and their second journey with Niccolò's son Marco as emissaries from Gregory X (1271-95) also fit into this diplomatic process. Some decades later (1289), Pope Nicholas IV sent the Franciscan Giovanni di Montecorvino, who founded a successful mission in Khanbaliq (Beijing) that lasted until 1369; it was this which Odoric was aiming to visit.

If the first emissaries were met with hostility, by the time of William of Rubruck (1254-5), Möngke Khan would host a debate at Karakorum between Buddhists, Muslims and Christians about their faiths. In 1266, Khubilai asked the Polos to send holy oil from Jerusalem along with a hundred missionaries. Two were sent, who did not complete the journey; Giovanni was sent in response to a second request, and the process continued until the end of Mongol rule in China (1368) and the Ming expulsion of foreign religions. As the khanates successively converted to Islam, western interest faded, and Buddhism disappeared from the parts of Asia bordering Europe.

Reading Buddhism in Medieval Europe

We have to ask three questions about the reception of missionary accounts. How widely did these texts circulate, and who read them? Secondly, given the slow rate of circulation, where and when were they read? As seen, something can be said about this within the limitations of what is known of textual history and distribution of pre-modern books and the complexities of the linguistic situation.

Thirdly, with what little evidence we have, we can ask not so much what the texts say to us as what medieval readers might have made of them. It is sometimes assumed that the religious framework within which such authors wrote was identical to how a reader might interpret their accounts:

> It was always customary to describe other religious traditions in terms of the Christian religion, which offered the only model then understood for such descriptions. (Beinorius 2005: 11)

There is some truth to this, in the deployment of images of monsters or the search for the Christian 'Prester John'; but early Christian sources were on some points well-informed about Indian religion. More generally, the kind of educated Europeans who had access to these sources – or to the thirteenth- and fourteenth-century narratives, could draw not only on Christianity but on sophisticated classical discourses about local and barbarian philosophies, the various religions of the pagan world, and the pseudo-anthropological information of the Old Testament and classical accounts of barbarians.

In some ways, medieval Christian authors could allow themselves considerable sympathy with Buddhism, so long as they adopted a broad framework which denied it ultimate value. A 'virtuous pagan' reading of the life of the Buddha, in fact, runs from Clement of Alexandria to Edwin Arnold. Until the second half of the nineteenth century, it was not only heretical (and in many cases extremely risky) to hold that another religion might be true or have salvific value; the textual information to understand Buddhist claims in this respect was also not available. (When it was, some Irish people did indeed start to give their religion as Buddhist in the census.) However, from *Alexander and Dindimus* on, Christian authors and readers could see Buddhism, or Indian religion, as virtuous.

It is by now a truism to say that 'Buddhism' did not exist as a concept prior to the nineteenth century. It is true that western interpreters could not make the connections between all the different Buddhisms, divided by language and practice, which they encountered (less true of Asian Buddhists, who preserved clear origin myths reminding them of the arrival of Buddhism from elsewhere). Medieval Europeans often struggled to distinguish 'Buddhism' from 'Hinduism', 'Taoism' or 'Shinto' until they had translations which offered them Asian categories with which to do so. The immense variety of lived Buddhisms by the Mongol period, and the complex textual histories in Europe, also made it harder to disentangle the multiple accounts available. In this sense, the Church fathers – with fewer linguistic barriers and a greater interest in doctrine – were better placed.

This does not mean, however, that western observers failed to notice the coherence of a particular religion in a given time and place, even if they could not always connect that experience to other contexts; for this reason, this chapter uses 'Buddhism', only slightly anachronistically.

Medieval Europeans in Buddhist Asia

Giovanni da Pian del Carpine (Journeyed 1245–7)

Giovanni, from near Perugia, had been a companion of Francis of Assisi and was sent as a papal legate from Lyon to the Khan's court near Karakorum, an immense journey which generated two texts, a *History of the Tartars* by Giovanni and a *Tartar Relation* perhaps based on the experience of his companion Benedykt Polak. Giovanni has most to say about traditional Mongol religion, but includes a second-hand account of Chinese religion, perhaps based on accounts by Nestorian Christians at the court, whom he mentions as reliable sources:

> The men of Cathay are pagans, having a special kind of writing by themselves, and, as it is reported, the Scriptures of the Old and New Testaments. They have also recorded in histories the lives of their forefathers: and they have monks, and certain houses made after the manner of their churches. They say that they have many saints also, and they worship one God. They adore and reverence Christ Jesus our Lord, and believe the articles of eternal life, but are not baptized. (Komroff 1929: 37–8)

Nestorians, of course, were well aware that Chinese pagans were not as Christian as this suggests. Giovanni's account brings to mind the Eastern Rites controversy, where seventeenth century Jesuits failed to convince the Vatican of the closeness they saw and pursued with Chinese customs. His Christianising write-up was perhaps an over-egging of the 'virtuous pagans' cake, aimed at stressing their openness to conversion.

Giovanni's mention of monks, churches and (later) alms reads like a description of Chinese Buddhism, then in the ascendant, while other elements (histories and multiple saints) could equally refer to Confucianism or Taoism. Others again may be misunderstandings (eternal life as Nirvana or the Pure Land, for example). What is clear is the sense of Chinese religion and culture as civilised, on a par with Europe: up to the arrival of adequate translations, European visitors as late as the eighteenth century tended to notice the structural organisation of Chinese religions more than their doctrinal contents.

Giovanni's history was widely circulated (Morgan 2007: 23); it won him an archbishopric in Montenegro and was inserted into Vincent de Beauvais' *Speculum Historiale*, part of the most widely-distributed medieval encyclopedia, the *Speculum Maius*. The *Speculum* also included a large proportion of another *History of the Tartars* by Simon of St Quentin, companion of Ascelin of Lombardy (travelled 1245–8); the original is lost. Giovanni's version was reworked by Hakluyt in his *Voyages*.

William of Rubruck (Journeyed 1253–5)

William's *Travels* had a restricted circulation by comparison: only four independent manuscripts are known, but all are in England (Morgan 2007: 23), so Irish knowledge is possible. They were later translated and published by Hakluyt. William was, perhaps, too accurate an observer to be popular at the time; it is precisely this which makes his account so fascinating today. Travelling to Möngke Khan's court at Karakorum, William met a range of ordinary Europeans at the court (such as his interpreter, the son of a French goldsmith); like James, many such Europeans encountered Buddhism without publishing their experiences.

William did not see the connections between the different Buddhisms he encountered, and could confuse different religions at second hand:

> Living mixed among [the Chinese], though of alien race, are Nestorians and Saracens all the way to Cathay … The priests of the idols of the nations spoken of all wear wide saffron-colored cowls. There are also among them, as I gathered, some hermits who live in forests and

mountains and who are wonderful by their lives and austerity … [The Nestorians] have sacred books in Syrian, but they do not know the language, so they chant like those monks among us who do not know grammar …[25]

The bishop rarely visits these parts, hardly once in fifty years. When he does, they have all the male children, even those in the cradle, ordained priests, so nearly all the males among them are priests … They are all simoniacs, for they administer no sacrament gratis. (Rockhill 1900: 157-9)

Most of these sound like references to Buddhist monks, perhaps Tibetans.[26] William's first-hand information is more concrete, including the first European mention of 'om mani baccam' (Lopéz 1998: 116) and an account of inter- and intra-religious rivalry between Catholics, Nestorians, Muslims and 'Tuins',[27] culminating in a famous debate instigated by the Khan (Weatherford 2004: 173; Sutin 2006: 49-50). In William's understanding, the 'Tuins'

all hold this heresy of the Manicheans, that one half of things is evil, and the other half good, and that there are two (elemental) principles; and, as to souls, they believe that they all pass from one body into another. (Rockhill 1900: 231)

William wanted to debate the existence of a single all-powerful God, while the Buddhists were more interested in 'the destiny of the soul after death'. They asked him 'If your God is what you say, why did he create half the things evil?', to which William replied that evil did not come from God, and 'all that is, is good'. They followed up by asking where evil came from, but he changed the subject to the existence of God, where the Muslims and Nestorians agreed with him. The debate was suitably inconclusive:

When this was over, the Nestorians as well as the Saracens sang with a loud voice; while the Tuins kept silence; and after that they all drank deeply. (Rockhill 1900: 235)

As a result, Möngke – plausibly enough, but remarkably for a medieval European text – is allowed to state that the Mongols

25. Syriac is still used by the Nestorian church today (Mike Tyldesley, pers. comm).
26. Tibet traditionally had very high rates of ordination, while ordination as a rite of passage is more common in SE Asia; the reference to ordination in the cradle could be a misunderstanding of the recognition of *tulkus*.
27. Buddhists and Taoists: *tao-in* (Beinorius 2005: 11).

believe that there is only one God, by whom we live and by whom we
die ... But as God has given us the different fingers of the hand, so he
gives to men divers ways [of religion]. (Rockhill 1900: 235)

Other Travellers

A series of other travellers left less knowledge of Buddhism which
might have made it to Ireland. André de Longjumeau's account
(1245–7, 1249–51) was drawn on by William, by the French chronicler
Guillaume de Nangis and by Jean de Joinville's *Life of St Louis*.
This latter only survives in three medieval manuscripts, but was
printed in French in the sixteenth and seventeenth centuries (Smith
2008: xxxv). Joinville devotes a substantial section (paras. 471–89)
to the reports of 'two Dominican friars', envoys from King Louis
to the Khans. Continuing Giovanni's Christianising tendencies, he
spuriously relegates non-Christian religion to the 'Tartar' past, and
ascribes their success to conversion to Christianity (2008: 264–6).

Giovanni da Montecorvino (1289–1328), an immensely energetic
missionary, preached in India and founded the Catholic diocese
in China which Odoric visited, and which survived until 1369.
His letters to the Pope in 1305 and 1306 have survived, but I have
found no evidence that they were known in Ireland. The Dominican
Jordanus Catalani (travelled 1321–30), first bishop for the Indies,
wrote a *Mirabilia* which noted similarities between the religion of
the 'Great Tartar' and Catholicism:

> In that empire are idol-temples, and also monasteries of men and
> women as with us; and they have a choral service and sermons just
> like us; and the great pontiffs of the idols wear red hats and capes
> like our cardinals. 'Tis incredible what splendour, what pomp, what
> festivity is made in the idol sacrifices. (Jordanus 1863: 46)

The *Mirabilia*, however, only exist in one MS.

Lawrence of Portugal (1245) was instructed to travel by Innocent
IV but left no further records. He may have died or abandoned
the journey. Lastly, Giovanni de' Marignolli (1338–53) visited the
Chinese diocese and was held prisoner in Ceylon on his return; he
noted his memories as asides in a history of Bohemia, and they were
not published until the eighteenth century.

Marco Polo (1271–95)

Marco Polo's *Travels* are too well-known to introduce.[28] They were as well-known in medieval Europe as Odoric, and we can 'place' them in Ireland, in the 1460 translation *Leabhar Ser Marco Polo*, done probably in Lismore monastery in Co. Waterford for Finghin MacCarthy and his wife Catharine Fitzgerald (Yule and Cordier 1903: 102–3). The Irish version interpolates an unusual justification for its existence:

> There was then in that city a princely Friar in the habit of St Francis, named Franciscus, who was versed in many languages. He was brought to the place where those nobles were, and they requested of him to translate the book from the Tartar into the Latin language. "It is an abomination to me", said he, "to devote my mind or labour to works of Idolatry and Irreligion".
>
> They entreated him again. "It shall be done," said he; "for though it be an irreligious narrative that is related therein, yet the things are miracles of the True God; and everyone who hears this much against the Holy Faith shall pray fervently for their conversion. And he who will not pray shall waste the vigour of his body to convert them."

Polo has much to say about Buddhism.[29] Firstly, at the Khan's court, are *Bacsi* (bhiksus) and *Tebet* (Tibetan lamas), appearing as ritual specialists:

> They know the diabolic arts and necromancy better than anyone, and even though they use the very devil, they make believe that the marvels come from their high sanctity and through divine will …
>
> [W]ith great chants and great happiness they perfume the idol with the scent of the good spices which they have obtained … (Polo 1990: 122–3, my translation)

He also discusses the *Sensin*:

> They practise severe abstinence according to their customs, and their life is very hard: for their whole life they only eat gruel, that is the crust, the husks of grain which come from the wheat … And even though they eat nothing else, they also fast several times in the year …

28. On the debate as to whether Polo was genuinely a first-hand eyewitness, see Wood (1998) and de Rachewiltz (1998). It does not substantially alter the issue of European reception.

29. I have been unable to find a translation of the Irish text or its immediate source in Pipino (Bellonci 1990: 38); the discussion here relies on the underlying Franco-Italian version.

> Strange to say, the other monks consider as heretics those who
> live according to the rule of such a strict abstinence, because not
> all idolaters worship the idols in the same way, but they have very
> different rules. The *Sensin* would under no circumstances take a wife:
> they have shaven heads and beards, they wear a robe of yellow and
> black hemp ... (Polo 1990: 123)

Polo, then, distinguishes between different schools (Offermans
2005: 18): here perhaps between Nyingma lamas and Kadampas?
Secondly, he discusses the tale of 'Sagamoni Borcan' (Shakyamuni
Buddha) in Ceylon, and (unusually) recognised the link to the very
different Buddhism of the Khan's court. For Polo,

> This Sagamoni was the first man who was made into an idol. Because,
> according to the legend, he was the best man who ever lived; and he
> was the first who they worshipped as a saint, and the first idol they
> ever had. (1990: 273)

There follows a biography which includes the father who
surrounds his son with luxury because of worries that he will not
want to be king, the sights of a dead man and an old man:

> Having fully understood these things, the dead man and the old,
> the son of the king returned to the palace and said that he no longer
> wanted to stay in this sad world, but that he would go to seek that
> which never dies and which had created him. He thus left his father's
> palace and went into high and cliffy mountains, and lived there his
> whole life, in austerity and chastity, practising great abstinence. And
> certainly if he had been a Christian he would have been a great saint
> in the company of Our Lord Jesus Christ. (1990: 275)

Polo, like later travellers, mentioned pilgrimages to Adam's Peak,
which he describes as the Buddha's tomb. He recounts a legend that
not only the Buddha's teeth, but also his hair and begging bowl
were preserved there. The Khan, according to Polo, sent for the two
largest teeth, the hair and the bowl and the whole people 'religious
and not', went in procession to meet them.[30]

The text has a difficult balancing act around intra-religious
relations, made more complex by the prestige it has to attribute
to the Khan. After noting the Khan's celebration of Easter and
Christmas, Polo acknowledged that the Khan also celebrated 'the

30. When later Irish papers used the Kandy tooth as a symbol of Buddhist superstition this part of the back-story was missed.

principal feasts of the Saracens, of the Jews and of the idolaters'. He gave the Khan's explanation for this, with his own gloss:

> There are four prophets who are adored and venerated in the whole world: the Christians worship Jesus Christ as their God, the Saracens Mohammed, the Jews Moses, and the idolaters Sagamoni Burcan. I honour and revere all four, and honour in them the [traditional Mongol] greater God who is in the sky, and to him I pray so that he may help me.
>
> But, going by what he showed, the Great Khan judges the Christian faith as more true and better ... (1990: 130)

'Sir John Mandeville' (c. 1357)

Finally we can mention the partly spurious *Travels of Sir John Mandeville*. In large part based on Odoric's travels, some derives ultimately from Giovanni da Pian del Carpine and some from the Alexander legend. *Mandeville* was more popular than any but the *Golden legend*, with about 300 surviving manuscripts (as against 73 for Odoric and 80 for Polo). It was rapidly translated into English and Latin and into Irish by the mid-fifteenth century (Meserve 2006: xii–xiii).

Mandeville repeats Odoric's tale of the monks 'that be good religious men after their faith and law' who feed animals and say that the latter reflect their virtue in a previous life, together with vaguer tales of the 'Great Chan's court' and his philosophers, represented simply as ritual specialists (2006: 136–7). In the *Alexander and Dindimus* passage (2006: 192–5), he notes

> Albeit that these folk have not the articles of our faith as we have, natheles, for their good faith natural, and for their good intent, I trow fully, that God loveth them ... albeit that there be many diverse laws in the world, yet I trow, that God loveth always them that love him, and serve him meekly in truth, and namely them that despise the vain glory of this world. (2006: 195)

This neatly combines the *Alexander* critique of worldly things with the concern of other authors to legitimise Eastern religion. In this rather vague form, *Mandeville* brought Onesicritus, Giovanni and Odoric's experiences to a wide range of medieval readers.

Reflections: Medieval Irish Knowledge

The conditions which enabled Franciscan friars to travel to China soon ended. By the end of this period, however, well-read Irish people had many opportunities to come across information on Asian Buddhism, especially in the Church fathers, the *Alexander legend* and the *Golden legend*, the *Speculum historiale/Speculum maius*, and the widely-published *Travels* of Odoric, Polo and 'Mandeville'. Other accounts (Giovanni da Pian del Carpine, William of Rubruck) also circulated, while *Barlaam and Josaphat* (but not Aesop) was recognisably a tale of Eastern holiness.

Contra naïve accounts of simple transmission, it is clear that communication was shaped by the economic, political and cultural relationships within different world-systems, from the early encounters with canonical Buddhism mediated by the medieval Church and secular literature through to the diplomatic and trading encounter with the Asia of the Khans. *Contra* equally naïve cultural determinism, it is surprising how much recognisable and accurate material survived even lengthy transmission processes (Stoneman 1995, Millar 2009).

Asian Buddhisms, with all their diversity, were not always recognised as interlinked or distinguished from the immense diversity of other forms of 'idolatry': Rubruck and Polo stand out as unusual in their ability to do this even partially. More typical is Odoric, failing to connect his Chinese monasteries to Tibet or distinguish them from Taoism and Confucianism, despite spending three years at a well-established Catholic bishopric in China. A modern reader can pick out the Buddhist fragments in Odoric from his tales of the Jaganatha festival or the Old Man of the Mountains, and join the dots between Rubruck's pieces of information, but the medieval reader could not.

One major task of nineteenth-century scholarship, then, was organising material which was already available. Thus the Irishman, James Tennent, in 1859 devoted four chapters of his *History of Ceylon* to ancient and medieval knowledge – one on Greek and Roman authors, one on Indian, Arabic and Persian authors, one on Chinese knowledge and one on the 'Moors, Genoese and Venetians'. The material in the first and fourth of these was almost all available to medieval Irish readers.

The travel accounts show how many *different* readings of the same material could be given by authors – and, no doubt, by readers. Longjumeau rewrites the Mongols as being Christian; Pian del Carpine turns Chinese monks almost into errant Christians;

Jordanus is fascinated by the parallels; Odoric and 'Mandeville', with the Alexander legend, make Buddhists virtuous pagans;[31] for Rubruck Buddhists are honest opponents, and only for Polo are some devil-worshippers, while his Irish translator interpolates an excuse for being interested in the subject. Rubruck and Polo both allow the Khans, with all the prestige their texts give them, to express religious tolerance openly, and 'Mandeville' proposes that all religions are the same in the eyes of God. Clearly, there were multiple medieval ways of engaging with Buddhism; but on the whole these authors responded positively and sought ways of justifying the discussion of 'idolatry' in Christian contexts where heresy was a death sentence.

Readers are also not bound to authors' interpretations, as we know from later European Buddhists, who often drew on texts and translations by Christian scholars. As Hall (1980) puts it, a reader can certainly follow the official reading of events (non-Christian religions are inferior, and therefore Buddhism is too). They can, however, also take a consciously oppositional view (I am unhappy with Christianity and more impressed with these virtuous pagans) or a negotiated reading (I would not want to be seen to disagree with the church, but this religion is both ethically good and non-Christian).

The popularity and diffusion of the medieval travel accounts (or the Alexander legend) makes it clear that such accounts of 'otherness' were of great interest in medieval Europe, in the sense of 'information exchange': the world was larger than conventionally presented, other ways of being existed, and other places were equally or more civilised. In particular, a medieval Irish reader could have had a sense of Asian religion as well-organised, theologically sophisticated, given to asceticism or virtue, and *other* than the only religion they knew first-hand.

The Wild Irish Girl *and the Dalai Lama:*
Early Modern Circuits of Knowledge

Who read, and what was read in the eighteenth century? What made people read, and how did they view culture, knowledge?

31. In a sense Dindimus' presentation as the monotheist foil to Alexander's polytheism wraps the legitimating mantle of Christianity around Indian religion.

What ideology did their culture reflect? (Jean-Paul Pittion, cited in
Kennedy 2001)

The roads East which closed in the mid-fourteenth century were
reopened in the sixteenth and seventeenth centuries, on radically
changed terms. The new European efforts to develop trade routes
and colonies were an integral part of the construction of the
capitalist world-system (Arrighi 1994). Made possible by explorers
and traders, the new relationships enabled Jesuit missions across
Asia. All wrote about their experiences, and in new ways – with a
more ethnographic attention to everyday experience and (for the
Jesuits) more study of language and doctrine. These accounts were
collected, printed and distributed as a conscious part of the new
trade and conquest, and in the process became far more available
than ever before.

Irish people participated in these ventures, notably in the East
India Company, where there was an important Irish role from
the top in figures like Thomas Sutton, Comte de Clonard, via the
Irish chaplains (Cullen 2006: 22–9, 16) right down to Irish Catholic
privates from the 1680s on (Lennon 2004: 171–2). Irish merchants,
and no doubt ordinary sailors, also travelled to Asia. Thomas Ray,
son of a merchant family from Youghal, organised various East
India ventures 'with a striking Irish participation' between 1714–20,
to India and China, which made him the wealthiest man in Ostend
(Parmentier 2006: 372–9). By the end of the early modern period
(roughly 1500–1800), these sinews of capitalism – labour, trade and
knowledge – had distributed information about Buddhism very
widely throughout Europe.

Around this point Sydney Owenson (later Lady Morgan) became
Ireland's first commercial woman writer with her 1806 *The wild Irish
girl*. The novel went through nine English and American editions
in its first two years (Kirkpatrick 2008b: xix) and another seven
between 1811 and 1834 (Lennon 2004: 142); the start of a publishing
career that saw her become the first woman writer to receive a
government pension (Kirkpatrick 2008a: ix).

The wild Irish girl is a key work of cultural nationalism. Owenson
had rejected her mother's English and Protestant background for
her father's Irish (Galway) and Catholic identity (Kirkpatrick 2008a:
vii). Writing 8 years after the United Irishmen's 1798 rebellion and

its brutal repression, the novel attempts to resolve these family and political conflicts. By

> charting the progress of an English narrator who gives up his prejudices towards Ireland and the Gaelic Irish, Owenson suggests that difference might be loved rather than hated. (Kirkpatrick 2008: xv)

Her hero is gradually drawn into an extended encounter with the Irish language and literature, the Connacht landscape, Catholic priests (many penal laws were still in force) and of course the 'wild Irish girl' herself. His deepening love for his new country parallels an imagined Asia (Lennon 2004):

> I now listen to the language of Ossian with the same respect a Hindoo would to the Shanscrit of the Bramins. (Owenson 2008: 161)

At one point, the narrator stumbles across a rural mass-house:

> This sermon was delivered by a little old mendicant friar, in the Irish language. Beside him stood the parish priest in pontificalibus, and with as much self-invested dignity as the *dalai lama* of Little Thibet could assume before his votarists. (2008: 134)

Thus in a massively successful novel, Owenson could assume that her readers knew who the Dalai Lama was. By 1806, in other words, the knowledge of Buddhism which was earlier available to clerical scholars, and later to elites, was part of broader educated knowledge. A reader of Thomas Astley's popular (Teltscher 2006: 102) *New general collection of voyages and travels* (1745–7), for example, would have known that the Dalai Lama was

> This Sovereign Pontiff of all the *Tartarian* idolaters, and whom they acknowledge as their God. (cited in Lopéz 1998: 21).

Or a reader of Oliver Goldsmith's *Citizen of the world* (1762), an Irish contribution to the genre of fictional oriental travellers to the west, could have enjoyed 'Lien Chi Altangi's' observations on western society and his critical asides on Buddhism (Watt 2006: 74fn17).

Owenson's comparison of the parish priest with the Dalai Lama also highlighted the conflicted and opposing cultures *within* Ireland, which meant that an English-speaking and Protestant culture found the Catholic church as alien and exotic as Tibetan Buddhism. As we shall see, there was no unified Irish culture to remake Buddhism, but rather a conflict *between* cultures, not restricted to Ireland but part of a broader conflict within the UK and Europe. There were competing channels for distributing knowledge (commercial print versus religious institutions), which in turn were constrained by language, literacy and the politics of Reformation and anti-Catholic repression in Ireland.

The Many Worlds of Early Modern Ireland

Kearney writes, of the Irish freethinking radical John Toland,

> Perhaps one of the reasons why Toland presented himself as a contra-
> diction (as Leibniz and others argued) was because the Irish mind
> was a cleft-mind? Not uniform but pluriform. Not homogenous but
> diverse. Anglo *and* Gaelic, Catholic *and* Protestant. Native *and* planted.
> Regional *and* cosmopolitan. I am not arguing that no other European
> cultures of the period experienced similar divisions … (1997: 131)

We need to rethink our impression of Europe as naturally divided into internally homogenous cultures, projecting backwards the outcomes of nineteenth- and twentieth-century nationalism. Early modern Ireland was contested territory: to the earlier conflicts between Gaelic, Viking and Anglo-Norman were added new coloni-sation from the Elizabethan period on and the repeated irruption of the Wars of Religion, producing new divisions around language, religion, political allegiance and external points of reference. All of this shaped the encounter with Buddhism.

Ireland had always been a province of a wider world:

> The importance of earlier contacts – diplomatic, political, economic
> and cultural – between Ireland and Scotland and Europe cannot be
> overstated and often dated back to the early Middle Ages. (Ohlmeyer
> 2006: 459).

For Catholics in particular, wider links became particularly necessary from the mid-sixteenth century:

> [T]he enforcements of the acts of supremacy and uniformity meant
> significant civil disabilities … Before this, the Irish clerical and profes-
> sional *élite* had frequented the English and Scots universities but as
> religious differences hardened these became uncongenial. Many
> travelled further afield, to the Low Countries, France, Spain and
> the Italian peninsula. As early as the 1560s Irish names begin to
> appear in significant numbers in European university registers.
> (O'Connor 2001: 14)

As the English state attempted to impose its power through plantation and penal laws, so too Gaelic lords engaged in a strategy of confessionalisation and state-building. From Hugh O'Neill in the 1590s through the seventeenth and eighteenth century:

> in the last third of the century of lights, the aspiration to construct a Catholic *régime* in Ireland displayed new vitality. It managed to strike a deal with both agrarian agitation and republican radicalism, producing a form of Catholic nationalism which, for weal or for woe, acted, in partnership with liberalism, to modernise Ireland in the nineteenth century. (O'Connor 2001: 12–13).

The Catholic church was part and parcel of this: the Jesuit arrival in Ireland was in the context of conflicts between the newly Anglican Henry VIII, the Irish parliament's declaring him king (rather than lord as hitherto) of Ireland, and appeals from Irish chieftains to the Papacy (McRedmond 1991: 13–15).

Along with the irruption of wider conflicts into Ireland, so too Irish communities exported themselves abroad (O'Connor 2001, O'Connor and Lyons 2006, Lyons and O'Connor 2008). From the Elizabethan wars on, the native aristocracy sought education, employment and political futures abroad (Ó Dúshláine 2001: 79); through the Cromwellian period and Jacobite risings up to the French Revolution a series of diaspora communities developed on the continent, including Irish regiments in Spain, France, Austria and Sweden; student communities and eventually Irish colleges supported by France, Spain and the Papal States; merchant communities in Nantes, La Coruña or Cádiz; individual professional migrants, and poorer refugees (Lyons and O'Connor 2008: 3).

On average 700 people a year, mostly men, emigrated to the continent in the seventeenth century, with perhaps 34,000 people travelling to Spain, Flanders and France in the Cromwellian 1650s:

> [T]he figures for both Ireland and Scotland represent a considerable proportion of the populations of both kingdoms and could, certainly during the early decades of the seventeenth century, equate to at least ten per cent of the adult male population. (Ohlmeyer 2006: 472)

The comparison with Scotland shows the relative normality of this situation:

> A number of common themes immediately emerge: diplomacy and international relations; the Grand Tour and education; political, religious, commercial and military migration; migration networks;

and the formations of communities abroad. Other themes – return migration and the impact that Europe had on Ireland and Scotland, particularly with regard to the transfer of knowledge and people – are less well documented, but are equally worthy of study. (Ohlmeyer 2006: 459)

There was thus an extensive circulation of people and ideas between Ireland and the continent, particularly strongly in Catholic gentry families. Irish Dissenters, for their part, might orient themselves to the Lutheran or Calvinist areas in the Baltic region, the United Provinces, or Central Europe (Ohlmeyer 2006: 460–8). The net impact of all this was to create two or three separate and often opposed circuits of knowledge both within and outside Ireland:

> up until the mid-1740s, the Irish colleges, regiments and merchant houses on the Continent functioned as alternative educational and career networks for those in Ireland who found the official Anglican state uncongenial. In this way, Irish migration to Europe, in all its diversity and complexity, was a crucial factor not only in modernising Europe but also in shaping the changed Ireland that emerged after the end of the Revolutionary Wars in 1815. (Lyons and O'Connor 2008: vii)

Early modern Irish knowledge, then, was not confined to Ireland. Merchant sons might be sent to the continental branch of the family business for some years or decades and then recycled back home; priests were trained abroad for Ireland; officer sons abroad could return to inherit; families travelled too. Knowledge was also not unitary: information and institutions based, or linked, abroad were already structured by religious affiliation, political allegiance and linguistic context.

Linguistic Diversity and French Books[32]

The linguistic implications of these international circuits were considerable. In 1642, for example, an Irish Franciscan discussed academic priests and chaplains based in France, Italy, Austrian and Spanish territory who were fluent in Latin, Spanish, Dutch, English and/or Irish (Ohlmeyer 2006: 461); Italian and German were also implied by their bases. Literary and intellectual work in Irish was developed on the continent from 1607, at the Irish College in Louvain and other seventeenth-century Franciscan centres, often intended for use in Ireland (Dillon 2004: 383).

32. This section draws particularly on Kennedy (2001).

The island itself was linguistically divided, with Irish still the majority language until the eighteenth century. Within and outside the island, the Irish world was as multilingual as it had been in the medieval period. Jean-Pierre Droz, in College Green, published a *Literary journal* from 1744–9 whose subscribers could read abstracts of the latest books in French, Latin, German and Dutch and order them from his shop (Kennedy 2001: 100–1).

French as a language was important to both Catholics and Protestants. From the mid-seventeenth century Huguenot refugees arrived, and French remained in use until the early nineteenth century. Catholic families might have members in French regiments, wine-trading branches based in France or children studying in the Irish colleges in Paris, Bordeaux, Douai, Lille, Nantes, Toulouse, Poitiers or Louvain, and French was sometimes the adopted language of upper-class families. French was taught in state, church and charitable schools in Ireland, even in provincial towns, and private academies specialising in modern languages, while others employed French tutors. Trinity's establishment of professorships in modern languages in 1775–6 was thus responding to local realities (Kennedy 2001: 22, 65, 128, 26):

> By 1800 … from being a phenomenon of the social elite [French-speaking] appears to have extended to the sons and daughters of the metropolitan and provincial middle classes. (Kennedy 2001: 65)

The net effect was that French-language information on Buddhist Asia was as significant for early modern reception as English-language. In particular, the second half of the eighteenth century saw a shift in French-language imports and publishing from the religious needs of the Huguenot community to a broader, second-language readership with more general interests, including scientific, philosophical and literary ones (2001: 91).

Thus, Bayle's *Dictionnaire* was widely available – confusing Buddhism and Hinduism but giving a clear description of Zen meditation (Sutin 2006: 111). Raynal's *Histoire philosophique et politique des deux Indes* was published in Dublin perhaps in 1778 (7 vols., £2.5s.6d) with English translations printed in Belfast in 1776 and in Dublin in 1776, 1779 and 1784 and excerpts in the *Magazin à la mode* in 1777. Prévost's *Histoire générale des voyages* was in a 1784 catalogue, though at £17.13s for nineteen volumes this was for the wealthy or libraries alone, as was La Harpe's 1782 *Abrégé de l'histoire*

générale des voyages (22 volumes, £11.7s). No fewer than five Dublin
booksellers imported the *Encyclopédie* (Kennedy 2001: 95, 85, 140).

While as Kennedy notes the personal libraries known to us from
wills etc., are mostly those of conservative groups such as nobles,
parliamentary and ecclesiastical elites (2001: 167), nevertheless the
most widely owned author was Voltaire (2001: 135), with other bestsellers including Bayle's *Dictionnaire* (36), Raynal's *Histoire des deux
Indes* (34), the *Encyclopédie* (24), Herbeleto's *Bibliothèque orientale ou
dictionnaire universel* (22), Montesquieu's *Lettres persanes* (22 private
libraries) and Prévost's *Histoire générale des voyages* (5). Thus 'Ireland'
was part of broader flows of language, knowledge, texts and people
within Europe and indirectly with Buddhist Asia, bringing the
eighteenth-century European encounter with Buddhism into Dublin
bookshops and provincial homes in French as much as English.

Empire-building Knowledge

A particularly important source of knowledge about Buddhism
lay in secular collections of travel narratives, bringing together
the medieval accounts with recently-published narratives by
merchants and Jesuit missionaries and oral accounts by returned
sailors. Building on sixteenth-century collections such as Giovanni
Ramusio's (1550) *Navigationi et viaggi* and Richard Willes' (1577)
History of travel in the west and east Indies, a milestone was Richard
Hakluyt's *Principal navigations, voiages, traffiques and discoueries of
the English nation* (first edn. 1589, second edn. 1598, rev. 1599–1600)
and his other works. Hakluyt's work was 'the true prelude to the
building of the British empire'; for Asia his main interest was in
generating knowledge for traders (Williamson 1946: 11, 14–5).

The Hakluyt Society's census of original copies[33] makes it possible
to trace Irish knowledge. Marsh's Library in Dublin bought a 1598
edition from England in 1705; the Trinity library has two copies of
the same edition (one possibly acquired in the early seventeenth
century) and one of the 1599–60 edition donated by the presumably
Huguenot Claude Gilbert (1670–1743). Cashel's Bolton Library holds
two among the collection of the mid-eighteenth century Anglican
Archbishop: a 1598 edition with the seventeenth-century inscription
'Pat'k Fitz Symons' (evidently Irish) and a 1599–60 edition once

---

33. http://www.hakluyt.com/hakluyt_census.htm

owned by William King, Archbishop of Dublin (d. 1729). The National Library also owns a 1598 edition. Albeit expensive, this kind of knowledge was evidently circulated in Ireland, particularly by Protestant divines, from the seventeenth century on.

Hakluyt's work was continued by Samuel Purchas, who first published three editions of his own *Purchas his Pilgrimage, or Relations of the World and the Religions observed in all Ages and Places discovered from the Creation unto this Present* (1613, 1614, 1615). Having acquired the rights to Hakluyt's work he produced *Hakluyt's Posthumus or Purchas his Pilgrimes* (1626), whose four volumes ran to 4,262 pages and over 4,250,000 words. This monstrous tome drew on over 1300 authors, including Hakluyt's texts, manuscripts of recent voyages, other printed works and oral accounts. Purchas went beyond even his contemporaries' appetite for knowledge, and *Posthumus* was not reprinted until 1905; Marsh's library nevertheless holds two editions.

The later seventeenth and early eighteenth century saw a flourishing of such collections (Crone and Skelton 1946), many relating to Buddhist countries and covering issues of religion. A sample of sources can be found in the title of a 1705 collection by John Harris, FRS:

> Navigantium atque Itinerarium Bibliotheca: or, a compleat Collection of Voyages and Travels: consisting of above Four Hundred of the most Authentick Writers; beginning with *Hackluit, Purcass*, &c. in English; *Ramusio* in Italian; *Thevenot*, &c. in French; *De Bry*, and *Grynae Novis Orbis* in Latin; the *Dutch East-India* Company in Dutch: and continued, with Others of Note, that have published Histories, Voyages, Travels, or Discoveries, in the *English, Latin, French, Italian, Spanish, Portuguese, German, or Dutch tongues* ... [and so on.]

Ireland had gone from famine to feast, as far as the availability of knowledge about Buddhist Asia went. The list of single-author works and collections from this period known from Ireland includes the Huguenot François Caron's *A true description of the mighty kingdoms of Japan & Siam* (1645, English 1663 and 1671);[34] the Jesuit Johann Grueber's *China and France, or two treatises* (1660s);[35]

---

34. This was a true bestseller, translated into all major European languages. Among other things it accused Japanese Buddhist priests of practising sodomy and employing prostitutes (Offermans 2005: 28).

35. Marsh's holds 1696 French and Italian editions.

the English sailor Robert Knox's *An historical relation of the island of Ceylon* (1691);[36] Simon de la Loubère's *Description du royaume de Siam* (1691);[37] Philippe Avril's *Travels into divers parts of Europe and Asia* (English translation 1693);[38] Melchisidec Thevenot's *Relation de divers voyages curieux* (1696);[39] John Harris' *Navigantium atque itinerantium bibliotheca* (1705),[40] already mentioned; the Jesuit *Lettres édifiantes et curieuses* (1707 and later editions; second English edition 1762);[41] du Halde's *Description géographique, historique, chronologique, politique et physique de l'empire de la Chine et de la Tartarie chinoise* (1735, English translations 1736 and 1741);[42] Bernard Picart's *The ceremonies and religious customs of the various nations of the known world* (1741);[43] Thomas Astley's *New general collection of voyages and travels* (1745-7, drawing on Grueber and translated into French by the Abbé Prévost from 1746 on);[44] and others.[45]

Astley's collection reads like a *summum* of what Europeans knew about Central and East Asian Buddhism. Drawing on the Jesuit du Halde's sophisticated analysis of Chinese Buddhism and material from embassies to the Chinese court, it also included the 'Map of Great Tibet drawn from that made by the Lama Mathematicians in 1717', the accounts of Jesuits Ippolito Desideri and Orazio della Penna in Tibet, with other accounts of Korea and a summary of 'the Relations of *Marco Polo, Carpini,* and the other early *Missioners* into Tartary' (Crone and Skelton 1946: 103-8).

The accuracy and time lag of this knowledge varied, even in the early nineteenth century: Richard Phillips' periodical series *A Collection of modern and contemporary voyages and travels* (1805-10) only drew on recent work, but John Pinkerton's (1808-14) *General*

36. Trinity holds three originals, and Marsh's one. This popular work influenced *Robinson Crusoe* (Sutin 2006: 115).

37. Marsh's holds one.

38. Trinity holds one.

39. Marsh's library holds a copy of this, which includes Grueber and Caron as well as Martinius' *Novus atlas Sinensis.*

40. Marsh's library holds a copy.

41. Trinity holds the French edition, and Maynooth and Trinity the English translation.

42. Both editions were held in Ireland; see above.

43. Maynooth library holds the 1739 French original and Trinity and Marsh's the English translation.

44. Trinity holds two copies of this French edition.

45. As can be seen, the Jesuit literature circulated as effectively in Ireland via commercial publishing as via the Society's own circuits.

collection of the best and most interesting voyages and travels in all parts of the world still relied on mid-eighteenth century accounts of China and Tibet. By this point, in any case, the traditional solution of catch-all collections was no longer feasible (Crone and Skelton 1946: 136–8).

Such literature was entertainment for the educated: a clergyman in 1720s Hillsborough wrote to his London brother asking for books such as 'travels and sea journeys into the remoter parts of the world' (Barnard 1999: 68–9). If the major collections were expensive, others were sold in monthly parts at 1s each, making them available much lower down the social scale. Mid-eighteenth century dedications and subscription lists show that interest had spread beyond the gentry to 'merchants, factors, brokers and customs officials', while smaller and cheaper collections which pirated or abridged the major ones were widely published (Crone and Skelton 78, 89, 109–19). If Owenson's readers had read cheap knock-offs of Astley, for example, they knew not only who the Dalai Lama was but could comment (thanks to du Halde) on the concept of *sunyata*.

Academic Knowledge Before *Buddhist Studies*

Such sources are barely explored for the reception of Buddhism in the West (Lopéz 1998, Offermans 2005 are exceptions), yet this is how knowledge of China came to Enlightenment Europe (Millar 2009), how Leibniz and Hegel encountered the Jesuit interpretation of Buddhism as quietistic (Offermans 2005: 30–1), and how words such as 'Buddha' appear in Oxford English Dictionary citations from 1681, 'dharma' from 1796, 'Buddhism' and 'Buddhist' from 1801 (Bluck 2006: 4).

The rise of Buddhist Studies was just around the corner, with Michel-Jean-François Ozeray's (1817) *Recherches sur Buddou ou Bouddou* and Edward Upham's (1819) *History and doctrine of Budhism* being followed by the founding dates of contemporary Buddhist Studies, Brian Hodgson's 1837 circulation of key Sanskrit and Tibetan manuscripts to scholars and Eugène Burnouf's 1844 *Introduction à l'histoire du buddhisme indien*.[46] From the 1850s, Irish universities were teaching Oriental Studies; yet Buddhist Asia was a subject of educated discussion long before this.

---

46. Trinity holds a 1911 translation.

To give a sense of the scale of prior knowledge, there is a 43-page bibliography of works published on China alone before 1850.[47] We need to be wary of privileging the knowledge of 'real' Buddhism generated through doctrinal study and archaeology over the 'religion of eyewitnesses (missionaries, travellers)' represented in the pre-Buddhist Studies literature (Offermans 2005: 17).

Scholarly interpretations of the travel collections were available in Ireland through bodies such as the Dublin Society (founded 1731), which subscribed to sixty journals in the eighteenth century, including the *Philosophical Transactions of the Royal Society*, containing geographical and archaeological papers and material from the Society's programme of voyages (Crone and Skelton 1946: 68), and the *Journal des Savans*, the *Mémoires* of the Parisian Royal Academy of Sciences and of the Berlin Academy, the *Acta Eruditorum Lipsiensa* (Leipzig) and the journals of the Göttingen Royal Society (Brown 1987).

There were class and regional dimensions to this scholarly knowledge: reading societies and commercial lending libraries developed in Dublin, Cork, Belfast and Galway by the end of the eighteenth century but were less widespread in rural market towns. Brown (1987) compares the major cities to Liverpool or Manchester and 1790s Dublin to Continental patterns of reading practice in this regard. To this particular circuit, however, we have to add the competing circuit of Catholic, particularly Jesuit, institutions.

Catholic Circuits of Knowledge

If the knowledge represented by commercial travel collections and scholarly journals was particularly aimed at empire-building and favoured by Anglican divines, it was nonetheless also available to Catholic gentry and merchants. It also overlaps with the key Catholic source of knowledge, the sixteenth and seventeenth century Jesuit missions to Asian Buddhist countries. Travel collections drew on the Society's annual letters, which summarised reports from Jesuits abroad and circulated:

> to the different Jesuit houses, schools, universities, scholars, and to the rich and the powerful. The revised missionary reports became a part of the teaching materials at the Jesuit educational establishments,

47. http://www.idc.nl/pdf/172_titlelist.pdf

> were quoted at the Sunday sermons, or were prepared as pieces of art
> at the Jesuit theatres, where this genre was able to reach out also to
> non-Jesuits. (Offermans 2005: 18)

Sometimes this literature was purely exoticising, 'from first to last
... an Arabian Night's Entertainment' for one nineteenth-century
historian, and overly detailed accounts of Buddhist doctrine were
censored (Sutin 2006: 64–5). Nevertheless there was extensive scope
for engagement with Buddhism, varying of course in quality. Matteo
Ricci and Francis Xavier criticised Chinese and Japanese Buddhism
respectively for tolerating male homosexuality – a widespread
theme in the travel literature (Offermans 2005: 24–9).

More remarkably, Ippolito Desideri made an 18-month journey
to Lhasa, arriving in 1716 and winning both permission to stay and
a challenge to debate Tibetan lamas. In preparation for this event,
which unfortunately for later scholars never happened, Desideri was
given extensive opportunities to study Buddhist texts, composing
his own refutation of 'the Views of Rebirth and Emptiness' in
Tibetan (Sutin 2006: 100–6), noting

> Although I believe the articles of [Buddhist] Faith to be absolutely
> wrong and pestiferous, yet the rules and directions imposed on the
> will are not alien to the principles of sound reason; they seem to
> me worthy of admiration as they not only prescribe hatred of vice,
> inculcate battling against passions, but, what is more remarkable, lead
> man toward sublime and heroic perfection.

It is often observed that Desideri's book on Tibet remained
unpublished for centuries (Beinorius 2005, Sutin 2006), but his
annual *letters* were included in the Jesuit collections, and thus
widely available to educated Catholics.

Jesuit views moved from an early sense of Buddhism as idolatrous
to the more sophisticated position of du Halde's 1735 *Description
géographique, historique, chronologique, politique et physique de l'empire
de la chine et de la Tartarie chinoise* (English trans. 1736, 1741), which
distinguished between an exterior and superstitious Buddhism and
an authentic, interior atheist version relying on *sunyata*:

> Learn then, said he to them, that there is no other Principle of all
> Things but Emptiness and Nothing: From Nothing all Things proceed,
> and into Nothing all will return, and this is the End of all our Hopes
> (cited in Offermans 2005: 22).

Du Halde went on to cite Confucian scholars in his analysis of Buddhism as nihilistic.

Jesuit Knowledge in Ireland[48]

The availability of Jesuit knowledge in Ireland was massively constrained by context. Arriving during the wars of religion and Tudor plantations, discussions of rebellion at Louvain boosted their image as enemies of the crown; the first Jesuits were hanged, drawn and quartered in Ireland in 1572 and 1575.

The Society was still essentially clandestine at the start of the seventeenth century, but colleges were in operation in Dublin, Drogheda and Waterford by the late 1620s, with schools and classes in Kilkenny, Cashel and elsewhere. Educational strategies, particularly in Leinster, benefitted from tolerance in the 1630s and there were 13 residences, most with schools attached, by 1640. These were supported by the Jesuit creation of the Irish College in Salamanca in the 1590s and control of the Rome college from 1635, and by seminaries in Lisbon, Santiago and Seville.[49] By 1649 an inspector found a well-organised order offering free education and in most cases teaching five hours a day.

The Cromwellian wars from 1649–52 and the expulsion of Catholic landowners were followed by a brief flourishing in the Restoration, but after the 'Glorious Revolution' the Dublin parliament passed a massive series of 'Penal Laws' (1695–1728) which included a ban on most categories of Catholic clergy in Ireland and forbade teaching and study abroad. In this period a Jesuit was worth £50 to a priest-hunter, more than a bishop. By the 1720s persecution was ebbing, and schools were founded in Dublin in particular (Mary's Lane in 1718, Fishamble St around 1750) before the Society's suppression in 1773. Thus the annual collections of missionary letters, circulated to Jesuit establishments and patrons, will have been available in Ireland at various times during this 200-year period as well as in commercial forms.

When the Society was re-established in 1814, a new era of exchanges with Asia had developed. It nevertheless became a central part of upper-class Catholic education in Ireland, culminating in

48. This section draws extensively on McRedmond (1991).
49. Ignatius' ideal Jesuit education included where 'necessary or useful' languages 'such as Chaldaic, Arabic and Indian' (McRedmond 1991: 111).

the role of Jesuits as directors of the newly established University College Dublin in 1882. Among the Jesuit missionaries, St Francis Xavier has been consistently popular in Ireland, so that outline knowledge of his encounters with Buddhism has been transmitted in many forms, from twentieth-century prize books to Bouhours' 1682 French biography[50] and the 1664 Latin one by de Bartoli:[51]

> It is in any case certain that Xaca [Shakyamuni] was one of the most famous gymnosophists of India. His father was a king in the Gangetic basin and his surname "Buddha" means a wise or lettered person. He lived about a thousand years before Christ. (cited in Beinorius 2005: 12)

Irish students abroad, often in Jesuit-led institutions, were particularly well-situated to attend the Jesuit theatres or read the annual *Letters*. As Chambers notes,

> A major portion of those people who would naturally have formed a native Catholic intelligentsia either based themselves in Europe or were strongly influenced by their continental education … From the establishment of the Irish colleges network within the European Catholic university system in the late sixteenth century until the disruption of the French revolutionary wars and the foundation of the "Royal College of St Patrick" at Maynooth in 1795, the intellectual life of Irish Catholics remained vigorous, diverse and European (2001: 57).

Irish Reception of Jesuit Material

Some traces of this can be found in the libraries of Trinity College, Dublin (est. 1592) and Maynooth (est. 1795), the intellectual centres of Anglican and Catholic Ireland respectively,[52] and in the Dublin library of Archbishop Marsh, incorporated as Ireland's first public library in 1707. Du Halde's compendium on China and 'Chinese Tartary', for example, seen by Samuel Johnson as the most accurate account (Millar 2009: 13) is to be found in Trinity and Marsh's (1736 edition) as well as Maynooth (1741). Du Halde was a director of the Jesuit journal *Mémoires de Trévoux*, of which the Dublin Society acquired a retrospective series running up to 1763 (Brown 1987: 22).

Trinity holds a 1693 translation of the Jesuit Philippe Avril's *Travels*, discussing China and 'Great Tartary' and including extracts from Hakluyt and Purchas, while Marsh's holds this and the French

---

50. Maynooth holds a copy.
51. Maynooth holds an 1858 translation, and Trinity has an 1825 *Italian* collected works.

original (also 1693). Marsh's also bought the 1653 work of Irish
Franciscan Raymond Caron, *Apostolatus evangelicus missionariorum
regularium per universum mundum expositus*, surveying the work of
missionary orders, and a 1660 edition which Maynooth also holds.
Jesuit sympathy for China was contested by Jansenists; Eusebius
Renaudot's 1718 *Anciennes relations des Indes et de la Chine* uses
medieval Muslim travellers' accounts for this purpose.[53]

The final compilation of Jesuit letters, the two-volume 1762
*Travels of the Jesuits, into various parts of the world, particularly China
and the East-Indies*,[54] was 'sold by all the Booksellers of Great-Britain,
Ireland and New-England' (cover page). Maynooth holds a copy of
this, inscribed 'Nicholas Callan' – Professor of Natural Philosophy
from 1834 and inventor of the induction coil – showing how long
such a work might circulate in private hands before donation.
Trinity also holds this edition, and French versions dating between
1707 and 1823.

After this period, church-circulated knowledge about the Jesuit
missionaries in Buddhist Asia merged into that from more recent
missionary societies,[55] and into the secular travel narratives.

Plebeian Knowledge

It would be easy to conclude that knowledge about Buddhist Asia
was the province only of the gentry and higher clerics; but this
is an artefact of what survives. Print arrived in Ireland in 1551,
and textual culture increasingly dominated over the following
150 years (Gillespie 2005: 39). Literacy was widespread though
not universal, marked by class, urban-rural and gender divides. If
as Gillespie notes in one Kerry estate two-thirds of native tenants
and 83% of settlers could sign their names between 1653 and 1687,
illiteracy could still be found higher up the scale, in the civic elite
of Belturbet in the 1680s or Meath churchwardens in the 1750s,
and Barnard suggests that plebeian literacy may have taken off in

52. Pre-1795 works were donated at a later stage by Catholic families or clerics
or bought second-hand.
53. Maynooth holds a 1733 translation. Thanks to Susan Durack and Barbara
McCormack for this reference.
54. A translation of *Lettres édifiantes & curieuses*.
55. We should note here the Irish missionary Robert Hanna (1762–97), sent by
the French Vincentian order to China. There is no record of his having sent any
information on China back to the west (Shan 2012).

the cities alone (1999: 61).[56] By the 1770s about 50% of Irishwomen could read (Kennedy 1999: 79). Literacy also went increasingly beyond the ability to sign a document:

> In the 1790s there were fifty printers in Dublin alone, thirty-four provincial presses and at least forty newspapers. Besides the 1841 census revealed that 54% of Catholics could read and that 35% could read and write. (McManus 2002: 239).

Books were widely available from the sixteenth century on: up to the end of the seventeenth century books were imported from France, Holland and England to small towns such as Coleraine, Dingle, Drogheda, Galway, Ross, Wexford and Youghal as well as cities like Belfast, Cork, Derry, Limerick and Waterford which remained important in the eighteenth century (Kennedy 2001: 5). Pedlars transported books inland from the late seventeenth to the early nineteenth century (Ó Ciosáin 2010: 71-4).

By the late seventeenth century the physical costs of books were in part overcome not only by cheap editions and serialising, but also by sharing, even between religious opponents. Institutions such as coffee houses (from the late seventeenth century in Dublin, Limerick, Cork, Kilkenny, Clonmel, Wexford, Galway and elsewhere) and public libraries (from the early eighteenth century) extended this process further.

From the mid-eighteenth century postal services, canals and improved roads enabled an expansion of national and provincial newspapers and the distribution of British and continental papers, literary and scholarly periodicals. Newspapers were often read in coffee houses and by individual subscribers (Kennedy 2001: 6-9). Teachers, priests and gentlemen would also read papers to labourers and small farmers (Ó Ciosáin 2010: 216).

Thus, below the level of the two developing circuits of distribution – a Protestant, 'English' and imperial one and a Catholic, 'Irish' and diasporic one – middle-class and plebeian readers were increasingly able to share in the new knowledge of Asian Buddhism. It is

56. For comparison, the World Development Report, relying on 1994-6 research, rated 23% of Irish adults as functionally illiterate. Denny et al., (1999) explained this away as a cohort effect; but the 2009 PISA report estimated that 23% of male teenagers were functionally illiterate (Walsh 2011), suggesting that the development of literacy has stalled – and that we should be wary of looking down on previous centuries.

a mistake to think that modern Irish history shows a progression from ignorance of the wider world towards greater awareness; the kinds of material artefacts (books, newspapers) and skills (reading, foreign languages) which we might see as prerequisites for under-standing were far more widely distributed than we might assume, particularly for the eighteenth century.

Hedge Schools and Their Rivals

Culture in Ireland is often 'ordinary' (Williams 1999). The mandarin assumptions of a Bourdieu (Bourdieu and Passeron 1990) that the poor are deprived of culture are simply untenable in the colonial and post-colonial world, where the cultural possessions of elites often became the oppositional knowledge of many different social groups. It is not that knowledge is not distributed in classed ways: it is that poverty need not mean ignorance. Literacy was widespread though not universal, and reading material of many different kinds circulated widely.

As chapter five shows, a Dublin-born 'hobo', drifting between jobs and countries, could defeat university-trained missionaries in debate. Early modern Ireland contained far more of U Dhammaloka's peers – returned sailors and soldiers – who had encountered living Buddhists than it did genteel commentators. In the nature of things, however, their accounts have not survived.

The Irish poor, rural and urban, (often) cared about education and (sometimes) got the chance to act on this. Between the Penal Laws in the late seventeenth century, forcing Catholic education under-ground, and the national education act of 1831 which established both state- and church-led education, unofficial 'hedge' schools flourished, dominating Catholic education by the late eighteenth century. Often in rudimentary conditions, 'wretched huts, built of sods in the highway ditches', they were massively popular, and poor parents made huge sacrifices to send their children, supporting teachers who were themselves poor, if educated (McManus 2002: 239–40).

In particular, their main form of literature – chapbooks – were everywhere:

> Four Dublin booksellers were engaged in printing them exclusively in 1825. One bookseller had four presses in operation, publishing some 50,000 books annually. Other presses were located in Cork,

Limerick, Belfast and Galway. From all these sources, it was
estimated that the circulation of chapbooks grew to about 300,000
per annum. (McManus 2002: 11)

By far the most popular kind of chapbook in eighteenth and
nineteenth century Ireland were medieval romances and similar
texts (McManus 2002: 170). William Carleton's (1830) 'The Hedge
School' expected that their advertisements would mention among
others 'the works of Alexander the Great' and Aesop's Fables; other
titles known to have circulated include *Life of Mahomet, Chinese tales*,
and so on. Marco Polo, the *Golden legend* or Mandeville may also
have been used.

In the early nineteenth century, the (Protestant) Kildare Place
Society set itself the task of competing with the hedge schools and
supplanting chapbooks. By 1824 it was responsible for 100,000
scholars and over a thousand schools, provoking a struggle over
control of Irish education which in some ways continues to this day:
here as elsewhere, the study of Buddhism and Ireland is inevitably
torn between the different kinds of relationships created by these
competing elites. Rather than medieval romances, the Society's
literary assistant, Rev. Charles Bardin, focused on voyages and
travels, producing at least 24 books on the topic between 1821 and
1832 at the height of the Society's influence (McManus 2002: 49–53,
218). Nonetheless, chapbooks continued to be used until well after
the Famine (Ó Ciosáin 2010: 57).

Even at this level of basic education for the poor, then, medieval
and early modern encounters with Buddhism were present. Rather
than see Buddhism as only lately coming into the view of ordinary
Irish people, we should rather think of these multiple circuits of
knowledge – commercial, Jesuit, plebeian – as continuously touching
on what was known of the other end of Eurasia, building on the
more restricted distribution of medieval and classical knowledge
before that.

Awareness and Identification: Conversion and Utopias Revisited

As I have shown, *some* knowledge about Buddhism was continuously available in Ireland from the seventh century on. This
expanded considerably – in content and in distribution – in the
later medieval period; in the early modern period, massively
more information became available through an even greater

diversity of channels. This knowledge did not necessarily translate into sympathy or identification with Buddhism. As Offermans notes (2005: 17), sixteenth-century Jesuits 'already knew more, in particular concerning Buddhism as a lived tradition, than many an Orientalist of the nineteenth century'. Yet as far as can be established, this ethnographic encounter took until the later nineteenth century to induce any degree of identification – or any *active* interest on the part of Irish writers.

Thus we cannot sustain the conventional assumption that interest in, sympathy for or commitment to Buddhism flow naturally from knowledge of Buddhism. The latter was a necessary, but in no way sufficient condition. In some contexts – the medieval period when writers insisted on the virtue of Buddhism, or the late twentieth century – Buddhist Asia could be an attractive 'Other' for some Irish people; at other times, equally or more detailed information could be available without evoking such responses. Indeed contemporary Irish Buddhists are by no means uniformly well-informed.

Clearly the *structure* of available knowledge makes a difference to how people respond: we can perhaps reframe Offermans' comment as the observation that those brought up Christian were perhaps unlikely to convert on the basis of external accounts of rituals, even where they seemed familiar. Yet Marco Polo provided a clear (and brief) life of the Buddha which does not seem to have had the same dramatic effect as the 1879 *Light of Asia*, even though Christians were primed to respond to such biographies (and saw parallels). For their part, readers of the Jesuit texts in particular could have put together some indications on aspects as recondite as Zen meditation and the *sunyata* doctrine.

Research on conversion frequently comments (eg Stark 1987) that the best situation is one where the new religion is neither too similar nor too different from the old. Astley drew precisely this conclusion in 1747, in anti-Catholic mode:

> the greatest security the Bonzas [in Tibet and China] can have against the Progress of Popery among them, is the great Conformity between the two Religions: For, by the Change, their Followers see they will be just in the same Condition they were before; there being nothing of Novelty to induce them, excepting what arises from the Difference of a few Forms. Besides, they must naturally have a greater Respect for the Saints, Images, and Ceremonies of their own, than those of a foreign Manufacture. (cited in Lopéz 1998: 30)

Less mischievously, we might say that for much of the early modern period in particular, when Irish people sought alternatives to the religion of their birth, they did so 'not under circumstances of their own choosing', but in the context of the Wars of Religion and the conflict of denomination, language, culture and political affiliation which structured everything (including of course the circuits of knowledge, and the ideological frameworks within which that knowledge came packaged). This situation continued until the late nineteenth century, when the rising power of Catholic nationalism created a new kind of crisis for old affiliations. It is not that a particular type of information *produces* conversions; but that a particular local politics of religion makes certain choices possible and meaningful.

This restates the power/knowledge connection stressed by Foucault (1981) and Said (1995), but with a different focus, on the power created over the supposedly knowing subject, and a closer attention to the economic, political and cultural relationships within which knowledge of Buddhism was transmitted, distributed and received in Europe – and to the needs, purposes and choices of dissidents in different times and places.

Religion, Power and Repression

Readers' responses never took place within the world of the text alone, any more than religion usually does. One key fact was the role of religious repression in constructing the boundaries of what could be said and thought. This structures many of the contexts discussed so far. Classical knowledge was transmitted through a church which imposed orthodoxy with the support of state violence; the Crusades made trade through the Arab world impossible and later prompted the exploration of possible alliances with (and conversion of) the Khans; early modern Ireland and Europe were massively structured by the conflict between the Catholic, Reformed and Anglican churches. Repression is also more intimately present in areas such as the medieval attempts to legitimise discussion of Buddhism by likening it to Christianity or deploying the 'virtuous pagan' trope, in Anglican legislation against Catholic education, and in Jesuit editing of missionary letters.

We can briefly note two other barriers to unsuitable forms of religious belief: blasphemy legislation and censorship; and denominationally-exclusive institutions and informal sanctions. As the overarching reach of a single national church broke down in Britain, blasphemy became an issue of criminal rather than canon law. In England, the Blasphemy Act of 1650 had a massive effect on the Ranters, leading to the transmutation of their radicalism into 'prophetic dogma and ... sectarian organizing zeal' (Thompson 1993: 27). Religious persecution in these islands was *also* aimed at radicalism outside the main churches, and the offence of blasphemy was designed precisely for those who did not owe allegiance to them.

A 1697 Act criminalised disbelief in Christianity, the Bible and until 1813 the Trinity (Bradney 1999: 83). As late as 1883, the publishers of the British *Freethinker* were tried for blasphemy and GW Foote was sentenced to a year's hard labour. Harry Boulter, in 1909, was similarly jailed as was the socialist freethinker, John Gott, for nine months in 1921. In Ireland, the Blasphemy Act of 1697 and the common-law offence remained in operation until the 1920s; the 1937 constitution prohibited blasphemy although this was not carried into new legislation. It was not until 1999 that the Supreme Court ruled that it could not say what blasphemy now consisted of.[57] A new offence of blasphemous libel was introduced in 2009, but has not yet been tested in the courts. Thus, until independence at least, to be openly Buddhist was illegal.

Blasphemy legislation was only the most visible aspect of a censorship process which was in many ways inherent in the structure of western Christianities: once orthodoxy was measured by views and ratified by states, self-censorship was a constitutive aspect of the writing process. Largely defined around religion and the expression of political loyalty, censorship was notoriously to remain a central feature of Irish intellectual and artistic life throughout much of the twentieth century.

Secondly, the cultural structure and key institutions of post-Reformation Ireland were, and often are, explicitly or implicitly denominational. As we have seen, education and careers in the early modern period were massively structured by this fact, as were charitable institutions, hospitals and so on. Oxford, Cambridge and Dublin universities were all religious institutions, with dissenters barred from the English institutions until the 1850s and religious tests remaining in all three until the 1870s. Catholics, for their part,

57. *Irish Times*, Apr 29 2009: 1.

needed a dispensation from their bishop to attend Trinity until
1970. Whether in Anglican or Catholic institutions, the holders of
knowledge were not neutral agents in Ireland's religious conflicts,
nor intended to be.

The broader history of sectarian institution-forming in Ireland
meant that all sorts of informal social consequences attached to not
being part of a well-established denomination, let alone standing
outside Christianity altogether: employment, marriage, access to
schooling, jury service, parliamentary service and so on were all
tied to religious persuasion throughout the early modern and much
of the modern period.

If medieval states were Christian, early modern ones were
confessional:

> the process of confessional or religious definition was grafted onto
> the ongoing process of monarchical consolidation which in turn
> influenced the way subjects lived. These were the driving forces
> behind state-building in early modern Europe ... On the basis of their
> respective confessions of faith, the four main religious communions
> developed into internally coherent, exclusive communities ... In time
> it permitted magistrates to impose limits on popular behaviour by
> attempting to inculcate new moral standards. (O'Connor 2001: 10–11)

This process also operated beneath the level of the state, as two
Quaker examples show. In the 1650s, Quakers arrived in colonial,
Anglophone Ireland, then in the process of the Cromwellian wars:

> Howgill, Burrough and Elizabeth Fletcher had settled Meetings from
> Dublin to Cork, and created mayhem in the English Army. Henry
> Cromwell, Commander-in-Chief of the Army in Ireland, saw Quaker
> agitators as a menace to military control of Ireland. (Davies 1998: 236).

Quakers oriented themselves to 'patience and industry', but soon
faced their own internal dissidence:

> a group of Quakers in Chapelizod obtained a copy of the printed work
> of the sixteenth-century German mystic Jacob Boehme ... On the basis
> of reading the book and discussing its contents they arrived at rather
> unorthodox theological views for which they were censured by the
> Quakers. (Gillespie 2005: 14)

The religious structure of early modern and modern Ireland
was marked by both these relationships, of internal control and
external conflict. If we want to identify the conditions under which

widespread knowledge of Buddhism did not lead to identification with it in one situation but did in another, we have to include the basic fact of a power structure in which religious orthodoxy was enforced.

Antiquarian Interests

What knowledge *did* lead to was attempts to fit a Buddhism which was seen as morally virtuous or institutionally sophisticated into local frames of knowledge. We have seen this with medieval texts; in Ireland, Buddhism was fit into alternative accounts of Irish history, which survived well into the nineteenth century in opposition to Whig accounts of English colonisation as civilizing agent (Lennon 2004).

Thus Kerry-born Henry O'Brien speculated in 1834 that round towers had been constructed by migrant Buddhists (Murphy 2011: 78). The towers, he thought, were phallic symbols; the Irish word Budh meant both sun and phallus, and hence Buddhists worshipped both. The radical Yorkshire magistrate Godfrey Higgins, in 1827–9, also thought that Ireland had many Buddhist remains; for Higgins the first human race had one language, one colour and one religion, which was closest to Buddhism and Druidism (Hutton 2007: 182). By 1894, however, James Bonwick rejected the thesis that round towers were Buddhist relics (1894: 272–3).

The tradition would reappear in Theosophy, and in Evans-Wentz' *Fairy-faith in Celtic countries* (1903), which argued that fairy stories point to an ongoing belief in reincarnation, and is still alive in contemporary 'Celtic Buddhism' and elsewhere. In more academic form, the theologian J. Kennedy published a series of articles in the *Journal of the Royal Asiatic Society* on early links between Buddhism and Gnosticism (1902), Babylon and India, and so on, writing that Basilides' Gnosticism

> was Buddhist pure and simple – Buddhist in its governing ideas, its psychology, its metaphysics; and Christianity reduced to a semi-Buddhist ideal as a result. (cited in Beinorius 2005: 9)

Knowledge alone, then, led to a need to reduce cognitive dissonance, whether by fitting new knowledge into old histories, or by resolving the challenge posed by Buddhism to assumptions of unquestioned Christian superiority, but not to anything more.

Conclusion

To the best of my knowledge, this chapter is the first attempt at a reception history of Buddhism, not simply for Ireland, but for Europe in this period. By treating books as material facts and translation, rewriting, compiling, plagiarising, printing, distributing and so on, as material processes rather than as disembodied words, it shows, first, that a series of different knowledges about Buddhism circulated continuously if unevenly in Ireland and the broader Irish world. Secondly, these processes, and the situation of different kinds of Irish people within these (Protestants and Catholics, diaspora and on the island, wealthy and poor) were shaped by the changing world-system relations within which knowledge and people were both embedded. Thus Ireland becomes not an isolated case apart but a vantage point from which to explore broader European processes.

Reading is by no means the only aspect of the encounter with Buddhism: it is a privileged form of this particular situation, perhaps a specific characteristic of 'information exchange' at the ends of world-systems along with the occasional transmission of exotic goods and the migration which became more significant towards the end of this period. By the period discussed in part II, far greater numbers of Irish people found themselves directly involved in Asian politics in the era of high imperialism and anti-colonial Buddhist Revival; and Ireland itself was increasingly reshaped by the Anglo-Irish relationship to empire and Catholic nationalism's bid for power.

Part II

Caught between Empires: Irish Buddhists and Theosophists (1850–1960)

Chapter Three

The Two Empires: Ireland in Asia, Asia in Ireland

Chapter two has shown three things. Firstly, knowledge of 'elsewhere' does not simply happen; it is transmitted and shaped through concrete, if sometimes surprising, historical relationships, linked to the rise and fall of world-economies and world empires. Secondly, by the time Europeans came to convert to Buddhism in the later nineteenth century, the relevant knowledge had been continuously available for centuries. Thirdly, the European response was structured by the local facts of religious conflict and repression.

Part II of this book explores a situation which had changed in these respects. With British global hegemony (Arrighi 1994), Ireland became related to Buddhist Asia in new ways, and knowledge about Buddhism came to be produced within the social relations of high imperialism. This affected Orientalisms both mainstream and dissident, with the use of the Asian Other to critique the here-and-now (Clarke 1997), and the development of anti-colonial (Lennon 2004) and anti-missionary solidarity. Europeans, and Irish people, started to become Buddhist converts and sympathisers, facing far less severe formal sanctions for this, although informal social costs remained high.

The Politics of Religious Identification

European and Global Contexts

Religion had long been political within Europe, and the English and French revolutions and associated radicalisms had added new dimensions to the mix. In the later nineteenth century, as popular mobilisations undermined the attempted restorations of *anciens régimes*, states had far greater need for popular legitimation and parliamentarianism spread.

One outcome was the development of 'pillarisation', within which different, and opposing, subcultures organised their own political, cultural and social institutions. Sometimes these 'cleavages' (Lipset and Rokkan 1967) divided Protestant from Catholic, as in Ireland, Germany and the Netherlands; sometimes they divided religious subcultures from liberal or anti-clerical ones as in France or Italy; sometimes they divided the socialist, communist and anarchist worlds of organised labour from those of the upper classes and petty bourgeoisie.

All this meant that religious identity was an increasingly significant *choice* – of ethnic identification, social position or political strategy. From being a taken-for-granted part of a traditionalist way of life, religious affiliations became subcultural 'worlds apart', increasingly structured by popular mobilisation, against each other and the new liberal worlds introduced by the French Revolution, and often allied to traditionalist élites seeking to restore an older *status quo*. These choices, collective or individual, were more about politics than theology:

> For at least a century and a quarter it has been commonplace for observers of Irish life to note that the differences between Protestants and Catholics in Ireland have nothing to do with religion *per se* and everything to do with divergent cultural traditions or with economic discrimination. (Akenson 1991: 12)

Or, as Robbie McVeigh puts it

> Sectarian labels are about more than religion ... they approximate more to notions of ethnicity – involving nationality, politics, culture, "race" and boundary maintenance as much as faith and religious organisation. Religious identity ... remains the main signifier of ethnic difference in Ireland. (1995: 627)

This is not an Irish peculiarity, although the absolute domination of the ethno-religious cleavage is (McLeod 1997: 20). Where the southern Irish rural population was until recently overwhelmingly practising Catholic (1997: 54), much of Europe has been marked by disparities between traditionally dechristianised or anti-clerical and traditionally devout regions.

Religious identity was bound up with history, with economic interests, forms of popular organisation and imperial projects; all within a rapidly changing landscape. These are the years of the Paris Commune, the unification of Germany and Italy, and of the First World War; years in which religion lurched from its previous role of alliance with monarchy and reliance on traditional behaviour towards a new role of popular mobilisation which found shape in Bonapartism, fascism and postwar Christian Democracy.

Globally, these are the years of most intensive colonisation: in Asia, the replacement of the East India Company by the British Empire, the conquest of Burma, the 'opening up' of China and Tibet through opium wars, the repression of the Boxer rebellion and the Younghusband expedition – and the years in which the anti-colonial movements (religious, nationalist and socialist) that would lead to postwar independence were formed.

The British Empire in particular moved decisively in the later nineteenth century from a hands-off policy towards local religion, allying with local elites to maintain control for political and economic purposes, towards an increasingly close alliance with missionary Christianity to legitimate empire at home. This produced anti-colonial movements in religious shape, such as the Buddhist Revival by the new educated, lay elites of countries like Ceylon and Burma, with which Irish Buddhists allied themselves.

Sectarianism in Ireland: the Political Implications of Religious Choice

In Ireland, the defeat of the 1798 rebellion and the 1800 union with Britain created space for Daniel O'Connell's political Catholicism, characterised by Eagleton (1995) as the world's first modern social movement. As this removed legal barriers to Catholic elites in particular, the Catholic church was increasingly offered a role in organising Irish life through education, health and the provision of welfare. Irish Protestants, for their part, increasingly saw identification with London as the main underpinning of their own social position.

Williams' (1981) useful classification distinguishes dominant (hegemonic), residual and emergent elites. Between 1850 to 1960 a once-dominant Anglo-Irish elite became residual, while the once-emergent Catholic nationalist elite became dominant: Land War and Land Acts undermined the economic basis of the aristocrat-tenant rural order, while Home Rule, Unionism and independence created new political structures (and states). The years following the 1840s famine saw

> a "devotional revolution" in which the clergy established a dominant influence over the religious life of the people, and patterns of Catholic life were established that have remained up to the present day (McLeod 1997: 50).

In 1869, the Anglican church was disestablished, paralleling the construction of the massive Catholic institutional complex (Nic Ghiolla Phádraig 1995). The rising Catholic elite slowly remade Irish society in its own image, while Protestant elites sought with increasing desperation to retain the old order. Other social groups – notably the peasantry, the urban working class and women – were subordinated to these identifications, with short bursts of independent action. Religion did not only mean ethnicity; it also meant loyalty to these ethnic leaderships.

The 'Two Empires' and Their Circuits of Meaning

In this context, the Irish encounter with Buddhism was shaped by the continuing division between the two different circuits of knowledge. The Protestant elite increasingly understood itself in colonial terms: not only in the shift from an earlier nationalism to a closer identification with Britain, but also in its role as imperial service class.[1]

At the top, the diplomatic corps and Indian Civil Service, officer commissions in the military and navy, together with university scholars and museum curators, defined this relationship, constructing a circuit of power/knowledge which combined ethnic identification in Ireland with race in Asia. As the life histories of its dissident members (chapters four and five) show, this class forged bonds of solidarity in serving imperial power abroad and its own interests at home, connected through networks of family and friendship (see Crosbie 2012 for a detailed discussion).

So too, the emergent 'nationalist service class' – the organic intellectuals of Catholic nationalism – developed what was described as a 'spiritual empire' abroad, a massive missionary effort based in Ireland, while the popular press and commercial entertainment at home retailed its own narratives about 'native' culture, including Buddhism.

There were of course overlaps – Protestant missionaries, members of the Catholic middle classes seeking careers through empire and

1. 'Service class', in contemporary Marxist sociology, denotes managers, civil servants, technical experts and other professionals whose work assists in the organisation of capitalist firms and the state in its various aspects. Typically marked by a code of 'service', considerable workplace autonomy and discretionary power, they are distinct both from the ruling (capitalist) class and from small property-owners.

plebeian soldiers and sailors – but there were nonetheless two distinct sets of institutions involved.

There was thus not one Orientalism but two 'official' ones, each with their own dissidents. Irish Buddhism has related not to a single dominant 'national culture' but has been caught in the conflict between *two* conflicting cultures, and is only now beginning to emerge from this. While these two engagements with Asia were oriented towards power, at home and abroad, they also provided a setting for 'class desertion' from both of these projects. Some Irish people rose in the world through participation in power; others identified with the colonised. Sometimes, as with Maurice Collis, a single life could contain both experiences.

Dissident Orientalisms

If Said (2003) is right to see European knowledge of Asia as constructed through processes of power, Clarke (1997) is equally correct to observe that such knowledge was often drawn on strategically by European *dissidents* to critique local power relations, from eighteenth-century imaginings of the outsider's view of Christianity to twentieth-century counter-cultural uses of Buddhism. Lennon (2004) identifies a tradition of drawing parallels between Ireland and Asian countries, underlining their similar positions with relation to metropolitan culture and empire: as Yeats wrote of Irish peasants, 'had they not lived in Asia until the Battle of the Boyne?' (cited in Murphy 2011: 79). Moreover,

> Nineteenth-century Ireland occupies a curious historical position as both victim of, and participant in, imperialist expansion. This description is valid, provided it is recognised that the two imperial roles do not somehow cancel each other out. Irish participation in empire does not lessen the credibility of an Irish anti-imperial critique (Ryder 2006: 12).

While this chapter highlights Irish involvement in British Empire and Christian missionary effort, chapters four and five explore ways in which Irish people used religion to critique empire and their own culture. Some did both: turning in disgust from empire to the defence of cultures they had come to love; justifying empire while simultaneously defending the societies it was destroying; or mixing active opposition to Christianity with arguments in support of capitalist modernisation.

Chapter four discusses the politics of Irish Theosophy, which in Britain and the US was a key matrix for early Buddhism but in Ireland took different directions. It argues that Theosophy represents defection from the politics of Irish Protestantism towards an alternative strategy which would enable them to remain active in the politics of the new Ireland – or, indeed, the new India – and to do so in religious terms.

Chapter five argues that rather than identifying with old or new elites, or seeking a 'third way' to political engagement in Ireland, the early Irish Buddhists followed a strategy of defection and 'going native' within the organisations of modernist Buddhism in Asia. Most such Buddhists were also defecting from the declining Protestant identity, along with some plebeian Catholics.

These choices were formed within, and as responses to, the social and political relationships of mainstream Orientalisms. To be a Buddhist, a Hindu or a Theosophist was not simply to worship differently or have a different inner experience to a conventional Anglican, Catholic or Dissenter. It was also to practise a different kind of politics. It meant writing in different modes, and finding different careers (not as academic, civil servant or priest, for example). It meant separation from social goods provided through churches – access to particular kinds of jobs and services or the links of ethnic community; outmarriage of any kind routinely meant disinheritance. Finally, and most crucially, it meant crossing a racial barrier which defined both empire and religion.

'Dissident Orientalism', to coin a phrase, was not simply another discourse: in a world where religion, ethnicity, career and social identity were intimately connected it had enormous implications for one's whole life. As chapter five will show, these implications were so great that most Irish Buddhists of the period 'went native' in Buddhist Asia.

Imperial Identifications

The longterm after-effects of this ethno-religious polarisation lead us to think of 'British', 'English' and 'Irish' as nationally and geographically-bounded situations. This situation remains a live one in Northern Ireland in particular; but in the period in question people born or living in one place could use any or all of these identifications depending on who they were talking to, with different implications for their relationships to Buddhist Asia. Robert Hart, for example, variously described himself as British, Irish, English and an Ulsterman (O'Leary 2009: 31). Conversely, those we might now call Glasgow Catholics often called themselves Irish; while Ulster Protestants might be described as Scots.

The situation was entangled. For example, Buddhism was debated in the *Dublin University Magazine* (for 1873) and the *Dublin Review* (for 1875, 1888 and 1890). The former was a key intellectual organ for the Protestant Ascendancy, the latter important to Catholic self-understanding. However, in 1873 the *Magazine* had just acquired a Northern Irish editor, after some years of being run by a London printer. Shortly afterwards, in 1877, it would be bought by the Trinity-educated Robert Cook, husband of Theosophist Mabel Collins.

The *Review*, for its part, had been founded with O'Connell's backing, and its main contributors were Maynooth academics (Hayley 1987: 37). However as the 'leading Roman Catholic journal in Britain' (cited in Franklin 2008: 16) it became an organ of the Catholic intelligentsia across the British Isles and eventually merged with the London-based *Month*. Its articles on Buddhism were penned by clerical scholars based in England, France and Belgium respectively. Thus even when boundaries were being fixed as never before, key institutions were far more broadly based than we might now expect. So too, Irish people who became Buddhists or Hindu nationalists were published by Asian organisations, by western spiritualist, theosophist or atheist periodicals and by the commercial mainstream.

More broadly, in 1861 or 1911, just as in 2011, if something was published in Britain or the US it was often available in Ireland, and the American and British encounters with Buddhism were known in Ireland too. However, questions of national reception and distribution, as well as creation, are significant ones, and this chapter focuses on what is known to have been read or written in Ireland; related to these metropolitan encounters but inflected in very specific ways.

Furthermore, as Nagai has shown, the cohesion of the British Empire depended in part on the use of analogy, creating similarities in policy:

> British subjects … daily read Irish and Indian news side by side in
> *The Times*, and could make their own analogies and comparisons to
> form their opinions about the working of the British Empire.

Conversely, oppositional Irish or Indian intellectuals could draw on both direct contact and analogy to 'form anti-colonial resistance and national identities' (2006: 4–5). If as McMahon (2010) shows reflection on Indian partition was informed by Ireland, so too Irish and Indian nationalists thought about colonialism comparatively (O'Malley 2010), while Burmese nationalists published accounts of the War of Independence (Hans-Bernd Zöllner, pers. comm.) While the 1919 Amritsar massacre was shaped by the Irish experiences of the officer commanding and the provincial governor (Grace 2010), Justice Daniel Twomey in Burma could leave as his *magnum opus* an integration of British and Buddhist law which mirrored Irish relationships between the Crown and the Catholic church.

The Hindu convert Sister Nivedita from Dungannon linked the common sense of Britishness she perceived in the then 'United Kingdom of Great Britain and Ireland' with her attempts to define a common Indian identity (Hayes 2010), and consistently opposed Buddhist claims to separation from Hindu hegemony. Irish Buddhist sympathisers such as Lafcadio Hearn or Maurice Collis, for their part, interpreted Asian Buddhism through Anglo-Irish eyes, adopting Yeats' strategy of disidentifying with establishment religion and exalting peasant religion to the circumstances of Japan and Burma.

Thus people saw Ireland in Asia and Asia in Ireland, practically and politically, as well as in emotional and religious ways; analogy and comparison consistently underlay their positions, even when they are not made explicit. 'Irish nationalists' fascination with Indian mysticism' (Nagai 2006: 5) was no accident. More generally, the Irish abroad were able to draw on their experience of cultural difference at home (see e.g. O'Leary 2009). As Crosbie (2012: 219–20) notes, TCD-trained civil servants also drew on cultural nationalism and the ethnographic study of Irish peasant life to understand Asian culture.

One characteristic episode involved three Irish civil servants who we shall meet again. In response to requests from Siam and Buddhist-Hindu conflict over the Maha Bodhi temple, the local Commissioner, William Hoey, proposed strengthening links with Buddhist countries by donating relics of the Buddha to the Siamese king. The acting Chief Secretary, Vincent Smith, proposed to give the relics but not the containers because of their archaeological interest; the Lieutenant-Governor, Sir Antony MacDonnell, took 'a keen interest' in the whole affair (Allen 2009: 205–8). At the 1899 handover Hoey praised the 'great preacher of peace' and stated

we are entitled to congratulate ourselves that we live in an age of
toleration and of wide sympathy with the faiths professed by others
(Allen 2009: 211–2).

– an aspiration whose Irish resonances cannot have been lost on any
of the three.

The Imperial Service Class and Its Circuits of Knowledge

Nothing in a decade of doctoral studies, followed by research for
my first book, had given me the slightest inkling that the intellectual
and popular cultures of [the Victorian period] had been so steeped in
Buddhism. (Franklin 2008: viii)

The Army and the Dharma

Empire was an interconnected circuit. Catholic privates were
commanded by Protestant officers; those officers in turn might
donate their loot to a Dublin museum. Imperial adminstrators were
educated in Irish universities, and in turn might retire to academia
to train the next generation. Where soldiers went, missionaries
followed; all sent back news and stories, which fed popular literature,
and brought back religious items undesrtood as 'art' which inspired
painters and poets. This chapter separates out aspects of these
stories; at the time they were all jumbled up together.

The most common Asian encounter with Ireland was at the point
of a bayonet:

Most Irish [in India] were soldiers: former peasants, artisans and clerks
turned privates and non-commissioned officers, led by a sprinkling of
Irish and Anglo-Irish officers (Cook 1987: 509).

There had been Irish soldiers in the East India Company since the
1680s (Lennon 2004: 171–2) and covert recruitment increased from
the 1750s (Crosbie 2012: 70). Numbers grew rapidly after the ban on
Catholic privates was removed in the 1790s (that on officers lasted
another century). By 1813 there were recruiting offices in Belfast,
Dublin, Enniskillen and Limerick (Sen 2003). The army exported
ethnic and class conflict abroad (Nagai 2006: 19–20).

Despite Ireland's far smaller population, Irish soldiers in the
Bengal Army between 1825 and 1850 were only just outnumbered by
British ones; over half the white soldiers in India in 1857 were Irish
(Sen 2003). Still in 1911, there were about 12,200 Irish-born soldiers
in India (Bartlett 1997). Bayly claims that nineteenth-century Cork

may have had more direct contact with India than with Dundee (2000: 387–9).

The everyday meanings of this are dramatised in Kipling's *Kim* where the Catholic and presumably Irish (Cronin 2006: 132) Father Victor talks Col. Creighton into using money sent by a Tibetan lama for Kim's education to put him in St. Xavier's rather than giving him to the Protestant regimental chaplain. Creighton responds:

> I – er – strongly recommend sending the boy to St. Xavier's. He can go down on pass as a soldier's orphan, so the railway fare will be saved. You can buy him an outfit from the regimental subscription. The Lodge will be saved the expense of his education, and that will put the Lodge in a good temper. (Kipling 1908: 159)

This 'India' was considerably larger than today's: the 'Army in India' and the Indian Civil Service were responsible for present-day India, Pakistan and Bangladesh; border regions with Buddhist populations (Nepal, Sikkim, Bhutan, Ladakh and the Chittagong Hill Tracts); the conquest and (until 1937) administration of Burma; and the bases for imperial presence in Tibet. More loosely, 'India' often also meant Ceylon, with its Buddhist majority.[2] Elsewhere, the imperial presence in Buddhist Asia also included Chinese treaty ports, Singapore and the other Straits Settlements in present-day Malaysia.

Irish soldiers, sailors and policemen encountered living Buddhism in a variety of different contexts, while diplomats engaged with the independent Buddhist kingdoms of Japan and Siam. In present-day India, Pakistan and Afghanistan, diplomats and officers uncovered the textual history and archaeology of ancient Buddhism (Lopez 1995, Allen 2003).[3]

In 1801 the presumably Irish Captain Mahony, an 'officer of the *Bombay* establishment, sometime resident in Ceylon' (Harris 2006: 225) wrote a sympathetic account of Sinhala Buddhism, focusing on rebirth and nibbana. The article, submitted in the 1790s, draws on dialogues with a Buddhist monk, Sinhala manuscripts and Dutch questionnaires distributed to monks in the late eighteenth century (Harris 2006: 171–2, 17, 225 fn 24). For Mahony, Buddhism was

2. Unfortunately, much of the literature on 'Ireland and India' is not specific as to *which* India is meant, a problem paralleling chapter two's discussion of 'Ireland'.

3. To complete this overview, Irish people were present as missionaries in Manchuria (Presbyterians), Korea (Catholics), Japan (Presbyterians and others) as well as China, Burma, India and Ceylon.

founded in a mild and simple morality. Bhoodha has taken for his principles, Wisdom, Justice and Morality (Mahony 1801: 40).

The power/knowledge nexus within which Mahony was writing, however, was neither mild nor simple. As well as the long and complex conquests of present-day India, Pakistan and Bangladesh and the suppression of the 1857 rising, the Sri Lankan kingdom of Kandy took three wars to conquer (1803, 1815, 1817–8), as did Burma (1823–6, 1852–3, 1885–6). Britain fought two wars in Afghanistan, with its Buddhist past (1839–42, 1878–80) and invaded Tibet (1903–4). In China, two wars were fought for the opium trade (1838–42, 1856–60), while Britain intervened in the Taiping and Boxer rebellions (1850–64, 1899–1901). Convict uprisings were put down in the Straits Settlements (1852, 1853). Japan and Thailand were the only Buddhist countries *not* theatres of British military operations (or conquered by other European powers).

No attempt was made to hide the brutality of these operations. Here, for example, is Kipling, then (1888) a young journalist and poet in India, describing reprisals against a Burmese village during the counter-insurgency campaign:

Long was the morn of slaughter,
Long was the list of slain,
Five score heads were taken,
Five score heads and twain;
And the men of the First Shikaris
Went back to their grave again,

Each man bearing a basket
Red as his palms that day,
Red as the blazing village –
The village of Pabengmay,
And the 'drip-drip-drip' from the baskets
Reddened the grass by the way.

They made a pile of their trophies
High as a tall man's chin,
Head upon head distorted,
Set in a sightless grin,
Anger and pain and terror
Stamped on the smoke-scorched skin.[4]

4. 'The grave of the hundred head', 1888.

Irish involvement in empire, then, was also involvement in routine violence:

> [The Connaught Rangers believed] that what had been conquered by the sword must be kept by the sword; but not being issued with swords they used their boots and fists to such purpose that they were more respected and feared by the natives than any other British unit in India. (Benson 2010: 16).

Irish people, including from the 26 counties, remained involved in British colonial administration and the military after independence. One of our interviewees had served in the Royal Navy in Asia in the 1960s:

> In all this time I'd been based in Singapore, in Hong Kong ... I sailed with, or met, Buddhists. And these people were always gentle people ... The Gurkhas were in the Army ... They are peaceful people, they are from Tibet. (interview B)

Loyalty to Empire

'Ireland and empire' – and narrower variants such as 'Ireland and India', 'Ireland and China' etc. is, rightly, an increasingly important area of study (e.g. Cook 1987, Holmes and Holmes 1997, Lennon 2004, Foley and O'Connor 2006, Nagai 2006, O'Malley 2008, McCormack 2009, Silvestri 2009, Benson 2010, Bubb 2012, Crosbie 2012). It is also a highly contested one: the subject matter is vast and spread over a long period, while disciplinary approaches vary from literary postcolonialism to conservative historiography.

Much of the strictly historical literature, while rhetorically damning as insular the nationalist assumption that Irish-born people in this period saw themselves as 'Irish', took nationalist perspectives and attempted to resist empire, is in its own way equally provincial. Insisting on the extent to which they saw themselves as 'British', were loyal to empire, participated in its creation and so on, there is no awareness of the extent to which other 'British' people *resisted* empire, and no recognition of a wider world in which conquest, colonisation, government, exploitation and so on took place. Thus a characteristic observation is that

> Many Irish in fact displayed a pride in belonging to the empire and simultaneously nourished hopes for a more autonomous Ireland at a time (c. 1880–1922) when both Irish nationalism and British imperialism were compelling ideologies. (Cook 1987: 508)

This is not a paradox but simply another way of expressing the success of the imperial service class at maintaining hegemony globally and locally. To rule, in Ireland as in India, those ruled had to believe that they could gain local advantage without challenging the overall power structure. This is a basic fact about organising armies (Gramsci 1978): troops who put down a rebellion have to separate this from grievances at home. Similarly, contemporary revisionism involves a complete disconnect from what involvement in imperialism meant *outside Ireland* (Newsinger 2006, Gott 2011). At the time, there was little doubt:

> To India we will go, my boys,
> To India we will go:
> To hunt those murdering Sepoys,
> To India we will go. (Benson 2010: 14).

Kipling's loyal Irish soldiers (chapter five) illustrate how widespread this position was (Bubb 2012). However, it was never uncontested: the nationalist Charles Gavan Duffy criticised Irish complicity with imperialism, while Thomas Davis called for direct support for Afghan rebels (Ryder 2006). At a popular level, the ballad 'The bowld sepoys' (1858) starts

> It's of the bould Sepoys I'm going for to tell,
> Who turned on their tyrants and thrash'd them right well;
> Who hoisted their green flag o'er England's old Jack;
> And laid all about them with whop, whop, whack, whack! (Benson 2010: 14)

There was nothing inevitable or universal about supporting imperialism. Present-day sophistry often asks us to judge people in terms of the views of their day, as if those were homogenous: yet the later nineteenth-century century saw regular mass demonstrations in London in support of anti-colonial struggles, often involving Irish migrant labourers (Rothstein 1983: 49–51), while Kipling felt the imperial project to be constantly under attack (Gilmour 2002). Imperialism was a political choice, not an accident of history.

People could also change their positions: oral historian Terry Fagan (pers. comm.) collected a story of a working-class Dublin soldier who was jailed and dishonourably discharged for refusing to shoot on an Indian crowd out of common experiences of poverty. Like George Orwell, it seems that James Connolly (Nevin 2005) went from soldiering (in Orwell's case, police work) to socialism and anti-colonialism, as did Maurice Collis (below).

It is not news that the majority position in late nineteenth-century Catholic Ireland was 'home rule within the British empire'; this is precisely what was dramatic about the 1919 electoral shift to Sinn Féin and independence. At this level, we are discussing *processes* rather than static givens. The business of politics was to change existing facts, or sustain them in the face of pressure from below. Speaking of Amritsar, where the Irish-Indian General Dyer killed at least 379 people, Unionist leader Edward Carson argued that Dyer

> had tried to prevent "the conspiracy to drive the British out of India ... developing into revolution" ... To these Irishmen, saving the Raj was equivalent to maintaining Ireland under the Union. (Nagai 2006: 132–3).

Arguments over Asia, including those over Asian religion, were simultaneously arguments about Ireland, as we shall see. More broadly, as Silvestri puts it, we need to examine

> the multifarious ways in which empire impacted Ireland, and how Irish participation in and opposition to empire in turn impacted other parts of the British Empire (2009: 4).

This was equally true in relation to Buddhism.

Ruling the Raj

Irishmen not only helped to conquer Buddhist Asia; they also helped to rule it. At the top, Sir James Tennent from Fermanagh was civil secretary (number two in the administration) of Ceylon from 1845–50. Hercules Robinson, ex-Indian Civil Servant from Westmeath, was Governor from 1865–72, followed by Sir William Gregory (1872–7), husband of Augusta (McEvansoneya 2009).[5] Sir Antony Macdonnell from Mayo rose to become Lieutenant-Governor of the Northwestern Provinces (1895–1; see Allen 171–2). Similarly, Lord Dufferin, from a Co. Down family, was Viceroy of India from 1884–8, presiding over the final conquest of Burma.

Irish diplomats, often the sons of Protestant clergymen, might travel even further afield: John Quin climbed the diplomatic ranks in Japan from a start as translator in a treaty port (Starr 2009). Sir John Newell Jordan also started as an interpreter, eventually becoming

5. Both Tennent's and Gregory's appointments were consolation prizes: Tennent's career was stymied by his support for Catholic emancipation (Jones 2006). Conversely, Gregory had hoped for a better appointment but had an infamously Tory career in Ireland.

Chinese Secretary (O'Leary 2009: 35). Meanwhile Henry Charles Sirr was vice-consul for Hong Kong from 1843 and subsequently a magistrate in Ceylon.[6]

From 1855, the Indian Civil Service (ICS) was opened to competitive examination, leading to a rapid rise in the recruitment of Irish candidates, from 5% of appointees between 1809 and 1850 to 24% of those recruited between 1855 and 1863, with a peak of 33% in 1857. The Irish did so well at the language requirements that the weighting of Sanskrit and Arabic was lowered to restrict their numbers. This was above all a career for middle-class Protestants (13% of Irish recruits were from gentry or aristocratic backgrounds, but 80% were from professional, mercantile, business and strong farming backgrounds (Cook 1987: 510–5). This had a major impact on Irish academic Orientalism.

Such figures had a major impact on European understandings of the Buddhist world. Tennent's *History of Ceylon*, lavishly illustrated and over 1,000 pages long, went through five editions in 1859–60 alone and remained the standard history into the twentieth century (Jones 2006). It discussed among other things Sinhala Buddhist chronicles and literature, Buddhist monuments and 'The influences of Buddhism on civilization'. Similarly, Sirr's Sinophile *China and the Chinese: their religion, character, customs and manufactures* (1834, 2 vols) was followed by his *Ceylon and the Cingalese: their history, government and religion, the antiquities, produce, revenue, and capabilities of the island* (1850, 2 vols), another commercial success (McEvansoneya 2009) quoted by Captain Nemo in *20,000 leagues under the sea*.

Knowledge moved both ways. Gregory's family had made its fortune in eighteenth-century India (Robert Gregory became a director of the East India Company), and the family home at Coole contained Indian art, books on India and Ceylon and a 'Ceylon room'.[7] William's Irish predecessor Robinson had set up an Architectural Commission to photograph Buddhist inscriptions, and consulted Robert Childers (below) when commissioning a catalogue of Buddhist manuscripts.

Having been involved in creating what is now Ireland's National Museum, Gregory built on Robinson's work and brought what

6. In the twentieth century, Irishmen were central to British intelligence on India (O'Malley 2008: 5).

7. This discussion is based on McEvansoneya 2009.

Fig. 3.1 Sir William Gregory as art critic. Caricature by James Tissot for *Vanity Fair*, 1871.

Buddhist scholar Monier-Williams described as 'wisdom, judgement and scientific ability' to existing plans for Ceylon's national museum. Drawing on the Irish experience, Gregory was keen not to alienate religious authorities. He also drew on the Royal Irish Academy's model in linking the collection of artefacts to the study of texts and including a library as an integral element of the museum.

Beyond this, Gregory also imitated George Petrie's work in Ireland, bringing researchers to work on Ceylonese inscriptions and epigraphy. After retirement, he remained closely involved and made several return visits, being described by Buddhist scholar Sinatu Raja as 'our unofficial representative in Britain'.

In Burma, similarly, Irish names recur among the colonial elite. Sir Daniel Twomey of Carrigtwohill retired as chief justice of Rangoon after the trial of U Dhammaloka (chapter five) and having made a major contribution to integrating Buddhist canon law with Anglo-Indian civil law[8] (Bocking 2011). As with the military, this continued after independence, when few Irish members of the Indian Civil Service resigned (Silvestri 2009: 8). A good example is Maurice Collis from Killiney, at one point senior magistrate in Mandalay.

Civil Servants and Asian Buddhism: the Example of Maurice Collis

Born to a family of Anglican gentry,[9] Collis entered the ICS in 1912 as an administrator in Burma. The experience moved him from a naïve acceptance of colonialism towards recognising its exploitative nature, native resentment and British racism. By 1920 he was accused of being 'pro-Burman' as he deepened his interest in Burmese culture and contacts with Burmese people (Derné and Jadwin 2006: 194).

With the War of Independence and Black-and-Tan atrocities, Collis became sympathetic to Irish nationalism and drew parallels to Burma, a perspective which grew with the 1930–2 Saya San rebellion:

> As a younger man I had felt deeply the estrangement which had arisen between the Irish and the English, an estrangement which would never have been, I thought, if the English had recognised in time that the Irish demand to manage their own affairs was natural and right. A similar estrangement was growing between the English and the Burmese. (Collis 1953: 196)

8. He was also grandfather of anthropologist Mary Douglas.

9. His uncle was TCD graduate George Grierson, Superintendent of the Linguistic Survey of India and author of scholarly articles on Indian *bhakti* religion.

In 1929, criticising an employer who had bullied a servant to suicide, he caused a furore:

> no Englishman had ever before been rebuked from the bench in Burma (Collis 1953: 177)

The next year he went one further and jailed a lieutenant who had caused a traffic accident injuring two Burmese women, with the upshot that military authorities and the business community demanded his removal, leading to a series of increasingly marginal posts; he eventually resigned and turned to writing as a career. As George Orwell commented on the event,

> The truth is that every British magistrate in India is in a false position when he has to try a case in which European and native interests clash … he is part of a huge machine which exists to protect British interests, and he has often got to choose between sacrificing his integrity and damaging his career.[10]

In 1931, home on leave, he had hosted a delegation of Burmese nationalists who were negotiating over home rule with Britain, and introduced them to 1921 Treaty signatory Robert Barton and republican Maud Gonne MacBride, both of whom offered advice (Gonne's was to get everything in writing) and AE (George Russell) (chapter four). As Derné and Jadwin comment, 'experiences on the domination side of colonialism might transform those who adminstered the colonial project' (2006: 190).

Empire's loss was literature's gain, as Collis' thirty books drew extensively on his Burmese experiences and other encounters between Europeans and the wider world, positive and negative: works on Marco Polo and early modern Europeans in Burma (Friar Manrique), Siam ('Siamese White') and China and works on the Opium War or the Spanish conquest of Mexico. Collis saw these as meetings of equal cultures: he noted in 1920 that Burmese philosopher Shwe San Aung

> was attempting a synthesis of Buddhist and Western metaphysics, a matter of particular interest to me because my study of Oriental thought, amateur though it was, had already led me, as it had led A.E., to think that such a synthesis was possible. (1953: 37)

---

10. *The Listener* 9.3. 1938; attributed to Orwell at http://georgeorwellnovels. com/reviews/review-of-trials-in-burma-by-maurice-collis/

Yet like the Anglo-Irish folklorists of the day, Collis' interest was as much in folk magic as it was in Buddhism; one of the positives he noted in Buddhism was its inclusion of past religions (1953: 139–40). Like Hearn's revaluation of 'old Japan' in the midst of the Meiji, or Augusta Gregory's revaluation of ghost and fairy tales in the midst of the rationalising processes of Victorian Catholicism, the colonial outsider's position allied them with the past, the traditional and the peasant. Collis' writing connects ancient manuscripts, known history, archaeological discoveries and contemporary peasant belief. Discussions of peasant folklore as pagan survival were transferred directly from west to east:

> What rituals were enacted in these dark passages? The monks, to whose keeping had been entrusted the two shrines, must have had their reasons for placing in them representations of the older gods. The only reason I can think of is that they believed these deities would grant them benefits which could not be demanded of the Buddha, just as you might ask Venus for what it would be improper to mention to the Virgin. (1953: 137–8)

At times this identification went further: at the magic hill of Taung-ni, he experienced the traditional mysterious smell which was understood to represent the presence of the hill spirit, an experience confirmed by the village headmen (1953: 106–7). As in Ireland, this one-way identification was hard to sustain when the peasantry revolted. Collis was perhaps more self-aware than Yeats in this situation; writing of Saya San's rebellion (1930–2), he observed:

> All the Burmese one had met in Rangoon, the members of parliament, the bar and the professional class, pinned their faith on the grant of a new constitution and were as much surprised as was the government. It was a magical rebellion ...
>
> All those sweet fairies among whose haunts I had been wandering nearly twenty years were now summoned with music and dancing, aroused with offerings of fruit and flowers, adjured with incantatory verse ... since in the past they had always stood by the old kings and the sacred land, so now they would rally, extend their protection, give counsel and lead the van. (1953: 192–3).

If for Mahony in the 1790s a strong positive response to Buddhism could be part of an officer's perspective, by the time Collis had become a supporter of Burmese and Irish nationalism the tension could no longer be sustained. A quarter of a century previously, the Irish agitator Dhammaloka had turned the wearing of shoes on pagodas by Europeans into a political issue of respect for native religion (Turner 2009). When Collis visited the Arakan pagoda as senior magistrate in Mandalay, this rule was quietly relaxed and the pagoda trustees dealt with an objector. But the emotional distance between Buddhist sympathiser and colonial official could no longer be bridged:

> The half light, the strong scent of the incense, monks passing, the sound of gongs, distilled a sense of devotion more intense than I had ever noticed at a Buddhist shrine before, where in general all is gently devout. My conductors were fallen on their knees; I alone remained standing, a conspicuous figure with my shoes on. It suddenly struck me that I was committing a rudeness, and I wished I had not come ... I grew more uncomfortable and felt like an outsider, or worse, like an oppressor who was taking advantage of his office. (1953: 57)

Race and power ran through religion, dividing the barefoot Irish monk from the shoe-wearing colonial judge and foreshadowing the end of British rule in Burma.

Bringing It All Back Home

A statue in the National Museum, a nineteenth-century Burmese Buddha in *parinirvana*, appears repeatedly in *Ulysses* (Ito 2003), including Molly Bloom's monologue:

> look at the way he's sleeping at the food of the bed ... like that Indian god he took me to show one wet Sunday in the museum in Kildare street all yellow in a pinafore lying on his side on his hand with his ten toes sticking out that he said was a bigger religion than the jews and Our Lords both put together all over Asia imitating him as hes always imitating everybody I suppose he used to sleep at the foot of the bed too with his big square feet up in his wife's mouth. (Joyce 1960: 693)

Molly's 'Indian god', presented by Col. Sir Charles Fitzgerald shortly after the conquest of Burma as 'a trophy of Britain's newest colony exhibited to the people of her oldest' (Ito 2003: 58), was probably looted.

In 1853, before the highpoint of Asian conquests, the Irish Industrial Exhibition included many items from Buddhist countries, including Lt John Elliott's 'Burmese umbrella, taken by exhibiter from the state barge of Bandiola, the commander-in-chief of the Burmese army'; J Gallagher (HMS *Arrogant*) lent 'A collection of Chinese and Japanese curiosities'; Arthur Huband an 'Indian idol, first brought to Calcutta by a vessel from Rangoon; marble head taken from the Great Pagoda'; Viscount Gough's[11] collection included 'four imperial standards of China taken at Chin-Keang-Foo; ... model of Chinese joss-house, with an idol in it ... Chinese gong of a curious shape, used in the temples'; and the Royal Asiatic Society's collection included a 'Japanese joss-house, used by the people for the reception of Buddhist idols in their domestic worship; ... piece of ancient sculpture, representing Buddha and his disciples' (Sproule 1854: 475).

Similarly, a 1991 Chester Beatty exhibition brought together Buddhist holdings from its own collection and the National Museum. These include Burmese items such as a *Vinayapitaka* collection removed from the Royal Palace at Mandalay, Chinese items such as a jade *Prajnaparamita* text taken from the Peking Summer Palace in 1900 during the Boxer Rebellion, a wide range of Japanese items such as a wooden pagoda from Nara and stone carvings from present-day India, Pakistan and Afghanistan (anon. 1991: 8, 16, 34, 40).

Between them such provenances represent the main sources of Buddhist items in Ireland until recent times: looting (Burma, China); purchase (Japan); and archaeological/antiquarian appropriation (India etc.) The exhibition also included Thai texts and various Tibetan items (some of the latter no doubt taken during the Younghusband invasion).[12]

Some Irish figures were major collectors: thus Lt-Col. Charles 'Hindoo' Stuart (1757–1828) collected a vast amount of Hindu and Buddhist art, which became a key part of the British Museum's collection; George Annesley, Lord Valentia (1771–1884) who brought artists like Henry Salt to illustrate the archaeological sites he visited; or Lord Dufferin (1864–1902), whose collection from his time as Viceroy of India (1884–88) included loot from the final conquest of Burma such as 'an enormous Burmese bronze temple bell, stone temple-lions, a model of a Burmese temple', while his wife was presented with a gold Buddha statue by 'the troops of the Burma field force' (Lynch 1988: 177–8, 181–3).

11. The catalogue wrote that this 'illustrious Irishman ... so well maintained the honour of his country when commanding her armies in our Indian Empire' (Sproule 1854: 473).

12. One other category was described by Matteo Ricci as 'battle prizes': pieces of Buddhist art given him by Chinese converts to Christianity (Sutin 2006: 95).

Curators of the Buddha

These various activities fed into a series of Irish museums. Returned officers and civil servants donated Buddhist material which they had looted, bought or dug up to the Dublin Museum of Science and Art, now the National Museum of Ireland (Audrey Whitty, pers. comm.) The museum was a major subject of contestation in the years 1876–1907 (Crooke 2004), and motives for donations doubtless varied between its original goal of showcasing global crafts for the betterment of Irish industry, a museum of national cultures, and disposal of the collections of deceased relatives. Between 1877 and 1922 the museum received over seven *thousand* items of Asian art (Whitty 2009); many remain unidentified.

Other sources included the East India Company's museum holdings; broken up in 1879 and divided among a range of museums, Dublin was in second place after the V&A. Other donations came from various sources: Japanese and Chinese material from the collection of Gerald, 5th Duke of Leinster; Japanese collections from Mrs Thom, wife of Alexander (Audrey Whitty, pers. comm.); and purchasing at exhibitions in Calcutta, Manchester, Dublin and Cork (Foley and Rider 1998). In such cases the original acquisition is usually beyond reconstruction.

Two collectors deserve special mention. Albert Bender, son of Dublin's chief rabbi, had emigrated to San Francisco and later donated a dramatic collection of Tibetan thangka paintings and other Buddhist and non-Buddhist artefacts (Whitty 2011).[13] From a multilingual and cosmopolitan family (O'Connor 2009), Bender was well-read and could cite George Roerich (Whitty 2009). By a twist of fate, the museum's then director Adolf Mahr was *Ortsgruppenleiter* of the Nazi Party in Dublin – a fact that only became clear to Bender late in the negotiations (Audrey Whitty, pers. comm.)

In 1934, prime minister Éamon de Valera opened the Augusta Bender Memorial Room of Far Eastern Art, which remained on display until it was closed in 1973 to make way for the Wood Quay finds from Viking Dublin. By this latter point the rest of the Museum's Chinese and Japanese art had already been moved to storage and Asian art was no longer being collected (Wallace 2009).

Secondly, Chester Beatty, who visited Japan in 1917–8, made his Dublin library available to scholars in 1954 and to the public in 1968.

13. These were mostly purchased via the ex-military Henry Hart, in China's warlord period.

With a particular interest in religious items, it contains a range of Buddhist texts and artefacts. A third museum existed at the Dalgan Park, Meath headquarters of the Columban missionaries, with five public rooms up to the 1990s holding material from Burma, China, the Philippines, Korea and Japan respectively (Boland 2005).

On a smaller scale, there were private collections in Dublin and elsewhere. Coole Park's 'Ceylon room' has already been noted; James Tennent's collection of art and artefacts, including Ulster artist Andrew Nicholl's sketches of Buddhist sites in Ceylon, was auctioned as recently as 2004 (Jones 2006).

Thus Irish people were able to build up a first-hand picture of Buddhism as geographically and culturally diverse and through texts, images painted and plastic and ritual objects – and to do so as easily in the late nineteenth century as in the early twenty-first. For educated Buddhists such artefacts could be significant. As one interviewee recalls of the 1970s,

> I used to go into the Museum a lot, and although they don't have very good [Buddhist] collections, I think they had more Buddhist items on display then. For example, there's a collection of masks that belong to Trinity College, that were collected, it must have been the time of the Raj. And these would have been from Sikkim and from Tibet. And there were some nice Buddha images on display. (interview C)

Artistic Interests[14]

Museums fed into a much broader artistic interest in Buddhist Asia, particularly China and Japan, in eighteenth and nineteenth century Ireland. Japanese prints were shown in the 1853 Dublin exhibition; for the 1865 exhibition Sir Rutherford Alcock, Britain's first representative to Japan, lent his library (including works on Japanese religion). Irish diplomat John Quin researched lacquer production in mid-nineteenth century Japan, while in 1868 Edward Godwin was commissioned to design a Japanese wall for Dromore Castle. In the 1880s, Irish impressionist Roderick O'Connor travelled to France to collect Japanese woodblocks. The success of the *Mikado* on its 1886 arrival in Ireland thus fitted into a broader interest in matters Japanese; the bulk of exhibits in the 1985 NMI exhibition 'Decorative arts of Japan' were acquired between 1879 and 1897. This general level of interest no doubt contributed to the receptivity towards Far Eastern ideas and culture which Hearn and Yeats identified as Buddhist.

14. This discussion draws largely on Starr (2009).

Provincial Perplexities

Museums, however, did not always know what they had (much of the National Museum's collection has only recently been classified: Audrey Whitty pers. comm.), or want it (Mahr had been reluctant to accept Bender's Oriental collection). In 1907 the Cork Technical Instruction Committee found itself debating the future of a 12-foot long wooden statue of the Buddha, which 'has been lying in the Art Gallery since its arrival at the School of Art. The Committee decided on a previous occasion that the effigy was not worthy of being erected in the institution',[15] but found itself the object of tongue-in-cheek media comment:[16]

> Mr Sisk, who presided at yesterday's meeting of Cork Technical Instruction Committee, asked Alderman Kelleher to propose a resolution to move "Buddha" out of the Art Gallery and put the figure out in the yard.
>
> Alderman Horgan – Don't be hard on her. Leave her where she is for the present.
>
> The Chairman said that there was an enterprising poor man in the city who was prepared to give a price for her. He was after opening a factory for the manufacturing of "kindling," and was prepared to pay a reasonable sum. He thought he ought be encouraged.
>
> Alderman Kelleher – Who brought Buddha here?
>
> The Chairman – She was sent by the Department.
>
> Alderman Horgan – Send her back again to them.
>
> The Chairman – They won't take her.
>
> Mr. Mulligan (Head Art Master) suggested that the statue might be sent up to Fitzgerald Park, and Mr. O'Keefe (Head Science Master) thought it might be put on the top of Blackrock Castle.
>
> No action was, however, taken in the matter.

The Committee was embarrassed by the publicity given to these deliberations:

> A letter was read from a Dublin gentleman stating that he had seen by the papers that the Committee wanted to get rid of a statue of Buddha. "I would consider it an honour," he wrote, "to have it in my house, and would willingly pay package and carriage up here."
>
> The Chairman – Don't read any further. Put it by. We have heard enough of that, and we don't want to hear any more of it.

---

15. *Irish Independent*, June 18, 1907: 2.

16. The 'Oirish' variants in these reports – 'she', 'after opening' etc. – are presumably sneers.

Canon Nicholson – We never passed a resolution to get rid of the statue.

Chairman – In my opinion, we have heard too much about it already.

Mr. M'Carthy – And it is going into English papers, too.

The matter was not further discussed.[17]

Fig. 3.2 The Buddha statue that the Cork Art Gallery didn't want (now in University College Cork library). Thanks to Brian Bocking and Michael Holland. Reproduced with permission from UCC library.

17. *Irish Independent*, July 2 1907: 3.

Thus the presence of an artefact implied no particular knowledge or appreciation about its nature; but the Committee were naturally sensitive to being portrayed as provincial philistines. Happily, in 2010 Brian Bocking and Michael Holland rediscovered this (5-metre) Sri Lankan statue[18] in the University College Cork archive, which also contains other, smaller Buddhist items.

Irish Universities and Orientalism

Overlapping the circuits of soldiers, museums and artefacts were those of civil servants, universities and texts. Buddhism was an important intellectual 'way in' to Asia, both as the 'Asian philosophy' then in highest regard and as a route into a wide variety of languages.

The opening of the Indian Civil Service to examination in 1855 led to the foundation of Irish Orientalism (Mansoor 1944) as a scholarly discipline. The centre of this was Trinity College Dublin (TCD), which developed privileged relationships with the ICS training process;[19] however Queen's College Belfast, which taught Sanskrit and Arabic, nearly matched TCD's Indian-language programme, while University College Cork taught Indian geography and history (Lennon 2004: 175) as did Galway (Cook 1987: 511).

In 1882, Queen's awarded honorary degrees to 26 graduates, of whom 14 were in the imperial service – an indication of the centrality of the imperial service class to universities of the day (Guinness 2004: 23). Further down the chain, Dublin's High School, alma mater of Yeats, Charles Johnston and the other two founders of the Dublin Hermetic Society, prided itself on the number of ICS members among its ex-pupils (Guinness 2004: 23).

Typically, those who taught Oriental studies had themselves spent time in Asia, usually developing a scholarly interest while technically employed as civil servants or diplomats (occasionally as soldiers or missionaries). An exemplary figure in this respect is Thomas Watters (1840–1901).[20] The son of a Presbyterian minister from Co. Down (Bushell 1905: viii; Anon. n.d. [b]), Watters completed an MA at Queen's and entered the Consular Service in 1863. Starting as a translator in Peking, he remained for 32 years 'in all parts of the Chinese empire', retiring as consul in Foochow.

18. Thanks to Kate Crosby for this identification.
19. It had already changed its medical training to enable recruitment for the Indian Medical Service (Scott 1987: 510).
20. I am indebted to Hilary Richardson for information on Watters' life.

Fig. 3.3 The British Consulate in Taiwan where Thomas Watters was acting Consul in 1866. Thanks to David Oakley.

Watters' obituary noted that 'His early philosophical training fitted him for the study of Oriental religions and metaphysics, which always remained his chief attraction' (Bushell 1905: ix). TW Rhys Davids, co-founder of the Pali Text Society, wrote that 'Mr. Watters probably knew more about Chinese Buddhist Literature than any other European scholar' (1905: v).

In *Kim*, the hero helps his lama search for the River of the Arrow, mentioned in accounts of the Buddha's early life. The search for such sites, inspired by Schliemann's discovery of Troy, was a highpoint of archaeological rivalry and public interest in the 1890s (Allen 2009). Scholars searched northern India and Nepal using the Pali texts and the accounts of later Chinese pilgrims as evidence for where to find sites long buried or hidden in the jungle.

Watters' *magnum opus* (1904–5) was a two-volume commentary on the most important of these pilgrim accounts, Xuanzang's journey to India, discussing the latest research on this real-life Buddhological quest; it was the scholarly equivalent of a treasure-map. His other book-length works covered Laoze, Confucian temple tablets and the Chinese language, along with journal articles on topics such as the 18 lohans (arhats) and Kapilavastu (the Buddha's home town). He was also expert in Pali and Sanskrit and collected Korean artefacts.

In Watters' account of the pilgrim's return we can hear something of the spirit which animated such Orientalists:

> He had been where no other had ever been, he had seen and heard what no other had ever seen and heard. Alone he had crossed trackless wastes tenanted only by fierce ghost-demons. Bravely he had climbed fabled mountains high beyond conjecture, rugged and barren, ever chilled by icy wind and cole with eternal snow. He had been to the edge of the world and had seen where all things end. Now he was safely back to his native land, and with so great a quantity of precious treasures. (1904–5: 11–12).

Watters goes on to enumerate treasures such as palm-leaf books, Buddha statues and 'curious pictures' – precisely what scholars such as himself brought home to Ireland. His comments on 'Yuan-chuang' show the humanist tolerance with which this minister's son could view someone else's religious affiliation:

> As a Buddhist monk Yuan-chuang was very rigorous in keeping the rules of his order and strict in all the observances of his religion. But his creed was broad, his piety never became ascetic, and he was by nature tolerant …
>
> [T]he Buddhism to which Yuan-chuang adhered, the system which he studied, revered, and propagated, differed very much from the religion taught by Gautama Buddha. They knew little or nothing of Yoga and powerful magical formulae used with solemn invocations. It was not on Prajnaparamita and the abstract subtleties of a vague and fruitless philosophy, nor on dream-lands of delight beyond the tomb, nor on P'usas like Kuan-shi-yin who supplant the Buddhas, that the great founder of the religion preached and discoursed to his disciples. But Yuan-chuang apparently saw no inconsistency in believing in these while holding to the simple original system. (1904–5: 14–15).

So much, one might say, for the embittered sectarian polemics of turn-of-the-century Ireland: there should be scope for disagreement, even criticism, but open-mindedness is a virtue in itself, a perspective that recurs with Theosophists and Buddhists of the day.

Another Queen's graduate was William Hoey, who also 'devoted much care to the task of identifying the various places mentioned in early Buddhist works relating to the life and labors of Buddha' (Mansoor 1944: 30; see Allen 2009: 117–8 for his search for Kapilavastu). Hoey, proficient in Sanskrit, Persian and Hindi-Urdu, excavated what he believed to be the ruins of Sravasti and the Jetavana Grove, identified a vase as containing the Buddha's ashes and translated Oldenberg's seminal (1882) *Buddha: his life, his doctrine, and his order* for his doctorate (Allen 2009: 79, 145–6). In the introduction to the latter he wrote

> To thoughtful men who evince an interest in the study of religious beliefs, Buddhism, as the highest effort of pure intellect to solve the problem of being, is attractive. It is not less so to the metaphysician and sociologist who study the philosophy of the modern German pessimistic school and observe its social tendencies. To them Dr. Oldenberg's work will be as valuable as it is to the Orientalist. (Hoey 1997: iii–iv)

On retirement in 1903 Dr Hoey became Reader in Hindustani and Indian History at TCD (Allen 2009: 223). Here too, Buddhist countries were a key focus of research interest. Robert Atkinson, Prof. of Romance languages from 1869 and of Sanskrit and Comparative Philology from 1871, was also expert in Chinese, Tibetan, Tamil and Telegu (McDowell and Webb 2004: 272), while a later Professor of Oriental Languages, TW Haig (1865–1938) specialised in Indian history.

The circuit of work in Asia followed by university teaching was followed by John Van-Someren Pope (1850–1936), son of the Methodist missionary G.U. Pope who compiled a Burmese dictionary. The younger Pope learned Pali and Burmese as Director of the Dept. of Public Instruction in Burma: deeply sympathetic to the Burmese, he was put in an impossible position by the pressures of colonialism, unable to satisfy nationalists and eventually forced out of office (Alicia Turner, pers. comm). Subsequently he became Professor of Modern East Indian Languages at Trinity and an eminent Pali and Tamil scholar and translator (Mansoor 1944: 28).

Vincent Arthur Smith (1848–1920), historian of India and Sinhalese art, joined the ICS after Trinity, dedicating his spare time to ancient history and amateur archaeology, writing scholarly articles and a 1901 *Asoka: the Buddhist emperor of India*. In India, he collaborated with Hoey on a number of Buddhist archaeological projects while pursuing alternative locations for Sravasti. Subsequently he too became a Reader in Indian History and Hindustani at Trinity (Allen 2009: 23–5, 81–3, 114–7, 147–8, 223–4).

We should also mention, in this mobile academic world, Robert Childers, who moved from a career in the Ceylon Civil Service to become the first Professor of Pali and Buddhist literature at

University College London. Having married Anna Barton of Wicklow, he was father of executed Irish nationalist and bestselling author Robert Erskine Childers and grandfather of Irish President Erskine Hamilton Childers. His *Dictionary of Pali* was a 'pioneering work of Buddhist doctrine based on his own scholarship and dialogue with members of the monastic Sangha' (Harris 2007: 15), and he was a strong Buddhist sympathiser.

If the Irish Orientalists were particularly strong on languages, law was another important area, drawing on Irish experience of the problems of merging colonial law with local customs and religion. Daniel Twomey has already been mentioned; another good example is Whitley Stokes, who studied law at Trinity and then Irish languages and literature while a lawyer in London. In 1862 he joined the Indian legal service, where he became president of the Indian Law Commission in 1867. His *magnum opus* was *The Anglo-Indian codes* (1887–91), but he also published over 300 articles and 30 books on subjects including Irish, Breton and Cornish literature and linguistics.[21]

The process of Irish independence, and subsequently post-war decolonisation in Asia, ended this relationship, but slowly. E.G. Hart, appointed Chair of Arabic, Persian and Hindustani in 1926, was not a scholar but 'a typical Indian Army eccentric, who dabbled in mysticism and Yoga' (McDowell and Webb 2004: 449). Still in the inter-war years, a Desmond Parsons (Parsons 2009: 66–7) could move to Beijing to learn Chinese and teach languages. Living in a traditional *hutong*, Parsons translated Chinese folktales before realising his dream of photographing the cave paintings in Dunhuang, dying on his return (1935).

Back at Trinity, Van-Someren Pope's job was cut in 1923, probably for economic reasons (McDowell and Webb 2004: 449), and in the 1950s and 1960s the South and East Asian elements of the Trinity degree disappeared until all that was left was the study of Semitic languages. As late as 1946, however, a student graduated in Sanskrit and Pali (McDowell and Webb 2004).

This scholarly Orientalism represents a substantial degree of sympathy, but in the religiously-delineated atmosphere of Irish universities it would have been out of the question for anyone to publicly identify themselves as Buddhist in the way that Tweed's

21. *Irish in India* exhibition, TCD, 2010.

'rationalist Buddhists' did elsewhere.[22] Perhaps some of the anonymous Buddhists in census returns noted in chapter five were academics.

Texts and Dissemination

These scholarly developments meant that libraries such as Trinity's had substantial Oriental holdings, although not without problems. In 1803

> the Ship on board which was the remainder of the Oriental Works for the Trinity College Dublin had been captured, and carried into the [French] *Mauritius*. A new set shall be prepared by next season.
> (cited in Benson 2010: 23)

Trinity acquired the first 312 volumes of *Bibliotheca Indica*, published by the East India Company and Asiatic Society of Bengal from 1848, and an Oriental Languages Society developed. By 1900, the library already held five Pali manuscripts from Burma, including the *Visuddhimagga*. Its holdings were sufficiently significant for a Burmese envoy in 1872 to visit it – and declare that a supposedly Pali manuscripts was actually in Shan (Harding 2011: 23).

Later, the Chester Beatty library would collect sufficient Burmese manuscripts to have a catalogue (Frasch 2004: 2) and a range of Sanskrit Buddhist texts (Sinéad Ward, pers. comm.) It is not impossible that a dedicated student could have taught themselves to meditate from the *Visuddhimagga* or, more plausibly, texts in the *Sacred Books of the East* series; Foster's biography of Yeats notes the popularity of the latter series, including *the Buddhist Sutras* (1881; cited in Lennon 2004: 424 fn12).

With the *Dublin University Magazine's* article 'Buddhism and its founder'[23] we move into the broader sphere of associated public opinion. The leading forum for the nineteenth century Protestant intelligentsia, the *Magazine* published nearly every major writer of the day. It combined a romantic vision focused on 'the internal, the authentic, and the essential' in Ireland with a cosmopolitan vision that 'looked outward, renouncing separatism as hopelessly provincial' (Hall 2000: 2–3, 13). At its peak it printed 4,000 copies

22. This remained true until the 1990s to the best of my knowledge, although there were Buddhist academics in the 1970s. My own 'coming out' was a cautious one, in institutions which retained a number of overtly Catholic elements.
23. Aug 1873 (vol 82): 206–18.

monthly and had a wide readership, including in the countryside (Hayley 1987: 36).

In 1869 its editorship had passed from Sheridan Le Fanu to the London printer Charles Adams,[24] who sold it on in June 1873 to its former editor, Durham Dunlop. Dunlop was critical of missionary activity, and of Ultramontanism, which the *Magazine* identified with intellectual narrowness (Hall 2000: 217, 221, 226). The 'Buddhism' article shows a rationalist and broadly sympathetic understanding:

> Sometimes gorgeous, and touched with the spirit of oriental poetry, but often simply puerile and ridiculous, the supernatural machinery which has been invented for the grand epic of the life of the Buddha is purely exoteric ... [but] we have the spectacle of a sincere lover of truth giving up all that men hold dear – power, riches, pleasure, love – that he might attain true wisdom and communicate it to his fellow-men. (cited in Almond 1988: 65–6)

The academic and middle-brow publics for such material co-existed with a broader popular interest and with the excitement generated in spiritualist and Theosophical circles. Even the daily press could be interested at a fairly serious level: the *Nation* reviewed Spence Hardy's *Eastern monachism* over two issues in 1852, for example. In 1924 the *Freeman's Journal* could devote a lengthy article[25] to a joint SOAS/Sociological Society conference on 'the Oriental religions of the Empire and various modern movements arising out of them', followed by discussion of 'what has been called "The Sociology of Religion".' The *Irish Literary Gazette* gave over its front page to summarising Max Müller's review of Stanislas Julien's *Buddhism and Buddhist pilgrims* in 1857,[26] concluding with recommendations for further reading. Today's Irish media do not ask as much of their audience.

Protestant Missionaries

Along with the soldier, the civil servant, the judge and the professor came the Protestant missionary. Research is in its infancy (however see Comerford and O'Leary 2009), but their numbers were substantial, perhaps as great as those of Catholics (Hogan

24. According to the Wellesley index, Adams wrote or more likely plagiarised the article on Buddhism.
25. Aug 20: 8.
26. Sept 26 (vol I no IX): 129–30.

1990: 7). The 'Irish Auxiliary', founded 1714, worked in India and Japan among other places, and was joined in 1814 by the Church Mission Society and Irish involvement in British-based organisations. Three Trinity graduates arrived as missionaries in China in the 1840s (Comerford and O'Leary 2009: 74). The Dublin University Far Eastern Mission, founded in 1885 'to work with the church in China in mission, education and pastoral care', is still in existence, as is the Church Mission Society. Comerford and O'Leary argue that Irish experience led Church of Ireland missionaries to push for the indigenisation of the Anglican church in China (2009: 80–6).

At an early point, the Irish Methodist Adam Clarke (c. 1760–1832) became responsible for two Sinhala monks who sailed to England as would-be converts in 1818. The academic and preacher, Clarke, three times President of the Methodist conference, was known for his support for overseas missions. Nevertheless he wrote

> These men cannot be treated as *common heathens:* they are both *Philosophers* – men of profound erudition in their way ... deeply read in the most speculative, most refined and purest ethics of the brahman and Budhoo systems.

In 1820, he published a set of Christian principles he had prepared for them, arguing that the Holy Spirit was in everyone's heart and that

> Those who have acted conscientiously, according to the dictates of this heavenly light in their minds, shall not perish eternally; but have that measure of glory and happiness suited to their state. (cited in Harris 2006: 34)

– an inclusive view which some Buddhists might well have agreed with. By contrast, Dr Barcroft Boake, an Anglican graduate of Trinity and principal of the Colombo Academy in the mid-nineteenth century, saw Buddhism as

> not so much a religion, as a system of Philosophy recommending as the greatest excellency attainable by man an apathetic indifference to all external things. It can therefore have no hold on the affections of the people. (cited in Harris 2006: 56)

Similar contrasts continued in later generations. In 1889–90 Thomas Berry (1854–1931), later Bishop of Killaloe, gave the Donnellan lectures in Trinity on *Christianity and Buddhism: a comparison and a contrast* (Berry 1891), a well-informed but hostile

Fig 3.4 Maynooth Library copy of the 1903 edition of T.W. Rhys David's *Buddhism*; the library also holds 1877 and 1925 editions.

polemic. Yet the Presbyterian missionary, Frederick O'Neill (1870–1946), subsequently Moderator of the General Assembly, was strongly sympathetic to local religion in Manchuria (Harris 2006: 235). The Irish Mission to Manchuria lasted from 1869 to 1919, involving 90 missionaries (Rosemary Presbyterian Church 2009).

Knowledge about Buddhism, and competing accounts, circulated through these various networks in surprising ways. If T.W. Rhys Davids was the first European scholar to openly align himself with Buddhism (Sutin 2006: 140), nevertheless his *Buddhism* was published by the Society for Promoting Christian Knowledge in 1877. In turn the Catholic library at Maynooth acquired a copy, implying that the book was distributed in Ireland.

A Child's Experience Reworked: Helen Waddell[27]

In the 1930s, Helen Waddell (1889–1965) was known as 'Ulster's darling', popular for the novel *Peter Abelard* and her work on medieval goliards (Burleigh 2005: ix). Her literary career began, however, with a focus on Japan. It offers a rare insight into the emotional realities of Irish Protestants in Asia, by virtue both of her literary skill and its sources in childhood memory.

Her father, Hugh Waddell (1840–1901), was born in Co. Down, trained in Belfast and was sent to China in 1869 as a Presbyterian missionary. Invalided to Ireland in 1871, he was returned to Spain; but wanting to 'preach the Gospel to the heathen' turned to the United Presbyterian Church of Scotland, which sent him to Japan in 1874 (Burleigh 2005: 1–2).[28]

With a break of three years caused by her mother's death, Helen lived in Japan until the family's final return to Ireland in 1900. If one's father was an open-minded missionary like Waddell – who broke with his church for being too severe on a native pastor, spoke good Japanese and had pretensions as a Chinese scholar – it was possible for a young Irish girl in Japan to visit Japanese homes and Buddhist temples unaccompanied. She reports her brother visiting a Japanese house as a child:

27. Much of this section relies on Burleigh 2005 and Waddell's pieces collected there.
28. It is tempting to posit a family relationship with the Scottish Presbyterian medical officer to the Younghusband expedition, Laurence Austine Waddell, an amateur Buddhologist who bought his own Buddhist temple in order to interview the priests about their practices (Sutin 2006: 194–6), but I cannot verify this.

pointing severely to the Buddha on the Butsudan, [he] denounced the
worship of idols with great fluency. And the dears, instead of being
angry, bowed profoundly, and set the Buddha into a cupboard. Now
did you ever know finer manners than that? (Burleigh 2005: 44)

Living in Belfast in her twenties and thirties, Waddell drew on
these experiences in a wide range of pieces touching on Japanese
Buddhism and Shinto as experiences of ritual and emotion; later,
she moved towards writing about an imaginary Japan, relying more
on travel books, Lafcadio Hearn and her mentor, the missionary
George Taylor (Burleigh 2005: 30).

Her major Japanese work *The spoiled Buddha* ran for a week in
1915 at the Belfast Opera House. Burleigh suggests that it disappointed audience expectations of another *Mikado*, although the *Irish
Independent* noted:

> We imagine it to be more suitable for reading than playing since
> much of the quiet humour in this story of Binzuru, the disciple of
> Buddha, who fell from grace, would almost certainly be lost among
> the elaborate scenic beauty demanded by the stage directions.[29]

To a Buddhist reader, *The spoiled Buddha* is great fun, rather like
Dario Fo's renditions of medieval folk theatre using familiar figures
like Jesus and Lazarus. The male statues in a Buddhist temple
come to life to argue about their relationship to women. Waddell's
confidence with the familiar figures of Japanese Buddhism that she
had grown up with – very different from the situation of an adult
convert – enabled her to play fast and loose with orthodoxy, as did
the folk myths she drew on. Here Buddhism appears rather as a
stock of characters, the common heritage of a culture in which for
her as for Hearn 'Japanese' and 'Buddhist' are often inseparable.

Waddell's emotional relationship to 'old Japan' is of course
different, a child's love for the land of their youth, innocent of
Hearn's difficulties as an immigrant, employee and family member
in later life. If both were Buddhist sympathisers of a romantic kind
(Tweed 2000), though, Waddell had no desire for conversion. She
critiques folk Buddhism as a Christian: 'Kwannon of the single
grace' shows a pilgrim hoping for unlikely divine assistance.
Unlike Thomas Hardy's contemporary (1915) 'The Oxen', however,
she exempts her own tradition from this scepticism, and defends
Christianity as more optimistic (Burleigh 2005: 52).

29. Oct 20 1919: 2.

The spoiled Buddha works better as literature, and has something of the ironic humanism of Lord Dunsany's stories (chapter four):

> I know it's daring to make the bronze images move and speak: but it's part of the preposterousness of the conception that these images are indeed the Buddha and Binzuru and Daruma, flesh and blood transmuted into rigidity by the impassive years. I think the thought at the back of the play is that the narrow way of ascesis attracts either the finest natures or the weeds – narrow ill-minded people like Daruma, or great rich natures like the Buddha's ... withal, it is *life*, 'the passionate and humorous life of men' that comes before the Buddha at the last: he all but yields to it, having found the emptyness [sic] of Nirvana: but tradition is too strong. I *think* it is tradition. For the Buddha by this time knows that one finds the infinite here also. (Burleigh 2005: 55).

And indeed the play's final revelation is that the Buddha is silently in love with Kwannon, just as Binzuru is attracted by an image of female beauty.

An Imperial Service Class in Crisis

The circuits of knowledge discussed here responded to real problems: how could small numbers of people *both* remain in power in Ireland *and* help hold down so much of the world? If Buddhism was (wrongly) understood to be the world's largest religion, this was a problem for its conquerors, and an intellectual challenge for an ethnicity defined in religious terms.

In one sense the imperial service class – and its Irish component above all – was permanently in crisis. Yeats' image of Protestant Ascendancy was constructed in response to Catholic assertion; Anglo-Irish participation in the ICS grew only to be curtailed; indeed the age of high imperialism in the Buddhist world barely lasted more than a long if blood-stained lifetime: Burma, for example, was finally conquered in 1885 and became independent in 1948.

The Irish Theosophists discussed in chapter four, and some of the Buddhists discussed in chapter five, can be understood in the context of Irish people's participation in the colonial enterprise as military and naval officers, colonial administrators and professional Orientalists, curators, art collectors, missionaries – and indeed children of empire. Family background, professional training and in some cases early careers located them within this matrix, which they struggled against and in most cases abandoned.

Their forms of knowledge – esotericist, antiquarian, Asian Buddhist, communist, free-thinking – represented alternative modes of knowing to the orthodox knowledge of the Oriental scholar, theologian or judge, and involved them in different kinds of relationship with other people both in Ireland and Asia. They deserve to be assessed in terms of what they tried to say and do and who they allied with, in the teeth of the world's then hegemonic power and its associated religion.

Thus Maurice Collis or Hugh Waddell pushed at the limits of what was possible 'within the system'. Their honourable attempts to treat Asians as equals, and their respect for the cultures they lived within, were remarkable in their time – and stand as an indictment of those who 'did their job', took their pay and accepted the institutions they lived within. The dissent, resistance and defections represented by such individuals, and those who went further, were made possible in part by the crumbling of the local version of that hegemony within Ireland. That crumbling was a forerunner of waves of anti-colonial movements that would eventually bring about the end of the British Empire in Asia and construct, in Asia as in Ireland, new kinds of nation-state grounded in new alliances, with a new series of problems inherited from this struggle.

The Catholic Nationalist Service Class

Maynooth's Spiritual Empire in Asia

By contrast with Protestant missionaries, and imperial networks generally, the Irish Catholic missionary effort in Asia started later, but its impact as a circuit transmitting knowledge of Buddhism became as wide if not always as deep. After Catholic Emancipation in 1829, the church had become one of Ireland's main organising structures, with a massive institutional network of parishes, religious orders, lay sodalities, schools, colleges, hospitals and charities (Nic Ghiolla Phádraig 1995) – as well as industrial schools and Magdalen asylums. This was fuelled by the post-Famine shift from multiple inheritance of farms to single inheritors, which cut off the majority of Irish people from the possibility of ever marrying in Ireland, creating a boom in vocations for a church whose primary task was to police the sexualities this produced.

Once this was in hand, attention turned first to organising the global Irish diaspora, and missionary work beyond this was

relatively slow to develop, although there had been Irish participation in missionary organisations based elsewhere. A number
of Irish Vincentians worked in China, and their role as spiritual
directors in Maynooth from 1886 was key to stimulating interest in
the Far East. Irish de la Salle Brothers went to Hong Kong between
1875 and 1900 (Hogan 1990: 47, 50). There were also Irish religious
involved in the Burmese de la Salle schools, most visibly St Patrick's
Moulmein, founded 1860.[30] Later, an Irish Jesuit observed that
French secularism was leading to the takeover of missionary orders
by the Irish, among others (McCullagh 1929: 117–118).

It was in the early twentieth century that Irish societies for
non-Christian missions really developed:

> Between 1916 and 1937, five new Irish missionary institutes were
> founded – St Columban's Foreign Mission Society (The Maynooth
> Mission to China), canonically erected in 1918; the Missionary Sisters
> of St Columban, 1922; the Missionary Sisters of the Holy Rosary, 1924;
> St Patrick's Foreign Missionary Society (The Kiltegan Fathers), 1932;
> the Medical Missionaries of Mary, 1937. (McGlade 1967: 2)

Over 1,500 Columban missionaries alone went overseas (Boland
2005: 132). Until 1949, the main Buddhist mission ground was China
(where Jesuits and the Legion of Mary also went), with substantial
numbers in Korea and smaller numbers in Japan and Burma
(McGlade 1967: 53–82; Collins 2009: 226–288). Lay missionaries were
largely absent except for the Legion of Mary (Hogan 1990: 128).

The Maynooth Mission to China (initiated in 1916) was the
turning point of Irish missionary activity in the non-Christian world
generally, and Buddhist Asia specifically. The initial impulse came
from its founder Edward Galvin's interest in matters exotic (at one
point he had volunteered to work among Indians in Arizona; [Hogan
1990: 93]), coupled with John Fraser's 1911 address in Maynooth
on his missionary work in China. Opportunity was created by the
withdrawal of many European missionaries from China during the
First World War, and by the lingering impact of national tensions
within Ireland:

> The missionary movement unquestionably provided a form of
> idealism to which Irish nationalists from all traditions could subscribe.
> It also provided those who were weary with the perennial problem of
> political violence with a vehicle of national regeneration which they
> could recommend without reservation (Hogan 1990: 97).

30. Its emblem has both Patrick's shamrock and an Irish harp.

If Irish Buddhists were seeking a way out of sectarian identification, missionary activity enabled Catholics to overcome internal
tensions (around Home Rule vs independence, empire and world
war, and later the Treaty) by displacing energies abroad. As Collins
(2009: 76–7) notes, while the Vatican thought the Columbans were
Bolsheviks or draft-dodgers and the Foreign Office saw them as
'undeniably anti-English', mission was actually a way to avoid
confronting such issues.

The circumstances of the Irish presence in Asia – caught between
British colonialism, Buddhist Revival, later Japanese imperialism
and the rise of communism – were hardly propitious for its very
institutionally-focused strategy, and the only substantial results in
Buddhist Asia were among the non-Buddhist Kachins in Burma,
thanks to tensions with the Burman majority and British support
for mission schools.

Nothing to Say?

Boland comments:

> It struck me as remarkable that – to my knowledge – not one of
> these literate, educated Irish men and women, who must have had
> quite extraordinary experiences in the Far East in the early part of
> the twentieth century, had published a memoir … It is a missing,
> unrecorded story. (2005: 132–3)

This overstates the case (McGlade 1967, Barrett 1967, Hogan 1990;
subsequently Collins 2009). Yet other than Collins, these accounts
have very little to say about the world to which missionaries went,
what they actually did there, and how they related to 'heathens': the
interest is in the organisation and the missionaries themselves. By
contrast with the imperial service class, the Catholic missionaries
(and their historians) felt they already knew what they needed to
know of the rest of the planet:

> The work of the Church is everywhere and at all times fundamen-
> tally the same, a struggle of the kingdom of God against the empire of
> Satan, of truth against ignorance, error and prejudice, of virtue against
> vice. (McGlade 1967: 15)

Thus if McGlade mentions ten Vincentian sisters, one Irish, killed
in the 1870 'massacre of Tientsin' (1967: 11–12), nothing is said about
the disputed and complex politics of that event: it is martyrdom,

plain and simple. Much, however, is said about how *difficult* it was to be Irish in a decolonising world:

> No Irishman is likely to dispute the right to political independence, but the Irish missionary must be realistic ... There is suspicion, if not growing hostility, to the white man in general, or to the European, in many of these independent areas (1967: 16)

Worse yet was communism, but after a nod to poverty as cause it is another incomprehensible opponent:

> This godless ideology has touched the Irish missionaries most closely in the Far East. The Chinese Communist regime has expelled all of the once-strong force of Irish missionaries ...
>
> The story of imprisonment and torture of Irish missionaries by the Communists in China and Korea, of various types of persecution and even of death, has become well-known to the Irish people ... (1967: 17)

Asian society and culture, even Asian religion (which might have been expected to be of interest as the nominal adversary) appear as backdrop to the real focus, ecclesiastical organisation:

> In all the East, there is a sort of unity that is distinctive, just as there is in the West. It is compounded of a way of looking at life, an outlook on reality that is inscrutable to the westerner ... (1967: 51–2)

The strong impression is that the Irish Catholic missionary effort was 'Orientalist' in the worst sense: with no serious interest in understanding the worlds it encountered, registering exoticism or atrocity, but mostly focused on its own cadres. The one exception is the Jesuits. Faintly echoing the 'rites controversy', Irish Jesuits made the mistake of building their Hong Kong seminary 'in traditional Chinese style with landscaping to match', so that it was 'often mistaken for a Buddhist monastery', and were criticised for this (McRedmond 1991: 252–5).[31]

This hostility to those who breached the lines of race and culture in any way was common to white groups in Buddhist Asia, although it hardly helped the missionary effort. In imperial Orientalism, however, a (suitably distanced) interest in society, culture, economics, history and so on was part of the process of rule. It is hard not to conclude that Catholic missionary activity was actually

31. McCullagh (1929), writing in the Jesuit *Studies*, was at that point studying Oriental languages in Paris, and sings the praises of French Orientalist expertise, including in Buddhist Studies.

about the missionaries themselves and their Irish supporters, and uninterested in an understanding which might help the ostensible purpose of conversion:

> The initial reaction to Chinese tradition reads strangely, not alone by modern missionary standards ... but also when measured against the understanding of Chinese religion and culture arrived at by Matteo Ricci ... Consider the terms in which the Irish reported what they found: "a hideous shrine or temple", "grossest superstition, a mixture of Buddhism, ancestor-worship, devil cult, idolatry, magic", "Canton is a black pagan city", "superstitutious pagans, materialists, even enemies of religion", "the religion of fear and hopelessness which centres round their placating of devils" (McRedmond 1991: 256).

Despite Maria Griffin's best efforts we found it impossible to secure interviews with returned missionaries, those who had taught them or anyone familiar with matters from the inside. All enquiries ran into dead ends which were not paralleled elsewhere in our research, or in the experience of those more familiar with researching Irish Catholicism.

A range of explanations might be offered, starting with the age of survivors and a reasonable sense that their experience might be misunderstood: Collins' (2009) good and often critical insider history seems embarrassed by some of the ethnocentric or racist attitudes reported. Recent revelations of systematic abuse and for-profit adoption of children no doubt also affect how Irish religious perceive research.[32]

Anecdotally, many missionaries 'went native' and/or left the Church, often on marrying, while many who remained and became engaged in their new societies, found the Ireland they returned to uninterested in the struggles of the wider world. Lastly, as discussed below, Vatican attitudes have changed sharply around Eastern religion, which may no longer be a 'safe' subject.

The net effect, however, is that personal experiences remain a closed book, with only brief insights such as Father Galvin's purchase of a Buddhist altar for a chapel:

> One could not guess how the altar had come, divorced from all religious attachment or significance, to a corner of Hanyang, but here it was. (Barrett 1967: 148)

---

32. Some of the sample of priestly abusers examined by the Commission of Investigation into the Catholic Archdiocese of Dublin were returned missionaries (*Irish Times*, Nov 27 2009: 11).

We can, however, discuss the responses to Buddhism evident in missionary training and Catholic literature.

Missionary Training

Some courses on Buddhism or indeed meditation were delivered in various seminaries over the years. At St Columban's College in Dalgan Park, for example, an orientation to Buddhism was taught from 1946–63 for future missionaries to Burma and Korea; it was fairly basic and staff did not have direct experience of Buddhist practice (Paddy Dooher, pers. comm.) These seem, however, to have been fairly marginal to the main curriculum.

Bernard Murphy, who attended the All Hallows seminary in the late 1950s, shared some of his material from that period. The guidebook gives a flavour of this:

> The 1st four years are devoted almost entirely to Sacred Scripture, History, Liturgy, Canon Law, Sacred Eloquence and all the branches of Theology. Throughout the entire period there are classes in Elocution and in Music, Gregorian and Modern ...
>
> Prayer, the Sacraments, Conferences, Retreats, and friendly advice are the chief means used in the formation of character ... [Also encouraged are] Football, Hurling, Handball, Tennis, Cricket, Athletic Competitions and long walks. (Anon n.d. (d): 2–3).

The tone is overwhelmingly that of the self-referentiality of Catholic Ireland, and unsurprisingly the most effective work was done in the Irish diaspora. In the yearbook (Anon 1961) only the obituaries give a sense that the purpose lay abroad. By contrast with the ICS training, which privileged language and culture above all else, Catholic missionaries studied language and culture on arrival (if at all), so that

> The missionary, not knowing how to ask the simplest of questions or how to behave, felt incompetent and isolated, and commonly experienced depression and anger ... Columbans in China spoke with awe of Galvin's ability to read the local newspaper (Collins 2009: 28).

This actually represented a substantial step *backwards* by comparison with the experience of earlier Irish members of foreign orders such as Robert Hanna, who was trained in language and religion on arrival in Macao in the 1790s (Shan 2012). In the new context of Irish missionary training for a lifetime as 'expatriates', individuals who succeeded in making local connections were exceptional indeed. The combination of massive organising effort with the absence of preparation or thought about the world from which converts were supposed to come is remarkable. Like the British Army, the net effect was to transport the internal problems of Catholic Ireland, particularly its surplus of unmarriageable people, abroad.

Irish missionaries were being trained at best to keep the Irish diaspora within ethnic boundaries:

> American and Australian Columbans found themselves in an institution which was predominantly Irish and endured irritants like conversations devoted to Irish politics or Gaelic football (2009: 28).

In this context, the main mechanism for conversion was (as in Ireland) religious instruction in mission schools, for which Christian Brothers – notorious for their violence – were imported from Ireland (2009: 95, 103–4). This ran counter not only to Chinese government policy but also the advice of more experienced missionaries: it took a papal delegate to forbid compulsory attendance of non-Catholic students at religious instruction and worship and the slapping and beating of boys (2009: 105).[33]

At a higher level too, the training of such native laity and seminarians as could be recruited was not geared to cross-cultural dialogue:

> The formation of students for the priesthood, imposing Latin, and the philosophy and theology of the West, resulted in a small number of ordinations, and produced men divorced from the culture of their own country (2009: 177).

The positive side was that the main effect of Irish missionary activity was not the conversion of 'pagans', 'atheists' and so on but the provision of education, medical care, orphanages and crisis responses – not always conditional on religious affiliation. For our purposes, however, the massive Catholic missionary effort generated surprisingly little Irish knowledge of its religious opponents, even by comparison with its medieval predecessors.

33. Reviewing Hogan's book, Fr Denis Faul commented plaintively that 'the *robust direct methods* of the Irish didn't envisage the strong religious traditions of the Indians with Hinduism and Buddhism centuries old' (1992: 313; my emphasis).

Idolatry and Paganism

John Fraser inspired the Mission to China with statements like this:

> It was in Ningpo that I saw, for the first time, a person committing the sin of idolatry. It was an old woman prostrating herself before an ugly idol (Collins 2009: 34).

One of those influenced by his 1911 talk, John Blowick, became Junior Professor of Dogmatic Theology, writing in the 1917 *Catholic Truth Annual* that Fraser had convinced him that 'China was a pagan nation'. For Blowick, there was no salvation outside the church: righteous atheists and unbaptised children alike were consigned to Limbo (Collins 2009: 36–8).

The minority view, following the traditional Jesuit line, was represented by Galvin's colleague Joseph O'Leary, who wrote in the *Far East* in 1918 that Christians could build on various Chinese beliefs such as

> the belief in an incarnation, in a goddess [Guanyin] who is called a "Queen of Mercy", in the power of Satan especially at birth, in the immortality of the human soul, a punishment and reward after death, and the power of the living to help and offer sacrifice for the dead ... [and] a high code of morality. (cited in Collins 2009: 35)

Neither O'Leary nor Blowick had much clarity about the relationship between Confucianism, Taoism and Buddhism as scholars might then have seen them, let alone the ethnographic realities. Non-Abrahamic religions were still understood as 'pagan', hence polytheistic and lacking in sophistication – and thus not deserving of study. Pope Benedict XV (1914–22) saw other religions as 'the cruel slavery of demons', while bishops promoting the Maynooth missions issued pastorals on

> the countless millions of a mighty empire that still sits in the darkness of Paganism and the shadow of eternal death (cited in Collins 2009: 48).

Hence the Dalgan Park training focused on controversy with 'Christians living outside the Roman Catholic Church', who were seen as enemies, with brief dismissals of other religions on theological grounds:

> For Columbans in China in 1924 the words "pagan" and "heathen" and the name of Buddha were linked with terms such as "diabolical" and "darkness" (2009: 296).

It was in its own way a minor miracle when any information about Buddhist Asia came back to Ireland through such circuits.

Disseminating the Missionary Experience

Despite its ethnocentricity, the Catholic church represented by far the most effective *distribution* mechanism for awareness of Buddhist Asia in this period. The Catholic Book Society for the Diffusion of Useful Knowledge throughout Ireland (founded 1824), for example, produced half a million volumes in its first five years and five million by 1837; its successor the Catholic Society of Ireland (1845) was comparable (Loeber and Stouthamer-Loeber 1999: 152). Focusing specifically on missionary information, the Association for the Propagation of the Faith (founded 1838)

> was as much concerned with heightening missionary consciousness among Catholics as with the task of fund-raising. Its populist *modus operandi* was designed to serve both purposes. Employing a cell system based on tens and multiples of tens, the small weekly contributions of the poor were made to amount to substantial sums, and through this ingenious method large numbers of laity were made to feel intimately involved in the Church's missionary activity. (Hogan 1990: 62)

A Dublin edition of the APF's *Annals* had a monthly print-run of 12,000 copies by 1841. Although most missionary activity, then and later, was aimed at Irish emigrants, the *Annals*, like later missionary literature, highlighted the 'heathen' effort (1990: 66–7).

By the twentieth century, dissemination was massive. In 1930, the three main journals (the Maynooth *Far East*, the Holy Spirit *Missionary Annals* and the Society for Missions to Africa's *African Missionary*) had a circulation around 130,000, to which can be added four other magazines and the periodicals of the missionary sisters (Hogan 1990: 146). This became part of everyday life: Bernard Murphy, as a young boy in 1950s Cork, sold *The Far East* to friends and neighbours (pers. comm.) The main focus of such literature was on the spirit of adventure and the dramatic aspects of missionary work, and the 'scramble for souls' in competition with Protestants (Hogan 1990: 155).

Children were a target audience, and missionaries visited schools to give lectures, often illustrated by magic lanterns or (later) films produced by missionary orders:

> Missionary films took the form of both documentary and fiction, and
> all were essentially propaganda ... Scenes which displayed exotic
> locations, jungle vegetation and semi-civilised pagans had a huge
> impact on audiences ... (Bateman 2006: 121)

No doubt too devotional material on the missionary work of St
Francis Xavier (chapter two) was circulated to audiences in Jesuit
schools and UCD.

For a more educated (or adult) audience, things were slightly
more detailed. Thus 'the Rev. D. Nugent, CM, Ningpo, China'
lectured in Dublin's Mansion House on the history of Catholic
missionaries in China, starting in 1291 and touching on early Jesuits
before coming to the post-Boxer situation. Here too, though, details
on Chinese religion were thin:

> The missionary had to work against Chinese religions, Confucianism,
> Taoism, and Buddhism, with their concomitant superstitions, of which
> filial piety and ancestor worship are the principal. The missionary
> raised up temples to the True God as he advanced in his work of
> evangelisation ...[34]

Returning to *Ulysses*, Bloom's reflections passing Westland Row
church thus fit within a routine Irish experience:

> Same notice on the door. Sermon by the very reverend John Conmee
> S.J. on saint Peter Claver S.J. and the African Mission ... Save China's
> millions. Wonder how they explain it to the heathen Chinee. Prefer an
> ounce of opium. Celestials. Rank heresy for them. Buddha their god
> lying on his side in the museum. Taking it easy with hand under his
> cheek. Josssticks burning. (1960: 81)

As Ito (2003: 57) notes, Bloom consciously takes sides with
Chinese people against the missionaries, recalling both the Museum
statue and the Opium Wars – an important reminder that oppositional and negotiated readings (Hall 1980) of missionary literature
were possible.

Wider Catholic Reading

Beyond the missionary literature, the Irish church published little on
Buddhism; but some elements of a reception history are nonetheless
possible. The holdings of Maynooth library, in the country's
pre-eminent seminary and headquarters of the Catholic hierarchy,

34. *Freeman's Journal,* Apr 29 1924: 4.

Fig. 3.5 The Buddha teaching his disciples in the forest, by Olga Kopetzky for Paul Carus'
Gospel of Buddha.

show some interest in Buddhism from the later nineteenth century. Many books are donations or bequests from clergy rather than direct library acquisitions, widening their significance for reception. The texts include scholarly works and Buddhist apologetics alongside works by Catholic authors. The latter, typically by mid-twentieth-century French Jesuits, are mostly sympathetic, exploring topics like the integration of Zen meditation into Catholic spirituality (chapter six).

Early texts include an 1877 copy of T.W. Rhys David's *Buddhism: a sketch of the life and teachings of Gautama the Buddha* (with 1903 and 1925 editions) and an 1892 edition of Sinnett's *Esoteric Buddhism*, the founding text of Theosophy, with other works on Buddhism from 1900 and the period 1926–33. Most interesting is *The wisdom of the Aryas* (1923) by Ananda Metteyya (Gordon Bennett), founder of the Buddhist Society of Great Britain and Ireland, and *The message of Buddhism* (1926) by J.E. Ellam (BSGBI and Maha Bodhi Society), suggesting attention to western Buddhist organisation. There are also early editions of *The Light of Asia* and Paul Carus' *Gospel of Buddhism*, probably from bequests.

Mgr Donal Reidy, Dean of Kerry, bequeathed texts such as E.A. Wallis Budge's 1923 *Baralam and Yewasaf*; a Mgr Kissane left, among others, Louis de la Vallée Poussin's 1925 *Nirvana*. A 1943 Coffey bequest included Caroline Rhys David's *Buddhism: a study of the Buddhist norm* (also 1925), while Rev Dr Gerald Hanratty of UCD Philosophy Dept. bequeathed five texts on Buddhism including Henri de Lubac's 1953 *Aspects of Buddhism*.

There was thus a consistent if limited interest in Buddhism on the part of Catholic intellectuals from the late nineteenth century onwards. As an emergent elite, the Irish priesthood were mostly happy to rely on others to write about Buddhism, until the Church's own role in organising hegemony became unstuck in the later 1950s and early 1960s, and young Catholics became attracted to Buddhism (chapter six).

The Dublin Review *and Buddhism*

A related picture – of limited reception within elite circles – appears from the *Dublin Review*. Co-founded by journalist Michael Joseph Quin, Cardinal Wiseman and Daniel O'Connell for educated Catholic opinion, it mirrors the *Dublin University Magazine*. Published in London, the editor when it first covered Buddhism, William Ward, was professor of moral philosophy and dogmatic philosophy at St Edmund's College at Ware, while for the later articles editor James Moyes was professor at St Bede's in Manchester.

The authors were similarly international. William Francis Barry, author (according to the *Wellesley index*) of 'Modern society and the sacred heart'[35] was professor of theology at Oscott College in Birmingham. Charles de Harlez, author of 'The Buddhistic schools'[36] and 'Buddhist propaganda in Christian countries'[37] was professor of Oriental Studies in Louvain (and a specialist on Zoroastrianism, Sinology and Manchu language and culture). Philippe Colinet, author of 'Recent works on primitive Buddhism',[38] was another Louvain Orientalist.

Such texts represent not so much 'the view from Irish Catholicism' as the view educated Catholics were encouraged to adopt. As Gramsci (1971) notes, characteristic of church organisation was restraining its intellectuals from disturbing the uncomplicated allegiance of 'the simple'. Certainly the gulf between the level of some of these articles and the training of missionaries is huge.

Franklin argues that Victorian authors:

> do not appear to respond to Buddhism primarily as Congregationalists or as Catholics or Broad Church Anglicans or, for that matter, as humanist agnostics who still profess a Christian worldview and ethics. They nearly all write on behalf of Christianity as a whole ... (2008: 16)

However, even where *Dublin Review* authors use the language of 'Christianity' versus 'Buddhism', this is embedded in polemics about the Sacred Heart, attacks on liberal Catholicism or conspiracies of freemasons (see below). This was not a purely Irish phenomenon: the Mormon *Deseret Evening News* reported on the Irish Buddhist Dhammaloka in order to score sectarian points about the ineffectiveness of mainstream Christianity. Where the main cleavages were not between Christians and freethinkers or socialists but between different ethnic identities marked by religion, Buddhism was a terrain of sectarian conflict between different Christianities.

Barry's (1875) 'Modern society and the Sacred Heart' links D.F. Strauss, Thomas Carlyle and R.W. Emerson as exponents of the

---

35. July 1875, vol. 25: 3–38.
36. 1889, vol. 43: 47–71.
37. July 1890, 3rd series vol. 23: 54–73.
38. Jan–Apr 1890, 3rd series, vol. 23: 256–85.

'Modern Idea' along with Stuart Mill, Comte and Bruno Bauer (1875: 11). This 'idea', in Hegel's hands,

> may be paralleled with the overpowering imaginations of those Oriental mystics to whom we owe Buddhism. (1875: 13)

Franklin (2008: 79) notes that Dharma as universal natural law was widely compared to key scientific theories of the age such as evolution, atomic theory and the laws of thermodynamics. However, Barry's point is the differences:

> The Eastern withdraws himself into contemplation, subdues every moment of passion, and longs vehemently for only one consummation, that the semblance of life, which he has, may be taken from him, and pain may cease with annihilation. The Western cannot learn from this hopeless asceticism; he believes that the cycle of things is an evolution from mere potentiality to some large perfection; he worships progress, and looks out for the means of advancing society and mankind in its outward path. (1875: 17–18)

This distinction is not so much aimed at Buddhism as at its potential for legitimating 'the Modern Idea', within internal Church struggles after Italian unification and the Paris Commune, and the Vatican's rejection of modernity and democracy:

> The Roman Pontiff has told us all, that Liberal Catholics are, not indeed in intention but in effect, the worst enemies of the Church ... We do not speak of the Revolution; we are pointing to those who think a compromise between the Church and modern society not only feasible, but right and becoming. (1875: 36)

The article concludes in a crescendo celebrating the consecration of the Church to the Sacred Heart.

In 1875, then, Buddhism appeared rather distantly, as a potential support for internal dissenters. By 1889–90, Buddhism had become a problem in itself. Colinet's 'Recent works' is largely sympathetic (rejecting the charge of nihilism or that the Four Noble Truths lead to passivity), but takes aim at Buddhism on the question of the simple:

> The Buddhist theories, however, were quite incomprehensible to simple folk. (1890: 261)

This enabled a broader defence of keeping the simple, simple:

> The spirit of primitive Buddhism is quite different from that of the nascent Christian church. Here the ideal is faith, simple and ingenuous;

> the kingdom of heaven is reserved to those who become like unto
> little children. There, on the contrary, science – and what science! – is
> the indispensable condition of salvation ... (1890: 265)

Science, of course, was a problem much closer to home in this
period. Colinet was also concerned to dissociate early Buddhism
from Protestantism:

> it is believed that it is possible to find something analogous between
> those old times and the ardent combat between Protestantism and
> the Papacy. This is an error. In the eastern provinces where Buddha
> founded his religion the Brahmanic hierarchy was not organized.
> (1890: 264)

The overall tone is one of reasonable interest and disagreement
– and a concern not to add Buddhism's prestige to Protestantism.
Matters were very different for de Harlez, as we shall see.

Christian Moral Panics

The enormous popularity of *The Light of Asia*, the rise of Theosophy,
the occasional actual Buddhist – and the development of comparative
religious studies – provoked a minor moral panic among some
Christians in the late nineteenth and early twentieth century. On the
Protestant side, we have encountered Berry's (1889–90) Donnellan
lectures on 'Buddhism and Christianity' and Hannay's (1903)
insistence that there was no link between Buddhist and Christian
monasticism in the 1901–2 Donnellan lectures.

Catholics were equally concerned about the Buddhist threat to
Christian legitimacy and originality. Already in 1857 the *Dublin
Review* had devoted much energy, reviewing Père Huc's *Travels*,
to arguing that the similarities between Tibetan Buddhism and
Catholicism were really to be attributed to medieval Franciscan
missionaries (1857: 459–62).

Maynooth library holds the American *The Dhamma of Gotama the
Buddha and the Gospel of Jesus the Christ*, whose preface notes:

> The specious attempts to lay the Gospels under obligation to Buddhist
> teaching have shaken the faith of not a few Christians. The need of a
> thorough refutation is imperative. (Aiken 1900: vii)

Similar struggles were waged at a more popular level: the
Freeman's Journal[39] noted an article on Buddhism in the Catholic

39. Apr 17 1908: 8.

Encyclopedia and a year later Catholic Truth Society translations of French pamphlets on 'The study of religions'.

> For those who have not time for very deep study, but who desire to know something reliable.[40]

De la Vallée Poussin's contribution to the series (1910) is unambiguously Orientalist:

> It is absurd to suppose that Christianity can be injured by comparing it to Buddhism: see Buddhism as it is, and you cannot dispute the superiority of Christianity. But let us carefully note that this superiority … is primarily that of the Western mind over the Hindu. (1910: 29)

It concludes:

> Neo-Buddhism is, if I may be permitted to express my personal opinion, at once frivolous and detestable, and dangerous, perhaps, for very feeble intellects. (1910: 32)

As late as 1921, the CTS published Gerald Willoughby-Meade's *Buddhism in Europe*, which saw Buddhism as a greater threat than spiritualism (Humphreys 1937: 75–6).

As Franklin (2008: 20) notes, this 'Christianity-versus-Buddhism' debate took place across the British Isles and in different denominations. The primary fear was not so much Buddhist conversion, as that the world as a whole was Buddhist. Conventional turn-of-the-century estimates saw 40% of the world as Buddhist[41] and only 26% as Christian (Sutin 2006: 225). Buddhism was known to be half a millennium older, and comparative religion and Biblical criticism both raised doubts about Christian claims to uniqueness.[42]

These wider fears may explain the tone of de Harlez' (1890) 'Buddhist propaganda in Christian countries', which saw the intellectual tide turning against Christianity:

> who would believe that in this century, so full of light, after some 1900 years of the teaching of the Gospel, there could be found among Christians, men, and in no small numbers, who are again bringing

40. Mar 23 1909: 7.

41. This was based in part on counting all Chinese and Japanese people as Buddhist.

42. Franklin also argues (2008: 121–4) that Buddhism was threatening because it disrupted the historical contract between Protestantism and capitalism, prescribing spiritual activism rather than 'works' and opposing economic accumulation. This may well be true for Britain, but for obvious reasons does not appear in Irish debates.

into honour the most extravagant practices of magic, and are working openly for the conversion of Christians to Buddhism and to Kabbalistic doctrines? ... Distinguished minds, even renowned *savants*, have made themselves co-operators in this strange task, and are working at it silently but perseveringly, all the world over, but principally in England, America, and France. (1890: 54)

The threats included the 'Theosophic Society', but also academia in France where Church and State were increasingly separate:

there are others, no less celebrated, who are working their hardest to propagate in the France of St. Denis and of Clovis the religious ideas of the Brahmans and the Bonzes; who place Buddhism high above the doctrines of the Gospel ...

This is being done in the Collège de France, from those chairs of the Sorbonne where but lately the teachings of theology still echoed ... (1890: 55)

As with Colinet and Barry, Buddhism's intellectual prestige needed to be removed from local use:

"Rather Turk than Papist", said the disciples of Luther, "rather Buddhist than Christian," say their modern imitators. Sham Buddhists of course! For not one of them would consent to submit to the laws of this religion which they pretend to admire. (1890: 56)

Unfortunately de Harlez proceeds to discuss Col. Olcott, famous for having converted in Ceylon, and another Theosophist who had also taken the five lay precepts. The fear of Buddhism, however, was real enough to provoke a senior academic like de Harlez (professor at Louvain, member of the Belgian Royal Academy, canon of the Cathedral of Liège) to take seriously the claim that

There are 30,000 Buddhists in Paris.[43] There is a professor of Buddhism at the Sorbonne. (1890: 56)

In fact, there was a vast conspiracy:

Everywhere are books, journals and reviews multiplying themselves, together with the societies which publish and support them. Among their authors and their supporters some work openly, with their names displayed upon their banners; others work in secret, in an

43. The claim was by the eccentric Orientalist Léon de Rosny. A noted Sanskritist and director of the École des Hautes Études, it is hard to believe that de Harlez was not more directly familiar with him.

underhand manner, or with borrowed names, but with no less ardour
and perseverance. (1890: 58)

The conspiracy was manifested particularly in the (French) Isis
Society and the Theosophical Society, condemned for attempting
to reconcile Buddhism and Christianity or for their 'Buddhistic
tendencies' (1890: 58–9). Part of the problem was the *politically*
radical tendency of European Buddhists:

> But we must again notice a list of books recommended for reading
> of the adepts of New Buddhism. It will show better the spirit which
> animates the Theosophistic societies. (1890: 61)

There follow titles by liberal or modernist authors like Victor
Hugo, Lamartine, Baudelaire etc. De Harlez seems to have had
difficulty identifying non-Theosophist Buddhists, and the only fully
Buddhist work discussed is Olcott's *Buddhist catechism*, whose aim
was

> to draw Christians into apostasy, to persuade them to embrace the
> Hindu [sic] faith, and to prevent the Buddhists and Brahmans from
> becoming Christians. (1890: 62)

Unsurprisingly, de Harlez was worried by the popularity of the
text:

> It can easily be imagined what effect such pamphlets will produce
> upon the minds of Orientals, to whom all ideas of Christianity are
> absolutely unknown, and who are beforehand satisfied with the
> perfection of their own beliefs. (1890: 65)[44]

Matters had reached a crisis globally:

> The activity of these Neo-Buddhist societies does not exert itself
> upon the Buddhists, Brahmans, or Christians alone; their propaganda
> extends itself also to other religions. (1890: 72)

Exhibit A was the Zoroastrian Theosophist Dhunjibjoy Medhora:

> most likely he is a Freemason also.

The tone of panic which runs through the article is striking:
for the Catholic professors who wrote, published and read this in
Belgium, England and Ireland, Buddhism and Theosophy were real
existential threats. Similar themes would recur in the late twentieth

---

44. De Harlez was apparently unfamiliar with the modernist theory of projection.

century: an oscillation between fear and anathema and assertions of superiority, interspersed by elements of more or less well-informed dialogue.

An Irish Contribution: John Howley

A rare Irish author in this period is John Howley (1866–1941), Professor of Philosophy at University College Galway from 1914–35. Interested in the philosophy of asceticism and mysticism (Brown 1941: 603), he wrote *Psychology and mystical experience* (Howley 1920) to respond to the issues opened up by William James:

> There is such curious kinship between the methods employed by Buddhist and Sufi, by Neo-Platonist and Christian, that writers like Vaughan have inferred from them the fundamental similarity of all mystical experience. (189–90)

Covering a wide range of different literatures on meditation, Buddhism appears mostly *en passant* as one of many examples of a fundamentally homogenous 'East'. A lengthy citation on the *jhanas* underpins a recurrent contrast between 'Indian' and theistic mysticism:

> With the Buddhist the process of emptying consciousness is for its own sake, with the Sufi there is the hope of being filled with the Divinity: the end in view is very different. (1920: 199)

In a later review, he discusses his own thinking at greater length:

> When I began the study of these questions a quarter of a century ago, I confess I was rather puzzled by the severity of the Roman censures of quietism, but ... I had only realized the latent sensuality lurking in quietist systems; I had not appreciated the abysmal pride to which Yoga technique, fully and rigorously worked out, necessarily leads. *Tatwamsi* and *Nirvana*, the *scientia matutina* and the *scientia vespertina* of the Ninth Circle! ...
> I think the *scientia vespertina* of the Arahat is even more terrible in its perversity than the *scientia matutina* of the Jivan Mukta! (1935: 141-2)

Howley accepted similarities in mystical psychology, but saw 'Eastern' approaches as self-delusional and theistic ones as real encounters with divinity – so that nothing would be learned by further pursuit of the former. Impressive by the standards of his ecclesiastical peers, Howley is not on a par with scholars like Watters; indeed by far the most substantial Catholic scholarly engagement with Buddhism before figures like William Johnston in the later twentieth century was no cleric but the judge Daniel Twomey (Huxley 2001). The Irish Catholic church, as institution, prioritised the construction of local and diaspora power structures as against knowledge of the wider world.

Buddhism in Popular Culture

Buddhism filtered into Irish popular consciousness in many ways: in personal encounters as soldier or sailor; via slide shows in church halls or museum exhibits; through newspaper articles and poems like Edwin Arnold's 1879 *Light of Asia.*

Written by the editor of the *Daily Telegraph* (circulation quarter of a million), *The Light of Asia* was one of the most successful books of the day (Tweed 2000: 29, Link 1959, Beinorius 2005: 20). It went through over a hundred printings and sold nearly a million copies (about as many as *Huckleberry Finn:* Kinnard 1998: 826). Translated into six languages, it was turned into an opera, a Broadway play, two cantatas and a movie (Clark 1997: 88).

It is hard to imagine that such popularity in Britain and America did not translate into Irish awareness. One Irish Buddhist thinks –

> [It] helped at the time to instil an appreciation and understanding of Buddhism (formerly many people had seen it as a branch of Hinduism). From the UK, it is very likely that this understanding/ knowledge percolated through the interested educated community in Dublin at the time. (Ani Tsondru, pers. comm., citing John O'Neill)

Yet despite the anxieties of Protestant and Catholic clergy alike, the *Light of Asia* seems not to have received a single review in the Irish press. When the movie was shown in Dublin the *Irish Independent*[45] summarised the story as that of a 'Prince who renounces throne, home, and love to go out into the world and minister for suffering humanity', without mentioning the word 'Buddha'. The same was true for references to the opera.[46]

There is, however, other evidence. The book *was* sold in Ireland by Gill and Sons on O'Connell St for 3/6 alongside other bestsellers like Jules Verne and Charles Kingsley.[47] In other contexts, Arnold

45. Nov 23 1927: 11.
46. Nov 2 1929: 6, Sept 3 1935: 12.
47. *The Nation*, Nov 9 1889: 12.

Fig. 3.6 Cover of Sir Edwin Arnold's *The Light of Asia* (1884 edition).

was introduced as 'the author of "The Light of Asia".'[48] By 1926, *The Independent* could mention a new 'limited edition of Sir Edwin Arnold's famous "Light of Asia"',[49] again without mentioning its topic. Most press references to 'Light of Asia' in Irish media are to racehorses or greyhounds, indirectly attesting to its popularity.

A veil of polite silence, in other words, was drawn in the popular Catholic press despite its popularity and discussion in the *elite* Catholic media – confirming Gramsci's analysis of the Church's 'firewalling' of the simple.[50]

Popular culture, then, was not free from the field of force of Ireland's two competing hegemonies – most newspapers were relatively clearly aligned. However, it had other agendas, most obviously making money.[51] Nineteenth-century Ireland had an extensive and lively press (Hayley 1987) which included much general knowledge information along with political news, gossip etc., and Buddhism could fall under this category.

Authorship was international – and only occasionally indicated in the paper itself. Plagiarism was normal practice, while Irish audiences also read British and American periodicals, so a bounded picture of the 'Irish press' is bound to fail. Research is skewed by the fact that digitisation is more advanced for newspapers than for magazines, which made up much of the market. Lastly, as *The Light of Asia* shows, self-censorship was the norm; we see what an author or editor thought would be acceptable – to the public, to religious authorities, or to the state.

On the latter, the political aspects of Asian Buddhism were mentioned when it was not inconvenient. Thus a piece entitled 'Buddhist martyr' in a 1906 *Irish Independent*,[52] before the rise of hunger strikes in Irish politics, noted the self-immolation of a Buddhist monk in Burma as an exotic fact with no indication as to

48. *The Nation*, Aug 6 1887: 5, Sept 22 1888: 5.

49. Aug 16 1926: 4.

50. Olcott's *Buddhist catechism*, despite de Harlez' concern, may not have been distributed in Ireland. Dublin booksellers were reluctant to carry Theosophical titles (chapter five).

51. Books, too, led a life of their own, not only through individual purchase: the eighteenth-century library had spread and now included everything from public libraries (often funded by the Carnegie Foundation) via private reading societies of the gentry and the loan of personal collections for exhibitions to reading rooms organised by factory workers (Legg 1999).

52. May 14 1906: 6.

its purpose. Conversely, it was acceptable to link the (thirteenth) Dalai Lama's flight to Chinese incursions into Tibet[53] and to add, in a tone of liberal interventionism:

> The Buddhist community of Darjiling will hold a meeting to-morrow protesting against the treatment of the Dalai Lama by the Chinese government, and hoping that India may help him in his hour of need.[54]

The Catholic Press and the Search for Knowledge

Articles on Buddhism appear primarily in the Catholic press. The Protestant *Irish Times* mentioned it more as an incidental feature of current affairs, or perhaps had less of a general knowledge brief than newspapers aimed at those climbing the social ladder: 'science and discovery' was the main framework for articles.

The *Nation's* reviewer for Spence Hardy's *Eastern monachism*,[55] however, may well have been Protestant.[56] Claiming 'daily intercourse with both Buddhists and Brahmans in India for years', the author, like many Victorian Protestants, is sympathetic to the Buddha for not being Hindu (Almond 1988: 70) and for imperial values such as self-control, bravery and energy. The Buddha is imagined as saying to himself –

> I am determined to try and set us all right, or, at all events, to try and bring people a little nearer to truth and piety than those beastly, sensual, foul Brahmins are.

On this reading, Buddhism's disappearance from India was a result of its non-violence in face of 'the grisly, blood-smeared, foul old giant' of Brahmanism. Part II[57] continues the same tone: the author resists the consensus that Buddhism rejects a creator god, values religion's moral character rather than 'speculative opinions', and gives Buddhism high marks for the former, at least 'when compared with Oriental religions generally'.

By 1855 the *Nation* was interested in the acquisition of Chinese Buddhist scriptures during the Taiping rebellion:

53. *Irish Independent,* Mar 2 1910: 5.
54. Mar 3 1910: 5; he was staying in the Druid Hotel.
55. Feb 28 1852: 14.
56. Founded by leading nationalists in 1842, *The Nation* had a circulation of 13,000 copies with a wider readership (Hayley 1987: 41).
57. Mar 13 1852: 11.

[the priest] is continuing to print the books purchased by Sir John Bowring; and this object is more interesting and important as the Nanking rebels destroy the libraries wherever they prevail. They will allow circulation to none but their own books ...[58]

Similarly, the *Freeman's Journal*[59] was enthusiastic about Aurel Stein's 'discovery' of the Dunhuang texts, rejoicing in the discovery of a new language, and stressing a search for western origins:

These discoveries ... offer hopes that the whole of Greek literature may yet be recovered. Everywhere the Asian explorer goes he finds traces very strong of a Grecian culture blending with a Buddhist culture – the art and literature of Greece, from even pre-classical days downwards to very late after Christianity, were known in India and China.

Such interests tied into a broader concern for exploration: the *Sunday Independent*[60] discussed the Japanese Buddhist Zuicho Tachibana's search for Buddhist archaeology. Tachibana,

although only 20 years of age, has completed a journey lasting nineteen months across Central Asia of some 5,000 miles ... The traveller has brought back with him over 4,000 manuscripts and a magnificent collection of ancient coins.

There were less-informed versions of the same tropes: thus the regional *Anglo-Celt*[61] noted the theories of Gustave d'Eichthal which 'endeavoured to establish a link between Buddhism and the creed as well as the customs of the American Indians'; while in the *Southern Star*[62] Edward Yates claimed 'Ancient Buddhism tradition-alized certain duties of a quest-like kind in order to restore fertility', discussing rain dances and the Holy Grail.

Like missionary periodicals, adventure was at a premium, as with the *Irish Independent's* serialisation of Heinrich Harrer's *Seven Years in Tibet*.[63] The *Southern Star*,[64] criticising Walder Savage Landor's account of the Boxer rising, claimed for its reviewer the authen-ticity of having seen events 'in the flesh': first hand experience of Buddhist Asia was not rare.

58. May 12 1855: 10.
59. Mar 11 1909: 6.
60. Mar 27 1910: 8.
61. Jan 20 1864: 4.
62. May 16 1936: 6.
63. Feb 2, 6, 8 1956 etc.
64. Jun 8 1901: 3.

Buddhist Prestige in Public Discourse

We have already seen the intellectual prestige of Buddhism, when safely positioned 'over there'. Thus the President of Queen's College, Cork, in the attempt to gain Catholic control of the National University, claimed in 1906

> It is a sad and most disheartening spectacle to see how the Government, in its ill-considered plans to provide higher education for the young men who represent three-quarters of the population, has so far ignored the views and requirements of the Church to which that majority belong ... If the Grand Lama and his followers could establish a large colony in Ireland tomorrow, it is not improbable that in the course of a year or so they would be conceded a University adapted to the religion of Buddhists.[65]

In the same campaign, the Catholic Archbishop of Dublin, attacking Trinity College's self-presentation as a bastion of liberalism, notes the Professor of Education's apparent admission that philosophy, ethics and history were denominational matters:

> It is perfectly obvious that you could not take a professor who has been brought up in the Buddhist philosophy and put him down to teach philosophy here ...[66]

The same trope continued until at least 1923, in the context of debates about Catholic schools in Northern Ireland.[67] Here Buddhism is used to mean 'another sophisticated religion, but one not relevant in Ireland'. As the *Freeman's Journal* put it in an attack on the 'New Theology':

> In Ireland, where the old Faith is the religion of the bulk of the people, we are not troubled with the religious unrest which manifests itself from time to time in non-Catholic countries ... The interest taken in this matter in Ireland was no more than would have been excited by paragraphs about some development in Mahomedannism [sic] or Buddhism ...[68]

At one level this represented an increasing recognition of the comparability of 'world religions'; an article 'Quest for truth in the pagan world' by 'An NUI graduate' could allow that 'the

65. *Irish Independent*, Aug 13 1906: 4.
66. *Irish Independent*, Mar 12 1907: 5.
67. *Freeman's Journal*, May 9 1923: 6.
68. Sept 26 1908: 5.

first questionings after truth' developed in 'the East', mentioning Buddhism along with Confucianism, Zoroastrianism and ancient Egypt before getting down to the conventional business of discussing Greek philosophy.[69]

Very rarely, Buddhism's intellectual or moral prestige could be extended to European Buddhists. Reporting on a British mission to Lhasa, which aimed to 'fill in many gaps that exist in western knowledge of the early history of India and of the Far East generally', the *Freeman's Journal* reported without sneering on the mission's goal of an audience with the Dalai Lama 'to present credentials and gifts from Buddhist societies all over the world'.[70] This did not detract from their authority:

> All of the members are British, and members of the Buddhist Church, and expect to be received by the Tibetans with sympathy and good will. But they have been selected for their scientific attainments and experiences, and are qualified to make accurate observations and studies of the country ...

Because of the Younghusband expedition (which, post-1922, the *Journal* could describe as the 'Guru Massacre'),

> It is certain that only Buddhists themselves would be received with the necessary confidence for unfettered research.
> The members of the present mission, as Buddhists going to Buddhists, possess credentials necessary for such study as has never before been attempted.

Such defences of 'insider research', however, were very rare. The *Irish Independent's* excerpt from William McGovern's report of the same expedition was entitled 'To Lhasa in disguise – Unknown country entered – Story of fascinating adventure', with no indication that McGovern was in the Buddhist Society of Great Britain and Ireland and had been ordained in Japan (Humphreys 1937: 41).[71]

Triumphalism and Saving Souls

Anti-Buddhist polemic also featured, notably around the Buddha's tooth at Kandy. The single most common Buddhist topic, it was universally treated as heathen superstition. Thus the *Westmeath Examiner* discussed the relic with complete disdain, insisting that

69. *Irish Independent*, Apr 13 1909: 4.
70. Jul 10 1922: 2; see also May 2 1923.
71. He is sometimes said to be the inspiration for Indiana Jones.

'the tooth, even if it were really genuine, was utterly destroyed' in 1560 despite Buddhist counter-claims.[72] There were Irish undertones to the commentary: while Protestant writers aimed to highlight parallels to Catholicism, modernising Catholic writers wanted to distance themselves from peasant religion of all kinds.

A second common theme was 'Buddhist becomes a Jesuit'[73] etc., in this case related to Japan. An early version discusses the conversion of a 'Buddhist hermit-priest' in Ceylon, highlighting his family status, education and religious accomplishments and concluding optimistically

> His conversion to Catholicity is, therefore, a most remarkable one, and is a great and severe blow to the fast-dying cause of Buddhism in Ceylon.[74]

The *Independent*,[75] speaking of an earthquake in Japan, rejoiced in 'the yearning after better things somnolescent in the hearts of many of these poor benighted pagans', instancing a follower of Amida whose writings the author felt showed Christian tendencies.

In reality, Irish Catholicism was notably ineffective at converting Buddhists or other Asians, and the growing stress on Buddhism's internal weaknesses reflected this failure. Thus, discussing a new Buddhist catechism, the *Southern Star* noted that it was the result of a royal competition

> in the hope that Buddhism will stem the tide of murders, thefts and brigandage that has been sweeping the country. Catholic missionaries express the opinion that the Buddhist religion will prove unequal to the task, and they look upon this catechism as a concrete expression of Buddhism which will give them the opportunity to refute that religious system.[76]

Ten years later, *The Independent* was still discussing 'Siam – new mission field':

> Catholicism they respect, but with its demand for self-discipline and for active good works it is not so attractive to them as their own

72. Apr 4 1885: 4.
73. *Meath Chronicle,* Apr 15 1933: 8.
74. *Anglo-Celt,* Apr 20 1907: 2.
75. Oct 27 1923: 4.
76. Aug 17 1929: 2.

version of Buddhism, which emphasizes the avoidance of evil rather than the doing of good.[77]

For Irish Catholic readers, then, Buddhism was a religion whose inferiority and prospective decline were already known in advance: exotic, but not attractive. *Western* Buddhists were usually beyond the pale. Discussing the poet Lionel Johnson's letters, the *Irish Independent* commented:

> In 1883, we find the boy attracted to Buddhism ... The Buddhist fit wore off ... This is meaningless and morbid ... Unhappily, the writer seems never to have grown fully beyond the emotional stage of his schoolboy utterances. They are sickly reading.[78]

Similarly, reviewing L. Adams Beck's novel *The key of dreams*, the *Freeman's Journal* noted:

> His hero, Dunbar, however, with all his enthusiasm about the mystic exaltation of Buddhism, treats the little Japanese Miyuki, a pathetic and charming creation, in a way which must be termed caddish.[79]

Buddhism as religious opponent, in Asia or Europe, was damned above all for character flaws – individual or racial – which contrasted with its intellectual or moral prestige when considered as philosophy or as ancient history.

Platitudes and Dancing Lamas

Moving beyond the press, we can mention John McCormack's 1912 recording of 'Nirvana'.[80] Written in 1900, this song was inspired by *The Light of Asia*. The song contrasts Asia's 'mystic Nirvana' with the west's 'human love aspiring to the divine' (Scott 1997), within a general trope of 'fallen civilisations'.

From the (would-be) sublime to the ridiculous, a 1920 Sanatogen ad is perhaps the first appearance of 'Buddha' as an authority for gnomic feel-good sayings ('By the force of my will I shall subdue this disease', followed by a quote from Kipling).[81]

A final stage of the colonial engagement with Buddhism, this time as pure entertainment, was the 1925 'affair of the dancing lamas'

77. Nov 18 1939: 8.
78. Nov 3 1919: 4.
79. Apr 5 1924: 9.
80. Thanks to Ani Tsondru for this reference.
81. *Freeman's Journal*, Apr 23: 1.

(Hansen 1996). The 1924 Mallory/Irvine expedition to Everest was largely financed by film-maker Capt. John Noel, and resulted in the silent *Epic of Everest*, with extensive footage of Tibet. Showings were preceded by a musical and dance performance by six Tibetan 'lamas' (in fact one lama and five monks), causing a major diplomatic rift between Tibet and Britain and giving ammunition to opponents of the 13th Dalai Lama's modernisation plans.

The film was shown – with lamas – at the Corinthian picture house in Dublin. Advertisements claimed:

> This is the first time in the history of the world that a Lama has set foot in a European country.[82]

Fig. 3.7 The 'dancing lamas' on the roof of the *Irish Independent* offices in Dublin, 1925. With thanks to Irish Newspaper Archives (www.irishnewspaperarchives.com) and the Irish Independent. Copyright Irish Newspaper Archives.

82. *Irish Independent*, Sept 16 1925.

One reason for visiting the newly independent Free State was presumably the Irish connections of John Noel (who had married a Co. Galway woman), expedition doctor Richard Hingston, and scriptwriter Col. Victor Haddick from Birr, a major figure in early Irish film (*Luck of the Irish*).[83]

In a later acount of the expedition, serialised in *The Independent*, Haddick records that the lamas 'felt a profound respect for the Dublin hospitality which they encountered'.[84] A newspaper picture showing lamas in sunglasses on the roof of Independent House in Abbey Street highlights both the connections existing in this period and the limited meaning they sometimes conveyed.[85]

Conclusion: the Two Empires, Buddhism and 'elsewhere'

Franklin proposes a

> theoryofculturalcounter-invasion[which]assumesthebi-directionality of hybridity and focuses on the impacts of colonization upon the colonizer. The British "discovery" of Buddhism was at the same time the beginning of the counter-invasion of Britain by Buddhism ... (2008: 9)

Mutatis mutandis, this is also true for Ireland; the sheer volume of material on Buddhism generated by the 'two empires' is considerable. This material, between 1850 and 1960, was received in many different ways, veering from an Orientalist focus on knowledge for practical and intrinsic purposes, via a view of Buddhism as dangerous religious 'other', to a tourist, cinematic or collector's view highlighting the exotic.

Both Catholic and Protestant elites could draw on exoticism to glamourise their own empire-building efforts, and Asian Buddhists were often useful for this. The pursuit of knowledge – for rule, for its own sake or for popular education – often drew on Buddhism as a valuable object of knowledge. At other times, this very prestige (and Buddhist numbers) made it appear a threat, in Europe as in Asia.

While elites (including media elites) had their own purposes, other social groups – newspaper readers, ordinary soldiers and sailors, museum visitors, cinema viewers, audiences at public talks,

83. I am indebted to Sandra Noel for this information.
84. Jul 6 1938: 6.
85. *Irish Independent,* Sept 16 1925.

groups of schoolchildren and indeed consumers of Sanatogen – had different fish to fry.

Thus Ireland had *multiple* Orientalisms – Protestant/imperial and Catholic/nationalist, but also commercial and (dimly glimpsed through our sources) popular. It also had *alternative* Orientalisms: Irish Theosophists, Hindus and Buddhists who drew on this general, if contested, knowledge to critique their own societies and either reposition themselves within a changing Ireland or abandon it altogether through engagement with Asian cultures, themselves becoming 'elsewhere' and 'other'.

Chapter Four

Esotericism Against Empire: Irish Theosophy

The 'Irih Theosophists' (notably W.B. Yeats, 'AE' (George Russell) and James Stephens) were central to the 'Irish Renaissance' of the later nineteenth century, and played a major role in Irish cultural life subsequently. In Britain and the USA, Theosophy was crucial to the development of western Buddhism; yet Irish Theosophy and Buddhism barely overlap. If chapter five discusses the first converts to Buddhism, here I discuss the problem of *non*-conversion, with a view to understanding Buddhism and Ireland.

Dublin Theosophy was not purely a literary phenomenon, but also a new religious movement opposed to exclusivist Christianity, and hence *both* the sectarian Protestantism of its participants' upbringing and orthodox Catholicism (Guinness 2003, 2004, 2006; Bryson 1977; Graf 2003); in other words, it was a challenge to the politics of 'two empires'. This chapter explores the role of Buddhism in the formation of Irish Theosophy and the religious politics of the choices *within* Irish Theosophy which explain the absence of a post-Theosophical Buddhist development. It also discusses the 1890s counter-culture of which Theosophy was part, to shed light on the cultural matrix within which religious alternatives could be articulated in Ireland.

The Politics of Theosophy: Class, Empire, Ireland

Theosophy, a 'late-Victorian hybrid religion' (Franklin 2008) was the product of two conjunctures. One was the rise of spiritualism and other forms of 'do-it-yourself' esotericism which offered forms of direct experience and practice that could be understood as religious, as scientific, as neither or as both, in the context of the late Victorian crisis of religion. Barrow (1986) highlights how late-nineteenth century *plebeian* spiritualism offered a 'democratic epistemology' making the otherworld available to ordinary people without priestly mediation – an analysis which can later be extended to Buddhist meditation.

Morrison applies this to Theosophy (and spiritualism)'s characteristic form, the occult periodical: in a time of the decline of formal legal sanction against public expression of non-Christian belief, the occult revival 'took place at a curious intersection between the private and personal and the flamboyantly public' (2008: 3). This public sphere was one in which

> disempowered groups began to create alternative institutions of publicity and to appropriate features of the commercial press for their own politicized purposes (2008: 4).

The other conjuncture was the experience of empire, and the encounter with a different Other World: the intellectual sophistication and religious diversity of non-Christian religions, and by extension cultures. Theosophy's key tenet, that all the world's religions were imperfect reflections of the truth, dethroned Christianity's claim to uniqueness, drawing both on comparative religious scholarship and the imperial relationships within which this scholarship and the practical encounter with other religions (as texts, artefacts or people) took place. As the humanist Theosophist 'John Eglinton' (W.K. Magee) put it,

> Any acquaintance with the doctrines of Buddhism or Brahmanism suggests that mankind might have developed along other lines than have been chosen by the Western races. (cited in Bryson 1977: 32)

In this sense Theosophy represented a kind of 'globalisation from below'; in Ireland this could mean both the development of local cultural nationalism and a religious identification with non-Christian cultures, leading to practical anti-colonial solidarity (Gandhi 2006: 115).

If the otherworld was universalised, there was also a nationalist pull to identify with a particular 'people'. Diaspora Irish Theosophists Annie Besant and W.Q. Judge both held that Ireland's destiny was as the spiritual leader of Europe (Guinness 2004: 30). Later, W.J. Evans-Wentz argued in *The fairy-faith in Celtic countries*, dedicated to his friends Yeats and AE, that tales of fairy realms masked a belief in reincarnation and that Connemara was an ideal setting for the experience of spiritual perceptions (Sutin 2006: 262–3).

This paralleled older antiquarian arguments according to which the ancient Irish had really been Buddhist, connecting Ireland and

Asia through spiritual affinity rather than imperial relationships or Orientalist knowledge. In Ireland, this also responded to the particular problems of *Protestant* defectors from the Anglo-Irish imperial service class: unable to identify with institutional Catholicism, they sought ways of being legitimately Irish which did not depend on a relationship to an organised church, like the fairy 'gentry', rooted in the land and hostile to clerical authority (Foster 2011: 119–20). Thus folklore and occultism could

> open a way into national tradition from a marginalized base, and [enable] a claim on intuitive, organic, traditional forms of wisdom. (2011: 103)

Thus even at the territorial height of the British Empire in the 1880s and 1890s, Theosophical universalism was undercut by a tendency to see perennial truth as particularly well expressed in a particular place or religion. Once attention shifted from safely remote and anonymous Tibetans, distances between those sympathising with Hindu nationalism in India and Buddhist nationalism in Ceylon (itself partly organised around contesting Hindu control of Bodh Gaya) grew.

So too 'Westernising' forms of sub- and post-Theosophical organisation developed, drawing on ritual magic (the Golden Dawn, grounded in classical antiquity and Kabbalah), esoteric Christianity (Anthroposophy in Germany, the Hermetic Society in Britain), local folklore and paganising antiquarianism (Wicca) or mixtures of these. In each, one 'ray of light' was privileged and counterposed to others.

The Society was not homogenous but a complex and unstable international alliance. Even within mainland Britain, Barrow's (1986) contrast between plebeian and elite spiritualism was paralleled by contrasts between the Society's metropolitan leadership and its more demotic regional branches (Mike Tyldesley, pers. comm.) Irish Theosophy took a different position again. Foster (1997: 50) locates Yeats, AE and Charles Johnston within 'a particular tradition of Irish Protestant interest in the occult ... [with] figures from the increasingly marginalized Irish Protestant middle class, from families with strong clerical connections, declining fortunes and a tenuous hold on landed authority.' Later (2011: 108–10, 113) he highlighted the earlier role of Swedenborgianism within this tradition. MacCorristine (2011: 49–50) reads Irish spiritualism as a similarly 'Ascendancy' phenomenon, though in ways which leave little space for radical Catholic plebeians like Patrick Breslin (chapter five).

Thus the 'outcomes' of Theosophy were not automatic results of its ideology but reflected the needs that individuals brought to their (often temporary) participation and the possibilities they pursued within it.

'Esoteric Buddhism' and the Politics of Irish Theosophy

In this sense, Theosophy was a 'borning organisation' (Payne 1995): a key matrix for the formation of alternative and new religious movements of all kinds:

> For those whose heterodoxy manifested itself expressly against mainstream Christianity, Theosophy and its contiguous offshoots offered a spiritual alternative in eastern religions, one that demanded a corresponding disavowal of the claims of "modern" western civilization. It was this tendency that brought the movement and its largely middle-class adherents into intimate commerce with parallel, secular, avant-garde critiques of western civilization, exemplified in the linked projects of dress and sexual reform, and homosexual exceptionalism; dietary politics, anti-vivisectionism, and vegetarianism and aestheticism, or the repudiation of bourgeois materialism and philistinism in the form of class or colonial avarice. (Gandhi 2006: 122).

Among other things Theosophy was central to the formation of Buddhism in Britain (Bluck 2006), where today's Buddhist Society, for decades the country's main Buddhist organisation, grew out of a lodge of the Society (Humphreys 1937),[1] and the USA, where 'esoteric Buddhists', influenced by the Theosophical presentation, considerably outnumbered all others in the Victorian period (Tweed 2000). Theosophy's foundational text, after all, was *Esoteric Buddhism*; H.P. Blavatsky represented the Society as deriving from Tibetan 'Mahatmas' and wrote extensively on Buddhism; while Col. Henry S. Olcott formally converted to Buddhism in 1880. Not all Theosophists became Buddhists; but any serious member had to engage with Buddhism.

The Irish Theosophists present a huge field of research, including as they do some of the greatest figures of Irish literature, centrally

1. The previous 'Buddhist Society of Great Britain and Ireland' had been founded by an ex-member of the Golden Dawn, Ananda Metteyya.

involved in the Celtic Renaissance which has become foundational for much later discussion of national identity. Here I restrict myself to their reception of Buddhism and the matrix within which they made their choices.

There were three choices to be made. The first and most fundamental was defection from the religious, family and career matrix of the imperial service class; as Joyce put it, Theosophy was 'a refuge for renegade Protestants' (Ito 2004: 11); it offered 'liberation from the stifling Protestantism of their Anglo-Irish class' (Bryson 1977: 32). The second was a choice of direction *within* Theosophy, between those interested in Eastern philosophy, following Blavatsky and Olcott's lead, and those searching for a western mystery tradition, most of whom eventually joined the Golden Dawn. The third and final choice, as Theosophy's links to actual Asian religious politics developed, was the tension among 'Easterners', between those interested in Buddhism and those interested in Hinduism.

These choices were hard ones; their purpose was to find in culture

> the territory on which to address the real terror of sectarian conflict which animated the predominantly Ulster-born Dublin theosophists ... the flight from Ulster Protestant sectarianism and the search for a future Irish nation that might take its shape from humanitarian and nonsectarian imaginings is key to the ideas of "that hermetic crowd, the opal hush poets": AE, Charles Johnston and ultimately James Cousins. Their understanding of empire, anticolonial struggle and nation-state as contingent phases in mankind's evolutionary development towards a society where cultural distinction is celebrated as the local inflection of a universal, free-moving, indeed Asiatic, spirit epitomises the tensions and ambivalences of cultural nationalism during the decolonising phase. (Guinness 2006: 70)

Below I follow a number of Irish Theosophists to explore their relationship to Buddhism and the wider religious politics within which we have to understand the choices of conversion – and non-conversion.

Charles Johnston (1867–1931) and the Origins of Irish Theosophy

It took nearly a decade for Irish people, other perhaps than Bowles Daly (chapter five) to notice Theosophy. The *Irish Times* attacked it twice in the early 1880s, describing Olcott's preaching in India as 'a farrago of the most arrant rubbish the mind of a man ever conceived'[2] and identifying Theosophy as

> a combination of Spiritualism and Buddhism, although in what proportion the peculiarities of the different schools are allowed to enter it is not very clear.[3]

The formation of a Theosophical milieu in Ireland, however, came from A.P. Sinnett's *Esoteric Buddhism* which Yeats and Charles Johnston read in 1884, the year they co-founded the Trinity-based Dublin Hermetic Society with AE 'to promote the study of Oriental religions and theosophy generally' (Guinness 2004: 21). The same year Johnston presented the inaugural paper, on Sinnett, published as 'Esoteric Buddhism' in the *Dublin University Review,* a short-lived cultural nationalist journal.[4] In the same issue was 'A.P. Sinnett (Lines suggested by the late Theosophical Movement in T.C.D.)', which it described as a 'satire on the young Buds': as with the *Irish Times,* Buddhism and Theosophy were seen as identical. One verse ran:

> I'm an Esoteric Swell
> A boss of the Buddhists as well
> A Theosophistico
> Occulto-Mystico
> Koot Hoomi Lal Singhi Swell (cited in Alldritt 1997: 44).[5]

Johnston co-founded the Dublin Theosophical lodge in 1886, replacing the Hermetic Society. Having taken Oriental Studies in Trinity, he went on to the Indian Civil Service, becoming a noted translator of Hindu works from Sanskrit (Oderberg 1996: 5) and eventually an assistant magistrate. He was a lifelong friend of Blavatsky and married her niece. Guinness (2004: 30) speculates on a later connection with Indian nationalism.

Politics, Spirituality, Aesthetic Choices: W.B. Yeats (1865–1939)

By the 1880s, the Society abroad was already in conflict around its relationship to Buddhism. In 1883, Anna Kingsford and Edward

---

2. Weekly Irish Times, Jul 28 1883: 5.
3. Weekly Irish Times, May 3 1884: 3.
4. Vol. 1 no. 6: July.
5. Less irenically, Joyce's *Portrait of the artist as a young man* shows (Catholic) students protesting at the 1899 debut of Yeats' *Countess Cathleen:* 'We want no amateur atheists. We want no budding buddhists' (2003: 246; see Murphy 2011: 80).

Fig. 4.1 W.B. Yeats in 1911.

Maitland had proposed in response to *Esoteric Buddhism* to split the London Lodge between

> Those Fellows who desire to pursue exclusively the teaching of the Thibetan Mahatmas ... [and] the study of Esoteric Christianity, and of the Occidental theosophy out of which it arose (Harper 1974 :5).

The result was the 'western' Hermetic Lodge, which left the Society in 1884. Harper (1974: 4) sees the Lodge as in opposition to the 'Easterner' Johnston's Dublin Lodge; the Dublin Hermetic Society, co-founded by Yeats, Johnston and AE, thus reflected and contained these tensions (Guinness 2004: 22 fn14).

In 1888, Yeats joined the ('western') Esoteric Section of the Society in London and in 1890 the Hermetic Order of the Golden Dawn, while AE remained with the Theosophists. Kuch (1986: 58) sees this not only as an East-West split but also between an occult path of knowing (Golden Dawn/Yeats) and a mystical path of being (Theosophy/AE).[6] It also, as Foster (1997: 106–7) notes, enabled strained nationalist connections to be drawn.

Despite this choice, explored particularly in his 'Castle of Heroes' project (Graf 2003), Yeats remained powerfully affected by Buddhism. His later aesthetic relationship was mediated through Japan, starting with correspondence with Lafcadio Hearn (chapter five). From 1913 he spent time with Ezra Pound, then working on the papers of Buddhist sympathiser Ernest Fenellosa on Noh theatre. Yeats thought that Noh received 'its philosophy and its final shape perhaps from priests of a contemplative school of Buddhism' [Zen], speaking of 'a deep of the mind that had hitherto been too subtle for our habitation' and concluding 'It is now time to copy the East and live deliberately' (1916).

This attraction appeared in later works such as 'The double vision of Michael Robartes':

> On the grey rock of Cashel I saw
> A Sphinx with woman breast and lion paw,
> A Buddha, hand at rest,
> Hand lifted up that blest ...

---

6. While Ananda Metteyya came to Buddhism from the 'western' Golden Dawn, this was a conscious change of path; *Wisdom of the Aryas* (1923) rejects his previous occultism in a way that parallels the ex-Gurdjieffian Jivaka's later rejection of super-natural powers.

[His] moonlit eyeballs never moved,
Being fixed on all things loved, all things unloved,
Yet little peace he had
For those that love are sad … (Yeats 1926b: 317–8).

Around the same time Prof. Yano of Tokyo Metropolitan University gave Yeats the first volume of D.T. Suzuki's Zen essays; afterwards, he received copies of Suzuki's *Eastern Buddhist* twice yearly until his death (Doherty 1983). Suzuki's *Zen Buddhism and its influence on Eastern culture* may have introduced a positive sense of *sunyata* in 'The Statues' (Shiro 1972). Yeats' remained an essentially aesthetic response to Buddhism, and his practical orientation was rather towards automatic writing and the elaboration of his occult cosmology.[7]

AE (George Russell, 1867–1935): Mystical Vagueness

Author, mystic and activist AE began his literary career in 1887 with a co-written article with Johnston in the *Theosophist,* and was intensely involved with Theosophy, co-editing the Irish Society's *Internationalist* (Allen 2003: 15) albeit with a shifting relationship to the international movement (Graf 2003: 57). Consistent with the broader theme of Theosophy as escape from the warring Irish tribes, he charged that religious power

> is the true problem which confronts us as a nation, and all else is insignificant beside. (cited in Graf 2003: 54)

In this view, the search for a native pagan mysticism was central to national political and literary revival. Theosophy was a key resource for his attempts to articulate this; and AE was 'Buddhist' in this sense: he described his two mystical influences as 'Madame Blavatsky and the sacred books of the East' (McFate 1979: 156 fn20). A natural mystic, he was perhaps the first Irish person to practise anything close to Asian meditation:

> No day passed in which he did not tuck his long legs under him, squat in the Eastern meditation posture, centre his mind into one point and visualise beauty, or truth, or power, or God (James Stephens, cited in Lennon 2004: 297).

7. The *Boston Globe* (Apr 10 1892: 20) describes Maud Gonne as Buddhist, but I have found no other support for this.

Fig. 4.2 AE/George Russell, c. 1902.

To Shaw, he wrote in 1921:

> Having divorced as much of the universe as is available the mind at last begins to gnaw itself in hunger, and that is the beginning of mysticism, magic, religion, & all the science of consciousness (Allen 2003: 120).

This is close to the Buddhist Society's understanding of meditation (Humphreys 1935) as a focus on consciousness to the exclusion of sense data. Other westerners took his Buddhism for granted:

> His doctrine is consistent: it is the doctrine of flux taught, not as certain of the Greeks taught it, but as it is held by the schools of Buddhism ... This poem ["Michael"], indeed, may be taken as the singer's message to his land and generation: the comment of a brooding Buddha on the phenomena of this Western island.[8]

Catholic comments were sharper-edged:

> Let Yeats believe in his fairies, AE in his Buddha, with the Irish trade-mark, and James Stephens in his *Uberseele*. It is their affair not ours. We have theological tenets of our own ... (*Dublin Review*, Oct–Dec 1925, cited in Allen 2003: 192).

In fact, AE's notion of Buddhism was extremely vague, as became clear when Maurice Collis brought the Burmese nationalist delegation to meet him over Christmas 1931–2:

> [he] anticipated in this case a discussion on Eastern religion that would give him a chance to quote his poems ... Though only politicians, [the Burmese] could have talked intelligently enough about their type of Buddhism, the Little Ferry Boat [Theravada], but he had never read its canon nor, for that matter, the Great Ferry Boat's [Mahayana], and was only at home in the [Hindu] Upanishads and Vedanta. The expectation that the Burmese, because they were Orientals, would be able (or want) to converse on Hindu metaphysics was a mistake which even a man of his attainments was liable to make at that date (Collis 1953: 202–3).

For AE, as for many other Theosophists, Buddhism often stood for broad intellectual or spiritual horizons rather than anything more specific. Nevertheless, these horizons enabled him to become 'a tireless agent of change for a new Ireland' (Bryson 1977: 36).

8. *Irish Times*, July 16 1926: 3.

James Stephens (1880–1950): Religious Universalism

AE's protégé, James Stephens, was a working-class Protestant who had been a sympathiser not only of the Dublin Lodge and AE's Hermetic Society but also of socialist organisers James Connolly and James Larkin (McFate 1979: 11). Never accepting Christianity (Pyle 1965: 55), he was influenced by Theosophy, Celtic myth and Blake before turning to Eastern philosophy in later life:[9]

> it was in Buddhism that he found the answer to his perplexities, and a satisfactory personal philosophy of life. (Pyle 1965: 55)

This, however, reflects his biographer's own confusion; she makes clear that his philosophy stressed 'Brahman, or God, [which] is the universal Self' (1965: 127). McFate's notes on Stephen's reading show that his knowledge of Buddhism was limited to D.T. Suzuki (McFate 1979: 114), whose 1927 *Essays* he annotated with verse fragments:

> Seeing there is no anyone
> Who would be come or gone
> Why dost thou spread a wing
> In air
> Who art not anything
> Or anywhere (cited in Pyle 1965: 122–3).

Stephens' primary references were the Upanishads, the Mahabharata and Vedanta (Lennon 2004: 317). He seems to have shared the Hindu nationalist perception that Buddhism is 'a reformed version of the original Hinduism' (Pyle 1965: 127); his papers include a poem entitled 'Brahm, and Buddha, and the Christ have told'. On occasion he identified as Buddhist (here joking about the 1798 rebels):

> They were quarter-hung and half-hung, and three-quarters hung and finally hung. And if there is any truth in the Buddhist doctrine of reincarnation these men were eminently fitted to be giraffes in the next world through the neck stretching they got in this one (cited in Pyle 1965: 176).

Along with a general uncertainty as to distinctions between Asian religions, Stephens also shared AE's mysticism (or perhaps meditation practice):

9. Several of his books achieved the ambiguous honour of being placed on closed access in the Maynooth library.

Light floods the mind!
And now the mind is pure,
Is naught-intent,
Is empty:

Is withdrawn into its solitude ...

Stars and the moon
Are lost in the light of life,
As the pure mind, withdrawn,
Is lost in the light of God. (cited in Pyle 1965: 157).

In this context we can also mention the mystical poet Susan Mitchell (1866–1926), friend and colleague of AE and member of the Hermetic Society (Pyle 1998: 83–91). Dependent on the Society and Theosophy for her knowledge of eastern religion, she was a more committed 'westerner' than AE or Stephens: 'Plain God is good enough for me'. Rejecting conventional Christianity as lacking spiritual fire, she was not above the occasional mention of the Ganges as 'River of the World' or drawing on Celtic mythology (1998: 85, 91, 110, 125). No doubt a similar creolising mix was more widespread than a focus on published authors suggests.

Theosophy and the 1890s Counter-Culture

The counter-cultural milieu from which modern Irish Buddhism developed in the 1970s was paralleled in microcosm by the Theosophical milieu of the 1890s, in particular by 'The Household', a theosophical commune at 3 Ely Place in Dublin where AE lived between 1891 and 1898 and which Yeats used as his Dublin base. Here, spiritual practices and experiments were combined with communal living, a theosophical magazine and even a vegetarian restaurant. Yeats and AE painted a series of murals of ethereal beings which are apparently still there. Unlike its latter-day counter-parts, however, this counter-culture in miniature did not lead to any deeper interest in Buddhism.

The house was owned by F.J. Dick, engineer and chair of Olcott's first Dublin talk (below). On the community's foundation it housed AE, Daniel Dunlop (editor of the *Irish Theosophist*) and two other young men, with membership subsequently varying (Graf 2003: 53). From 1895 it also housed what had been Blavatsky's printing press. The Household hosted weekly study groups on the *Secret doctrine* and other texts along with a Sanskrit study group and acted as a spiritual community: 'if any member saw a fault growing upon any other member, it was his duty to point it out' (Yeats 1926a: 193ff).

The 'Sunshine Vegetarian Dining Rooms', at 48 Grafton Street, were owned by Dunlop and his future wife Eleanor Fitzpatrick but run by Charles Johnston's sisters Ada and Georgiana, the latter a member of the Vegetarian Society. (Yeats 1926a: 193ff Yeats 1986: 234, Guinness 2004: 24; Meyer 1992: 33-4). The project was inspired by Thomas Lake Harris' Brotherhood of the New Life.[10] Operating 'for several months' in 1891,

> Hindu medical students, impoverished young authors and the Irish theosophists were brought together out of shared dietary necessity (Guinness 2004: 24).

The vegetarian interest outlived the restaurant; Yeats wrote for vegetarian magazines and Joyce attempted it for a while.[11]

Literary Reflections: Joyce (1882–1941), McKenna (1872–1934), Dunsany (1878–1957)

Other Irish writers encountered Buddhism through these routes, but their responses remained equally marginal to their main interests. Introduced to Theosophy by Yeats or AE, James Joyce purchased Olcott's *Buddhist catechism* in 1901 and reviewed Fielding-Hall's *Soul of a people*, which in his view presented Burmese Buddhism as 'a wise passive philosophy', contrasting this to western meat-eating and militarism (Ito 2003: 53).

Ulysses includes the National Museum's *parinirvana* Buddha and Stephen's recollections:

> Dunlop, [WQ] Judge, the noblest Roman of them all, A.E., Arval [the Esoteric Section], the Name ineffable, in Heaven hight …
>
> Yogibogeybox in Dawson chambers. [Blavatsky's] Isis Unveiled. Their Pali book we tried to pawn … Filled with his god, he thrones, *Buddh under plantain* (Joyce 1960: 191-2).

Other *Ulysses* references cover karma, Mahapajapati, Mahamaya, Mara and Rahula (Ito 2004: 18–19). Later in life, Joyce recommended the works of A.P. Sinnett to Stuart Gilbert. Ito (2003) sees Joyce

---

10. Capt. Pfoundes (chapter five) lived in a New Life commune in London with Charles Johnston in 1890.

11. Gandhi (2006: 69) gives a typical menu for such restaurants in 1888 London.

interested in Buddhism as an alternative to Christianity, especially reflecting his concern for nonviolence:

> No ravished country has ever borne witness to the prowess of the followers of the Buddha; no murdered men have poured out their blood on the hearth-stones, killed in his name. (cited in Ito 2004: 17)

Ulysses also mentions Stephen MacKenna, the translator of Plotinus. Marquez (1963) describes MacKenna as 'An Irish Buddhist', but his editor Doods writes

> Despite the images of Buddha that accompanied him in all the migrations of his last years, he was no Buddhist; he saw no reason ... "to believe in Karma, reincarnation and all that" (2007: 75)

Like Joyce, a major source of McKenna's attraction was 'the Hindu or Buddhist Ahimsa as the sole basis and law of morals (2007: 302, letter from 1933).

Lastly, we can mention the pioneer of fantasy fiction Lord Dunsany (1878–1957), who wrote short stories and plays on Orientalist themes. 'In the land of time' (from *Time and the gods*, 1905) includes a characteristically reworked version of Siddhartha's 'four sights' (1970: 27–37). Here king Karnith Zo sees a temple in ruins, then an old man, and then a funeral procession, in each case enquiring after its meaning and being told that the culprit is Time. He then sets out on a parody of the Buddha's quest, aiming to conquer Time (and, of course, losing). Dunsany's light-hearted polytheism, however, in which he sought implicit escape from monotheism, did not fit with the serious and abstract image then held of Buddhism.

Theosophy and Buddhism in Ireland: the Dog That Didn't Bark

Knowledge of Buddhism in Irish Theosophy

From 1892–7 Dunlop edited *The Irish Theosophist*.[12] It is notable for the absence of Buddhism by comparison with international Theosophical periodicals; Olcott, Judge and Johnston are the main contributors on the subject, but swamped by articles on 'The fire-fountain of Loch Laon', 'The magnetization of plants', 'The *Bhagavad Gita* in practical life', and so on.

12. It was surprisingly cheap, costing from 1d to 4d in the 1890s despite including AE's full-colour illustrations for his poems (Morrison 2008: 8). For an index see www.austheo.org.au/indices/IRISHT.HTM. AE's IT articles are collected at http://infomotions.com/extexts/gutenberg/dirs/etext04/itheo10.htm

A similar impression is gained from both Helen Waddell and Maurice Collis, who do not seem to have recognised the Buddhism they knew from Asia in Irish Theosophy:

> I became for a time [in 1919] a reader of theosophical books, fancying that Madame Blavatzky's [sic] inchoate *Secret Doctrine* might throw light both on Druidism and Hindu philosophy (Collis 1953: 21–22; for Waddell's reaction, see Burleigh 2005: 41).

Thus Buddhism was marginal both to the activities of the Society in Ireland and to the work of its most noted adherents and sympathisers.

This survey of the Celtic Renaissance indicates that the awareness of Buddhism, Theosophical engagement and counter-cultural milieu which in Britain or America were fertile grounds for Buddhism did not have this effect in Ireland, where other ethno-political choices were being made. This impression deepens if we note the failure of Buddhist missionaries to Ireland, and Irish Theosophists *outside* Ireland who engaged more deeply with Buddhism.

Two Buddhist Missionaries

Chapter five notes the limited evidence for Buddhist organisation in Ireland between 1903 and 1922. Here I want to discuss two religious activists who publicised Buddhism in Ireland: Col Olcott in 1889, 1894 and 1896 and the Rev. Will Hayes in 1929. As we might expect, Ireland was very stony soil.

In 1889, Olcott spoke in Dublin, Limerick and Belfast (1889a: 193–200), the first known public appearances by a Buddhist in Ireland. He had dramatically taken the Buddhist 'refuges and precepts' in Ceylon, and was recognised by many Asian Buddhists. Among other things, two monks apparently empowered him to give the refuges and precepts (perhaps to other Theosophists such as Bowles Daly) and he was successful in bringing Asian Buddhist leaders to agree to a set of 'fourteen fundamental Buddhist beliefs' (Kirthisinghe and Amarasuriya 2007: 9–13; cf Tweed 2000: 56).

Olcott had committed himself strongly to Ceylon, ignoring a call from Blavatsky's 'Mahatmas' to return to the west in favour of his lecturing there, and securing Theravadin approval for his *Buddhist catechism* which saw forty editions between its 1881 publication and his death in 1907 (Sutin 2006: 184, 226). His Theosophist Buddhism was not eccentric; as late as 1968 Christmas Humphreys, the Grand Old Man of British Buddhism, could write,

Fig. 4.3 Colonel Henry S. Olcott.

> I am yet unshaken in my view that the Theosophy of H.P. Blavatsky is an exposition of an Ancient Wisdom-Religion which antedates all known religions, and that Buddhism is the noblest and least-defiled of the many branches of the undying parent tree (1968: 18).

He spoke twice in Dublin, hosted by the Society, where he found 'some very earnest and thoughtful men and women, eager to know the truth and brave enough to proclaim it at every hazard'. At the Antient Concert Rooms, he spoke on 'the locally revolutionary subject, "Have we lived on earth before?"' and on 'The Irish fairies scientifically considered'.[13]

13. W.Q. Judge, visiting relatives, attended the second talk; cultural nationalist Douglas Hyde attended both (Guinness 2004: 30 fn 51).

Of the first talk, which noted that Theosophy 'was the search after the spirit which "glorified and exalted [man], and the glorified part was Buddah"', the *Irish Times* recorded 'a very large attendance, more than one half of those present being ladies and dignitaries of the clerical profession'.[14] After the second question, 'Why should Christian Irishmen, Protestant or Catholic, north, south, east, or west, listen to a public blasphemer coming into Dublin?', the *Times* noted 'The speaker's voice was after this barely heard over the din'. The audience refused to move a vote of thanks; the Chair moved it but did not put it to a vote.

Olcott was happy with controversy, but this indicates how much pressure could be brought on Irish people interested in Buddhism.[15] The *Freeman's Journal* attacked the Society in a leading article stating

> The study of Eastern literature, philosophy and religion is not fit for ordinary Westerns. (cited in Graf 2003: 52)

Olcott's Limerick talk ('Among the Orientals') was hosted by Robert Gibson (chapter five), the best-attested Buddhist in Ireland, while the Belfast talk (again on reincarnation) was apparently trying to rouse local interest: the Dublin lodge had requested a sympathetic Unitarian Minister to chair it. Again there was a large attendance of Christian ministers and students with scientists and members of the Secularist Society; the *Northern Whig* noted drily 'It is not very probable that the Theosophical Society will recruit its membership very heavily from [notoriously sectarian] Belfast' (Olcott 1889b: 197).

In 1894, Olcott gave general lectures on Theosophy,[16] perhaps learning from the previous response: 'It had been said that Theosophy was a Buddhist Society, but it might as well be said that it was a Hindoo, or Mahommedan, or other Society'. In 1896 a J.C. Meredith wrote to the *Irish Times* in response to 'American theosophists in Dublin', presumably Olcott again.[17] Berry's 1889–90 Donnellan lectures on Buddhism and Christianity were noted in chapter three; in 1891 he gave another counter-lecture to the YMCA on the same topic.

14. Oct 15 1889: 7.
15. *The Times* also notes that some bookshops refused to stock Theosophical books.
16. *Irish Times*, Aug 10 1894: 6.
17. Aug 4 1896.

Three decades later, the *Irish Independent* for May 14 1929 carried an advertisement reading 'Buddha Day will be celebrated in Dublin by a course of lectures on Buddhism' (evening lectures over 9 days and afternoon talks at the weekend). These were given by Rev. William Hayes ('Brother John'), Unitarian Minister of Chatham, Kent from 1929–44:

> An advocate of inter-faith co-operation, the Rev Hayes became the leader of the Free Religious Movement which sought to create "a Brotherhood of Nations through the Sisterhood of Religions" (Anon n.d. [b])

Hayes, a long-time friend of the London Buddhist Lodge who attended Humphreys' Buddhist wedding in 1927,[18] also celebrated Wesak in Chatham, in conjunction with Buddhist groups in London and Liverpool (Humphreys 1937: 71–72, 79).

The talks, however, were not in the Unitarian Church but in 'The Shrine Room' at 11 Harcourt Terrace. This seems to have been a joint effort between Vivian Butler-Burke (chapter five) and Hayes' 'Order of the Great Companions', advertised in the Buddhist Lodge's *Buddhism in England* as devoted to 'The Study of Comparative Religion and all that makes for the realisation of the Unity of all Life'.[19] The Companions published from Dublin and Kent between 1929 and 1932. Like Olcott, then, Buddhism was for Hayes a particularly favoured element of a universalist religious strategy – but one that seems to have found little resonance in the Ireland of the day.

Irish, Theosophical and Buddhist – Abroad

Chapter five discusses two Irish Buddhists, Capt. Pfoundes and John Bowles Daly, who both had spiritualist and theosophical links, but who seem to have developed these in London rather than in the Dublin lodge, outside the Irish political matrix.[20] The case of W.Q. Judge (1851–1896), the most prominent Irish 'Buddhist' Theosophist, underlines the importance of context.

Born and raised in Dublin, his family emigrated to New York in 1864 (Anon. n.d. [c]). Co-founder with Olcott and Blavatsky of the Theosophical Society, he became General Secretary of the

---

18. The bride, Aileen Faulkner, was Irish, according to two of our interviewees.

19. Vol. 3–4 (1928): 226.

20. They were also older than the Dublin theosophists, of an age to have been spiritualists first.

Fig. 4.4 William Quan Judge.

American Section and Vice President of the International Society, organising the Theosophical Congress at the 1893 World Parliament of Religions. He (and the American Society) split with Olcott and Besant in 1895.

Before the split, Judge was a frequent lecturer in Ireland (Guinness 2004: 30), which like other Theosophists he saw as having a unique spiritual destiny. AE in particular was deeply moved by him:

> I was overcome by a sense of spiritual dilation, of unconquerable will about him, and that one figure with the grey head became all the room to me ... Here was a hero out of the remote, ancient, giant ages come among us, wearing but on the surface the vesture of our little day (Iyer and Iyer 1988: 671–2).

Judge was far more 'Buddhist' in tone than the Irish Society[21] and his magazine *The path* (1886–1896)[22] contains a much greater proportion and depth of Buddhist material than *The Irish Theosophist*: 'A Buddhist doctrine', 'Prof. Max Mueller on Buddhism', 'Japanese Buddhist sects', 'A White Lotus Day address', etc.

Thus the Dublin Theosophists show that as in previous centuries, simple awareness of Buddhism, even when mediated through an otherwise supportive Society and with Buddhist visitors, did not lead to any deeper interest or commitment. Education and the willingness to defect from one's own birth culture were also not enough.

By contrast, Theosophists abroad, including Irish ones, often turned towards Buddhism, and as we shall see most known Irish Buddhists until the 1960s at least lived in Buddhist Asia. It is hard not to conclude that it was the specific matrix of Ireland which made the difference; but why?

Irish Theosophy's Anti-Colonial Politics – and Buddhism

Theosophy and the Imperial Service Class

Irish Studies have downplayed the politics of Theosophy and Theosophists, despite their well-known role in Indian and Sinhala cultural nationalism. Guinness (2006: 68) notes a tendency to see mysticism as refusing supposedly 'realistic and progressive activities like prose and philosophy' (citing Ganesh Devi's wonderful phrase)

21. See the collection of his articles at www.katinkahesselink.net/other/c/ c_wqj.html
22. Indexed at www.theosociety.org/pasadena/path/path-hp.htm

or more broadly an 'irrational escape from historical conditions during the decolonising period'. However,

> Instead of refusing modernity, movements such as theosophy promoted an idealism that tried to find in revised past practices indigenous models for a truly communitarian society that would be marked by a keen zest for social reform on a range of issues, including female suffrage, and a commitment to international cooperation (2006: 69).

As if in response to Devi, AE wrote:

> We rarely find philosophical writers referring to vision of their own, yet we take them as guides on our mental travelling, though in this world we all would prefer to have knowledge of earth and heaven through the eyes of a child rather than to know them only through the musings of one who was blind, even though his intellect was mighty as Kant's (Iyer and Iyer 1988: 151).

As with Barrow's plebeian spiritualists, the indefatigable organiser AE defended autodidact empiricism (grounded in meditation rather than séance) against the official knowledge of literary academia.

Chapter five analyses Irish Buddhism as in part a defection from an Anglo-Irish imperial caste in crisis. This is consistent with analyses of Irish Theosophy which see its members as (in Foster's words)

> from families with strong clerical or professional colorations, whose occult preoccupations mirror a sense of displacement, a loss of social and psychological integration, and an escapism motivated by the threat of a takeover by the Catholic middle classes (cited in Guinness 2003: 1).

By the 1880s, too, the Indian Civil Service was becoming considerably less accessible and less attractive to the Protestant Irish; the recruitment process had been changed to bring down Irish representation (from 33% in the late 1850s to 5% by the 1880s [Cook 1987: 511–2]). Those whose fathers had been gentlemen, clergy and doctors made up 67% of recruits in 1855–84 but only 17% in 1885–1914 as against newer middle-class professions (1987: 517). At the same time as external avenues were being closed off, disestablishment (1869) and the Land War (in the 1880s) were shutting down Irish careers, making defections particularly likely. Irish Theosophists needed a new place to stand, both in Ireland and abroad.

Guinness accepts Foster's analysis of a caste in crisis, but argues that Theosophy represents an engagement with history rather than a flight from it:

> the presence of so many members from an Ulster evangelical background in the Dublin Lodge can be read as a dissent from the increasingly sectarian identities on offer during the 1880s to the 1890s, in favour of securing a critical position, seemingly removed from, but none the less engaged in contemporary debates about Irish nationality (2003).

While sharing Guinness' analysis, I would stress that there was nothing 'removed' from politics in debating religious affiliations in the Ireland of this period. For most Irish people, politics was spoken as religion, as it was in India or Ceylon.[23] As we shall see, even the Irish atheist U Dhammaloka fought imperialism in Burma through religion; and matters were no more enlightened in Ireland, rather the reverse. Even James Connolly had to insist that his socialism was compatible with Catholicism (Cox 2010b).

Religion and Social Movements in Anti-Colonial Struggles

Theosophy's attraction was always political as well as cultural: in Britain

> theosophy enjoyed a core support among social reformers, epitomized by Anna Kingsford, anti-vivisectionist and dress reformer, and [Irish-identified] Annie Besant, labour activist, freethinker and birth control campaigner ...
> This sense of social mission meant that theosophy could compete with a career in the imperial services or the church in serving the Protestant middle-class conscience. (Guinness 2004: 22–3).

23. In Britain and continental Europe, the relationship between religion and politics was more complex. The British imperial effort was increasingly linked to and legitimated by missionary Christianity, in a world where military adventures now required greater popular support and mobilisation, and of course religious divides were important dimensions in some European polities. However – unlike Ireland or much of Asia – most western states had substantial *secular* political groups, whether expressed as anti-clericalism, Radicalism, atheism (of Marxist, anarchist and socialist varieties) or whatever. The significance of these issues also changed over time: Dhammaloka's atheism would have been less radical in British or American politics by his death c. 1914 than at his birth c. 1856. In Ireland, or Burma, challenges to orthodox Christianity were *more* politically loaded by the 1910s.

The Dublin lodge, for Guinness,

> made possible a liberal dissent from the increasingly narrow, and
> increasingly sectarian, narratives of identity available in Irish
> Protestantism ... By fuelling this dissent with prophecies of spiritual
> and racial revival, upheld by the principle of non-sectarianism
> embodied in international fellowship, and discursively structured by
> a syncretic approach to world religions, it facilitated the transition to
> a new Protestant home rule identity (2004: 26)

Thus AE, Stephens and Yeats could find a home in the newly
independent society. With a primary goal of remaining active
in public life in the new world of insurgent nationalisms, Irish
Theosophists were pushed from universalism towards more specific
choices.

In Ireland, Buddhism could not play this role as well as a
defensibly 'western' form of esoteric Christianity or ritual magic,
or an 'Irish' identification with pagan legend and peasant folklore.
Beyond Ireland, Hindu orientations could be relocated within the

> growing sense of mutual sympathy between Indian and Irish nation-
> alists in the late nineteenth century, which opened up the possibility
> of helping each other achieve self-government, made it easier to
> portray both India and Ireland as oppressed colonies which must be
> liberated and even prompted some attempts to form political alliances
> (Nagai 2006: 112).

In a religious world, the attempt to develop forms of religious
identification between India and Ireland was an important blow
against those who justified empire through Christianity. The
Hindu Theosophists abroad paralleled Irish Buddhists: defecting
from the Anglo-Irish imperial service class, rather than seeking a
place to stand in Ireland, they found this in anti-colonial religious
nationalism in Asia.

The Hindu Theosophists: Religion and Anti-Colonial Solidarity

Irish Theosophists who did not follow the Golden Dawn or explore
the fields of Faerie but became more coherently committed to
Hinduism than AE or James Stephens, then, did so abroad. This
drew on a long-standing Irish identification with India (Lennon
2004, Foley and O'Connor 2006, Nagai 2006), returned from the
Indian side (O'Malley 2008, Lennon 2009). We can mention three

cases: the poet James Cousins, the Irish-identified Annie Besant and the non-Theosophist parallel of Sister Nivedita.

James Cousins (1873–1956)

Cousins moved to Dublin as a young poet, teaching geography at the High School (and secretly organising Annie Besant's Dublin lecture in 1909: Cousins 2008). Working in a vegetarian food firm in Liverpool, he and his wife Margaret[24] then travelled to India as sub-editor on Besant's *New India*. Sacked after profiling the leaders of the Easter Rising, he remained based in India, converting to Hinduism at the end of his life.

Cousins began as a universalist Theosophist, in his 1919 'Ode to Truth' arguing that truth was partly refracted through the Buddha, Shiva and Christ (1940: 206–7). His opposition to sectarianism often led him to prefer locally 'given' religion:

> Not now, as once through swift salt-savoured rain,
> He watches men and women slowly pass
> With "God and Mary to you" to early mass
> By fuschia hedges in a Kerry lane …
>
> By other paths on the same quest he goes;
> Not to the rainy peak that Patrick trod;
> But hearing in strange speech the name of God
> Among the selvage of Himalayan snows. (1940: 468)

Often like AE and Stephens inclined to vagueness, his 1926 *A Tibetan banner* notes that it is 'condensed from a manuscript in the temple of Kalimpong' (1940: 319). The poem, describing Avalokitesvara preaching as a cuckoo to the birds, concludes:

> But whether you the scriptures scan
> Of man made God or God made man … [i.e. the Buddha or Christ]
>
> Still may your spirit's open eye
> The mystery of things descry.
> Whatever songs your lips indite,
> Still may the gleam of inner light
> Golden your thrumming finger-tips …

---

24. An active suffragette, she was imprisoned in Holloway, became India's first woman magistrate and was imprisoned again for opposing martial law. She played a significant role in links between Indian and Irish nationalists (O'Malley 2008: 58–60).

Their day of vision has begun
Who in the sunflower see the sun.
Life unto them on plain or hill
Holds something sacramental still. (1940: 317–8).

If this is not good poetry, like AE and Stephens it is at least genuine mysticism, rather than the rhetoric of 'all religions are the same' common to those for whom all inner experience is equally foreign. Consistently, in his writings Cousins 'replace[s] the idea of commonwealth with cosmopolitanism' (Guinness 2006: 74), in a Herderian sense of alliances between nations understood as spiritual ideals articulated by artists.

His *Wisdom of the west* articulated one aspect of this, inter-preting Celtic myths in Theosophical terms, while his interest in Hinduism led to a 'golden chain' view of caste as articulated by Hindu modernists (Guinness 2006: 77). Consistently, he celebrated the opening of Travancore's Hindu temples to Untouchables rather than contemporary Untouchable opposition to caste:

Now the right royal hand, whose hero-stroke
From galling custom's yoke
A million souls into their selfhood freed … (1940: 449)

Annie Besant (1847–1933)

Annie Besant, who wrote 'three-quarters of my blood and all my heart are Irish' (Cousins 2008: 186) had come from Catholic pietism via freethought, birth control and socialism to a distinctly theistic mysticism, joining the Theosophical Society in 1893 and becoming President in 1907. An indefatigable traveller, she lectured in Ireland in the 1890s and early 1900s (Guinness 2004: 30). Consistently anti-colonial, she wrote 'I used the light of Theosophy to illuminate political questions where great principles were involved' (cited in Viswanathan 1998: 203).

Her identification between Ireland and India and role as founder of the All-India Home Rule League in 1916 and president of the Indian National Congress in 1919 combined with Indian suspicion of her mentor Olcott's conversion to Buddhism[25] (Wickremeratne 1982: 245) to make a 'Hindu turn' almost unavoidable

---

25. Sinhala Buddhists for their part were suspicious of Theosophists' rationalist and anti-devotional tendencies; if Olcott was often exempted, Besant was a particular target (Harris 2006: 146–7).

Fig. 4.5 Annie Besant.

(Bayly 2000: 393–4). In her obituary of Olcott she claimed his and Blavatsky's mantle while minimising his relationship to Buddhism (Besant 1907).

Besant's leadership marks the Society's turning from flirtation with Buddhism towards closer identification with Hindu nationalism:

> of all religions Hinduism was closest to the religious wisdom which mankind had lost and it was the business of the theosophists to retrieve (cited in Wickremeratne 1982: 246).

This was a clear political choice: as Guinness (2006: 71) notes, *The Theosophist* had criticised her in 1894 for endangering the society's 'broad eclecticism' through her endorsement of 'Hindu revivalism and repeated invocations of India's Aryan heritage' in a period of sectarian attacks by Samajists on Muslims and forced reversions to Hinduism by converts to other faiths. Buddhist-identifying and -sympathising Theosophicals such as Humphreys left the Society (Humphreys 1968: 18).

Sister Nivedita (Margaret Noble, 1867–1911)

Nivedita's (non-Theosophist) career parallels that of other Irish Hindus in India. Born in Dungannon in 1867 to a family of Presbyterian ministers, her family moved to England where she founded a Froebel school and was attracted by Buddhist ideas for a number of years (Atmaprana 1991: 8–9). In 1895 she was converted by Swami Vivekananda and sailed for India in 1897 where she joined his order. She remained a committed Hindu nationalist until her death in 1911, running a women's school, writing at least 7 books[26] and was active as a public speaker (Ratcliffe 1913, Atmaprana 1991). Among other things she defended Hindu control of Bodh Gaya on the grounds that

> Bodh Gaya must be held for the great synthesis known as Hinduism ....
> Of this Hinduism, Buddhism, in all its phases, was an essential part.[27]

Theosophy and Anti-Colonial Politics

Thus Irish Theosophists *in India* took up positions aligned to local anti-colonial cultural nationalisms, in this case Hindu ones, and played significant roles in the process. Irish Theosophists *in Ireland*

---

26. These include various works on Buddhism, presenting the Hindu nationalist view that Buddhism is a form of Hinduism.

27. Cited in *Prabuddha Bharata* (Awakened India), vol. 103 (1998): 345.

Fig. 4.6 Sister Nivedita (Margaret Noble).

also developed new forms of self-identification to enable them to play a role in nationalist politics, and were successful in this.

If religion, not only in Ireland or Asia, but in the Britain of the evangelical revival, was increasingly political, we cannot separate off the rational and political from these identifications and their public meanings, in a world of missionary empire and religious nationalisms against empire. The personal meanings involved were no doubt different for different people: few of those discussed here and in chapter five had what the twenty-first century might recognise as a meditation practice, or engaged in ritual. However, one thing which was widely shared was an emotional commitment to a particular culture – Irish, Indian, Burmese, Japanese – marked out in particular as a love of landscape, of peasant life, of folklore and of religious myth. This position, with all its strengths and weaknesses, appears as shared by those who otherwise took radically different and opposed positions.

Those differences, as between 'Hindu' and 'Buddhist' orientations, nevertheless still need some explanation. If the sheer size of India, the shared history and the presence of Indian intellectuals in Britain (O'Malley 2008) played a particular role in driving Irish identification with India, there were nonetheless long connections with Ceylon, where Dharmapala had noted analogies to Ireland, and with the later Japanese nationalism of the Kyoto school.

The theistic and soul-oriented elements of Hinduism perhaps made it sufficiently close to Christianity to be comprehensible and meaningful while remaining sufficiently different to be worth exploring. Within Ireland, AE, Stephens and Cousins show us how an abstract or vague interest in Hinduism made it possible to argue that Christianity and Hinduism were 'really' one, referring to the same deity. Aijaz Ahmad's comment that 'orientalism is deeply complicit with high brahmanism, and theosophy arose as an anticolonial ideology out of this matrix' (Guinness 2006: 69) certainly applies to figures such as Besant, Cousins or Nivedita.

Nevertheless this can hardly be said of Buddhist Theosophists, and conflicts such as that over Bodh Gaya counterposed Europeans and Asians who drew on 'Buddhist' and 'Hindu' theosophy as transnational organising strands (see Kinnard 1998). Nivedita shared the brahminical view that Buddhism was included by Hinduism and therefore had no need of separate religious (or political) representation. Within Ceylon, Olcott's campaign for equal educational rights for Buddhists conflicted with orthodox Hindus: ironically so in view of present-day Sri Lankan politics, but neatly paralleling Irish debates. If in this period the British Empire went from hegemony to decolonisation, it is unsurprising that Theosophists moved from a general cosmopolitanism to a closer identification with *specific* local cultural nationalisms.

These experiences parallel those of early Irish Buddhists. Disaffected from Irish sectarianism (Catholic and Protestant), their alternative to both affiliations was to identify or sympathise with Buddhism, often as a contrast to religion as they had experienced it; thus Buddhism was valued above all for legal toleration and non-violence. It was also to identify with Asian *cultures* and *people* as they experienced them. Such allegiances were negotiated within a matrix marked by the rise of local, anti-colonial cultural nationalisms and struggles with an aggressive Christian missionary effort increasingly linked to empire.

Chapter Five

The First Irish Buddhists:
Jumping Ship and 'Going Native'

Resisting Both Empires

I have argued that Irish relationships to Buddhist Asia were mediated through the British Empire and the Catholic 'spiritual empire', and the local reflections of these in the Anglo-Irish imperial service class and the Catholic nationalist service class. The late nineteenth and early twentieth centuries, when the first Irish people became Buddhist, were marked by a decisive shift in power between these two, as the Land War undermined the economic basis of the old aristocracy and the nationalist service class led the Catholic peasantry in particular in religious revival (with disestablishment of the Church of Ireland), cultural nationalism, Home Rule agitation and finally partial independence.

All of this broke colonial and Anglo-Irish hegemony decisively, despite attempts at reasserting control and powerful counter-movements from Ulster Protestants. A new kind of hegemony was established in the South, with increased sectarian tension in the North in particular. This process was marked by intensive efforts at boundary-creation, identity formation and policing of difference in which religion, ethnicity and politics were tightly identified.

Dissent from these identities was often spoken in religious terms. The intense closure of Irish society in this period often meant that to stand outside the institutionalisation of cultural and religious division, one often had to literally stand outside Ireland:

> The Ireland of 1912 and 1913, however much Yeats may have wished
> to emphasize the universal implications of its folkloric traditions,
> was not, in reality, marked by much cosmopolitanism, spiritual or
> otherwise. (Brown 2001: 198)

While the first generation of Irish Theosophists sought to remain engaged with Irish politics and to develop suitable religious alternatives, the handful of Irish Buddhists known within Ireland at this time took a more quietist approach and do not seem to have sought such a public role. As with some second-generation Theosophists, most Irish Buddhists chose instead to 'go native' in Asia, allying with nationalist movements in Sri Lanka or Japan, resisting Christian missionary activity in Burma, or becoming Tibetan monks. Within Asia, the Buddhist Revival which they joined was itself a cultural nationalist response to colonialism, so that they encountered familiar processes in the new form of Buddhist modernism.[1]

Ethnicity, Family and Personal Marginality

The extraordinary closure of ethnic and religious identities in Ireland meant that to stand outside these was to stand outside 'normality' in very practical ways, and the first known Irish Buddhists were all marginal individuals. Thus this chapter discusses the eccentric Captain Charles Pfoundes practising fire rituals in Japan, the fictional *Kim* following a Tibetan lama in the Himalayas, the exiled Lafcadio Hearn defending 'old Japan', the adventurer John Bowles Daly running Buddhist schools in Ceylon, the ex-hobo U Dhammaloka[2] campaigning against missionaries across Asia, the eccentric Vivian Butler-Burke in Dublin, the spurious Tuesday Lobsang Rampa in Howth, the transsexual Lobzang Jivaka seeking transformation in a Ladakhi monastery, and the avant-garde writer Wei Wu Wei in Monaco. They were considerably more marginal than the Theosophists or contemporary Buddhists in other western states, who were often respected professionals.

Their marginalisation from the worlds they were born into was expressed in cross-racial marriages, transsexuality, new names and conscious action to tackle their own racism; in involvement with anti-colonial nationalisms and resistance to 'civilising' missionary activity. If race and gender stand out, this is because in Ireland as in Asia colonial power structures were organised through ethnicity and hence through family. 'Going native' as a problem teaches us something about the construction of the imperial service class in particular: what were Irish Buddhists marginal *from*?

Colonial officials as a class 'shared common adolescent experiences and some were connected by ties of blood or marriage.

1. Cox 2010a analyses early Irish Buddhists and sympathisers as solidarity activists.

2. U is a Burmese honorific, here meaning roughly "Venerable".

Scattered throughout the empire, contact was fostered by the *esprit de corps* of their chosen service' (cited in Nagai 2006: 76). Such conscious collective agency – to sustain an empire, to sustain Protestant Ascendancy or to challenge it from a Catholic position – relied on shared childhoods and professional socialisation; closely policed gender, sexual and family arrangements; and ethnic or racial closure.

In Ireland, marriage was virtually always within one's own religious denomination: outmarriage was understood as desertion, and routinely punished by disinheritance. Marriage outside one's caste (e.g. Charles Johnston's marriage to Blavatsky's niece) caused scandals which could preclude a successful career as civil servant, officer, academic or missionary.[3] Lafcadio Hearn's marriages – to a 'mixed-race' and later a Japanese woman – went even further.

Maurice Collis commented on his friend, the eminent Orientalist Gordon Luce,[4] who married the Burmese Ma Tee Tee:

> Today, and indeed in all other times except the short span of our rule in Asia, such a marriage is, and would have been considered a perfectly natural event … In marrying her, Luce was also well aware that he had erected a barrier between himself and the club population of Rangoon, which ranged from the Lieutenant-Governor, Sir Reginald Craddock, down to the latest joined assistant in the British timber firms. His wife could not risk entering the clubs, nor in general did their members invite her to their houses. Today this seems so absurd that the reader may refuse to credit it. But in 1920 it was sober fact. Luce was beyond the pale both of official and of mercantile society in Rangoon. (Collis 1953: 42–3).

Craddock, incidentally, was Irish (Crosbie 2012: 215). Family ties were crucial, as they remain in Ireland today, for sponsorship, mentoring and respectability. Comparing the biographies of Theosophists and Buddhists, Yeats or Eglinton could communicate with their fathers in particular: something which Hearn or Jivaka might have envied, but which also made it practically possible to pursue careers in a world of family and 'connections'.

---

3. His headmaster remarked 'He might have gone to the very top, but he made a fool of himself by marrying the niece of that charlatan Madame Blavatsky' (Cousins 2008: 187).

4. Brother of A.A. and uncle of J.V. Luce, both Fellows of TCD; J.V. reviewed Mansoor's *Story of Irish Orientalism* for TCD's *Hermathena* in 1945 (Lennon 2004: 192).

Family, gender and career were bound up in the production of this service-class 'respectability' (caste solidarity), in Ireland or India:[5] to 'go native' was to lose this, and to shame one's family at home if it became known. Collis again:

> It was about now that Sir Reginald Craddock told Luce to his face that he was a pro-Burman ... it was a very damaging term to have applied to you because it meant that you had for the Burmese a greater feeling of sympathy and fellowship than was sanctioned by British opinion at that date. To mix with them socially was alone enough to cause you to be called a pro-Burman ... The implication was that you were lowering British prestige; the Burmese would think less of us if we did not treat them as inferiors ... (1953: 44)

Such sanctions were not only informal. Writing in 1913, 'A veteran diplomat' noted that peers could now legally become Muslims or Buddhists:

> True, among the English officials of the civil service of India, [conversion to an Asian religion] is visited with dismissal, and would doubtless cost any officer of the army, the navy, or the diplomatic corps his commission. But this is merely a matter of discipline. (1913: no pagination).

All these constraints were if anything even tighter for the developing Catholic service class, and the only Catholic Buddhists identifiable before the late 1960s are of skilled working-class backgrounds.

Protestant Buddhists and Catholic Buddhists

All these relationships – class, profession, family and gender – were bound up with an ethnic identity inseparable from religion; were they processed differently? Rocha argues (2006: 7) that 'the adoption of Buddhism in Catholic countries, such as France and Italy, should be differentiated from its adoption in Protestant ones'. In fact France and Italy are better understood as pillarised societies (Lipset and Rokkan 1967), with centuries-long conflicts between Catholic, secular-liberal and socialist cultures. In Ireland, sectarianism shaped the reception of Buddhism in specific ways.

---

5. According to Dalrymple (2000), this ethnic closure developed in the later nineteenth century; in earlier periods one in three British men in India was married to an Indian. See also Benson 2010: 11.

The general western quarrel between Protestantism and Catholicism shaped images of Buddhism transmitted through competing circuits of knowledge. British researchers often identified a 'pure' Buddhism in ancient India, presenting the Buddha as a Luther-like figure rebelling against the priestcraft and hierarchies of Hinduism; Theravadin modernisers, in countries like Ceylon, welcomed this. Both perspectives involved constructing an image of Buddhism centred on self-reliance, with a founder of exemplary moral character and simple teachings (such as the *Dhammapada*) from the Pali Canon – a kind of 'New Testament' Buddhism. This never quite caught on for Tibet – hence the long-standing presentation of Tibetan Buddhism as a mixture of Buddhism and demon-worship, or alternatively as far more 'Catholic' than early Buddhism – or for Japan, where Japanese nationalism and the Kyoto school took a different turn.

These selective readings were geared to the concerns of European audiences. When Irish Catholics interested in Asian religion encountered this polemic and its imperial flavour, it hardly predisposed them in favour of Buddhism. As we have seen, Irish Catholic literature was neither as sympathetic to Buddhism, nor as informative, in this period.

Irish Protestants of the imperial service class had a number of good reasons for deserting the sinking ship of Ascendancy. The Catholic nationalist service class, by contrast, was in the process of consolidating its identity and developing hegemony, and I could not identify a single member who became Buddhist. The pressures, even lower down the scale, were intense: even Catholics working in solidarity with Indian nationalists preferred to draw political or economic, rather than religious, parallels (Lennon 2004). Of the Theosophists and Irish Hindus discussed in chapter four, only Annie Besant, Catholic Irish but in England, could overcome this.[6] Ireland contrasted with most of the rest of Catholic Europe even in 1848, when anti-clericalism and liberalism went hand in hand:

> there were very few Fenians, or other Irish revolutionaries, who abandoned their Catholic faith: it was too tightly bound up with their whole conception of what it meant to be Irish (McLeod 1997: 20–1)

6. Irish immigrants in Britain – particularly the poorest or most radical – often defected from the parish structures which formed the centre of immigrant life (McLeod 1997: 129).

Thus the few figures of Catholic background we can identify are plebeian rather than service class: Dhammaloka, Patrick Breslin, Mr Timoney and the 'whisky priest' discussed below. Indeed most 'Catholic Buddhists' were probably not of a class to record their experiences for posterity, but as we shall see writers familiar with the world of Irish soldiers in India present us with Indian-born Irish Buddhists as an unusual but not impossible situation. Dhammaloka shows us beachcombers turned Buddhist: no doubt some of these ex-soldiers, sailors and ex-policemen were also Irish. The difficulty of knowing more is shaped by class, and ownership of the means of intellectual production.

Buddhism and Gender

It was possible, in Britain, America or Asia, to be female and Buddhist (Madame Blavatsky, Marie Canavarro, Ida Russell, Alexandra David-Neel, Ruth Fuller Sasaki etc.) or Theosophist (Annie Besant, Anna Kingsford, Mabel Collins etc.) In Dublin, Dunlop's wife and Johnston's sisters ran the Sunshine Vegetarian Dining Rooms, while Sister Nivedita escaped from Dungannon to become a leading figure in Indian cultural nationalism.

By contrast, early Irish Buddhism seems somewhat short of women: we have the sympathiser Helen Waddell, some figures in the 1901 census, Dhammaloka's Irish-Australian sponsor Letitia Jephson and the 'Irish Gael' (below). This may be an artefact of our methods; perhaps the Irish membership of the Buddhist Societies and the Maha Bodhi Society was less exclusively masculine. More probably, the social costs of public conversion threatened women in particular ways; I return to this at the end of the chapter.

These various themes – ethnic closure, gender and family – come together in the remarkable story of 'An Irish Gael', whose 1928 'How I found Buddhism' begins thus:

> I was always an alien in my family and my race (I mean the European race) ...
>
>   Luckily ... I was born in a family where there had been two or three generations of mixed [Protestant-Catholic] marriages ...
>
>   I was never a Christian, and from my first years I fought contin-uously against all Christian teaching. My horrified family had never heard such views as I expressed. Only for the predominating Protestant element they would no doubt have looked on me as a "changeling" ... (Anon. 1928: 6)

This was an exceptionally tolerant (Irish-American) family for the later nineteenth century, which could live with mixed marriages, but had to be forced to abandon Christian socialisation:

> When I grew big enough to be sent to church with the rest I found an opportunity I had lacked before of attacking the foolishness and hypocrisy of Christian doctrine. As this was done in no calm spirit, it was finally decided that it would be better for my disposition not to send me to church at all. Another attempt to make me outwardly orthodox was tried some years later, but when it was found that I was visiting in turn all the nonconformist sects, and even the synagogues, Christian training was finally given up in despair. (1928: 6)

Even this highly determined young woman had a battle on her hands to step outside the bounds of respectability.

The Politics of Choice

Tweed (2000: 91) sees four background conditions to conversion: a personal crisis or the effects of a broader cultural crisis; the individual's inclination to seek and find a solution in religious community; the money, leisure and skills to pursue this; and a direct encounter with Buddhist beliefs and practices.

Ireland's two cultures were in different ways in crisis in this period, and Irish Buddhist lives were marked by the intersection of this with personal crisis. Furthermore, such crises were often understood in religious terms rather than socialist or psychological ones. It is less clear how useful the categories of resources and contact are, however.

The examples of plebeian Buddhists show that 'resources' are not always what they seem – a semi-skilled working-class Catholic could effectively become a celebrity preacher in Burma. In fact our identifications of converts are probably shaped by those who had the skill, leisure or wealth to *publish*.

We have also seen that both resources and contact had been present for many Irish people in the eighteenth and early nineteenth century without (as far as we know) any conversions; while apparently similar circumstances (for Hugh Waddell, Maurice Collis or Sister Nivedita) could lead in very different directions: to continued Christian missionary activity, to secular nationalism or to Hinduism.

It is important, then, not to see conversion simply as *result*, but also as (not necessarily conscious) *choice and strategy*: a choice of where to stand in a world where both empire and religion were massively contested facts, and a strategy of how to work with others and for what. Chapters three and four thus stand alongside this discussion of those who did choose Buddhism, as a way of illuminating the politics of remaining within imperial Protestantism and Catholic nationalism as well as 'conversion' to Theosophy or Buddhism.

Buddhism, Empires and Memory

This has a bearing on present debates. If we use the memory of the past to fight out the battles of the present, two of the latter are particularly important, and rely on the myth of the absence of choice in the past. Firstly, in recent decades, the Republic has seen welcome moves in many areas away from the state nationalism and Catholic hegemony of earlier periods. Together with this has come a strange rehabilitation of the British Empire – and the main mode of Irish involvement, military service. This is driven by a mixture of family pride in military ancestors and an increasing identification with empire rather than insurgency as Ireland becomes involved with 'EU foreign policy' and a transit base for the US military.[7]

One *reductio ad absurdum* is the proposition implicit in the National Museum's new permanent exhibition 'Soldiers and Chiefs', that any Irishman who ever put on a uniform – no matter whose and why – should be equally celebrated (literally, pro-Franco volunteers and the International Brigades side by side). So too is the increasing 'celebration' of the First World War, where Irish involvement is now presented as a moral good – rather than, as socialists, anti-imperialists and pacifists said at the time and most people agreed afterwards, a pointless bloodbath in the service of imperial ambition.

Thus, for example, Canny (2004: xv) writes of an Irish policeman in Burma who 'gave loyal service in return and always displayed gratitude for the livelihood and social uplift with which [the Empire] had provided him'. As with many such discussions, this is framed purely in terms of whether Irish imperial servants were being disloyal to 'Ireland'; we are told that 'if people are to be judged by moral standards, it must be by those they themselves cherished rather than by those of the present generation'.

---

7. Irish bodies in British uniforms still sometimes return from Afghanistan and Iraq.

But the history of Irish Buddhists – and indeed Theosophists, Hindus or secular nationalists who engaged in anti-colonial solidarity – tells us something else. Firstly, those moral standards (and their implications) were *contested*, at the time. Many people found the brutality of counter-insurgency and imperial policing, the exploitation and impoverishment of whole continents, the destruction of indigenous culture, the inherent racism of empire and the self-enrichment of many colonialists objectionable *in itself* (not simply in relation to 'Ireland') and on moral grounds which were thoroughly of their time. Secondly, a smaller number of courageous individuals faced the loss of career, social ostracism, public mockery and physical repression entailed in acting *against empire*. It is *these* moral choices which can quite legitimately be evaluated in terms of what they tell us about the people who made them, and the effects of different choices.

Secondly, a similar point can be made about the defence (usually by different people) of past collusion and collaboration in the religious power, carceral complex and licence to abuse which marked the Republic in particular for several decades. We are told variously that nobody knew any better, that it was a different time, and that it is not up to us to judge the past (even when the survivors are still alive and struggling for justice).

Yet the history of dissent shows that *not* everyone was content to follow their tribe in defence of Protestant Ascendancy or developing Catholic hegemony. Ordinary Irish people were thoroughly aware of the religious diversity of the world, and some (not many) chose identifications other than unquestioning support for their own elites. Resistance – including that of atheists and liberals, those who helped escapers from industrial schools or who intervened to protect children against abusers – was limited; but it was real, and gives the lie to attempts to avoid the question of historical complicity and present-day responsibility.

There can be no agreement on how to evaluate actions in the past, any more than there was at the time; but it is disingenuous to claim past consensus on these matters. Not everyone accepted the logic of empire abroad or religious power at home. Nor were those who resisted uniquely privileged; although we can certainly say that they were brave, not least in facing down the attacks from those who accepted the logics of power.

We also have to consider the *consequences of choices* – of imperial conquest and repression abroad, of volunteering for the First World War (in Ireland, there was no conscription), of collusion in the new and more oppressive religious domination from which the present-day Republic is still trying to extricate itself – or of involvement with the Buddhist Revival, to support Asian nationalisms on a secular basis, to resist imperialism and racism. These are complex issues (Sri Lankan or Japanese religious nationalism are no more desirable than British or Irish), but it is meaningless to assert that these choices did not have consequences in the outer world as well (as Buddhist moral theory has it) as on the individuals making them.

Maurice Collis' comment on Gordon Luce's marriage to a Burmese woman in a racist society is perhaps as good a summary as any of the longer term:

> In point of fact, Luce was one of the sanest men in Burma. What he nourished and advanced, has prospered; what his detractors upheld has withered away. (1953: 44)

If this cannot (yet) be said of empire and militarism, it can hopefully also be said of attempts to secure the religious domination of society. Those of us who live in later years have good cause to be thankful to those who resisted sectarian closure at its height, in the period covered in this chapter.

Early Irish Buddhists:
Extraordinary Choices, Extraordinary Lives

This chapter discusses the *known* early Irish Buddhists and the problem of Buddhism's 'hidden histories'. The literate and articulate figures identified here are almost exclusively those who had access to the published word and nothing to lose by writing about their experiences. Others may have lacked control of the means of intellectual production, or were in situations which made it impossible to publicise their actions for career, social or family reasons; we can occasionally give names, but not much more, to such individuals.

Their fractured relationship to family and Ireland played itself out not only psychologically but also socially (in terms of marriage and career) and politically; this often shows up in difficult personalities, shaped by their own suffering, and precarious financial situations. Perhaps unsurprisingly, their lives and writings show a tension between grand theories which draw on and mimic the imperial 'bird's-eye view', and the critique of imperial or religious hegemony involved in their new personal and political choices: like Vivian Butler-Burke, they became at once 'an alien in my family and my race'.

At the same time, these were extraordinary human beings, capable of making huge changes in their lives and successfully becoming members of another and radically different culture in positions (such as monkhood) of which much was expected. The derision of missionaries, English-speaking journalists and colonial officials was often balanced by marks of high esteem on the part of Asians who judged them as Buddhists and as allies. Despite lives on the edge, their intellectual, political and religious efforts speak for themselves.

I discuss these early Irish Buddhists in logical order, giving their Buddhist names when relevant and the best dates available for the period in which they identified, or strongly sympathised, with Buddhism. I start with census statistics between 1871 and 1911 and the few Buddhists who can be identified in Ireland, notably Robert Gibson. Moving to Irish Buddhists in Asia, I discuss Charles Pfoundes (1860s–1911) in Japan and Europe; J. Bowles Daly in Ceylon (1889 to c. 95); and Lafcadio Hearn, again in Japan (1890–1904). More nebulously, I use Kipling's *Kim* (1900–1) to explore the phenomenon of 'going native' and the remarkable pan-Asian figure of U Dhammaloka (1890s to c.1913), the most articulate plebeian Buddhist of his age.

Between 1914 and the 1950s, it is very hard to identify Irish Buddhists, although I can offer a handful of glimpses and some names. The early years conclude with three dramatic life-stories: 'Tuesday Lobsang Rampa' in Howth (1958–60s); 'Wei Wu Wei' in Monte Carlo (1958–86); and Lobzang Jivaka (1950s–62) in India and Ladakh. This brings us up to the late 1960s and early 1970s, when Buddhists start to become visible in Ireland more systematically (chapter six).

Some of these figures, such as Hearn, are well covered in existing literature, and my only interest here is in discussing them as Irish Buddhists. Others, such as Captain Pfoundes, have hardly been mentioned since their death; here I necessarily try to establish more basic facts. My main concern here is firstly to establish a picture of who these early Irish Buddhists were, and secondly to see what their lives tell us about Buddhism and Ireland in this period, when conversion had begun to be possible but only at the margins of what remained a very hostile context.

Who Is a Buddhist?

This question is a bit more complicated than we might think for this period, because of the actual meanings of 'Buddhist' in both western and eastern cultures at the time. Thus Tweed (2000), for example, treats Hearn as sympathiser rather than Buddhist, on the reasonable grounds that he said that he could not 'believe in' Buddhism. However, Hearn's position – a philosophical sympathy with what he understood of Buddhist doctrine – is not distinguishable *other than by context* from that of 'Wei Wu Wei', who at times did speak of himself as Buddhist.

The difference, of course, is that Wei Wu Wei thought in a European, patrician context within which 'being a Buddhist' was a philosophical position and a way of life, with no particular institutional implications or religious practice. It was only as a long-time Asian resident that Hearn, with his fascination for 'old Japan', could identify Buddhism as a kind of practice and devotion which he was unable to share fully.

Conversely, westerners in Asia such as the Dublin-educated beachcomber 'John' Askins were prone to doubt the meaningfulness of mere Buddhist ordination: 'whenever one of the boys went broke, it was get converted' (Franck 1910: 272–3). However, it was common for Asians to get ordained in order to get fed or escape a life crisis (poverty, losing a political struggle, scandal etc) – even if the sangha was sometimes purged of such individuals, or rules designed to prevent their ordination. These were established practices, and it is no surprise that westerners followed them.[8] In other cases again, such as an unnamed Austrian in Siamese government service, ordination may have been a condition of employment (Turner et al., 2010: 128).

'Who is a Buddhist?' is in some ways an unhelpful, if unavoidable, question. This chapter maps the first stages of the process where Irish people moved from knowledge, interest and sympathy with Buddhism to more easily defined positions, and so the different possible situations are of interest in themselves.

8. It was of course also common to accept an *Anglican* living without being particularly devout.

While the conclusion briefly discusses these various individuals from a normative Buddhist point of view, it should be said that the distinction 'Buddhist/not Buddhist' is not as central to Buddhism as it is to (for example) some forms of Abrahamic religion; in most schools it is not of salvific significance. Ethics, meditation, wisdom and enlightenment are rather more significant; and (as the Pali canon makes clear) it is problematic to judge these in others.

Census Statistics in Ireland (1871, 1881, 1891, 1911)[9]

The *Irish Times* (Dec. 3 1875) recorded the religious results of the 1871 census thus:

> When we come to count "single persons", we are in a labyrinth of varieties. There is an Idimite; a Reformer (a woman;) a "disciple of natural religion", and another of "Positivism, or the religion of humanity;" a philanthropist; a saint of no sect; a protestor against all priestcraft; a latitudinarian; a socialist; a Sabbatarian; a Buddhist; a Mussulman; a true Moslem; a Confucian; a Pagan.[10]

There had been no Buddhists in the 1861 census (Brian Gurrin, pers. comm.) It is just possible that this identification was a joke (but implausible at this early date, before *The Light of Asia* or *Esoteric Buddhism*).[11] They are more likely to have been in some more 'authentic' way Buddhist, perhaps even rare visitors or residents from Buddhist Asia.[12]

More probably, in this pre-Theosophical period, we are talking about one of Tweed's rationalists, dependent on the academic

9. I am greatly indebted to Brian Gurrin, Oliver Scharbrodt and Brian Bocking for the material used in this section. See Macourt 2011, 2012 and Scharbrodt 2012 for useful discussions of the problems of census data for small religions in Ireland.

10. The same article appears in the *Nation* for Sept. 4 (p. 13), showing that a sneer could be shared by Catholics and Protestants.

11. Despite the Anglican *Irish Times'* deliberately misleading presentation, the small numbers of people in 'all other denominations' come across as intensely serious, with detailed self-identifications or heart-felt confessions of faith. Religion, in this sectarian Ireland, was no laughing matter: as few as 1,044 people failed to specify their religion. According to the census authors, most were the children of Anabaptist groups.

12. There were seventy-three people born in Asia, including the near and middle East, in this census, including twenty-one schoolchildren, eleven seamen, three domestics and two soldiers. It is unlikely that any were Asian Buddhists, before the final conquest of Burma and just after the Meiji Restoration; though as in 1911 a Sri Lankan domestic servant is not impossible. Oliver Scharbrodt (2012) found small numbers of Indian Muslim and Hindu servants in the pre-independence censuses.

transmission of texts,[13] and probably associated with TCD (the entry is for a male in Co. Dublin). Oriental Studies were by now well established with substantial library holdings, but Trinity was still strongly confessional, and the Blasphemy Act was still in use.

From 1871 onwards, census totals list a consistent handful of Buddhists: a Dublin (city) male and a male in Co. Cork in 1881, both vanished by 1891 when there was a male in Ulster. The 1901 census shows a female Buddhist in Co. Dublin, a male 'Hindoo Buddhist' in Munster[14] and a male Buddhist in Galway. By 1911, there was a male in Co. Cork and five males in Dublin (not in the provincial totals). Subsequent (Free State) censuses do not contain detailed breakdowns of 'other religions' until 1991, when the statistical trail restarts.[15]

Nevertheless some names can now be put to these anonymous individuals.[16] Firstly, J. Bowles Daly (see below) *may* have been Dublin City's male Buddhist of 1881.[17] The 1901 male Buddhist in Galway was Joseph McCausland, a 30-year-old medical student from Donegal, then living at 31 Lenaboy in the south city. Medical students were rather more alternative at this time:[18] two of the five Dublin city Buddhists of 1911 (Ralph Mecredy and Francis Crosslee, both 22) were also medical students. Ralph Mecredy's father, also R.J., had been editor of *Cycling*, developing bicycle polo and winning races in 1891 to demonstrate the superiority of pneumatic tyres. His mother was the first Irishwoman to take part in a car race.[19] He himself survived the sinking of the *Lusitania* and went on to become a school medical officer in New Zealand.[20]

13. While *japonisme* was starting to become available via the Parisian avant-garde, the highpoint of this interest only occurs in the 1880s (Harris 2002: 366–8), and there were no self-consciously Buddhist artists this early.

14. This formulation may indicate another person responding for the whole household.

15. All identifications other than Catholic, Anglican, Presbyterian and Methodist were rare: the 1871 census only had 52,000 people in 'all other denominations', the vast majority Christian sects. There were only 285 Jews at this point and seven Swedenborgians along with these solitary figures.

16. Thanks to Oliver Scharbrodt for his work on household returns.

17. The household returns for 1871–1891 have unfortunately been destroyed.

18. However http://litndeb.nuigalway.ie/home-litndeb/previous-auditors lists McCausland, then auditor of the Literary and Debating Society, as studying arts.

19. *Otago Witness*, 7 July 1909: 59.

20. http://www.rmslusitania.info/pages/second_cabin/mecredy_rjr.html; *Evening Post*, Rorahi CIX, Putanga 143, 20, Pipiri 1925: 13.

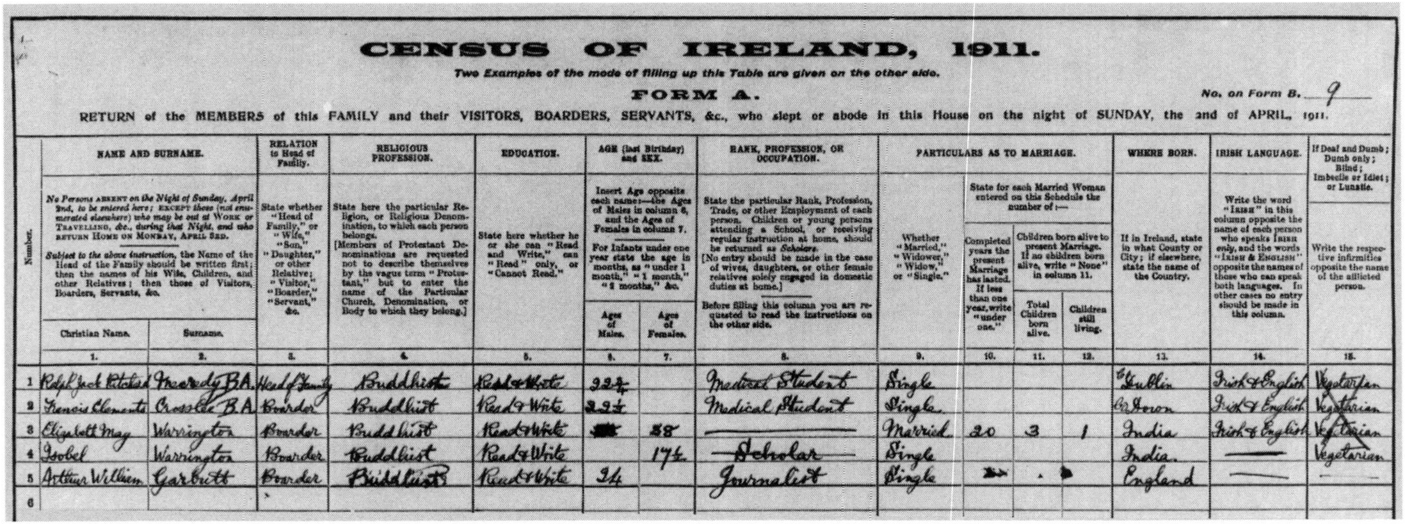

Fig. 5.1 Census record for the Dublin Buddhist household of 1911. Source: Central Statistics Office.

Mecredy and Crosslee's other Buddhist housemates, at 9 Gilford Road, were Elizabeth and Isobel Warrington (38 and 17), and Arthur Garbutt (24). Mrs Warrington, born in India, was probably the wife of Albert, head of the American Theosophical Society; in 1932 she would host the Adyar Theosophical convention.[21] Presumably Isobel (listed as 'scholar' and born in India) was her daughter. Arthur Garbutt continued as a journalist,[22] demobbed as a lieutenant in 1920 and appeared with his wife at a TCD music graduates' event in 1928.[23]

The 1911 male in Co. Cork was Narmo Kollagaran, a 28-year-old Colombo-born domestic servant living at 1, Ballyhooly Town. He was probably the servant of then-Captain William Sykes (listed as 'Church of India'), who along with a Lieutenant and a stock-jobber (called Norah) were visiting the homeowner, Herbert Beddington (who in 1906 was auditor of the London English Jew's College). What they were all doing together in Ballyhooly is a good Edwardian mystery.

Together with other known Buddhists in Ireland – Bowles Daly and Robert Gibson, *Light of Dharma* subscriber Richard Laffere, Maha Bodhi Society representative Ramsay Colles and Buddhist Society council member Oswald Reeves – these details give us a fleeting but plausible picture of the earliest Buddhists in Ireland (1881–1917): an enamellist, three writers, three medical students, two Indian-born white Theosophists, a Sinhala servant, a civil engineer and a butter judge. All the Irish-born figures seem to have Protestant backgrounds and probably a university education, mobile and inquisitive lives.

Incidentally, this evidence – where census identification precedes *public* self-identification by up to two decades – suggests that Buddhist Studies internationally could usefully push its census researches back into the nineteenth century as a cross-check for the more usual literary and organisational sources.[24]

A Rural Activist in Limerick (Robert Gibson, 1880s–1914)

The list of individuals can usefully start with Robert Gibson, perhaps the only Irish-born person to openly call himself Buddhist in Ireland

---

21. *World Theosophy Magazine*, Jun 1932–Dec. 1933.
22. See http://www.scoop-database.com/list/atoz_journalist/g
23. *Musical Times*, Sept 1 1928: 837.
24. Conversely, Gibson, Colles and Lafferre do not appear in the census.

in the hundred and one years between the first census returns of 1871 and D.A. Marks in 1972. All other known Buddhists filled census returns, published a century later, or quietly subscribed to societies or magazines based elsewhere. Eagleton (1995: 304) mentions 'The Limerick Cooperator W.L. Stokes, Buddhist and butter merchant, devouring *The Light of Asia* and the *Grocer's Gazette* with equal relish'. Eagleton's source R.A. Anderson, however, was referring to Robert Gibson, around 1889:

> A co-operative creamery had been started at Dromcollogher, in the west of County Limerick, by Messrs. W.L. Stokes, the Co-operative Wholesale Society representative in Limerick, and Robert Gibson, a bit of a character, primarily a butter merchant, but very good in his second character, as an esoteric Buddhist. He read the *Grocers' Review*, the *Grocers' Gazette* and the *Light of Asia* impartially. (Anderson 1935: 6–7)

Dromcollogher was the first of many co-operative creameries in Ireland and is sometimes cited as the birthplace of the movement. The story goes back to an anecdote in Digby's biography of co-operative leader Horace Plunkett:

> [Gibson] called himself an esoteric Buddhist, and while staying at Kilcooley was asked by Mrs. Ponsonby if he wanted anything to read. "Madam", he replied, "I have the *Grocers' Gazette* and the *Light of Asia*. What more can man want? But I thank you." (1949: 56).

Gibson was based in a 'strange and quaint' bungalow in Limerick (Young 1945: 26); a visitor noted 'He is not a political boss. He is just a person who seems to be always in the centre of things: hence "The Boss" or "Chief".' (1945: 28). It was perhaps this kind of personality which enabled him to call himself a Buddhist openly.

Russell (1978: 145) describes him as 'a Limerick grocer and spiritualist who actively promoted agricultural co-operation. His irascible though well-intentioned letters to the *[Irish] Homestead* afforded AE much entertainment when he answered them in his "Notes of the Week".' Similarly, the Ontario Minister of Agriculture and Food described him as 'a writer of the most violent letters I have ever seen in public print. I had the curiosity to meet him, and I never was so agreeably disappointed in my life. He was very genial and hospitable ...' (Ontario Dept. of Agriculture and Food 1907: 86).

The energetic Gibson had organised a stop of Col. Olcott's 1889 tour (Olcott 2003: 202) and hosted Olcott at his home; he also hosted Annie Besant's lectures (Young 1945: 26). As this suggests, the Protestant-born Gibson (Yeates 2000: 381) had a spiritualist background: the Society for Psychical Research had published a letter in 1884 (Gurney et al., 1886: 364). We do not know what his 'esoteric Buddhism' consisted of: as with his contemporaries, it could mean anything from an elegant way to say 'Theosophist' through to asking Olcott to give him the refuges and precepts.[25]

Gibson was also a temperance activist (Bolger 1977: 66 fn 28) and in later life manufactured 'Gibson's Universal Antiseptic Ointment', supposed to cure eczema, ringworm and other diseases:

> He daily treated without fee at his house in Limerick numbers of poor people.[26]

Gibson made public speeches for Home Rule candidates in 1910 (Gwynn 1911: 101); a 'Mrs Robert Gibson', whether his second wife or daughter-in-law,[27] was active with the Irish Women's Franchise League[28] and the Munster Women's Freedom League in 1913 (Urquhart 2000: 18). Professionally, Gibson was

> famous as a judge of butter, and whose knowledge of dairying in general was unlimited. A prolific writer and fearless critic, it has been stated that given a score or more of samples of butter, and no matter how these were shuffled, he could always place them in their proper order! (Murray 1935: 197)

Leaving aside such supramundane powers, Gibson – cooperative agitator, nationalist, suffragist ally, spiritualist, alternative healer, geologist[29] and Buddhist – deserves not to be forgotten. By happy coincidence, his Dromcollogher today hosts an organic farming college, thoroughly in keeping with this agreeable local eccentric.

---

25. Although he hosted Besant as well as Olcott, I am inclined not to read Gibson as pure Theosophist – both because he does not appear widely in their journals and because he was of an older generation, spiritualist before he became an 'esoteric Buddhist'.

26. The Pharmaceutical Journal and Pharmacist, vol. 94 (1915): 875.

27. He told a spiritualist tale regarding his wife 'since deceased' in 1884 (Gurney et al., 1886: 364).

28. http://www.limerickcity.ie/media/Media,4066,en.pdf

29. *Irish Naturalist*, vol. 2 (1893): 118.

An Orientalist in Japan (Captain Charles Pfoundes/Omoie Tetszunotszuke[30] c.1860s–1907)[31]

Mr. C. Pfoundes, the author of the article "Religion in Japan," lectured in the United States, 1876–1877, at Bowdoin, Yale, Boston Art Club, etc., on Japanese affairs, and in London and Provinces 1879 et seq.; he was elected Fellow of the following and other Societies: Royal Geographical Society, Royal Asiatic Society, Royal Society of Literature, Royal Historical Society, Royal Colonial Institute, and member of Anthropological Society, Society of Arts, Society of Economy and Fine Arts; and also by right of his service as a naval officer to the Royal United Service Institute. Since his arrival in Japan he has been initiated by special ceremony, the first foreigner thus admitted, to the Ten-dai, the Jo-do, and the Shingon sects, and to the esoteric arena of the latter, and authorised to wear the insignia of a Buddhist preacher. He also has been presented with medals by a number of Japanese Buddhist societies.[32]

The flamboyant figure of Captain Pfoundes is distorted by self-mythologising, although the reality seems more than lively enough for one life (Bocking 2013). Born in 1840, he claimed to have taken part in the second opium war against China, 1856–60 (Macmillan 1904: 501–2) and to have arrived in Japan in the 1860s (Thelle 1987: 110). He published a collection of his articles for the *Japan [Weekly] Mail* in 1875, claiming to have been more than a decade in Japan at that point (Pfoundes 1875: iii). This fits with the 1863 date of arrival he gave elsewhere[33] and his evident command of Japanese by 1870.[34]

His name, however, as appears from missing persons correspondence regarding his brother,[35] was originally Pounds. Reinvention ran in the family: his father, James Baker Pounds of Wexford, was an Anglican, trained in medicine, who had started out as a schoolmaster in Ireland (Quane 1950: 52 and House of Commons 1836: 27)

30. Pfoundes uses this name in Theosophical contexts; it seems (*Far East* 1/11 [1908: p. 507]) that Adachi Kinnosuke gave him this name as a translation ('heavy iron') of Pounds.

31. I am particularly indebted to Brian Bocking, Yoshinaga Shin'ichi and Gaynor Sekimori for comments and assistance with this section. See Bocking (2012, 2013).

32. *Open Court*, vol. IX/4 no. 387 (Jan 24 1895): 4374.

33. *Far East*, vol. 2 1897: pagination unclear.

34. The advertising material for his *Folk-lore of old Japan* (1880) states that he had 'lived the native life amongst the intelligent better class in that country', and this is borne out by the detailed observation of daily life, including home and family life, in Pfoundes 1875.

35. http://helendoxfordharris.com.au/historical-indexes/index-to-missing-people

before moving to Australia, first as a trader in mining machinery, subsequently as a prison MO and eventually coroner. His mother, Caroline Pounds née Elam, was a noted botanical watercolourist.

In the missing persons correspondence Pfoundes claims to have been commanding officer of HMCS *Victoria*, Victoria's first military ship (in fact he seems to have been a midshipman: Brian Bocking pers. comm.) He subsequently seems to have served in the Siamese navy.[36]

Pfoundes also shared the family habit of unstable employment; around 1869 he was proposing to start a Japanese-language newspaper, while in 1870 he was Superintendent Captain for the Yubin Jokisen Kaisha steamship company,[37] responsible for appointing the (white) captains and officers and general advisor and translator. One such officer recalled, discreditably:

> I was told that very few applications for employment would receive consideration unless the applicant offered to recompense Captain Pfoundes, if employed, and I found this to be the fact later on. (Mahlmann 1918: 122–3).

In 1871, Pfoundes abandoned this to guide Mutsu Munemitsu, already being groomed for his later career, around Europe (the party also included the later statesman Aoki Shuzo, then studying in Berlin). The two had letters from the British plenipotentiary in Japan and the Austro-Hungarian consul and were introduced to the Pope (von Siebold 1984: 166–75). Pfoundes was already fluent in Japanese at this point.[38]

By the later 1870s, he was making a career as an Orientalist with the 1875 collection of newspaper articles, a catalogue of Japanese art (which he was auctioning) and collections of folktales. In 1876–7 he lectured on Buddhism in the US but returned to Japan briefly before moving to England,[39] where he married Rosa Hill; the couple frequented scholarly and theosophical meetings.

36. 'The French colonies in China', *Open Court*, 3 (1903): 175–6. Here he claims to have commanded 'The Flying Fish' in Chinese waters in the early 1860s.

37. Thanks to Brian Bocking and Gaynor Sekimori for corrections here. Mahlmann implies a date around 1872 but repeatedly gets details wrong; *Acta Sieboldiana* gives 1870 for this employment, and he was in Vienna by 1871.

38. The two left with minor bills unpaid.

39. Thelle (1987: 110) gives slightly different dates, but the first-hand information cited at the head of this section is probably correct.

Until 1890 or so Pfoundes lectured on Japan at art schools in England[40] and addressed the South Place Ethical Society in the late 1880s (Pfoundes 1890a). Having separated from his wife, Pfoundes lived in Fellowship House in London around this period. This community was associated with the Fellowship of the New Life (led by Havelock Ellis' later consort Edith Lees, other inhabitants included the young Ramsay Macdonald and Agnes Henry, an anarchist friend of Malatesta [Nottingham 1999: 51–2]). The Fellowship had inspired the Sunshine vegetarian restaurant in Dublin; during this same period Pfoundes co-wrote a book on reincarnation with Charles Johnston (chapter four). Ellis described him as 'elderly, a Quixotic figure of a man, who knew and loved Japan, and went about lecturing on that subject, apparently his sole interest' (1967: 245).

According to Toshio Akai (2007: 58), Pfoundes was held in high respect by Japanese Buddhists by this point, and was appointed London correspondent of the (Japanese) Buddhist Propagation Society (BPS) around 1890.[41] This published literature for distribution at the 1893 World Parliament of Religions in Chicago (Mayeda 1893); Pfoundes was a member of the Parliament's advisory council (Barrows 1893: 45). Pfoundes also wrote several articles for the Japanese Buddhist publication *Kaigai Bukkyo Jijo* warning against Theosophy.

Japanese Buddhists were concerned by the rise of Christian missionary activity in this period, and it seems that Pfoundes returned to Japan to work for the BPS: he

> accepted the mission of going out to preach against Christianity in the principal centers of the country, sowing doubt and indifference. (Van Hecken 1963: 46)

Thelle (1987: 110) similarly describes him as giving 'many meetings [in which] he appealed to the national sentiment and attacked Christian missionaries for slighting Buddhism and despising Japan as a barbarian country'. A collection of these lectures was published in 1893 as *Bukkyō enzetsushū*.

---

40. *The Artist*, 1881: 377.

41. Founded as the Society for Communication with Western Buddhists in 1887 (Moriya 2005: 285). Pfoundes lectured on its behalf in London (*Light*, vol. 10 (1890): 136, 184) and published various pieces in its journal in 1889–90 (Akai 2007: 59ff). See Bocking, Cox and Yoshinaga 2013.

By 1898–9, Pfoundes was attempting to become a Japanese citizen (Ruxton 2008: 121); at this point the *Literary world* noted that he was

> exercising his various gifts as a lecturer and writer, a journalist and correspondent, in both the Japanese and English languages.[42]

As with other early Irish Buddhists, Pfoundes remains available to posterity because of this professional command of the means of intellectual production. Gentlemen scholars, such as the British Japanologist, Sir Ernest Satow, looked down on him, writing in 1879:

> I have seen notices of Mr Pfoundes or Pounds' Nippon Institute, and thought it too ambitious altogether. No communications have reached us from it, and I do not expect that any will. You really ought not to give it your countenance. The man is a charlatan and knows nothing. He wrote a Budget of Japanese Notes which were utterly valueless. Aston was asked to join it, but of course refused. I was surprised to see the names of so many people quoted in connection with the affair. (Ruxton 2008: 127).

Other scholars did not agree:[43] Pfoundes was a fellow or committee member in the most surprising learned societies, and was widely published in journals and other outlets covering the whole gamut from anthropology via family welfare and merchant shipping to spiritualism and Buddhism. Between 1878 and 1905 he gave papers and wrote on topics such as 'Oriental art – its use and abuse',[44] 'Notes on the history of Eastern adventure, exploration, and discovery, and foreign intercourse with Japan' (Pfoundes 1882), 'On some rites and customs of old Japan' (Pfoundes 1883), 'Divyatchakchus: the "infinite perception" of Japanese esotericism' (Pfoundes 1888), 'Japanese spiritualism' (Pfoundes 1890b) and so on. Endlessly prolific, he seems to have been good on facts if perhaps short on analysis.

In 1903, he was planning an 'Orientalists' International Union' from Kobe, following the 1902 Oriental Congress in Hanoi, which made a field trip to a pagoda

> preceded by the flag of the Irish Buddhist, which represented rays of light proceeding from the mystic svastica in the centre (1904: 501–2).

---

42. 1898: 232.

43. Bocking 2012 also defends the quality of *Fuso mimi-bukuro*.

44. Mentioned in *Transactions of the National Association for the Promotion of Social Science* (1883: 633).

Sometime after 1905, Pfoundes may have returned to London where among other things he curated a museum exhibition of Japanese temple pictures.[45] He died in Kobe in 1907.[46]

Where does all this leave Pfoundes *as Buddhist?* One of his key claims to expertise was that he had studied for 'nearly 9 years' in a Buddhist monastery or monasteries (Blavatsky 2003: 286; Lillie 1981: 102),[47] and hence had

> been initiated into many of the inner mysteries of that religion unknown to scholars who studied the subject from the outside.[48]

He claimed to have been ordained in Jodo Shinshu (which ran the BPS) as well as in the Tendai and Shingon branches of Shugendo, within which he claimed precedence

> next after the chief, as being both an *acharya* and an *uphadaya* (i.e. preceptor, etc.) and a member of the Arcand (Pfoundes 1905: 311).[49]

At the 1904 Hanoi Oriental Congress he displayed 'various vestments, scarfs, and rosaries that he had received as marks of his position in the hierarchy of Buddhist freemasonry'.[50] A contemporary photograph in *East of Asia* displays his full regalia, which Gaynor Sekimori comments consists of

> a medley of religious garb and paraphernalia: a Zen kesa, with two yuigesa: the yuigesa of the Sanboin (Shingon, Daigoji) lineage under that of the one probably from Shogoin (which was at that time under Miidera …) He seems to have a Zen prayer mat draped over his left arm (pers. comm.)

This kind of display (which Sekimori notes makes him look more like a collector of religious souvenirs) was of course characteristic of esoteric Buddhists in Tweed's (2000) sense, and this is often how

45. *The Times,* May 23 1911: 7.

46. *Buddhist Review,* vol. 3–4 (1911): 239.

47. As this reference suggests, he had once been a member of Blavatsky's Theosophical lodge but fell out with the Society (presumably after 1888 when he was still publishing in Theosophical contexts), after which he worked to challenge Theosophical interpretations of Buddhism and encourage Japanese suspicion of Theosophy (Akai 2007: 58, Yoshinaga 2007: 87).

48. *Times of India,* Jan 19 1903: 6.

49. Gaynor Sekimori notes that his statement that he held the 'sceptre of the chief of the order' probably means that he was acting as jisha (attendant) rather than being next in precedence (pers. comm.)

50. *Times of India,* Jan 19 1903: 6.

CAPTAIN PFOUNDES.

Fig. 5.2 Captain Charles Pfoundes (Pounds) in 1905. Thanks to Brian Bocking.

he presents himself. However, he also framed these explorations in a very modernist tone (here addressing the rationalist South Place Society):

> Buddhism teaches that mankind should work out each for themselves their own salvation, and rectify the ills caused by fellow-mortals by reasonable human effort …
>
> To those who seek a personal salvation, by merit or otherwise, this is not altogether denied; but to those who attain to the higher ideals something far higher, much less selfish, more noble, is offered.

Similarly, writing to Paul Carus' *Open Court:*

> It must be understood that religion is something more than donations
> to temples, attendance at service, employing bonzes at home,
> giving to them money and clothes, or entertaining them. Not mere
> prostration before the altar and shrine, the repetition of invocations,
> nor the "telling" of beads over and over, but something more than
> this is true religion, true Buddhism. "Ceasing to do evil, striving to
> do good, being mindful of our fellow human beings, loving kindness
> to all creatures, remembering the four truths, observing the five great
> precepts, not to violate the prohibitions, to walk in the eightfold path,"
> — in these alone consists true Buddhism (Pfoundes 1895c: 4597)

His list of 'practical lessons' from Japanese religion included:

> Toleration ... Unprejudiced, dispassionate inquiry into all things
> physical and psychological ... Sturdy independence of thought ...
> Refraining from forcing dogmatic opinion unwelcome ... Refusal to
> believe in much that is forced upon us by a professional, mercenary
> religious class ... (Pfoundes 1890a: 104, 107)

As this tone suggests, he shared with other Irish Buddhists abroad a strong opposition to Christian missionary activity.

In a figure like Pfoundes, we can see claims to personal experience, scholarship and Buddhism overlap in ways that are perhaps more characteristic of the present day than of the late nineteenth century. If his claim to have spent the better part of a decade in Buddhist monasteries and to hold formal rank in a Buddhist order can be shown to hold water, he would also be one of the earliest known *ordained* western Buddhists (Turner et al., 2010).

The claim is a strong, and unlikely one: it would have been remarkable for a westerner to have been ordained in Shugendo in this period (which saw the imperial separation of Buddhism and Shinto in 1868 and the banning of independent Shugendo in 1872), and the requirements for becoming recognised as an acharya are substantial. However, he does seem to have had inside information and to see Shugendo as its own intellectuals then saw it.[51]

Visiting Shugendo monasteries and writing for learned journals, spiritualist publications and popular magazines, Pfoundes is at one end of a chain of knowledge transmission about Buddhism which reached people like Robert Gibson in his Limerick activities – and

51. I am indebted to Gaynor Sekimori for the information in this paragraph.

one which is immediately recognisable 130 years later. Other kinds of relationship were also possible, however.

An Adventurer in Ceylon (John Bowles Daly, 1889 to c.95)

John Bowles Daly's life parallels Pfoundes' in some ways; unusually for the figures discussed here, they knew each other in 1889, when Daly was Honorable Secretary of a spiritualist society in King's Cross, London and Pfoundes chaired meetings at one based at Notting Hill Gate.[52] When Pfoundes failed to give an advertised talk to Daly's society, the latter improvised 'an interesting sketch of Buddhism'.[53]

Like Gibson, the two were old enough to start as spiritualists rather than Theosophists. Both started as professionals but later experienced fractured work lives. Orientalists as well as Buddhist Revival organisers, they engaged with Buddhism from afar and on the spot.

Born c. 1845,[54] educated in TCD[55] and with a doctorate in law,[56] Daly started out as the Anglican curate of Monkstown in Cork, living in Passage West.[57] On disestablishment in 1869 his annual living of £100 was commuted for £2,027, 8s 10d.[58] While this presumably gave him a modicum of independence, his subsequent employment record suggests that he remained constantly short of money, despite never marrying.

Daly's first move after disestablishment was apparently to work with the poor, where on his own account (speaking years later in Colombo):

> He found that the spiritual wants of the people (in the East End of London) were not met by the doctrines of Christianity ... Doles of food and coal tickets were given by some to procure good congregations. ... As for the rich, they go to church, "not because of their belief in the creeds of Christianity, but to keep up appearances and respectability. The intellectual class have for the most part abandoned the

52. *The two worlds*, June 1889 (vol. 2/85): 402.
53. *The two worlds*, Jan 3 1890 (vol. 3/112): 89.
54. *Brisbane Courier*, 21 Jan 1890: 2.
55. *The Critic*, 1892 (issues 515–40: 76).
56. http://en.wikipedia.org/wiki/Mahinda_College credits him with an LLD, confirmed by Jinarajadasa 1951: 389.
57. Dharmadasa (1992: 126 fn 39) confirms his Irish identification.
58. *Accounts and papers of the House of Commons* 1875: 46. Permanent curates received a life income rather than a lump sum.

> Church ... The desire of the nation is entirely centred on the material plane, and there is a great want of spirituality." (cited in de Harlez 1890: 57)[59]

By 1879 Daly was publishing in *The Theosophist* and addressing a spiritualist meeting,[60] thus anticipating the Dublin Theosophists by at least five years. At the same time, between 1884 and 1889, he wrote for the *Illustrated London News*[61] and published a range of books – *Glimpses of Irish industries; Ireland in '98: sketches of the principal men of the time; Ireland in the days of Dean Swift: Irish tracts 1720 to 1734* and *Radical pioneers of the eighteenth century*, and the novel *Broken ideals*.

These were political potboilers of a liberal and nationalist kind (Daly 1896: i–viii): both Catholic and Protestant newspapers approved of his *Irish industries*, which offered an analysis of what we would now call dependency (live cattle export undermining the development of local industry and banking siphoning capital out of the country) and calling for technical education and empirically-informed modernisation. As we shall see in his work in Ceylon and India, throughout his life the question of political agency was secondary to his exhortations to economic modernisation.

Already in 1879 he applied similar perspectives to Asia, reporting on the Buddhist Industrial School in Kandy for *The Theosophist*, along with other articles on Buddhist education in Ceylon. This bore fruit when he met Col. Olcott in London in 1889 and subsequently travelled with him to Ceylon. On his 1880 visit, Olcott had set up two parallel Theosophical Societies, a Buddhist Theosophical Society (BTS) in 1881, whose membership was mainly Sinhala, and a 'scientific' (freethinking and occult) branch: Daly was General Secretary for the latter, which failed to get off the ground (Olcott 1889b: 209; *The Theosophist* May–Sept 1890: cxxxviii; Malalgoda 1976: 246).

The BTS was an important part of the Buddhist revival, with a clerical division including leading monks from the different nikayas and a lay division including Sinhala Buddhist activists and foreign theosophists such as Olcott, Daly, C.W. Leadbeater and C.F. Powell (Blackburn 2010: 106ff; Malalgoda 1976: 246–54). Daly quickly

---

59. See Pfoundes (1895c) for what is evidently a rewritten account of Daly's experiences.
60. http://www.spirithistory.com/brtsoc.html
61. *The Theosophist*, May–Sept. 1890: cxviii.

followed the lead of these earlier figures in taking pansil (the five precepts) and so becoming a Buddhist in 1890 (Malalgoda 1976: 254), an event noted in the *Pall Mall Gazette*, the *Birmingham Daily Post* and other British papers.[62]

Daly joined the editorial staff of the Adyar *Theosophist*[63] and worked with Olcott, the young Dharmapala, and others on the Ceylon *Buddhist* (Guruge 1965: 704–5). Like the BTS, however, most of his activity was educational. Despite an 1815 treaty protecting the status of Buddhism, colonial policy had shifted to incorporating Christianity as an aspect of control, and particularly in education. The BTS schools were English-language, Buddhist counterparts to Christian mission schools modelled on the latter rather than traditional monastery education (Ames 1967: 29; Perera 2006: 43; Sirisena and Cox 2013). In 1891 Daly wrote in *The Buddhist*:

> that the condition of Buddhist temple *(pansala)* schools was very unsatisfactory due to lack of organization, materials, and finances, the want of discipline, and "slovenly methods of teaching". (Ames 1967: 28).

He was appointed general manager of the BTS schools in 1890,[64] and remained thus until 1893;[65] he also founded[66] and was first principal of Mahinda College in Galle from 1892–3 (Dharmadasa 1992).[67] He brought some energy to the task; *Lucifer* has him addressing thousands of villagers on a tour of the Central Provinces[68] and Sri Lankan histories record him as a 'pioneer of Buddhist education' (Kirthisinghe and Arasuriya 2007 [1981]). The challenge was substantial:

> My work in the Central and Sabaragamuwa Provinces is bearing splendid fruit. The people are now aroused to a sense of duty in regard to the education of their children. The shameful apathy of Buddhist parents in allowing their sons and daughters to be trained as Christians, has come to an end. I am literally inundated with applications from all quarters to open fresh schools.[69]

62. *The Theosophist*, 1890: civ has a detailed report.
63. *The Theosophist*, May–Sept. 1890: cv.
64. *The Theosophist*, Oct. 1890–Apr 1891: 187.
65. His 'farewell address' is in *The Buddhist*, vol. IV, nos. 31–4.
66. *The Theosophist*, 1909 (given as MDCIX) (30/1–6): 69.
67. http://www.mahindaclub.net/profile.html
68. *Lucifer*, Nov 15 1890: 261.
69. *Lucifer*, Mar–Aug 1891: 82, citing *The Buddhist*.

By 1898 there were 63 BTS schools, led by lay Sinhala, British and American organisers (Malalgoda 1976: 250). To give a sense of the significance of the BTS, a young Australian woman, Miss Pickett, who had only just arrived in Colombo, converted to Buddhism and became principal of Sanghamitta Girl's School before committing suicide. Her funeral had six or seven *thousand* mourners.[70]

Around this point, however, Olcott and Daly fell out badly, and Olcott gives a hilariously different picture of events: Daly

> had a certain sort of ability and any amount of self-push, but proved to be quite ignorant of Eastern literature … He went, as above said, to Ceylon; enlarged our Buddhist school at Galle into a weak College; did some hard work; gave rein to a furious temper; drove the boarding scholars out of the school building with a belt buckle on Wesak Day because their recitation of the gathas and silas annoyed him upstairs; was chosen a member of a Provincial Buddhist Committee; tried to wean from me the love of the Sinhalese; insulted and enraged some of the leading Buddhists; denounced wholesale the entire Sangha; and at last moved off to Calcutta, where he tried to prejudice the public against Theosophy, and finally became mixed up in several disagreeable public incidents. At last accounts he was in the Australian colonies (1889a: 183–4).

Olcott was perhaps not an impartial witness; and the generally positive reports of Daly's relationship to Buddhism makes it seem more likely that Olcott *wished* that Daly had turned away from Buddhism.[71]

Other contemporaries certainly noted Daly's 'choleric and irascible temper' (Harris 2006: 243 fn12), while his later *Indian sketches and rambles* apparently 'excited howls of indignation from respectable rascality and cowardly conservatism' (Daly 1896: ii). Olcott was equally fiery, but had a sense of diplomacy that Daly lacked. It is perhaps unsurprising that the latter's 1893 resignation was over failed fund-raising efforts (Harris 2006: 201). Nonetheless he had visited about thirteen hundred monasteries in his time in Ceylon, which hardly fits with Olcott's presentation (Dennis 1897: 534).

Daly apparently stayed in Ceylon for four to five years, to 1894–5, before moving to India as editor of *The Indian World* and the *Indian*

---

70. *Taranaki Herald,* Rorahi XL, Putanga 9201, 12 Whiringa-a-nuku 1891: 2.

71. Olcott's reference in an 1889 diary to events in 1892 makes it clear that the *Leaves* were rewritten before their publication in 1910. A John Bowles Daly appears in electoral rolls in Melbourne (1903) and Henty, Victoria (1914).

Daily News, where he continued to '[set] forth the beauties of the high moral teaching of the sacred Buddhist writings'.[72] As an expert on the subject, he was appointed[73] to examine the workings of the 'Buddhist Temporalities Ordinance', which placed monasteries' landholdings under the control of lay committees (Mills 1964: 129). His report, published in 1894, was noted by Max Weber as 'very instructive' (1967: 375).

While disestablishment was dear to the missionary lobby (Harris 2006: 41), Daly (himself disestablished) presumably supported it on modernist grounds – the lay committees paralleled the BTS' role in education. Incidentally, Pfoundes (1895c) saw the Meiji disestablishment of Buddhism as positive because it made the 'sacerdotal class' dependent on the Buddhist laity – and so would produce an improvement of priestly standards and a less ritualistic orientation from the laity.

Perhaps the ultimate difference between Daly and Olcott was the latter's need to retain good relations with the monastic sangha, while Daly (like many urban laity) had no great interest in local culture other than Buddhist doctrine and a top-down approach to change:

> The cultured native mind is peculiarly acute and intelligent, but wholly wanting in energy and organizing power. The men and women of Ceylon can do great things when shown how to organise and led, but seem to have absolutely no capacity to initiate. The education of the country is singularly backward, through want of personal effort: it is not to be expected that the British Government should initiate particular measures. My personal knowledge of the resources, or rather want of resources, of Ireland, has taught me to observe deficiencies here which might be easily remedied. A technical not a literary education would do much for the people of Ceylon, whose taste for art and decoration is remarkably true, its fruitful soil and the abundance of wood supplies readily all the means necessary. Just as at home, young men rush into Government offices for small pay, and the nobler arts are deserted for a literary education which presents too few outlets for talent. (Daly 1890a: 469–70).

This recalls William Gregory, and shows how a modernising approach to Buddhism could swing into Orientalism (at time of

72. *The Unitarian*, vol. 10 (1895): 465, speaking of him as editor of the *Indian World*.
73. Supposedly by the Indian government, but it must have been the Ceylon authorities.

Buddhism and Ireland

writing Daly had barely set foot in Ceylon) and support for any agency which might 'organise and lead'.

His one thread of continuity, from *Glimpses of Irish industries* through the BTS schools to *Indian sketches*, is that the future of colonial countries – Ireland, Ceylon, India – lies in modern education:

> I claim the credit of having first sounded the tocsin in this battle and unsparingly condemned the existing system of Education, which is old-fashioned, obsolete and absolutely worthless. (1896: i)

Yet this raises Marx's question: who is to do the modernising? Daly always imagined modernisation from above – by Irish capitalists, educated Sinhalese or foreign Theosophists; in *Indian sketches* he looks variously to European colonisers, the new urban Indian elites and modernising kings for help (1896: i–ii).

Daly as Buddhist

We can perhaps see family resemblances both to Gibson and to Pfoundes' Buddhism. All combined spiritualist interests with a strong modernising impulse – political in Gibson and Daly's case, but also religious in Pfoundes and Daly:

> [Buddhism's] substance can be contained in three "sentences": purify the mind, abstain from vice, and practise virtue ... Buddha proclaimed the absolute equality of mankind, irrespective of caste, and the pre-eminence of virtue over all other worldly distinctions. (Daly 1890a: 465–6)

Daly's engagement with modernising Buddhist politics thus combines with his earlier commitment to cultural modernisation and his spiritualism. It makes sense for someone whose attempts at political engagement, in Ireland or London, were frustrated by circumstances – and who seized the chance of involvement in an educational revolution which he had followed from afar since 1879.

Daly was for a time a Theosophist Buddhist, and in 1890 he was happy to be both. Nevertheless his Theosophy dates to Britain and Ceylon rather than Dublin, and he was not a creature of the Society in the way of his younger peers. Age, but also the more democratic practices of spiritualism (Barrow 1986), prevented this: if like Pfoundes he fell out with the Society, we do not find either needing to affiliate to one of the post-Theosophical organisations, but rather returning to splendid isolation (and a greater interest in Hindu thought once in India).

In terms of practice, although he wrote

> In this Buddhist religion meditation takes the place of prayer
> (1890a: 468)

there is no indication that it was ever a practice he followed, or that the love, pity and serenity (*metta, karuna* and *upekkha*) he discusses in the same article were meditation exercises he might have pursued. Instead, in the same issue of *The Theosophist*, he offered 'A few rules for exercise' (1890b) – of clairvoyance. After Ceylon, Daly remained

> strongly pro-Buddhist in his sympathies, and does not conceal his
> admiration for Buddhism as a religious system (Dennis 1897: 534)

India, however, seems to have overwhelmed him; or this is the impression given by *Indian sketches and rambles* (1896), which shows a massive disorientation, whether due to repeated culture shock or his precarious employment situation. The work oscillates between praising and abusing Indians (of many different kinds), English people, and virtually every other ethnic group he meets. He also shows uncharacteristic signs of anti-modernism:

> This talented young Indian gentleman is either ignorant of the
> spiritual conceptions of man and the universe, taught by his ancestors
> in the Upanishads and Vedas, or he has voluntarily thrown them over
> for the flippant and flimsy materialism of the West. He has exchanged
> a faith hoary with antiquity and replete with the highest wisdom for a
> pinch-beck materialistic creed … (1896: 33–4)

At another:

> Poor India, your glorious past is becoming a pale tradition of impossible
> existence, your ancient religion a tale told by a Theosophist, full of
> plaintive music, signifying nothing. The heavy hand of time presses
> on the heart of a country, once the cradle of religion and the home of
> the noblest aspirations. (1896: 134)

Elsewhere in the text he is fascinated by psychic powers of all kinds, and claims for himself the rather humble power of psychically directing his horse (1896: 170). Indian realities were evidently unbearable: running a cramming school in Calcutta (1896: 2–3) he became embroiled in a public exchange of letters with his own students, who noted wonderfully

> Dr Daly has done the duty of a teacher by teaching us the noble art of
> vituperation. (1896: 13)

It is to his credit that he reproduces an exchange in which he comes off the worse. Ultimately, he took refuge in a universalising and Promethean picture of spirituality:

> Man's experiments on the world within him will yield a rich return: for our ordinary consciousness is but a floating island upon the abysmal deep of that total individuality beneath it. The waves which wash under one end of our narrow standing place are continuous with the waves which wash under the other. Thus self-reverence, self-control and self-knowledge together with bodily chastity will enable man to be the ruler of his own spirit, the fashioner of his own fate, and perhaps also enable him to imbibe direct truth from the Eternal source before his work in this world is finished. (1896: 173)[74]

Despite everything, Daly *was* accepted into the Buddhist revival in Ceylon and played a real role within it. A Buddhist sympathiser for around two decades, he spent half a decade working directly for the revival movement. Like Pfoundes and Hearn, his involvement with Asian institutions was tied to his prestige as a western *professional* (writers and teachers). This situation, and their temperaments, set limits to their options, and they seem to have remained caught between worlds – Hearn continuing to write for western publishers while teaching in Japan, Daly working for the British administration after working for the BTS, Pfoundes oscillating between Japan and the West.

It also left them in peculiar positions vis-à-vis Asian modernists: Hearn employed as part of the Meiji modernising strategy, but defending traditional culture; Daly simultaneously allied with urban Buddhist elites and looking for external agents of change; Pfoundes exalting occult wisdom while acting for 'young Japan'. These tensions echoed their inherited situations – Pfoundes the self-made man searching for a role in the world; Daly as the disestablished curate, seeking an industrial revolution without political change; Hearn as the disinherited offspring of an imperial soldier.

An Exile in Japan (Lafcadio Hearn/Koizumi Yakumo, 1890–1904)

Lafcadio Hearn, interpreter of 'old Japan' to its modernising, Meiji present and the west, was author of thirteen books on Japan and one on China and numerous translations. He is well-known as an early

---

74. This may offer a partial explanation as to why he remained 'a grizzled old bachelor' (1896: 155).

Buddhist sympathiser, and is the subject of a collection by Kenneth Rexroth (1977) and detailed consideration by Tweed (2000).

Hearn had a very fractured family life and relationship to Irish culture. His father was an Anglo-Irish military doctor who (unusually) married Lafcadio's Greek mother while stationed in the Aegean. Combining 'the impeccably respectable professions of medicine and the army' (Murray 1993: 215), his father in turn had been a Lieutenant Colonel and Justice of the Peace, with a great-grandfather who was Archdeacon of Cashel.

The two-year-old came to Ireland with his mother until she returned to Greece following a nervous breakdown and his father divorced her. Alone in Ireland, he was brought up by an aunt, who having married a Catholic was semi-detached from the family. Boarded at schools in Britain (where he lost an eye) and France, he was sent to the US at 17, where he found work with the Fourierist, freethinking printer Henry Watkin (Cott 1991: 34) and began writing for the freethought *Investigator* on religion and Eastern philosophy (Murray 1993: 26).

Already in the mid-1870s, he was strongly attracted by the cultures of the Far East and 'enchanted' by the *Light of Asia*. By 1880, he was arguing that Oriental philosophy was superior to contemporary German thought; in 1883 he wrote:

> Buddhism in some esoteric form may prove the religion of the future … I have the idea that the Right Man could now revolutionize the Occidental religious world by preaching the Oriental faith. (cited in Murray 1993: 84).

His pro-Buddhist columns in the *New Orleans Times-Democrat* led to it being dubbed 'the Infidel Sheet' by local clergy (Sutin 2006: 12). Following the enforced breakup of his first marriage, to a local black woman, he travelled to Japan in 1890, where he became an English teacher and eventually university lecturer, married a Japanese woman, took a Japanese name and citizenship (at a considerable loss of earnings), adopted a Japanese lifestyle (Murray 1993: 156–7), including daily offerings to Buddhist deities (Cott 1991: 315) and was given a Buddhist funeral in 1904 at Jitoin Kobudera temple in Tokyo.[75] The day after his son's birth, he wrote

75. He had written in 1893, 'It is better to enter some old Buddhist cemetery here, than to moulder anywhere else' (1992: 264).

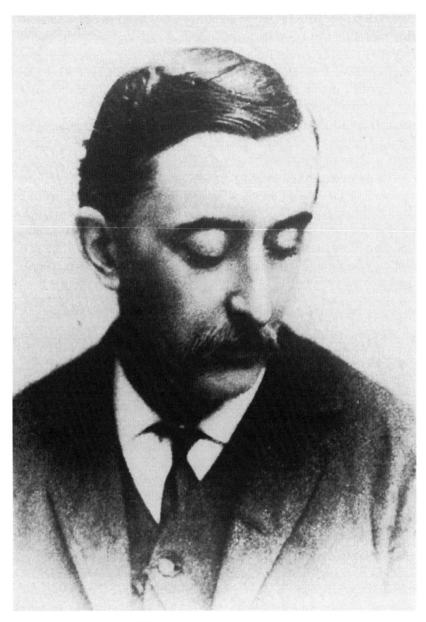

Fig. 5.3 Lafcadio Hearn in 1889.

The little man will wear sandals and dress like a Japanese, and become a good Buddhist if he lives long enough. He will not have to go to church, and listen to stupid sermons, and be perpetually tormented by absurd conventions (cited in Murray 1993: 168-9)

Hearn's Buddhism, then, was a matter both of philosophical conviction and of strong emotional attachment to a Japanese culture and folklore that he interpreted as largely Buddhist (Ronan 1997). He was interested in theories of change and development (world-cycles, karma and reincarnation) and devoted much effort, from his New Orleans period on, to relating Tendai and Shingon to Spencer and Haeckel, and trying to develop a theory of 'spiritual evolutionism'.

His agnostic and nonsectarian commitments kept him a sympathiser rather than an adherent (thus Tweed 2000: 74-5); in fact, like other Irish Buddhist sympathisers it was partly the lack of insistence on a monopoly of belief and practice that both made it attractive and prevented a closer commitment.[76] For Hearn, as for Pfoundes or Jivaka, sectarian claims to monopoly were anathema. He presents his first encounter with a Buddhist priest thus:

'Are you a Christian?'
And I answer truthfully: 'No.'
'Are you a Buddhist?'
'Not exactly.'
'Why do you make offerings if you do not believe in Buddha?'
'I revere the beauty of his teaching, and the faith of those who follow it.' (cited in Murray 1993: 124)

At another point, he writes 'if it were possible for me to adopt a faith, I should adopt [Buddhism]', or again 'I can imagine no means of consoling myself except by plunging into the study of Buddhism' (Cott 1991: 335). In this combination of grand theory, tolerant scepticism and romantic pull towards lived culture he recalls Thomas Hardy; this complexity gives power to his writing.

Hearn's 1896 'The genius of Japanese civilization' intertwines love of Japan with themes of impermanence, illusion and the suppression of desire:

76. This also enabled him to resolve the question of whether Japan was 'really' Buddhist or Shinto (*pace* Murray 1993: 148-9): in *Out of the East* (1897), he argued that Buddhism differed from Christianity and Islam in its capacity to incorporate other religions, and in particular to coexist with Shinto.

> Buddhism taught that nature was a dream, an illusion, a phantasma-
> goria; but it also taught men how to seize the fleeting impressions of
> that dream, and how to interpret them in relation to the highest truth.
> And they learned well. In the flushed splendour of the blossom-bursts
> of spring, in the coming and going of the cicadae, in the dying crimson
> of autumn foliage, in the ghostly beauty of snow, in the delusive
> motion of wave and cloud, they saw old parables of perpetual
> meaning. (1992: 85)

This perspective was deeply internalised: visiting a Buddhist
temple and wondering how a Buddhist might see *Romeo and Juliet*,

> suddenly, like an answer to that wonder, came a memory of the two
> hundred and fifteenth verse of the Dhamma-pada: *"From love comes
> grief; from grief comes fear; one who is free from love knows neither grief nor
> fear"*. (Dawson 1992: 76)

This vision was powerful enough across decades that the fifteen-
year-old Alan Watts converted to Buddhism after reading him
(Sutin 2006: 92). If Dawson (1992) suggests that Hearn's focus on
religion in his late essay *Japan* represents a loss of his pleasure in
Japanese culture, Rexroth holds that Hearn offered 'a sensitive and
durable vision of how Buddhism was and still is lived in Japan'
(1977: xi) – to which his own internal tensions add depth.

Like Collis, Hearn's romantic perspective on Japan paralleled the
Anglo-Irish relationship to 'Ireland', as paradoxical as Kipling's to
India or Waddell's to Japan: the emotional response to the place
and images of one's early years, in a context where the political and
cultural conflict made adult identification problematic. Sharing the
early Yeats' identification of the nature of a 'country' and 'people'
on the basis of peasant folklore, Hearn wrote to him in 1901 of
growing up with 'a Connaught nurse who told me fairy-stories and
ghost-stories' (Murray 1993: 33–5).

Like Yeats sceptical of modernising nationalism, Hearn opposed
the modernising orientation of the Meiji and the 'New Buddhism''s
calls for a reconstructed and purified Buddhism (Sharf 1995: 247).
His vision of peasant Buddhism is far more like Yeats' of simple
peasant wisdom and folk magic, distanced both from the institutional hierarchies of official religion and the encroaching rationalism
of modernity. There were powerful processes of dislocation at work:

> When one has lived alone five years in a Buddhist atmosphere, one
> naturally becomes penetrated by the thoughts that hover in it ... I do

not mean that I am a Buddhist, but I mean that the inherited ancestral
feelings about the universe – the Occidental ideas every Englishman
[sic] has – have been totally transformed. (cited in Dawson 1992: 128-9)

What brought Hearn, physically and emotionally, to this point,
was precisely Ireland's place in the world-system – the British
army's place in Greece and Ireland – and the sectarianism which
meant that the family abandoned Hearn and his convert aunt. His
father's marriage had already breached caste expectations: 'the
pukka ethos of the British officer corps would not have favoured
romantic involvement with a "native"' (Murray 1993: 212). Hearn
took this further, with choices sharpened by Victorian racism and
'respectability': the public news of his first marriage to a story-
teller born into slavery, the illegitimate daughter of a slave and her
Irish-born owner, raised a furore in the American South; while his
second marriage was the source of further racist attacks after his
death, one paper writing 'Lafcadio Hearn admitted no member
of his race to genuine intimacy' (Murray 1993: 307), an approach
repeated by early biographers (Cott 1991: 182-3).

This, no doubt, added to his refusal to engage with European
expatriates and the diplomatic world of Tokyo and his self-
perception (in 1895) as having 'gone native':

> The difference between myself and other writers on Japan is simply
> that I have become practically a Japanese – in all but knowledge of the
> language; while other writers remain foreigners … (cited in Murray
> 1993: 186)

These cultural and religious choices were deeply felt: he said that
missionaries should be shot on sight, and spoke of Jesuit attempts
at conversion as 'a crime against humanity, a labour of devastation'
(Murray 1993: 273, 293). Politically, he was consciously anti-imperi-
alist; the British consul (himself Irish) saw him as a nationalist 'in
the most extreme sense of the term' (Murray 1993: 285-6), and he
supported the Boers against the British and (like Pfoundes) the
Japanese against the Russians in these symbolically-charged wars.

While there is no evidence that Hearn knew Pfoundes or
Dhammaloka, he shared their concern for local authenticity and
hostility to Christian missionaries and their dependence on Asian
employment and political anti-colonialism – key themes for the
Irish in the Buddhist Revival.

A Fictional Character in India (Kimball O'Hara/Kim, 1900–1)

Further down the scale of respectability and fractured families, by far the most widely *represented* Irish Buddhist is the hero of Kipling's *Kim*, first published in serial form in 1900–1. *Kim* is based not only on the real-life Himalayan experiences of George Bogle (Teltscher 2006: 259–60) and the 'Great Game' of British and Russian spying, but also on the far more widespread experiences of Irish soldiers in India and their families. Before *Kim*, Kipling had been most famous for his Private Mulvaney (Nagai 2006:50), who shares many of his characteristics and drew on close observation of ordinary soldiers (Gilmour 2002: 44).

The son of an Irish ex-sergeant who has married an Irish nursemaid and taken a railway job,[77] Kim is brought up to bazaar life after his parents' deaths. Following a Tibetan lama met by chance, Kim is torn between this and the possibility of a 'western' life represented by school and the 'Great Game'. His life can stand for other Irish Buddhists who may yet be found in the archives of 'Irish India'. The Indian-born Kipling, whose primary audience was for a long time Anglo-Indian, had to write characters who were possible if unusual, and the many Irish characters in Kipling's stories played a particular role:

> Indo-Irish analogies and comparisons became especially important in representing imperial integrity in the late nineteenth century, and as such became the very site where the image of the British empire was contested ... [there was] first an "imperialist" mode of representation, which sought to interpret Irish participation in the Raj as the strongest proof of loyalty to the Empire; and secondly, an Irish and Indian "nationalist" mode of representation, which strove to form anti-imperial networks between India, Ireland and beyond, characterizing Indo-Irish connections as the cooperation between two colonies suffering from the common fate of being ruled and exploited by England (2006: 3).

Much of *Kim* revolves around his 'two souls' – the one, practical or cynical, represented as 'English' and working for the spymasters of the Raj; the other, romantic and 'Indian', seeking truth – and the different possible resolutions. *Kim* thus parallels T.E. Lawrence's self-presentation on the tensions of 'going native'.

---

77. Many demobbed Irish soldiers 'remained behind to work for the state railways, telegraphs or some other Public Works Department project' (Cook 1987: 509). Others became 'loafers' (Bubb 2012: 792).

Literary scholars debate the politics of the novel and whether Kim's 'Irish' component is allied more with the practicalities of the Great Game or the romantic quest for the River of Life (Kwon 2007, Franklin 2008). To my mind the strength of the novel, and its point, lies in how Kim, like Mahbub Ali, Hurree Babu or even Lurgan Sahib, with his mastery of fakir magic, resolves these tensions; and it is in resolving 'head and heart' that the novel works as a tale of adolescence. Readers of the time hoped to combine their emotional and spiritual hopes with their career, not to abandon their most cherished beliefs in the name of reality. Kipling, for his (Anglo-Indian) part, wants to show the compatibility of 'Indian' and 'English' – the pleasures of life in India and the value he sees in the British Empire (Gilmour 2002).

From a Buddhist point of view, the Lama is successful in his quest and wins 'Salvation for himself and his beloved' (1908: 413); if Kim is now a man and a successful spy, that makes him none the less his teacher's disciple from an Indian or Buddhist point of view. In 1900, *Kim* balanced between the real-life Tibetan Buddhist lama and Russian agent Aghvan Dorzhiev and the Irish Buddhist convert Dhammaloka – although neither was pro-British.

Kim is a good place to pause on the different meanings of 'Irish' and 'English', already discussed in linguistic terms. Cronin (2006: 135–6) discusses why Kim calls himself English rather than Irish and says that the text 'anxiously seeks to repress' this confusion of identity. Yet in the passage she quotes, where Kim represents himself as English to an English drummer-boy, the latter is talking about 'the Liverpool suburb which was his England' (Kipling 1908: 145). Liverpool was an intensely sectarian city with massive Irish immigration in the second half of the nineteenth century, and frequent Protestant-Catholic (or English-Irish) riots. Kim, then, is choosing *not* to be on the opposite side of this, and thus to make friends.

Nagai, by contrast, recognises the fact of the Liverpool Irish but assumes that these are 'two Irish boys who meet in India'. She recognises Kim's Indian accent but misses the drummer boy's (English/Protestant) one:

> The bugles 'ill go for dinner in arf a minute. My Gawd! ... It's awful doin' nothin' but school down 'ere. Don't you 'ate it? (1908: 145)

Liverpool, like Ireland, was not unitary, and this is part of Kipling's point; although this constructed friendship glosses over massive problems created precisely by empire and colonialism, there is nothing implausible in this being done through a strategic choice of identifications.

Kim as Buddhist

Kim's 'Indian' mentor[78] is a moderately orthodox[79] Gelugpa lama inspired by western accounts of the then Panchen lama (Norman 2008). His quest is that codified by Thomas Watters: the search for the holy places of the Pali canon, then in full swing among western Orientalists and avidly followed by some Asian Buddhists, in particular around the discovery of relics. Here, at the margins of Irish involvement in the British Empire and archaeological exploration, an Indian-Irish boy becomes the *chela* of a Tibetan Buddhist – and was accepted as such by local and global audiences.

Franklin writes that in

> the lama's Buddhist teaching and Kim's ecumenical practice Kipling reaches towards a vision of Eastern piety as both theologically profound and humanly practical (2008: 139, citing McCutchan).

He notes Mahbub Ali as spokesman for the key message:

> Therefore I say in my heart the Faiths are like the horses. Each has merit in its own country. (Kipling 1908: 204)

Franklin's point is that

> Kipling's purpose was not to place Buddhism above other religions. Rather, Buddhism provided a suitable vehicle for the dual message of genuine piety combined with religious tolerance, the only such vehicle Kipling perceived in an India torn by religious conflict. Kipling chose Buddhism because it was the only world religion without a history characterised substantially by violent suppression of other faiths. (2008: 140)

As with Watters, Collis and Joyce or Pfoundes, Hearn and Jivaka, such an understanding resonated with many Irish sympathisers.

---

78. And arguably mother-figure to Lurgan's father-figure: Kipling, son of a museum curator, probably knew the pseudo-etymology of lama as 'soul-mother'.

79. *The Light of Asia* influenced Kipling's view of Buddhism in a Vedantist direction (Franklin 2008: 235 fn 30).

Fig. 5.4 'The Lama', as executed by Kipling's father Lockwood for *Kim*.

Paralleling Kim

The fiction of *Kim* is grounded in the reality of imperial lives in India, which included not just 'Anglo-Indians' like Kipling himself, but a widespread practice where civil servants and soldiers of all ranks took local wives, as did (less publicly) missionaries. Whether such arrangements – and their religious implications – were permanent or dissolved on return home, most produced no records. As the Christian influence on the administration of India became stronger in the late nineteenth century and the 'Memsahibs' arrived from England, pressures towards racial closure increased and 'going native' in any sense – from wives to clothes – became unacceptable (Lynch 1988: 182, Dalrymple 2000). Thus, as part of his education:

> When tales were told of hot nights, Kim did not sweep the board with his reminiscences; for St. Xavier's looks down on boys who "go native altogether". One must never forget that one is a Sahib, and that some day, when examinations are passed, one will command natives. (Kipling 2008: 177)

Nevertheless, this 'going native' is the main possibility for attested Irish Buddhists of this period – those who published their stories. Kim, whose social invisibility is his primary advantage for the spymaster, can stand for the unknown number of those who did not, and were not recorded – or those, like U Visuddha and the anonymous Irish monks noted above, who appear only at the margins of history (Cox 2013).

Kipling's approach was shared by Bithia Croker from Roscommon, who having married an army officer and spent fourteen years in India before his 1892 retirement, was similarly aware of such lives. If *The road to Mandalay: a tale of Burma* recalls *Kim*, it equally recalls U Dhammaloka, or Lipton's and Murphy's encounters with Irish bhikkhus (below). One character is made to say 'I've heard more than once of these white *pongyes*' (Burmese bhikkhus) – there was no shortage even of Irish ones.

Chapter XX of *The road to Mandalay* features such a bhikkhu 'born in Cork and Madras':

> It was like this, sorr, I'm country-born; me father was a sergeant in the Irish Rifles, me mother was a half-caste – an Anglo-Indian from Ceylon – so I'm half Irish, quarter Cingalese. I was left an orphan when I was seven years old and educated at the Lawrence Asylum. I always had a wonderful twist for languages; it came as easy as

breathing to me to talk Tamil or Telugu. Well, when I was close on eighteen I enlisted and put in seven years with the Colours, mostly in Bengal; then we come over here and lay in Mandalay and, after a bit, I – somehow got lost.

In chapter XXVIII, he reappears as Michael Ryan and rejoins the army. In the closing lines of the book:

To the unspeakable grief of his comrades, he had gone West – but not to Ireland. (Croker 1917: no pagination)

Further up the social scale, the life of W.F. O'Connor (1870–1943), born in Meath, offers another parallel to Kim. O'Connor started in British intelligence, compiling a 1900 report on 'routes to Sikkim'; he was Younghusband's right-hand man on the 1903 invasion of Tibet, working alongside the Tibetophile Laurence Austine Waddell. No mean scholar himself, O'Connor spoke Tibetan, and was the Political Officer appointed under the terms of the treaty signed after the expedition (McKay 2005). In 1906 he published *Folk-tales from Tibet, with illustrations by a Tibetan artist and some verses from Tibetan love-songs*; later on he became a mystic (Audrey Whitty and Philip McEvansoneya, pers. comm.), publishing works such as *Quietude* (1940).[80]

A major part of the Political Officer's role was gaining goodwill through providing free (western) medical services to Tibetans by Ulster-born Capt. Robert Steen and later Lieutenant Robert Kennedy, educated in Queen's College Cork, who combined the medical and Political Officer role. Both cultivated the Panchen Lama in seeking Tibetan support for vaccination,[81] and subsequently the provision of British medical training for Tibetans. These were not minor posts; all three retired as Lieutenant-Colonels.

Lacking a European birth and education, a Kim could never have aimed so high (Ryan is allowed to die a Sergeant-major); but these examples, and O'Connor's subsequent evolution, support this reading of the story shadowing other, anonymous Irish encounters with Asian Buddhism.

---

80. Richard Cox has drawn my attention to the comparable life of Charles Howard-Bury, a Charleville-born soldier, explorer and enthusiast for Asian religion discussed in Davis 2012.

81. Sarat Chandra Das, a possible model for Hurree Babu, had already brought smallpox vaccine at the Panchen Lama's request in the 1880s.

A Beachcomber in Burma (U Dhammaloka/Laurence Carroll?, 1890s–1913?)

In 1900, some of Burma's senior sayadaws ordained an ex-hobo, ex-alcoholic Irishman with a level of ceremony which was evidently intended to give him the seal of official approval, and set him on a public journey of confrontation with Christian missionaries and ultimately the imperial state which was to last at least fourteen years and span not only Burma but also Singapore, present-day Malaysia, Siam, Cambodia, India, Ceylon, Nepal, Japan, China and Australia in an intensive process of pan-Buddhist organising.

The remarkable story of U Dhammaloka is the subject of ongoing research by Brian Bocking, Alicia Turner and myself (Turner et al., 2010, Turner 2010, Cox 2009b, 2010a, 2010b; Bocking 2010, Tweed 2010) which is constantly throwing up surprises, so the summary here is only a provisional account of what is known about the most original of all the early Irish Buddhists.

U Dhammaloka, as he became, had been born in southern Dublin in the 1850s, perhaps as Laurence Carroll, a Catholic grocer's son in Booterstown. If this identification is correct, he left school at fourteen to work in the family business but quickly emigrated, perhaps because older siblings stood to inherit. He failed to find work in Liverpool but worked his way across the Atlantic in a ship's pantry. Arriving in 1872, he became a hobo or migrant labourer, working on East Coast ships and then taking a variety of jobs – from shepherd to dishwasher – as he worked his way west to California, where he found work on fruit boats on the Sacramento.

The hobo part of his narrative was verified many years later, by three hoboes who were satisfied by his knowledge of how to jump trains and similar accomplishments; but the details beyond that are hazy. On his own account, he crossed the States fairly quickly and then found work in the mid-1870s on packet ships to Yokohama; after a few trips he was left behind in Japan, from where he made his way, eventually, to Rangoon.

Something like this must have happened, but when? The difficulty with this version is that we have no independent evidence of his presence in Burma before 1900, when he shot to public prominence as a celebrity preacher, prolific correspondent, temperance activist, publisher, international networker and – as a friend put it – 'terror to evil-doers'.[82]

82. *Englishman* (Calcutta), Apr 11 1912: 7.

Fig. 5.5 U Dhammaloka (Laurence Carroll?) in 1902. Copyright granted by Brian Bocking.

His own account implies that he arrived fairly rapidly in Rangoon, found work as a timber clerk but came across a Buddhist pamphlet which piqued his interest. Overcoming his love of drinking and fighting, he soon became a monk (or perhaps a novice) – probably in the Tavoy monastery where he was later based, which seems to have been something of a dumping-ground for the 'beach-combers' who occasionally converted to Buddhism.[83] On this version, he soon started teaching (by implication, English rather than the traditional monastic curriculum) and later began to travel and preach.

However, this account seems to suggest that he had been in the monastery for anything up to twenty years by the time of his higher ordination, was allowed to travel and preach despite only being a novice, and nevertheless failed to reach public notice despite everything we know of his later personality. One alternative possibility is that drifting, alcoholism and fighting had kept him busy, whether in the States or around Asia, up to a much later point (say the mid-1890s), when drying out in the monastery gave him a new burst of life, familiar to many mature students and late-comers to Buddhism.

Yet this does not explain how he learned the organising skills so evident in his public career – nor why he was so concerned with covering his tracks. I started with a question-mark over his Irish identity, for the very good reason that he gave a minimum of three different names, offered multiple contradictory accounts of his past (sometimes wildly implausible, such as having been a Catholic priest), and was a past master of the act of disappearance, to such a point that the date of his death is unknown – or at least, the date of his real death, because he or someone tried to fake his death some years previously.

All of this suggests that he may have had something a bit more serious to hide from than a past relationship with the bottle. Putting this together with his effective international activism, it seems at least possible that the missing decades of his life were spent in some more political activity which would still have had costs. There are many possibilities – Fenianism springs to mind, but there is no obvious context. Perhaps most likely is that he was involved in some of the bitter and often violent labour struggles of late nineteenth century US history, which might have given him some of the training and connections he seems to have had, and a past to conceal.

Whatever the truth, in 1900 he was reborn as 'U Dhammaloka', with the blessings of some of the most senior figures in the Burmese

---

83. Perhaps later he had the task of keeping order and instilling some basic monastic behaviour in this unruly crowd of ex-sailors, ex-soldiers and lost causes.

sangha, and took on defending Buddhism in the white man's world with great energy. The traditional centre of Upper Burma had only been conquered fifteen years previously, meaning that the hierarchy were still coming to terms with the new world (and seeking British recognition for a new head of the monastic order), and overt Burmese opposition to empire was likely to meet with a very harsh response (conquest had been followed by a brutal counter-insurgency campaign whose memory must have been very live).

As Dhammaloka interpreted matters, there were three related threats, summed up in phrases such as 'the Bible, the whisky bottle and the Gatling gun' – a triad which recurs in different forms and must have been a standard part of his preaching – or, to put it another way, Christian missionaries, alcoholism (and no doubt the general 'moral decline' attendant on proletarianisation) and the British Empire.

The bottle was a safe adversary: temperance was a respectable concern for whites no less than Buddhist monks, and Dhammaloka took an active role in the international Good Templar organisation. The British Empire was manifestly not a safe target, but opposition to Christian missionaries was feasible, though at times it meant skating on thin ice.[84] In this, Dhammaloka was importing an Irish model of using the defence of the popular religion (Catholicism or Buddhism respectively) against that of the colonial elite (Protestantism, or Christianity generally) in a mode of cultural nationalist organising which had already been brought to a fine art by Daniel O'Connell in the 1830s.

Dhammaloka's attacks on the missionary effort – delivered in cross-country preaching tours to mass audiences but also in English-language newspapers and tracts – drew not on Pfoundes' urbane rationalism or Hearn's sophisticated reflections, but the radical and plebeian traditions of polemic free-thought, or atheism:

> The Buddhist Tract Society is full of human sympathies; but as none of these are wasted upon the "Saviours" and "Gods", it has an abundance for the beings of earth … [It] fails to see the necessity of a vast host of able-bodied, well-fed Sky-pilots [missionaries] managers of matters between men and the big Papa in the Clouds, and it holds that if a man's soul is to [be] saved by man's work, the man that has the soul has got to do the work. (Dhammaloka 1910)

84. Tadhg Foley (2012) concurs with the analysis of Dhammaloka's anti-missionary work as a challenge to colonialism.

Fig. 5.6 Buddhist Tract Society logo, c. 1907–11. This image copyright Laurence Cox.

The Society – whose works, printed in the tens if not hundreds of thousands, were distributed in towns across Burma – republished, translated, epitomised and interpolated the works of European and American atheists, from Thomas Paine to Robert Blatchford. Like his authors, he was an effective polemicist in person as well as in print: he contributed to many papers and periodicals and carried a notebook of newspaper clippings tracking his activities.

Besides his Burmese home base, Dhammaloka's activities abroad have been explored by Bocking (2010). He spent long periods in the Straits Settlements – today's Singapore and Malaysia (in particular Penang and Ipoh). In Singapore, the best-documented of these, he set up a Buddhist Mission, founded a Buddhist school with support from the Chinese community, organised a Wesak ceremony that brought different Buddhist traditions together for the first time, ordained western monks and continued his anti-missionary and temperance activities.

In the independent kingdom of Siam, as Choompolpaisal's work is now showing (2012), he founded the country's first bilingual Buddhist school (and one of the first in all South East Asia), which is still in operation today.

Beyond these again, he is known to have visited Japanese religious gatherings; to have visited temperance organisations in Australia; to have travelled in India, notably the Buddhist Chittagong Hill Tracts and to have held a preaching tour in Ceylon. There is some evidence of his teaching in Cambodia and Nepal, and he also claimed (less plausibly) to have visited Tibet.

Such globe-trotting Buddhist activism, characteristic of the leading figures of the Buddhist Revival, was underpinned by networks of Asian patrons whom Turner (2011) has neatly unpicked. Burmese gem merchants, Chinese businesses and a Shan saopha all made his activity possible. Elsewhere (Cox 2010b) I have looked at his organisation in Burma. Here I want to lay out just one organisational sequence.

As a celebrity preacher in rural Burma, Dhammaloka was a 'field of merit' and was therefore the recipient of countless gifts in the form of jewellery, portable wealth used in such contexts. This would pose practical problems for anyone, let alone a monk forbidden to handle money. Conveniently, one of his close associates, Maung Maung, was a jewel merchant and ideally placed to handle these gifts.[85] Maung Maung was also active in the Society for the Propagation of Buddhism, which presumably provided the venues for part at least of his preaching tours. The analogy to present-day music promoters springs to mind. The money seems to have gone (at least from 1907 on) into the Buddhist Tract Society, which claimed to publish 'ten thousand copies each' of 'a hundred texts' – and with this amount of donations to fund it, probably did; the tracts were distributed in cities and towns around Burma.

As a bhikkhu, Dhammaloka lived up to the part. His ethical commitment to monastic discipline seems to have been very genuine, and there is no doubt that he had a genuine devotion to Buddhism. He was no dharma scholar, and it is likely that what drew him above all was the lived religion, in which he excelled on Asian terms.

We have contrasted Dhammaloka with the much better-known Ananda Metteyya: Metteyya was appreciated by Europeans for his role as scholar-monk, his gentlemanly status, his interest in 'bringing Buddhism to the west' (not always appreciated by Burmese patrons) and his orientation towards achieving recognition for Buddhism as a world religion alongside Christianity. By contrast, the plebeian Dhammaloka challenged Christian missionaries in Burma, and was popular among Asian Buddhists for his crossing racial lines and performance of correct ritual behaviour.

In keeping with his obscure beginnings and dramatic life, Dhammaloka's death is also shrouded in mystery. In 1910, he was charged with sedition for comments made in Moulmein, charges perhaps brought by the Irish teachers of St Patrick's School, already irritated at the presence of a student Buddhist association among

85. As a jewel merchant he was also part of international networks which enabled both him and Dhammaloka to travel internationally.

their pupils. The charge was upheld, in a high-profile appeal, but with only minor penalties (bound over to keep the peace).

Nevertheless something had changed, and Dhammaloka travelled to Australia, where his death was falsely announced, before returning to the Straits Settlements and Cambodia; as far as we know he never returned to Burma. The last certain record places him in Penang in late 1913, where he may have died.

Dhammaloka's story makes it clear that Irish Buddhism was neither exclusively Protestant by birth, nor exclusively educated; class privilege influences the survival of records, and Dhammaloka is probably unusual not as a working-class Buddhist but as a working-class *publisher* and celebrity, whose story was even covered in the Irish *Sunday Independent*.[86]

Otherwise, he shows us a classic Irish Buddhist: gone native in Asia rather than exploring Buddhism at home as many US and UK contemporaries did; allied with Asian organisations and networks against the missionary effort (and ultimately empire) rather than with Orientalist civil servants and universities; and drawing on Irish cultural nationalist repertoires to resist colonialism in a strange religious form of anti-imperial solidarity.

Lesser-known Irish Buddhists at the Turn of the Century

U Dhammaloka was by no means the only Irish bhikkhu in Asia; he is simply the best-documented one. In a recent article (Turner et al 2010) we showed that the history of early western Buddhist monks is more an organisational genealogy than anything like a full record, and identified over a dozen 'new' monks around the turn of the twentieth century. Beyond these, we came across multiple Irish monks while researching Dhammaloka. A story told by Sir Thomas Lipton, founder of the tea firm, recalled:

> the Buddhist monk he met, in the centre of China, who glared at him
> so fixedly that Lipton began to apprehend the rush and the knife of
> some fanatical enemy of the Christian and the foreigner, and then a
> little later, when the monk could separate himself from his fellows
> with their shaven heads and their habits and their beads, Lipton's
> surprise when he heard in excellent English with a slight brogue, the
> astonished inquiry, "What the d-l has brought you here, Lipton?" and

86. Aug 6 1911.

soon found that the shaved and habited Buddhist monk was as much an Irishman as himself. (T.P. O'Connor 1913: 50)

The O'Connors seem to have enjoyed such stories. T.P.'s wife Elizabeth has this one:

Doctor Patrick Murphy, when in the medical service in India, told me he was making a voyage from Calcutta to Bombay. On the boat were a number of Buddhist priests; they belonged to a silent order and were very devout. But, even buried in their habits and hoods, he thought he saw in a lean face, burnt a fine bronze, the intelligent gleam of a dark blue eye. And for some reason or other it seemed to him a familiar Irish eye. At first he dismissed the idea as impossible, but as he closely regarded the broad-shouldered, long-limbed man at his prayers, and saw how much more manly and free in action he was than is usual to the Indian, he decided if the opportunity arose to speak to him. When the boat arrived at Bombay, the priests not hurrying away were the last people to cross the gang plank, and the blue-eyed one lingered well in the rear.

Taking his chance, my friend said, 'An' will you have a drop of the craythur?'

The Buddhist priest raised his head like a war-horse who hears a trumpet, and, speaking in a low voice with a rich brogue, said, 'Faith an' I will'.

'Then follow me to the cabin,' said Doctor Murphy.

After a generous peg of whiskey, the doctor only had time to say, 'Where do you come from?'

The priest said, 'The West's awake, from Galway.' He then hurried up the steps and Doctor Murphy saw him no more.

What Arabian Nights' romance could be more entertaining than the adventures of that West of Ireland broth of a boy until he becomes, among many other things, a priest of Buddha. Nothing that Kipling ever wrote would be half so thrilling or so amusing as his experiences. The true and natural soldier of fortune, the man at home in every country, is always the Irishman, for it seems he alone can get into the skin of another nationality. (2009, orig. 1913: 130–1)

Neither O'Connor recorded the dates of these encounters, but they presumably refer to the first decade of the century.

For 1907, Kshirasagara (1994: 281) notes that an Irish bhikkhu, U Visud[d]ha (here the U indicates a Burmese ordination), officiated at the conversion to Buddhism of '1,000 workers and their families' – dalits in the Marikuppam gold-mines in Kolar – and implies that he was involved in the South Indian Buddhist Association.

As 'Bhikku Wisuddha a European Buddhist priest' he appears as associated with the Sakya Buddhist Society (also known as the Indian Buddhist Association – founded 1890 as the first major Tamil dalit organisation, supported by Olcott and Sumangala in Ceylon) and bringing a statue given in order of the late (European radical) bhikkhu Asoka from Ceylon to the Kolar branch of the association.[87]

The history of Irish ordination in Asia continued past this period. Eugene Kelly (pers. comm.) had heard a rumour of an Irishman ordaining in the 1930s or 1940s. Recently, Brian Bocking found a record which seemed to represent just this:

> Four Europeans were ordained Buddhist monks today at [Nyanatiloka's] Island Hermitage, Polgasduwa, in Dodanduwa.
>
> Two of them are from South Germany, while the other two hail from Dublin and East Prussia.
>
> They are Messrs. Joseph Pister, Otocraches Koff, Peter Ido and Shoharm Plodeck.[88]

By implication, the Dubliner was Peter Ido, but matters are more interesting than that.[89] The four were in fact Joseph Pistor (Nyanapiya), Otto Krauskopf (Nyanasisi), Peter Joachim Schönfeldt (Nyanakhetta) and Siegmund Feniger (who became famous as Nyanaponika). The two with apparently false names (Ido/Schönfeldt and Plodeck/Feniger) were Jewish, and this was 1936; presumably they had false papers.[90] Schönfeldt, in fact from Berlin, had been a member of the Symbolist poet Stefan George's inner circle before 1933; interned with the other Germans in Sri Lanka in 1939, he escaped to Tibet and subsequently became a well-known Hindu sannyasin as Swami Gauribala.[91] Whether there was a genuine Irish link to the presumptive false papers is unclear but unlikely (Keogh 1999); but if there was an Irish monk in this period it was not Nyanakhetta.

In the early 1950s, Robert Trumbull encountered an Irish Buddhist priest in Kalimpong (1956: 235), too early to be Jivaka who had not yet arrived in India.

87. *Ceylon Observer*, Nov 7 1908: 1669. Thanks to Alicia Turner for this reference.
88. *Straits Times*, Jun 13 1936: 19.
89. I am indebted to Ven. Nyanatusita for assistance with Peter Ido.
90. This did not prevent the German monk Nyanatiloka, who ordained them, being given a warning by the German consul in Colombo: http://www.payer.de/neobuddhismus/neobud0203.htm
91. http://aryasangha.org/german_swami_life-and-times.htm

There were also lay Buddhists during this period, such as Belfast-born film-maker and photographer William MacQuitty (MacQuitty 1991: 356). Having worked in India, Ceylon, Siam, Malaysia and China between 1926 and 1939, MacQuitty later knew the Dalai Lama (who wrote the foreword for his 1969 *Buddha*). His attraction to Buddhism seems to have been strengthened by his objections to organised religions and particularly to sectarianism:

> The virtue of Buddhism in his view was that it was actually a philosophy, not a religion, "and according to the Four Noble Truths, everybody is a Buddhist."[92]

Irish service in the British military continued after 1922, from both sides of the border (see Mr Timoney, below). We were lucky enough to interview one ex-serviceman, whose experiences in the 1950s and 1960s were no doubt shared by other sailors and soldiers in Asia. Such people could make the connection between what they had read about at home and what they encountered while serving abroad:

> Buddhism I knew about, I knew the name, and then somewhere there was a confluence [with his experience], and I recognised it. (interview B)

Years of Silence and the Missing Irish Buddhists

Thus in Asia at least, there was a slim but continuous Irish Buddhist presence from the 1860s to the 1950s. If in Ireland there seems to be a gap between the 1911 census and the later 1950s this is in part an artefact of the data and in part a genuine closure of what could be said in public in the early decades of the Free State.

As we have seen, there had been Buddhists in every census between 1871 and 1911, and when in the 1991 census it is possible to trace them again there were over 900.[93] In earlier publications (e.g. Cox and Griffin 2009) I was unable to name any Irish Buddhists in these 'years of silence', but since then the slow accumulation of accidental discoveries shows they were present, albeit often less visibly.[94]

---

92. http://quartetbooks.wordpress.com/2010/10/20/william-macquitty-and-the-titanic/

93. In 1961, for example, there were 5,236 people of 'other stated religions' in the Republic, and 6,248 in 1971 – excluding the main Christian denominations and Judaism. Between 1911 and 1991 the census did not count minor religions separately.

94. Scharbrodt (2012) comes to comparable conclusions for Muslims.

There was certainly a decline: if we look at 'other religions', these represented a consistent 0.4% of the population between 1901 and 1926,[95] dropping to 0.3% in 1936 and 1946 and then 0.2% in 1961 and 1971, from which point they picked up rapidly in 1991, 2002 and 2006: 1.1%, 2.3% and 3.3% respectively (MacGréil 2009: 6).

Astrology had a similar history. Sheerin (2003), looking at the Irish Astrological Society (founded in 1922), found a handful of early records with complete disappearance around 1940, from which point Roberts (2009) saw organisational quiescence up until 1972. In this case, the absence of an Irish organisation by no means meant the absence of Irish interest: Roberts notes 'the more sophisticated networks of English and American schools, organisations and journals' and that 'In actual practice, the English and American influence is almost overwhelming'. In other words, Irish astrologers in this period were members of overseas bodies, subscribers to journals abroad, or simply consumers of books published elsewhere. These 'latency networks' (Melucci 1989) then revived with the greater tolerance and interest of the 1970s.

But how can we trace small and unorthodox religions in a climate as hostile as the Free State and Dev's Ireland? Since there were a range of formal and informal sanctions facing those who were openly Buddhist in Ireland, we face EP Thompson's problem about researching people who were not keen to be identified by their neighbours or employers:

> If it was difficult to identify a Muggletonian two hundred years ago, we will find it more difficult to identify him today (1993: 69).

Even in more liberal Britain, Francis Story (Anagarika Sugatananda, 1910–71), who became a Buddhist at sixteen and spent much of his life in Asia, wrote:

> many people in the West still feel that being a Buddhist does not exact any public avowal. It is not like Christianity, in which a failure to declare one's faith openly is reckoned an offence meriting punishment hereafter. And in [Edwin] Arnold's time, more than now, an open declaration of Buddhism by a prominent and titled man would have caused something of a scandal (cited in Sutin 2006: 141).

---

95. Partition did not produce substantially different situations in this respect. The population of the Republic continued to decline until 1961, so the *relative* decline of 'other religions' is significant.

With the exception of Robert Gibson, all other Irish Buddhists *in Ireland* mentioned to date gave their information confidentially, to the census, and were only identifiable a century later when household returns became public. In fact, after Robert Gibson c. 1889, the next *publicly* Irish Buddhists in Ireland appeared in 1971 (Coleraine) and 1972 (Blackrock) respectively.

This avoidance of sanctions runs deep: Cosgrove's (2012) research found that 70% of members of new religions today conceal or have concealed their identities, whether by isolating themselves, avoiding discussion or in many cases 'passing' as Catholic, which they saw as an 'unsavoury, but necessary aspect of modern Irish life' (2012: 25). If this is true in 2012, it is no surprise that it was true in the heyday of church power and sectarianism:

> conversion is arguably one of the most unsettling events in the life of a
> society ... With the departure of members from the fold, the cohesion
> of a community is under threat (Viswanathan 1998: xi).

Irish Buddhists in this period must be sought in other, overlapping categories: Irish people involved in British or international Buddhist organisations; closet Buddhists; Irish people who were 'Buddhist' in other western countries; people from traditionally Buddhist countries living in Ireland; Irish people who did not think of their Buddhist sympathy, identification or practice as primarily religious, but rather as (for example) an aesthetic appreciation, a philosophical way of life, or an exploration of spiritual practices which could be used in Christian contexts; and 'night-stand' Buddhists and those who refused categorisation on principle.

Members of International Buddhist Organisations

The first kind of 'Irish Buddhist' can be identified through research in the archives and journals of the relevant societies. The Buddhist Society of Great Britain and Ireland (BSGBI) was founded in 1907 to prepare for Ananda Metteyya's 1908 mission to Britain.[96] On Metteyya's arrival, the society claimed 'ninety-five Buddhists in Great Britain and Ireland ... the great part are in London'.[97] On his

---

96. Its successor, the Buddhist Society, is currently working on its own and the BSGBI records (Louise Marchant, pers. comm.) Despite Maria Griffin's best efforts, she was unable to gain access to the records of the Theosophical Society in Ireland.

97. *Daily Mail*, Apr 22 1908. Thanks to John Crow for this reference.

departure, it had a mailing list of 700 names.[98] By 1909, it claimed 300 *members* (Maitreya 1956, though Bluck 2006: 7 suggests 150) and the quarterly *Buddhist Review* (Baumann 2002: 88). Around 1921 the *Review* sold 160–90 copies, sent out 45 free to public libraries and other free copies to 'nine Bhikkhus and ten Editors and press writers' (Humphries 1968: 12). Some, like the TCD library, were in Ireland. Irish people in London could attend public events as well as private meetings for an inner group committed to Buddhism (Baumann 2002: 88).

Metteyya's arrival in Britain was noted by the *Freeman's Journal* (Apr 24 1908: 7) and the *Irish Independent* (Apr 27 1908: 8) – the one more sceptically, the other describing him as 'a scientist of great attainment'. One of our interviewees was certain that a monk (which Metteyya was and Dharmapala could have been mistaken for) had visited Ireland at the turn of the twentieth century, and a visit by either – or come to that by William McGovern (chapter three) – is not impossible.

However neither press reports nor biographies (Harris 1998, Sangharakshita 2007a) indicate that either Metteyya or Anagarika Dharmapala, the indefatigable founder of the MahaBodhi Society, visited Ireland during their missions to Britain (1908 for Metteyya; 1893, 1897, 1904 and 1925–6 for Dharmapala). Dharmapala, for his part, had a particular interest in Ireland as a Sinhalese nationalist (Dharmadasa 1992: 125–6 fn 39 and 40) and wrote some articles on Irish parallels in resistance to colonialism.

Certainly both societies had some representation in Ireland. Between December 1901 and April 1905, perhaps longer, Ramsay Colles (born Richard William Colles, 1862–1919) was Irish representative for the Maha Bodhi Society.[99] Colles, son of a Kilkenny engineer and born in Bodh Gaya 'under the shadow of the great Maha-Bodhi Temple', was a minor literary figure, author of a *History of Ulster* and correspondent of Swinburne and Walt Whitman (Johnson 1983). Below I discuss Vivian Butler-Burke, correspondent of the Society's *British Buddhist*.

Between mid-1910 and 1917[100] Percy Oswald Reeves (1870–1967) was a member of the BSGBI's council. The English-born Reeves

98. *Irish Times*, Oct 1 1908: 4.

99. *Maha Bodhi*, 1903 (12): 5–6 and other issues. Colles was based at 42 Dawson St. Thanks to Brian Bocking for this reference.

100. *Buddhist Review*, vols. 2 (cover), 5–6: 226 and 7–8: 26.

had come to Ireland in 1902 to teach metalwork at the Dublin Metropolitan School of Art (now NCAD), where he taught until 1937 and was heavily involved in the Arts and Crafts Society. In 1916, when he did the enamelling for UCC's Honan Chapel, he was 'the leading enamelist in Ireland'.[101] Later, in 1922, the *Buddhist Review* noted a W. Fowkes as an Irish representative to the foundation of the International Buddhist Union (Nyanatiloka and Lama Govinda also took part). Slightly prior to this, the BSGBI had reimbursed Fowkes the princely sum of 7s 'for propaganda' (postage?) from the publication fund.[102]

Ani Tsondru and John O'Neill of the Karma Kagyu centre suggest that the BSGBI might have 'sent teachers to Dublin to give the occasional talk' (pers. comm.), and this is certainly possible; the Maynooth library holds a contemporary edition of Metteyya's *Wisdom of the Aryas* (Bennett 1923), published by the Society, and a 1926 copy of *The message of Buddhism* by J.E. Ellam, also of the BSGBI and simultaneously the UK representative for the Maha Bodhi Society.

The 'Ireland' in the BSGBI was not pure rhetoric, in other words; and we can add a third Buddhist organisation to the mix, the *Light of Dharma* magazine, published in San Francisco by the Jodo Shin mission between 1901–7 but aimed at a wide audience. Among its subscribers between 1904–6 was 'Richard L. Laffere', of Marlborough Rd and Gilford Rd in Dublin.[103] Laffère was one of the few listed as receiving two copies of each issue, implying some minimal distribution (most other multiple copy orders were for bookshops or Buddhist institutions). Born 1867, he worked as a surveyor in Siam, present-day Malaysia and India, suggesting that he encountered Buddhism abroad.[104]

The BSGBI's successor, the Buddhist Society, has the benefit of two detailed histories by Christmas Humphreys (1937, 1968) albeit dedicated to Buddhism 'in England'. This second society, unlike the

101. http://honan.ucc.ie/viewImage.php?recID=51

102. *Buddhist Review*, 1922 (12/1): 3; 1919–21 (9–11): 139. Thanks to John Crow for this reference.

103. Thanks to Thomas Tweed and Brian Bocking for this information.

104. *Minutes of the Proceedings* [of the Institute of Civil Engineers] 1910 (vol 179): 368. Ralph Mecredy and the other 1911 Dublin Buddhists are given in the census as living at 9 Gilford Rd while the *Light of Dharma* lists Laffère at no 7; presumably there was some connection. Laffère had died in 1909.

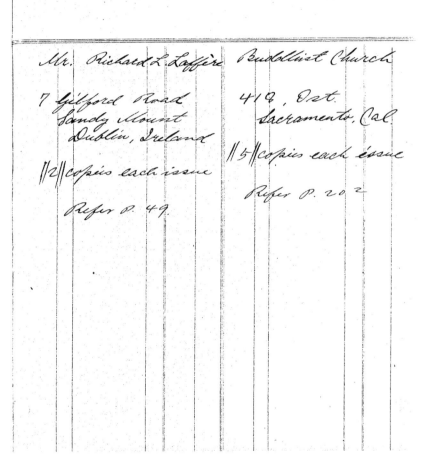

Fig. 5.7 *Light of Dharma* subscription record for Richard Laffère, 1904–6. Thanks to Thomas Tweed.

first, placed meditation at its core (Bluck 2006: 7; see Humphreys 1935 for a manual). The Society was hostile to Christianity, which no doubt affected its reception in Ireland. Its 1937 history mentions a rapid spread of Buddhism, with many students *outside* Buddhist societies (as we would expect Irish members to be); the 1968 account mentions events in Scotland, Liverpool and Leeds but no Irish groups. However, for 1964 it noted only twelve provincial groups and 1,000 members, making it clear that most members had no local group (Bluck 2006: 12). The recollection by one of our interviewees that in the 1970s 'there would have been members of the London Buddhist Society' in Dublin (interview C) is thus entirely plausible; and the Society's subscription records will hopefully advance matters.[105]

Nevertheless, prior to the 1970s Irish members and subscribers of international Buddhist organisations were almost never *publicly* active as such.

Closet Buddhists, Immigrant Buddhists and Irish Buddhists Abroad

Of other possible routes to research, 'closet Buddhists' are most likely to be identified by family historians, and it is in part with a view to encouraging such 'hidden histories' that this book is written. One, however, appears in Frank McCourt's memoir *Angela's Ashes*. In Limerick about 1940, Mr Timoney is a veteran of the British Army, whose Indian wife had been killed in a disturbance. He is described as 'a known Buddhist and a danger to good Catholics around him' and institutionalised on the intervention of the local bishop (McCourt 1998: 178).

Buddhist immigrants to Ireland, whether born Buddhist or convert, can in theory be researched, albeit with some difficulty (not least given the paucity of census data between 1911 and 1991): there are no obvious ethnic categories to look for and no easy sources. Lobsang Rampa (below) is the first clear case after Narmo Kollagaran.

Irish Buddhists living in other *western* countries certainly became a significant category from the 1960s on; but they were not absent earlier. If Aileen Faulkner was Irish, so too was the Buddhist Society's Maurice O'Connell Walshe (Walshe 1980: 3; Schmidt-Leukel 2006: 4). Perhaps two to three thousand Euro-Americans identified as Buddhist between 1893 and 1907, with tens of thousands of sympathisers (Sutin 2006: 26); no doubt in Britain as in the US, some were Irish by birth or identity.

One example is the poet and editor Maxwell Dunn (c.1895–1963). Born in Dublin, Dunn was probably exposed to Buddhism by a childhood tutor who had spent time in India (Croucher 1989: 50). In 1925, newly arrived in Melbourne, he co-founded a Theravadin 'Little Circle of Dharma' (Sherwood 2001: 61, but see Croucher 1989:

---

105. D.T. Suzuki visited Dublin in 1958, presumably as the guest of a local contact (Suzuki 1969: xvi).

26). Ordained a Soto Zen priest thirty years later, in 1955, he was the first Buddhist chaplain at the Olympic games (Pierce 1996).

More tantalisingly, Colin Middleton Murry writes in his autobiography of an interwar visit to his parents in England by

> an old Irish Buddhist with a snowy white beard and twinkling blue eyes called Mr. Loutet. He was exactly like a character out of one of the fairy tales to which I had become addicted and he had one especial talent which seemed to us wholly magical – he was a skilled ventriloquist (1975: 67)[106]

Identifying such people, however, is looking for a needle in a haystack.

'An Irish Gael'

Alicia Turner recently discovered a fascinating 'How I became a Buddhist' in the London Mahabodhi Society's *British Buddhist* for 1928, by a female 'Irish Gael'. The author describes herself as having had 'a very troublous and lonely life' and having 'withdraw[n] more and more from the worldly life'.

She speaks of herself as having grown up with

> an intense love and reverence for Nature, an absolute faith in a spiritual, unseen world, a sense of comradeship with the beings of that world ... and a feeling of love and thankfulness for all beauty (Anon. 1928: 6).

Brought up with her grandfather's fairy stories, she describes her childhood as

> in spirit very close to Nature, very independent and uncompromisingly sincere, believing absolutely in the existence of the spiritual world, but utterly indifferent as to the fate of my "immortal soul" (1928: 6).

Like AE the 'Irish Gael' was clearly a natural mystic, having seen what she later interpreted as a banshee before her little sister's death, experiencing 'flash[es] of the truth' around the insubstantial nature of reality, karma and reincarnation, in ways which she interpreted as the result of an 'invisible Teacher'. On reading the *Light of Asia:*

> It was my religion that I found expressed, I needed to know nothing more, I *was* a Buddhist. (1928: 7)

---

106. Thanks to Mike Tyldesley for this reference.

In her adult life she struggled to follow the Buddhist path, with the support of 'the Shining Ones of Ireland, our Sidhe or Devas', which she described as 'a living experience, a comradeship; they have been almost the only friends I have had' (1928: 7–8). She acknowledges the difficulties posed to Buddhist orthodoxy by this experience, resolving it in part by identifying fairies and devas, deities who in Buddhist legend often support spiritual practitioners.

'An Irish Gael' was probably Vivian Butler-Burke, an Irish-American friend of Micheál MacLiammóir who settled in Ireland in 1921 (MacLiammóir 1947: 178ff). Butler-Burke was an heiress, a vegetarian, a Republican, a correspondent of Tucholsky and Gandhi and a member of the Maha Bodhi Society. Research is still underway, but it seems she was approached in 1927 to set up a Buddhist centre and proceeded to do so at her Dublin home, 11 Harcourt Terrace.[107] In February 1929 she hosted a series of talks by Sri Lankan reformer A.P. de Zoysa and proposed to found a Buddhist study circle.[108] In 1935 she hosted Will Hayes' Wesak events here (chapter four). Butler-Burke remained the MBS contact for Ireland up to 1936, dying in 1937. Rediscovered by accident, her foundation of Ireland's first Buddhist centre has been forgotten for over seventy-five years. Other, equally isolated, Irish Buddhists in this period who did not write such accounts are lost to posterity.

Sympathisers: Patrick Breslin[109]

Sympathisers who did not identify as Buddhist is another category hard to research directly, but which includes such remarkable figures of the period as Collis or Waddell – and Patrick Breslin, who has the unfortunate honour of being one of three Irish victims of Stalin's purges.

A leading young leftist who had rejected Catholicism at the age of fourteen, Breslin was a member of the Communist Party and its successors the Workers' Party of Ireland and the Irish Worker League. He was simultaneously influenced by the astrologer Cyril Fagan (see above) and was a regular at 1920s Theosophical meetings in South Frederick Street (McLoughlin 2007: 14–17). Sent by James

---

107. *Buddhist India*, 1927 (vols. 1–2): 242.
108. *Maha Bodhi*, 1929 (37): 179.
109. Thanks to Fergal Finnegan for this reference.

Larkin to the International Lenin School in Moscow, he defended psychic phenomena:

> One day, in a Rudas seminar on dialectical materialism, this chap suddenly became very vocal. He introduced the topic of spiritualism: he was convinced that "materialisations" did take place and that spiritualism was therefore materialistic and thus all right. An extraordinary discussion ensued … Rudas promised this lad an English translation of a piece by Engels on spiritualism (cited in McLoughlin 2007: 35).

Breslin was subsequently purged from the School, more for his petty-bourgeois origins and general independent-mindedness than for his spiritualist leanings. In fact, the criminal psychologists who examined him as a prisoner years later noted that his statements were 'concrete, real and in line with the views expressed in literature [on "mystic sciences"]' (McLoughlin 2007: 35–38): in Russia as in Ireland, socialism and spiritualism were not automatically opposed.

At his purge session, Breslin claimed the ability to predict the future but held that the tenets of Indian mysticism were unprovable. He remained in the Soviet Union as journalist and translator, and was still being reported for 'religious-mystical' statements in the mid-1930s. His eventual condemnation to the gulag system, where he died in 1942, had more to do with the fact of being 'politically unreliable' and that his first wife had already been purged.

Katya, a Russian translator of Japanese, had worked for Russian intelligence. Born in 1904, her interest in Japan stemmed from a mystical experience when visiting the Buddhist temple in St Petersburg – the first in Europe, serving migrant Buryats and Kalmyks – as a teenager. The tradition in his second wife's family has it that Breslin too was very interested in Buddhism (Fergal Finnegan, pers. comm.). As with Dhammaloka and Kim, Patrick Breslin gives us some flavour of the 'other histories' of plebeian, ex-Catholic, Irish Buddhists and sympathisers in Asia in this period.

Night-stand Buddhists and Anti-Labellers

Finally, there were no doubt what Tweed (2002) calls night-stand Buddhists, not-just-Buddhists, creolising Buddhists and so on. In particular, as we have seen, many Irish Buddhists resisted classification as part of sectarianism. Here, for example, is Jivaka (below) on his ordination:

> A Christian order would be out of the question, as there was none
> which would tolerate my heretical views ... To become a monk,
> therefore, I must become a Buddhist.
>
> This labelling of religions had long seemed wrong to me. Names
> produced bigotry and intolerance, and the feeling that one was oneself
> right and the man who called himself by another name wrong. But
> with the world as it was one had to have a label. I decided to apply to
> become a novice monk, but not to become a Buddhist until the day of
> my ordination. (1962: 34)

Thus he would not have formally identified as Buddhist had
he not intended ordination – despite his commitment not just
to Buddhist ethical practice but to meditation and Buddhist
philosophy. As we have seen, there is little overlap between those
who identified as Buddhist in the 1901 and 1911 census and those
active in Buddhist organisations in the same period, as we would
expect given widespread resistance to categorisation.

While the last three years seeking Irish Buddhists have produced
a steady trickle of names, they have also underlined how difficult
it was not only to be 'Buddhist' and 'Irish' in any sense, but in
particular how hard it was to do so *publicly* and *in Ireland*. It is small
wonder that most 'out' Buddhists until the 1970s were those who
had 'gone native' in Asia. The same sectarianism which pushed
many to leave the religion of their birth also stigmatised this move
and made later attempts at identification harder.

By the late 1950s, there is once again some substantial documen-
tation on Buddhists in Ireland. The late 1950s and early 1960s were
transitional years, and not only in Ireland. In the earlier period,
the British Empire had brought substantial personal contact with
Buddhist Asia and a fair degree of public knowledge in various
forms. The new kinds of relationship established through the
'hippie trail' and refugees from countries such as Tibet or Vietnam
were yet to develop in 1958, and western knowledge was perhaps
at a hundred-year low (evidenced in part by Lobsang Rampa's
success).

The meaning of being Buddhist was also changing. In the imperial
period, western Buddhists in Asia were likely to focus on doctrine
and religious politics as central, following lines set out both by
western education and by much of the Buddhist Revival. Wei Wu
Wei was one of the last of the gentleman philosophers for whom
Buddhism was above all about 'how we should live'. By contrast,

when Michael Dillon (later Jivaka) arrived in India, it was starting to be expected of serious Buddhists, lay or monastic, that they should meditate,[110] a practice which would become *the* defining character-istic of Buddhism for westerners from the 1960s onwards.

A Fantasist in Howth (Cyril Hoskin, alias Tuesday Lobsang Rampa, c.1957–9)

The story of Tuesday Lobsang Rampa, Tibetan lama and author of the best-selling *The third eye* (1956) and some twenty other books, is justly famous (Lopéz 1998). Tibetologists asked to referee this ultra-exotic work objected strongly, and were so offended by its subsequent publication that they hired a private investigator, who in short order discovered the author to be Cyril Hoskin, a plumber's son from Devon.

Rampa, however, seems to have believed sincerely in his new identity and held until his death that Hoskin's body had been occupied by Rampa's spirit after an accident. He thus added a twist to the question of what makes one authentically Buddhist by adding the possibility of becoming a Buddhist through possession.

After publication of *The third eye* (but before the Hoskin revelations), Scotland Yard asked Rampa for his Tibetan passport or residence permit, whereupon Rampa moved to Ireland (Lopéz 1998: 98) where his then disciple Michael Dillon (see below) bought or rented him a house in Howth. He lived here up to 1959 (Mutton n.d. 63) with his wife and their friend and secretary, Sheelagh Rouse, before all three moved to Canada for tax reasons (Rouse n.d., Hopkins 2002).[111]

These were the years of the Hoskin revelations, and he dedicated *The Rampa story* to 'his friends in Howth ... for the Irish people know persecution, and they know how to judge Truth' (Rampa 1960: 3). Dillon, whose transsexuality was similarly exposed by the tabloid press in 1959, may have felt a sense of solidarity with Rampa. He certainly understood himself to be Rampa's only personal disciple (Sangharakshita 1979: 14–15).

Rampa's Buddhism was, to put it mildly, unorthodox, combining then-available popular writing on Tibet,

---

110. It was probably also expected of Peter Ido at the Island Hermitage.

111. While in Ireland he rescued a Siamese cat which later 'telepathically dictated' *Living with the lama* to him (Hopkins 2002: 143).

> supplemented with an admixture of garden variety spiritualism and
> Theosophy; the books contain discussions of auras, astral travel,
> prehistoric visits to earth by extraterrestrials, predictions of war, and
> a belief in the spiritual evolution of humanity. (Lopéz 1998: 103)

Lopéz' tongue-in-cheek defence of Rampa raises the question of who has the authority to speak about Tibetan Buddhism, and the counter-interests of academics in controlling the subject. Rampa could also fit comfortably into Lennon's Irish antiquarianism between Betham and Celtic Buddhism – or Tweed's occultist Buddhists.

Bharati (1974), one of the Tibetologists consulted by Rampa's publishers, was still hostile sixteen years later, but concluded his critique by observing 'I never saw why … Hoskins must be Tibetan (which he is not) if he has something important to teach' – incidentally mirroring Jivaka's judgement.

If Rampa's Buddhism is not what Tibetan Buddhists practise, he and his companions nevertheless identified as Buddhist. Early editions of his books, while he was still in Howth, advertised shamrock Buddhas for sale (Dharmachari Akshobin, pers. comm.) – the wearing of which may yet prove to be the first Buddhist practice in Ireland, at least for a given value of 'Buddhist' and 'practice'.

A Raconteur in Monte Carlo
(Terence Gray/Wei Wu Wei/0.0.0. 1958–86)

Christmas Humphreys' account of post-war British Buddhism notes that

> A new writer appeared in the field of Buddhist metaphysics in the person of "Wei Wu Wei", whose pseudonym but lightly veils a brilliant Irish mind now resident in Monte Carlo. (1968: 63, 79)

This was Terence Gray, an Anglo-Irish aristocrat from a Lisburn family who had had a distinguished theatre career in Cambridge between the wars[112] and a colourful personal life, marrying a Rimsky-Korsakov and later a Georgian princess.

Already in the mid-1920s Gray had been attracted to Buddhism (Cornwell 2004: 83), but his Buddhist writing arose from his 1954–5 translation of Hubert Benoit's *La doctrine suprême*, a work on Zen influenced by Aldous Huxley. Gray may have been associated at this

---

112. His theatre is now part of the Cambridge Buddhist Centre (Cornwell 2004: xviii).

time with the Parisian *Les amis du Boudhisme* (Cornwell 2004: 309); certainly he knew both Benoit and Christmas Humphreys, who recommended him to the publishers.

Gray wrote around this time 'It seems to me that the world at present has great need of Buddhism', although he was keen to present this in his own voice and avoid the explicit presentation of Buddhist doctrine as such (2004: 313, 323–4). He wrote seven such books between 1958 and 1974 and a posthumous collection of essays, and became a regular correspondent of the Buddhist Society's *Middle Way*. This was nurtured by a series of journeys to Asia, visiting Lama Govinda and Douglas Harding (author of *On having no head*) in India, John Blofeld in Thailand, Buddhist monks in Hong Kong and so on, creating what his biographer describes as 'his own Buddhist empire' – or at least his own Buddhist pilgrimage route (2004: 330, 335).

From today's perspective, Wei Wu Wei's Buddhism seems determinedly literary. In works like *Ask the awakened*, *The tenth man*, *Fingers pointing towards the moon* or *Why Lazarus laughed*, he combines Buddhism (particularly Zen) and Taoism to present an aphoristic philosophy of life in direct continuity with the whimsical wisdom of earlier Anglo-Irish raconteurs such as Dunsany. A critic might say that it offered not so much a life transformed by Buddhist practice but a version of Buddhism as fascinating ideas, not particularly distinguishable from Taoism, rather similar to his younger contemporary Alan Watts. Thus he wrote, in *Open Secret*,

> *The practice of meditation* is represented by the three monkeys, who cover their eyes, ears and mouth so as to avoid the phenomenal world. *The practice of non-meditation* is ceasing to be the see-er, hearer or speaker while eyes, ears and mouths are fulfilling their functions in daily life (Errey n.d.)

Yet Wei Wu Wei was driven by a genuine humanism, and as a good twentieth-century modernist his goal seems to have been to disrupt the written form as a way of enabling the reader to arrive at a different perspective:

> There seems never to have been a time at which sentient beings have not escaped from the dungeon of individuality. In the East liberation was elaborated into a fine art ...
>
> In the West reintegration was sporadic, but in recent years it has become a widespread preoccupation. Unfortunately its technical dependence on oriental literature ... has proved a barrier which

rendered full comprehension labourious and exceedingly long. Therefore it appears to be essential that such teaching as may be transmissible shall be given in a modern idiom and in accordance with our own processes of thought. But this presentation can never be given by the discursive method to which we are used for the acquisition of conceptual knowledge, for the understanding required is not conceptual and therefore is not knowledge ... (1970)

As with Watts, Huxley or Suzuki, the practical meaning of this was often to substitute a certain kind of *reading* for other kinds of spiritual practice. This of course had a long history in western philosophy (Hadot 1995); Wei Wu Wei follows Nietzsche in trying to use shock to break through everyday understanding.

More radical than his contemporaries, who tended to embed the shock in a discursive flow of comment on the irrational, Wei Wu Wei drew on his experience as a theatrical innovator to attempt a similar practice in literature. If the final result is unconvincing, at least part of this has to do with our own distance in time, as readers, from both, and the difficulty of reading Wei Wu Wei as writing in an artistic rather than philosophical mode, attempting to jolt us into a new emotional orientation to ourselves and our situations.

A Transsexual in Ladakh (Michael/Laura Dillon/Sramanera Jivaka/ Lobzang Jivaka, 1950s–1962)[113]

Michael (Laura) Dillon is best known as the world's first female-to-male transsexual through plastic surgery, and has been the subject of two biographies (Hodgkinson 1989, Kennedy 2007) focussing on this side of his life, a chapter by his one-time teacher Sangharakshita (2007b: 40–56) and a one-man play by Buddhist actor Phil Kingston (2006). He shared with Hearn and Kim a fractured family background (an orphan, s/he was brought up by elderly aunts in England after the family home at Lismullen in Meath was burnt in the War of Independence) and with Daly a prior interest in theosophy.

Having studied in Cambridge as a woman before WWII and transitioned to a male identity during the war, he returned to Ireland as a man and qualified in medicine at TCD while undergoing what was then pioneering (and illegal) surgery in Britain. Disowned by his brother, the 8th Baronet of Lismullen, he developed a deep interest in philosophical and spiritual questions, writing among

113. Thanks to Dharmachari Lalitavira for assistance on Jivaka.

other things a pioneering work on transsexuality (Dillon 1946). From reading Ouspensky, he drew quite Buddhist, and practice-oriented, conclusions:

> It was clearly stated that the purpose of man was to evolve, that he had no Self, as he fondly imagined he had, that "I" was not a unity but a multiplicity of moods, and that the first step anyone must take was to reduce the number of these "I"s and try to unify the Self. And one step towards this was to rid oneself of negative emotions, to which, normally, we are all slaves. This made sense. It satisfied my lust for truth. *It was practical. One could start to work that very day.* (Jivaka 1962: 28–9; my italics)

After Ouspensky and Gurdjieff, he encountered Lobsang Rampa (above), thus becoming perhaps the first Irish person to *believe* they were being ordained into the Tibetan tradition as well as, later, the first of whom this was actually true. He later wrote:

> Much of what he told me purporting to be of his own life I now know to be false … [but] what he said of the universe and man's place in it made good sense. (cited in Kennedy 2007: 148)

Working as a ship's doctor in 1958, Dillon's transsexuality was leaked to the press; a deeply private individual, he fled to India and encountered more authentic forms of Buddhism. In Kalimpong, Dhardo Rimpoche directed him to Sangharakshita at the 'English vihara' (Kennedy 2007: 142–3). He arrived with a robe and girdle with which Rampa had initiated him into the 'Secret Order of the Potala', but his faith in Rampa was considerably undermined when Sangharakshita showed him

> just such a monk's robe in my cupboard, presented to me by Burmese pilgrims whom I had met in one of the holy places. It was of the same yellowish-brown colour as the one Jivaka was wearing, consisted of the same number of patches, and bore in one corner the same manufacturer's label in Burmese script (Sangharakshita 2007b: 48).

As Kennedy notes, however,

> the Secret Order of the Potala was an apt metaphor for his situation. Dillon *did* belong to a secret organization with only about a dozen members worldwide. He *did* have special knowledge. Unlike nearly everyone else alive during his time, he knew what it was like to live in both a male and a female body. No one around Dillon seemed to grasp that his experience had given him unique insight into the human condition. (2007: 148–9)

Fig. 5.8 Jivaka (Michael Dillon) in Kalimpong with Sangharakshita, c. 1959. Permission granted by Clearvision.

Sangharakshita, with whom he had a difficult relationship, gave him the name Jivaka at his request to aid in anonymity (the original Jivaka had also been a doctor), and taught him to meditate. In Sarnath, staying with the Maha Bodhi society, he studied Buddhist texts (Kennedy 2007: 151) and was ordained as a Theravadin sramanera (novice) in spring 1959 (Sangharakshita 2007b: 46–53). He failed in a subsequent attempt to be ordained as a monk; this hinged on the interpretation of *vinaya* rules about persons of 'intermediate sex'. Sangharakshita writes that he incurred Jivaka's anger by informing the Sarnath abbot of this, but Jivaka claimed subsequently to have raised the issue himself (Sangharakshita 2007b: 53–4, Kennedy 2007: 158). [114]

Whoever was responsible, it barred Jivaka from full Theravada ordination; through Herbert Guenther and a Lama Lobzang, he turned to the Tibetan tradition, and the Ladakhi diplomat Kushok Bakula Rinpoche offered him a passport to Ladakh and ordination as a *getsul* (novice), with the promise of full ordination once the controversy was over (Kennedy 2007: 156–60, 171). [115]

After his novice ordination, Jivaka spent three months in 1960 studying under Rizong Rimpoche at the (Gelugpa) Rizong monastery in Ladakh. With Indo-Chinese border tensions, he was unable to extend his travel permit and was forced to leave the monastery (Kennedy 2007: 180, 184) but was promised higher ordination and library work on his return (Jivaka 1962: 175).

Having already collapsed from exhaustion at Rizong in 1960, he suffered typhoid in Sarnath in 1961 and died in May 1962 in Dalhousie while travelling to Kushok Bakula to seek another permit. Between his surgery and drugs, the poverty, malnourishment and harsh conditions he subjected himself to in the monastery, and his urgency to return, his death bears witness to how far he pushed himself in the desire to change. [116]

Unmaking the Privileged Self and Tackling Racism
Jivaka did not spare himself in the attempt to become Buddhist. He had already given away all his wealth, some £20,000, on becoming

114. Despite their falling out, Jivaka's *Life of Milarepa* recommends Sangharakshita's *Survey of Buddhism* (1994: 23).

115. He had also taken Bodhisattva vows with 'the Dalai Lama's teacher' in early 1959; elsewhere (1962: 125) he mentions receiving an initiation from Dudjom Rimpoche in Kalimpong.

116. The circumstances echo the end of James Hilton's 1933 best-seller *Lost horizon*, when the hero Conway makes a last, desperate attempt to return to Shangri-la. The last line, as the narrator hears how Conway's trail has been lost, is his question 'Do you think he will ever make it?'

a Theravadin novice.[117] Although in Rizong he was offered special treatment, he insisted on following the normal rules of ordination seniority, putting himself below Ladakhi teenagers, sharing the frugal food and living conditions of the poorest monks, and working as a cleaner in the kitchen. This came in part from a wish to tackle his own racist prejudices and to be treated 'normally':

> Would I be beaten black and blue, or would they have a hereditary awe of a "Sahib"? If so, *my purpose in going would be defeated* (Jivaka 1962: 16, my emphasis).

Already in 1959, he

> began to realise just how much work he'd have to do to overhaul his mind, to strip it of the snobbishness … He acknowledged that he found it difficult to make his ceremonial bows before the Sarnath monks who were his superiors. It is hard, he noted, for an Englishman to get on his knees – particularly when he was bending before a dark-skinned man. (Kennedy 2007: 152-3)

The attempt to go native was also an eminently practical one: already understanding basic spoken and written Tibetan, on arrival he worked hard to learn Ladakhi (Jivaka 1962: 16, 128, 148; Kennedy 2007: 175). It led to some wonderful moments of internal struggle:

> One morning while seated on the floor of the kitchen with the other getsuls [novices] and genyens [young boys], using a bit of twig for cutlery to spear the tiny lumps of dough out of their watery environment, I had a sudden vision of my London club – the bed with its Dunlopillo mattress, the tail-coated waiter wheeling a breakfast trolley into my room and handing me the morning paper. As I look at the trolley I see the cornflakes and milk, creamy from the cow, not from water buffaloes as in India, and sugar, as much as one wants; under the silver cover is crisp brown bacon and scrambled eggs on fried bread, and a rack of toast and marmalade. I abruptly put an end to this unwise piece of daydreaming, and looked at my cup with the greenish water and leaves floating in it and a bit of dough stuck on the side above the water line. Then I looked at my companions, three dirty boys in ragged dressing-gowns, two smoke-blackened youths, and a couple of gelongs who were breakfasting with us. Their faces were friendly and sincere … The moment had passed, and the London club was forgotten!

117. The request startled his lawyers so much that they took nearly a year to comply (Kennedy 2007: 154).

> After breakfast and washing up there would be apricots to
> distribute, tea to be made, wood and water to be fetched, and lunch to
> be prepared and served. (1962: 61)

The struggle, then, was resolved in favour of Ladakh and against
privilege. His determination to change himself so dramatically
– across barriers of gender, then class and finally race – demands
great respect and bears witness to a remarkable ethical practice.

Jivaka as Buddhist

Jivaka is the first Irish Buddhist known to have had a meditation
practice. His basic training was with Sangarakshita in Kalimpong;
in Sarnath, his primary aim was 'to become proficient in meditation'
and 'gain the mastery over my wandering mind' (1962: 41). In
Rizong, however,

> the early hours we kept in the kitchen prevented me from continuing
> with my two-year-old practice of an hour's meditation after getting
> up. This I missed badly, and with the lack of privacy it was not
> possible to fit it in during the day (1962: 69).

The focus on meditation marked a break with his earlier esoteric
perspective: if on arriving in India 'he wanted to know how to
read people's thoughts ... and how to see what was happening at
a distance' (Sangharakshita 2007b: 46), soon he would write that
occult powers 'come incidentally with mental development and
self-discipline, and should never be sought for their own sake'
(Jivaka 1994: xi; cf. 5–8). Similarly – by contrast with earlier Irish
Buddhists, from Hearn to Wei Wu Wei – he criticised the tendency
to identify 'being Buddhist' with having a particular set of *ideas:*

> the perception [of the fundamental principles of Buddhism] gained
> by meditation is different from that which comes from ordinary study
> (1994: 10).

His *Growing up into Buddhism* (1960), written for teenagers, gives a
wider sense of what he felt 'being Buddhist' entailed: on the one hand
a straightforward account of the eightfold path, the four noble truths
and the no-self doctrine from a modernist perspective, it shows strong
influences from Gurdjieff and Ouspensky in stressing conscious
living, making clear choices and resisting habitual tendencies.

Between 1959 and 1962, he wrote a series of books covering
the gamut of Buddhism: another Maha Bodhi introductory text,

Practicing the Dhammapada, a rewriting of Evans-Wentz' *Life of Milarepa*, a *Critical study of the Vinaya* and articles for the *Maha Bodhi* on topics such as 'Causation and Nagarjuna' and the Surangama Sutra.[118] He also wrote a fascinating account of his time at Rizong, *Imji getsul* ('English novice'),[119] and an unpublished autobiography in which he 'outed' himself (Kennedy 2007: 189).

One of his first pieces (1959) was a very critical review of the ex-Untouchable (dalit) leader B.R. Ambedkar's *The Buddha and his Dhamma*[120] (Queen 2004), where he argues that Ambedkar 'preaches non-Dharma as Dharma for motives of political ambition and social reform' and defending the monastic life to which he aspired against Ambedkar's criticisms:

> Bhikkhus, he thinks, are for the purpose of self-culture and social service, especially social service, which explains the critical and aggressive attitude of "New Buddhists" when they meet with any. (cited in Queen 2004: 136, 139).

The review repeats caste Hindu attacks (Queen 2004: 140, 147 fn 5), and it may be that arriving in India with an Irish image of tolerance, Jivaka was upset by the newly-converted dalits' insistence on separating themselves from Hinduism. We have seen above that he was resistant to labels: *Growing up* ... argues that Buddhism recognises an absolute which is not different from that underlying other religions, but that it is more consistent in refusing to define it. Consistently, at one point in his Indian writings he suggested that Buddhahood could be equated with Christhood (Jivaka 1994: 17).

It is hardly surprising that he was not immediately *au fait* with Indian religious politics on arrival; it is far more impressive how rapidly he remade himself to become part of the new world. Travelling with Rizong monks for a ritual, Jivaka wrote:

> Somewhere, years before, I had read of rain-making lamas. Could I really be among them, engaged in making rain? It seemed fantastic. There are some things you read of in books but never think could happen to you. Surely this was one of them? I looked down at my dress; yes, the red robes of the "lama" were on me, and all around were "lamas" seated cross-legged on the floor ... (1962: 109)

118. *Maha Bodhi*, 1959 (67): 215–23; 1960 (68): 126–9.
119. Reviewed by poet Austin Clarke (*Irish Times*, May 26 1962: 8).
120. *Maha Bodhi*, 1959 (67): 352–3.

Jivaka's life and death command respect as a Buddhist practitioner who spared no effort to change himself; it is no surprise that
he is also celebrated by Ireland's Transsexual Equality Network.
The last word on his life comes from the foreword to his *Milarepa*, a
story which he says

> is an inspiration to all those who feel that circumstances weigh against
> them and that their ends are unattainable. (1994: ix)

He concludes

> Every human being – every being – is a potential Buddha. It is up to
> him to actualise Buddhahood in himself. (1994: 22)

The Meanings of 'early Irish Buddhism'

What 'kind of Buddhists' were these first Irish converts?
Generalisation is obviously problematic, and the quantity and
quality of information is varied. It is easier to discuss the world-
systemic relationships within which people worked out what their
Buddhism might be. Early Irish Buddhists allied themselves with
modernising Asian movements that responded to colonialism,
missionaries, Orientalist scholarship and the renewed contact with
other Buddhist countries by rethinking and remaking what it meant
to be Buddhist.

Dhammaloka's 'Buddhist dialogue with freethought' as we
might now put it, represents a thoroughly rationalist interpretation, publicised widely via the Buddhist Tract Society. Daly
was similarly able to work with the new, educated laity and the
Theosophical Society against the resistance of traditionalist, temple-
based Buddhism to construct a modernist alternative and defend
Buddhism's scientific credentials against Christian missionaries;
while Pfoundes did much the same with the Buddhist Propagation
Society.

Hearn, for his part, romanticised Buddhist culture on behalf of a
highly modern Japanese nationalism – but not the openly modernist
schools in Japanese Buddhism. His cultural nationalism, however,
prefigures the Kyoto school in particular; like Collis and Yeats,
his is a romantic modernism attempting to preserve the rural and
traditional in the midst of change.

In Rizong gompa, of course, Jivaka had no real alternative; but
like Hearn his interest in evolutionary philosophies could draw on

past reading, the Maha Bodhi Society and his difficult relationship with the western Buddhist moderniser Sangharakshita. Wei Wu Wei, finally, was an ultra-moderniser, to the point of writing Buddhism almost without Buddhists and with everything presented in non-religious terms.

In these various ways and situations, then, Irish Buddhists were part and parcel of the transformations that produced contemporary Buddhism (McMahan 2008, Lopéz 2002). They were also heavily involved in personal change: to be Buddhist was to adopt another way of life, and most obviously to cross the race bars of empire. This is perhaps the main difference separating *these* 'Victorian Buddhists' from those studied by Almond and Franklin. The latter, remaining at home and working as traditional academics, novelists, journalists and so on were subject to 'limits of dissent' arising from their class situation. Their access to the written word (and hence posterity's access to them) depended on this.

Most early Irish Buddhists, however, had different institutional allegiances: Dhammaloka and Jivaka became monks, Daly abandoned the priesthood and allied with Sinhala modernisers, while Pfoundes and Hearn took up Japanese employment. It is really only in Europe, for Robert Gibson and Wei Wu Wei, that Buddhism did not mean a radical change of class position and lifestyle.

Along with this came other choices. Hearn became a Japanese citizen,[121] something Pfoundes attempted. Jivaka's challenge to his own racism and class position is particularly striking. Dhammaloka had less to say on the matter, but it is clear that becoming a Buddhist monk meant losing the relative security and privilege he had won for the first time in his life as a literate white man in Burma. Thus early Irish Buddhism meant, above all, some lived solidarity with Asian Buddhists and a crossing of racial lines. Beyond this, Hearn's scandalously interracial marriages, Dhammaloka and Daly's celibacy, and Gibson's marriage to a suffragette were not exactly conventional choices, to say nothing of Jivaka's transsexuality.

These issues of class, race and gender, of course, remain live ones in Ireland, and it is no accident that the *next* Buddhist wave in Ireland (chapter six) was closely associated with the counter-culture – and with travel abroad – or that it came intertwined with the

121. Leading to the loss of his post at Tokyo University.

women's movement, gay liberation, environmentalism, community organising, the peace movement and so on.

In the wake of these movements, it is now possible (albeit with sometimes severe difficulty) for people in Ireland to be 'out' transsexuals, for working-class Dubliners to acquire third-level education, for people from broken homes and mixed marriages to make careers rather than be sent abroad or into industrial schools – and, of course, to live in Ireland as an 'out' Buddhist. These are recent achievements, to which the counter culture and Buddhism have contributed hugely.

Finally, Buddhism represented a development of free thought, spiritual exploration and the abandonment of 'actually-existing Christianity': the sectarian Catholicism and Protestantism of their Irish backgrounds and the missionary Christianity they encountered in Asia.[122]

These routes ran through a mixture of atheism, spirituality and Theosophy, and for many of them, as for Watters, Joyce or Collis, the attraction of Buddhism lay precisely in its tolerance[123] and perceived pacifism, qualities sorely lacking in the Ireland of the day outside perhaps of Quakerism. As Lennon delicately puts it, tolerance has not been a dominant theme in Irish literature (2004: 369).

We have seen Jivaka's and Hearn's reluctance to identify as Buddhist; tolerance is also explicit in the writings of Wei Wu Wei and Hearn, working in Far Eastern Buddhist contexts for which some form of syncretism or coexistence with Taoism, Confucianism, Shinto etc., is unexceptional. Pfoundes stresses tolerance and rationalism; and with Pfoundes, Dhammaloka and Jivaka there is also a willingness to cross boundaries between Theravada and Mahayana.

Buddhist Humanism as Prefigurative Dissent

In this sense too, contemporary Buddhists in the Republic are the inheritors of these past struggles. As sectarianism has waned in the South, non-violence has become widely acceptable, a broad religious tolerance has become commonplace, and popular Christianity too

122. Period matters: opposing missionaries was far more important in the imperial period (for Dhammaloka, Pfoundes, Hearn and Daly) than subsequently (for Jivaka or Wei Wu Wei).

123. Not in the imperial sense (Nagai 2006) or that of modern *Hindutva* approaches to Buddhists and Sikhs.

has changed. Thus Buddhism, for those who actually engaged with it, represented a choice of another way of life which the rest of Ireland has taken rather longer to work out through other channels.

Many of the positions taken by Buddhists a century ago are ones which the descendants of the Catholic and Protestant service classes now find far easier to take. To misquote John Hume, we can say, only partly tongue-in-cheek, that today's Irish Christianity is becoming Buddhism for slow learners: it has become more tolerant and less sectarian, largely peaceful rather than stridently patriotic, less driven by the constraints of class, race and gender.

In other words, if contemporary Irish Buddhism is less counter-cultural than it was (chapter seven) this is only partly because it has become less radical. It is also because 'middle Ireland' has finally taken on board some of the critique of 'actually-existing Christianity' made over a century ago by early Irish Buddhists and Theosophists – and some of the critique of cultural conformity made by the feminists and counter-cultural activists of the 1960s and 1970s.

In the period this chapter covers, this was not the case. These people were marginalised and their 'authenticity' as Irish or Buddhist routinely attacked. By comparison with British or American Buddhism in the period, subordinate parts of their own cultures (Almond 1988, Tweed 2000), 'Buddhism' and 'Ireland' were almost impossible to hold together, and it was easiest to be Buddhist by defecting from one's class, 'going native' in Japan, Ceylon, Burma or Ladakh and abandoning both the local culture and its imperial context.

The psychological disruptions in the lives of the Dublin Theosophists were even stronger for Buddhists. Hearn (like Kim) was to all intents and purposes an orphan, as was Vivian Butler-Burke; Pfoundes' family relationships were deeply fractured; Dhammaloka was a hobo; Daly abandoned his church; Jivaka was disinherited and 'outed'; like Wei Wu Wei, he could never go home. While the Theosophists re-established themselves within Irish society and received many honours in later years, the Irish Buddhists received no such recognition; most survived by their pen and died poor.

Irish Theosophists avoided 'Buddhist' options in order to continue public lives in the age of independence. To be Buddhist, in Ireland, was to reject the religious choices that defined the public sphere. Foster, Deane and others suggest that these moves are a retreat from conflict: but Pfoundes, Dhammaloka, Daly, Judge and Wei Wu Wei hardly shunned controversy. Jivaka and Hearn, less consciously political, were nevertheless peppery public figures. Rather, it was a question of which conflicts they saw as worth fighting, and what for. Instead of defending the caste or tribe of their birth, people like Pfoundes, Dhammaloka, Hearn and Jivaka came to identify outside themselves, and at some cost.

As Harris (2007: 30) puts it, such groups

> were "dissident" in that they were a reaction against a culture which stressed the hegemony of Christianity, the rhetoric of Empire, and the superiority of Western civilization. They not only mounted a religious challenge to Christianity but also a social challenge to the imperialistic culture Christianity had spawned.

Irish Buddhists, caught between the rearguard actions of the Anglo-Irish imperial service class and the new rising Catholic nationalism, found both personal and political solutions in opposing the world of European, Christian domination of the globe – as part of alliances across, and against, the capitalist world-system in its high imperialist phase.

Irish Buddhism as Solidarity Movement

Elsewhere (Cox 2010a) I have analysed this form of Buddhism and sympathising as part of processes of international solidarity, alongside other kinds of alliances. Cultural nationalism and anti-imperialism in Ireland were mirrored in Buddhist Asia by an inter-national Buddhist revival, and the making of links is not surprising.

Many of the figures discussed here were located within or worked for Asian-led organisations: the Buddhist sangha (Dhammaloka, Jivaka); lay Buddhist organisations (Pfoundes, Daly); Japanese educational institutions (Hearn); Soviet institutions (Breslin), within a general framework of anti-colonial nationalism. Their political activities of course varied hugely, from Collis' personal acts of solidarity via Breslin's journalism to Hearn and Dhammaloka's much more effective publicistic activity and to Daly and Dhammaloka's organisation-building. So too did their political perspectives taken on their own terms, in a scale running from Daly's technocratic modernism via Collis' liberal nationalism and Dhammaloka's pan-Asian cultural revivalism to Hearn's visceral anti-imperialism, Butler-Burke's republicanism and Breslin's communism.

There was an important nexus between their own religious evolution and cultural nationalisms in Asia. Daly, Hearn, Breslin and Dhammaloka all shared an early rejection of Christianity along free-thinking, agnostic and/or spiritualist lines, not as independent personal decisions but as mediated through spiritualist and theosophical societies, free-thinking and anarchist organisations. In Asia, the choice of developing or deepening an interest in Buddhism led them into alliance with the cultural nationalisms of Ceylon, Burma and Japan. These cultural nationalisms represent key ways in which newly hegemonic developmentalist nationalisms and would-be hegemonic nationalist elites set out to conquer or remake 'civil society', in opposition – as far as our Irish Buddhists are concerned – to missionary Christianity.

The Limits of Dissent

Tweed's account of conversion notes the 'limits of dissent': his American Buddhists

> rejected some element of the dominant religion and culture, but they
> did so within the context of a broader consent (2002: 12)

This cannot be said of Irish Buddhists of the period, whatever their personal limitations; at the extreme, in a Dhammaloka or a Jivaka, we can see the 'ruthless critique of all that exists' elevated into the guiding principle of a life. American Buddhists struggled to overcome theism, belief in a permanent soul, the belief in action in the world as a value in itself, and optimism (Tweed 2000; see Franklin 2008: 23 for a similar position). Irish Buddhists did not have the same problems.

Free-thinking certainly offered a straightforward escape from Christianity for figures such as Hearn, Dhammaloka and Jivaka; in other cases (Daly, Breslin) we can see a classic loss of faith. It is only at the margins (for example in Joyce or Wei Wu Wei) that theism is at all significant, and there mostly as a gesture of tolerance, not wanting to exclude any religious position. Similarly, Irish Buddhists seem not to have been worried by the abandonment of belief in a permanent soul: those whose views are best known (Hearn and Jivaka) were interested primarily in theorising karma.

Those American Buddhists who relied like Žižek (2001) on second hand sources sometimes worried that Buddhism lacked this-worldly action. Irish participants in the Buddhist Revival did not face this problem, although Wei Wu Wei in Europe and the recently-arrived Jivaka have elements of posing the contrast, and resolving it in favour of inaction. Nor, finally, have I encountered any sense of a struggle over Buddhism as pessimist.

As noted, the main stumbling block to Irish Buddhism was probably that its sub-Theosophical version was too similar to generic Victorian beliefs, while its orthodox Asian versions were too far away from anything that could safely be subscribed to publicly in the Ireland of the day.

This reading has the merit of explaining why Hinduism, paganism and ritual magic *were* accessible options to the contemporaries of our Irish Buddhists, and have continued to be so until this century. They enable a continued orientation to theism and soul-belief, and – crucially for the Irish setting – they can be easily creolised with Christianity. A Vedantist understanding of God, a cultural nationalist reading of Celtic mythology or ritual magic as a reflection of Christian ritualism are all widespread sentiments in ordinary Irish religious practice today (Cosgrove et al., 2011).

Irish Buddhists, nonetheless, shared one key feature with their American brothers and sisters:

> in their natural idiosyncracy, their cultivated marginality, or their genuine cultural nonconformity, most Euro-American Buddhist sympathizers stood apart from their contemporaries (2000: 79)

It was to take a century for this situation to change in Ireland.

Going Native, Quietly:
Class, Gender and Shame

'Going native', both in religion and in other ways, was a long-standing feature of European presence in Asia, already familiar in the sixteenth and seventeenth centuries. It brought up extreme discomfort, verging on shame and disgust, for contemporaries because of its breach of lines of race, religion and power (inextricably intertwined in the colonial situation) and remains a problem for modern writers:

> this tendency to "go native" in India has by and large been either ignored or suppressed by historians of the Raj (Dalrymple 2000).

Dalrymple gives as an example the Irish mercenary George Thomas, the 'Rajah from Tipperary', who carved out his own state in Haryana at the end of the eighteenth century; he found it easier to dictate his autobiography in Farsi and Hindi than in English. Another figure is the Bengal Army general 'Hindoo Stuart', author of *The vindications of the Hindoos*:

> Not much is known about this strange Irishman who came out to India in his teens, but he seems to have been almost immediately attracted to Hinduism and within a year of his arrival in Calcutta had adopted the practice – which he continued to his death – of walking every morning from his house to bathe in and worship the Ganges according to Hindu custom ... when he visited Europe in 1804 he took a collection of his Hindu household gods with him (Dalrymple 2000).

This collection became the core of the British Museum's Oriental collection. For Dalrymple, the turning point in the meaning of 'going native' was the mid-nineteenth century:

> With the British victory, and the genocidal spate of hangings and executions that followed, the entire top rank of the Mughal aristocracy was swept away and British culture was unapologetically imposed on India; at the same time the wholesale arrival of the Memsahibs ended all open sexual contact between the nations. The White Mughals died out and their very existence was later delicately erased from embarrassed Victorian history books; they have since been studiously ignored ...

Except, of course, that this is only true for those members of the élite who went native openly. There seems not to be much research on 'going native' in Asia at all (Turner et al., 2010, Cox 2013) by contrast with the situation in the Americas, where radical historians have increasingly explored the phenomenon of *plebeian* 'going native'.[124]

---

124. There seems to be more research on literary *representations* of 'going native' in Asia than on the phenomenon itself. Occasionally, as with *Kim*, there is some Asian reality behind the image; more commonly, what this literature reveals is the nature of colour lines as understood in the west. Thus Sidney Owenson's *The missionary* (later republished as *Luxima the prophetess*), in which a seventeenth-century Portuguese missionary falls in love with the daughter of a Hindu priestess and arrives at a greater religious tolerance as a result, has been discussed by both Viswanathan (1998: 27–31) and Wright (2007: 93–8). Humanist though the text is, it is evidence rather for Owenson's 'critique of the sectarian savagery at the heart of European history' (Viswanathan 1998: 27) than for the actual nature of such encounters.

The whole area – whether Irish people becoming Buddhist or other situations – bears greater attention, although the research problems are substantial. The discoveries of Capt. Pfoundes, U Dhammaloka and Bowles Daly were all accidental.

If changes around 'going native' were part of the broader processes which saw British imperialism find greater legitimation at home through closer links with missionary Christianity, then, those who 'went native' by that token severed ties with what had once been 'home' and lost their place in the racial/colonial order. No doubt far more people 'went native' than were ever recorded by European papers; it would have been a considerable source of shame to the same families whose children's successful careers within the empire would have been a source of pride.[125]

I recently heard an older Irish man discuss how an acquaintance, to the day of her death, was spoken of as 'that poor woman' because her son had left the priesthood to marry. If this was true in postwar Ireland for something which meant the existence of (legitimate!) grandchildren, it is hard to imagine how earlier Irish families could have made public what might have been known privately about relatives' conversion to, or sympathy for, a 'pagan' and 'idolatrous' religion.[126]

Professional Buddhists

Because of this, most Irish Buddhists who were known at the time were in a sense Buddhists *by profession*. Between them, the figures discussed in this chapter wrote at least thirty-four books during their 'Buddhist periods' (Pfoundes wrote five, Hearn thirteen, Daly one, Jivaka six and Wei Wu Wei wrote eight). To this we can add a formidable body of writing in periodicals (Japanese newspapers, Theosophist periodicals and scholarly journals for Pfoundes; Indian newspapers for Daly; American magazines for Dhammaloka and

125. O'Toole 2009: 48–9 notes the high proportion of marriages between Chinese men and Irish women in America and Australia, and the likelihood that their descendants are now seen as Asian-Americans rather than part of Irish America. He does not discuss the question of religious behaviour.

126. As I was writing the first draft of this, the Commission of Investigation into the Catholic Archdiocese of Dublin produced a report on church authorities' role in covering up child sexual abuse – not in the distant past, but between 1975 and 2004. Their primary motivation was 'the avoidance of scandal and the preservation of the good name, status and assets of the church and its priests' (*Irish Times*, Nov 27 2009: 9).

Hearn, who also published in Orientalist journals and the Kobe *Chronicle*; the *Maha Bodhi Journal* for Jivaka, the *Middle Way* and other Buddhist journals for Wei Wu Wei) and Dhammaloka's activities as publisher and polemicist.

These public Buddhists escaped the social penalties for westerners who openly practised or sympathised with Buddhism through their role in Asian or Buddhist organisations – the Buddhist Tract Society, Buddhist Theosophical Schools, Japanese educational institutions, the Maha Bodhi Society, Indian newspapers, the Buddhist Propagation Society and European Buddhist bodies – a role which valued them particularly as writers and to which they responded with gusto.

Those not in this situation had nothing to gain, and much to lose – for themselves or their families – by 'outing' themselves, whether in Ireland or Asia. Helen Waddell faced incomprehension at *The spoiled Buddha*, while Maurice Collis was forced to resign for his sympathy for Burmese culture and people. Both could shoulder the cost and become well-published authors despite this. But we must assume that the various once-anonymous Buddhists whom we can now trace in the last censuses of colonial Ireland were not in the same situation; this was in all probability far more true in Asia where crossing the lines of race and power was a subversive act.

Remarkable Individuals

Consistent with this, the *known* early Irish Buddhists were remarkable individuals more generally. Some had substantial university education (Daly qualified in religion and law, Jivaka with his original BA and retraining as a doctor). Pfoundes (as naval officer, journalist and interpreter), Dhammaloka (in his many jobs), Daly (as curate, missionary, journalist and author) or Wei Wu Wei (as dramatist and translator) had already held multiple jobs before beginning their 'Buddhist careers'. Hearn and Wei Wu Wei had 'made their name' in these professions, while Jivaka's transsexual odyssey is an achievement worthy of even greater respect.

As Buddhists, they had to perform demanding, and highly-scrutinised, public roles: as monks (Dhammaloka, Jivaka) or teachers (Daly, Hearn), even if allowance was made for foreign origins.[127] They had languages to learn: Japanese (Pfoundes and Hearn) is

127. Jivaka discusses this at several points in *Imji getsul*.

notoriously difficult; Ladakhi (Jivaka) had no written form other than standard Tibetan; Dhammaloka could acquit himself in several languages. These were also people able to cut their ties with home, adapt to a foreign culture and engage in public controversy while being vulnerable to vicious attacks from journalists and missionaries.

One interpretation is that becoming a Buddhist for Irish people between 1850 and 1960 was extremely difficult, and only exceptional individuals could contemplate it, let alone succeed in becoming Buddhist. Alternatively, we may know these particular people *because* of their exceptionality: not only the mastery of the 'intellectual means of production' which enables us to recover parts of their experience, but also in possessing the background which enabled this, and the relative freedom from repercussions to present themselves publicly as Buddhists.

For their anonymous counterparts, we do not know whether the difference was in lacking the education and ability to publish, or in the freedom from repercussions. Both, of course, are matters of gender as well as class.

Gender Revisited

This question of shame and respectability makes it possible to revisit the relative absence of Irish Buddhist women. If Hearn was attacked for his 'mixed-race' marriages, and Jivaka's going native was the result of a tabloid 'outing' and a lifetime's experience of stigmatisation – women's respectability, then as now, was far more intensively policed than men's (Skeggs 1997). The cost to an Irishwoman, of any class or denomination, of marrying an Asian, would have been substantial. Vivian Butler-Burke, as American-born, orphan and heiress, nevertheless struggled with isolation and mockery; even her friend MacLiammóir, a gay actor not known for his conventionality, found her eccentric in the extreme.

The records of women travellers (Robinson 1990), however, make it clear that strong-minded women could travel independently in Asia, while Helen Waddell's experiences show that, at least as a child, a western girl born in Asia might have licence to explore the host culture. Women's relationship to Buddhism in these contexts was not always linked to men, and we may yet find Irish women Buddhists in Asia before the 1970s. The sources are more likely to be found in family histories and census returns, and whatever records exist for those who 'went native' quietly in Buddhist Asia

– marrying out, becoming nuns or otherwise vanishing from the pages of the European history of Asia.

... and Buddhist Practice?

Offermans (2005) has rightly criticised the assumption that the main European encounter with Buddhism was through texts. For European Buddhists *in Asia* the main encounters were through organisations, through ritual practice or through the wider culture. Although translations were available, the texts relevant to Asian Buddhism were traditionally studied and used in non-European languages, with the double barrier of a new language and a new script. When Dhammaloka carried out an ordination in Pali, in 1904 (Bocking 2010), this was almost certainly on the basis of his ability to memorise, and it is doubtful if he understood what he was saying in more than any general sense.[128] Hearn's approach, absorption in what he saw as a Buddhist culture, was extended to his children and his language; he also followed the Japanese model which defines being Buddhist as registration with a temple to arrange funerals.

Dhammaloka's orientation to monasticism (Cox 2010) was similarly rule-bound, and focused in particular on monastic discipline (although he was proud of what he had managed to study in terms of doctrine, he avoided preaching on it). Jivaka, for his part, negotiated the discipline imposed by three different monastic situations. He was intensely ethical as well as attempting a personal meditation practice (Kennedy 2007: 149, 158). While he had been given Tibetan initiations, it is unlikely that he understood the *samaya* obligations; he would have followed them diligently had he understood them. Pfoundes' negotiation of his monastic experience and subsequent relationship with the various orders is unknown.

Daly had a modernist Buddhism, suitable for the laity, available to him and had taken the precepts. There is no way of knowing if he attempted to meditate, but we can presume that the activist orientation and social ethos of the Buddhist Revival was attractive to him. Wei Wu Wei, finally, was very interested in mysticism, but seems unlikely to have associated any particular ethical or spiritual practice with this other than seeing the world differently.

---

128. In my Buddhist study group we regularly recite a lengthy Pali text from memory which probably none of us could translate word-for-word, and in some cases not at all.

Being an Irish Buddhist, then, meant the whole range of 'Buddhist' approaches then present in Asia – living in a given culture, following monastic precepts, attempting to meditate or living a 'philosophical life' were all available possibilities, perhaps best understood in the wider picture as experiments or *essais*, very much dependent on the availability of suitable institutional contexts.

In many cases, it took a lifetime's struggle to arrive at this point: Daly, Hearn and Jivaka arrived at Buddhism, and Asia, at the end of their lives, while Dhammaloka had had a full life before ordination. Another way of putting this is to say that at the high-point of imperialism, to abandon one's starting point in Ireland and become another person, in another religion and culture, in another continent – across barriers of race, power and language – was quite enough in itself. That many of these early Irish Buddhists went on beyond that to play real roles *in Buddhism,* on its Asian home turf, is remarkable.

Part III

Buddhism *within* Ireland:
from Counter-Culture to Respectability (1960–2013)

Chapter Six

The Founders: Social Movements, Counter-Culture and the Crumbling of Catholic Hegemony

The foundational period of present-day Irish Buddhism was distinct in many ways, both from its immediate past and from the period of stable institutions which will be examined in chapter seven. If earlier journeys to the East were primarily those of defectors from the declining imperial service class, supplemented by plebeian Catholics, those from the 1960s to the 1990s were shaped by the crumbling of Catholic hegemony in the new state. As a counter-cultural part of wider social movement challenges to post-colonial power, dissidents from the public sector service class explored Buddhism and laid the foundations for its present, more mainstream and respectable image.[1]

In the declining years of the Church's 'moral monopoly' (Inglis 1998a), a range of social movements seemed to offer escapes – individual or collective – from the cage of gender roles, class expectations and ethno-religious identity typical of 'closed modernity' in general but heightened in the monocultural Republic, the only state in western Europe where the vast majority of the population were still regular church-goers (McLeod 1997: 133).

Buddhism, with its core myth of stepping outside expected social roles, spoke to those seeking ways out of this situation, and the counter-culture which developed from the late 1960s to the 1990s could find space for this. Women's movements, in particular those which challenged religion as social control, also at times created a search for alternative and less oppressive spiritualities. Alongside these indigenous developments, 'blow-ins' from counter-cultures elsewhere and Buddhist missionaries from western countries also

1. Part III uses 'Ireland' to refer to the Republic except where specified: the two parts of the island diverged increasingly in this period as regards their receptivity to religious alternatives, with sectarian tension restricting developments in the North.

created a wide range of Buddhist institutions. Over all of this, the shadow of war in the North highlighted particular readings of 'religion', encouraging those sympathetic to Buddhism to avoid tight identifications and to highlight nonviolence and tolerance as key concerns.

Buddhism and the Counter Culture: Aikido and the Christian Brothers

As this book has shown, the idea that Ireland 'traditionally' knew little about Asia is a mistake. Rather, the immediate past – between the 1920s and the 1950s – marked a nadir of knowledge. Irish newspaper readers and college students in 1955 had far less chance of knowing something accurate about Buddhism than did their counterparts in 1855.

In the early 1960s, awareness of Buddhism in Ireland appears as fragmentary and marginal. There were, however, some straws in the wind. In 1963, travel writer Dervla Murphy found herself working, almost by accident, with refugee Tibetans in Northern India (Murphy 1966); by 1969 she was celebrating Buddhist New Year in Ireland with Tibetan noblewoman Rinchen Dolma Taring.[2]

In 1960, the *Irish Times* noted that HRF Keating, 'who used to be well known around Trinity', had written *Zen there was murder*, set in something like a Zen retreat and with the roshi as detective. Keating's novel – drawing probably on the summer schools run by the London Buddhist Society – includes a journalist like himself:

> 'To write up is to write down,' said Mr Utamaro.
> 'To write down?'
> 'Yes. To place in a poor light, make fun of' …
> 'You are right as a matter of fact,' she said. 'There's no point in trying to disguise it.' (Keating 1963: 63)

The reviewer opined that 'there is a great affinity between the Irish way of life and Zen Buddhism – even if we haven't thrown up any real Beatniks yet'.[3] This was about to change, but not overnight.

---

2. Her memoir includes a wonderful epilogue in which she brings a young Tibetan to Inis Oírr in the Aran Islands (Murphy 1966: 186–91).

3. Jun 8 1960: 6.

Irish Buddhism and Elite Formation

Two facts underlay the declining awareness of Buddhism in mid-twentieth century Ireland. Firstly, the imperial service class collapsed: the numbers and power of the Anglo-Irish declined, Oriental Studies was wound down, and from the 1940s 'empire' was increasingly in the past tense. The last 'early Irish Buddhists' from this milieu, Jivaka and Wei Wu Wei, were educated abroad. Secondly, the rising Catholic service class had little use for Asian culture and religion. What knowledge there was, was mainly restricted to elites, and there are few defectors from emergent elites.

The 1958 Whitaker report, which moved state policy from import substitution towards the goal of a 'small, open economy', also brought about a greater exposure to foreign media and influence and a more international orientation. At least as important, however, was the development of new kinds of credentialised – hence university-educated – careers. Ireland in 1911 had had a narrow majority of households dependent on owning productive property – mostly farms, with some small businesses and large capitalists. By the 1970s, the fastest-growing social group owed their employment to holding educational qualifications (Breen et al., 1990).

This process meant the continual expansion of third-level education to sections of the population which previously had no need of it, and hence a very different relationship to knowledge. Desmond Fennell wrote, à propos of his awe on encountering the cultured continental bourgeoisie:

> We of the Irish Catholic peasantry – the largest by far of the groups which make up Ireland – are recent in another sense. History robbed us of nearly everything which we brought with us from the remote past ... We came naked into the modern world. (Fennell 1959: 9–11)

As chapter two shows, however, the availability or distribution of information cannot explain everything. As with the imperial service class, what created receptivity to knowledge of Buddhism was the declining hegemonic power of the old elites, particularly the collapsing alliance between the old guard of nationalist ex-revolutionaries, the clergy, small national capital and farmers.

As power shifted to international capital and new elites of 'self-made men', and cultural authority from the clergy to the media (Inglis 1998b), new struggles developed. A large new urban working class was created, which rapidly became unemployed with the long recessions of the 1970s and 1980s; second-wave feminism challenged the gendered social order; communities opposed nuclear power in Wexford and multinational chemical plants in Munster (Allen and Jones 1990); and republican and socialist activism grew across the island.

The revival of interest in Buddhism, then, took place in a moment of hegemonic crisis. If the state and capitalism weathered this crisis successfully, they did so at the cost of the declining power of the Catholic church, its gendered morality and definition of community. Popular mobilisation was no longer associated with state-building and religious identifications, but now challenged both.

An Irish Journalist in Buddhist Asia

This moment of crisis can be felt in the 1956–7 Asian travels of then-progressive Catholic journalist Desmond Fennell. On the one hand there was a sense that 'to know our world one must know the East' (Fennell 1959: 12) and a feeling of cultural inferiority:

> I had heard that for the educated and sophisticated of Asia, Christianity seemed crude alongside Buddhism, Hinduism or accumulated Chinese wisdom. It was said that Westerners were regarded as machine-men ... I was conscious that I came of Irish peasants, potato-eaters. (Fennell 1959: 85)

Stephen Little's account of listening to Buddhist tapes as a young man thirty years later shared something of this:

> He [Sangharakshita] spellbound us with his knowledge of the arts and the artist, of western culture and the religions of the world. I clearly remember the atmosphere of interest and excitement in the room as my friends and I scrambled to pick up everything he said. (1998: 3)

Fennell illustrates the change in the Irish Catholic reception of Buddhism, and much else. On the one hand, he was well-informed on basic facts; but his sudden judgements showed a very different intellectual inheritance:

> The political leaders of Burma today – and they include some men of intellectual eminence – are convinced Marxist socialists ... At the same time, several national leaders, most conspicuously U Nu, are devout Buddhists ... The simultaneous adherence to mutually exclusive sets of beliefs is a widespread phenomenon of the Asiatic mind that has been termed by Professor W.E. Hocking "plural belonging" ...

> For one reason or another the atmosphere generated by Buddhism
> in Burma has not encouraged a spirit of enterprise. Ninety per cent of
> the business firms in Rangoon are in the hands of foreigners, mainly
> Indians and Chinese. (1959: 101–2)

The 'one reason or another' lay in a brutal imperial inheritance and
Rangoon's history as a colonial port (information readily available
from authors like Collis), while the combination of Buddhism and
commitment to social change had long roots in traditional Buddhist
kingship and Burmese nationalism (Sarkisyanz 1961: 59). Fennell,
however, already *knew* from his reading what Buddhism 'really
was':

> Buddhism ... has always preached another way for the overcoming
> of human suffering – the elimination of desires! If we have no desires,
> we are immune from much unhappiness. It is obvious that such an
> attitude does not lead eventually to the Welfare State which is the
> declared aim of Burmese policy. That is why a substantial section of
> the Burmese *elite* has borrowed from socialism the modern-Western,
> non-Buddhist attitude. (Fennell 1959: 103)

This contrasts with Maura O'Halloran's later perspective:

> How can one be Buddhist and not be socialist? How accept and allow
> the perpetration of a system based on desire? A system that functions
> as trigger and effect of the desire for money and commodities? A
> system that, to feed itself, must resort to crass commercialism and
> ever spiraling desire. (1995: 109–110)

Fennell observed old women in a Chinese Buddhist temple
in Malaysia, a Zen priest teaching calligraphy and a Buddhist
graveyard in Tokyo (1959: 120, 145–6) – but from this same
perspective of already knowing whatever was worth knowing.
Despite disavowing any intellectual inheritance which 'might be
orthodoxly colonial or orthodoxly anti-colonial, evangelical or
romantic' (1959: 85), he concluded in full orthodoxy:

> Belief and love – after the hunger of the belly these are man's greatest
> hungers ... Europe injected the whole world with her own hungers
> for belief and love – and she gave doctrines for the beliefs to cling to,
> ethics which enabled love to expand. Thus did Europe in the twentieth
> century after Christ make the world One. (1959: 272)

The nominal dissociation from colonialism was thoroughly
compatible with celebrating missionary Christianity – and with an
intensely provincial view of world history.

For more plebeian Catholics, though, as sectarianism waned in the South a situation arose where (in the early 1970s) –

> People didn't know hardly anything about [Buddhism], so they couldn't pigeonhole it, they couldn't say that it was this or it was that. So the overall feelings that the public in general had was that Buddhism was kind of benign. You know, that it was something harmless. And gentle. It had the image of serenity and so on … (interview C)

For older generations, awareness of Buddhism had been restricted to its newsworthiness. For the Dalai Lama's 1973 visit:

> People knew, like my mother for example sometimes used to recall listening to the radio in 1959 when the Dalai Lama was escaping from Tibet, and the escape took a long time and apparently this caused a lot of interest, and people were identifying with his plight … But I wouldn't say there was any excitement [about the visit]. It was a government honour … and he didn't give any public talk or any public appearances. (interview C)

Such knowledge was far from offering any sense of what being Buddhist might mean:

> I think mainly the difficulty is that in the beginning it was more that we were jumping in at the deep end with something we didn't really know the shape and size of. Then we were just trying to find our way with it and we were being introduced to quite advanced practices early on. And we would have been doing chanting and saying mantras and a little bit like "OK? How is this? Where do you want to go with it?" (interview A)

Abandoning Fennell's sense of knowing everything worth knowing, Irish Buddhism's founding generation had to work out everything for themselves. Printed resources too usually came from abroad, with difficulty:

> There was hardly anything available then [in the mid-sixties] and there was a few books on yoga which might have had some mention of meditation and Buddhism. But the first kind of hardcore Buddhist book that I came across, strangely enough, would have been the *Tibetan Book of the Dead* … (Interview C)

Another interviewee recalled:

> There were two bookshops off Canal St and Capel St and I would have just browsed those … I didn't have titles that I knew were out there, that I was looking for, I just saw what was there … There was no place to go at that time. (Interview D)

Buddhism as Dissident Orientalism

As it had been within late colonial Ireland, Buddhism was again appropriated for cultural critique within a newly uncertain service class, speaking for the needs suppressed by existing institutions. From 1960 onwards, cultural dissidents from the Catholic service class in particular used Buddhism in various ways to escape the cage of ethno-religious, family and caste expectations. O'Halloran wrote of her rejection of Catholic socialisation in the later 1970s:

> I thought about the alternatives that confronted me when I first came to Japan last November – the usual job as an English teacher didn't interest me. Either monastic renunciation or sensory wallowing drew me. A soul seeking surrender? It was either accident or providence that the first happened first. Either way was a search for liberation – freedom from inhibition, from other people's values, from their suffocating puritan ethic born from the delusion of a retributory hereafter. (1995: 100)

Little wrote of his route to Buddhism in 1992:

> I was a dreamy child, fond of my own company and living in my imagination for the most part ... Not surprisingly I went to college and studied physics. During the summer breaks I followed my passion for drawing, painting and playing the drums. I spent three years at Trinity College before I couldn't go on anymore and dropped out. (1998: 1)

This was not a service-class experience alone. To working-class Paula Meehan:

> What was flowing in under the guise of the counterculture, or what was called "alternative" ... we latched onto that like drowning puppies as an alternative to what we would be getting through the schools certainly and through the messages that our own culture was sending us as working-class kids. (2009: 247–8)

The starting-point was necessarily breaking with socialisation and the options presented to young adults: what came next had to be worked out in practice, or by making the right connections:

> I had written a commentary on a poem by Patrick Kavanagh. I think it was "Canal Bank" and my teacher in his comment upon it said "there's no need to go into Zen Buddhism to explain this poem". – "Oh, Zen Buddhism?" I hadn't actually gotten any books on Zen Buddhism. So I went and bought a book called *Zen flesh, Zen bones* by Paul Reps. So that was probably the first actual book on Buddhism I would have

gotten. And fairly soon after I got a book by Shunryu Suzuki called *Zen mind, beginner's mind* – very good book. (interview D)

Another interviewee, becoming interested around the age of 12, was able to study Buddhism, teach himself meditation from books and become vegetarian. Buddhism was in part attractive because it was seen as lacking the sectarian habits of Irish Christianity:

Buddhism traditionally has been largely non-proselytising and it's supposed to be like that. It isn't aggressive ... From the beginning things can be quite relaxed in its encounter with other ways of thinking. And it doesn't have the idea that it's the one true approach ... Buddhism is seen as provisional because the ultimate truth can't really be expressed (interview C)

At times, sectarian closure itself was a force driving people out, in this case the church ban on Catholics attending TCD before 1970:

So within there, the nucleus of these people [Asian Buddhists] and I'd never met it in Ireland. Simply the reason, because even to come to Trinity College was a mortal sin! ...

So I was excommunicated from the Catholic church. I applied and got it [admission] ... I decided to do some seafaring, and that's where I was steered from Trinity, the Royal Navy, the Admiralty ... (interview B)

Dissident Orientalisms found a route East as an internal critique of their own culture rather than a way to exercise power over other cultures. In the 1960s and 1970s this was set within an awareness of political struggles in Asia:

The first Buddhist teacher I would have come across would have been Thich Nhat Hanh during the Vietnamese war in the late 60s, and I would have read his poetry in a newspaper called *Peace [News?]* at that time ... I'd always been completely moved by what he'd written and also of course by what was happening in Vietnam. Seeing the monks there burn themselves – a bit of a wake-up call ... (interview A)

Another future Buddhist noted of this period:

I just seemed to have a fascination with things Eastern. I used to annoy my father by bringing home the *China Pictorial* from Easons with Mao on the cover. I used to get them as reminders and get them cheap and bring them home and he would have these arguments about communism, as you would. (Interview D)

Fig. 6.1 Peter Cornish working at Dzogchen Beara c. 1974, shortly after his arrival. Permission granted by Matt Padwick.

Buddhism in the *Irish* 1960s, then, was as much a political phenomenon in a shared post-colonial world as a 'world faith' or a lifestyle commodity. It was situated within the broader context of global upheaval:

> It was the 60s and it was the 70s. There was something happening I think then, there was an opening. And I think of Zeffirelli's film *Brother sun, sister moon* about St Francis, but it was very much a hippy-type almost consciousness. (Interview D)

This consciousness had broad perspectives and local discontents:

> there were a lot of radical forces in play, disruptive forces ... All those ideas – around socialism, around colonialism, around revolution – were filtering through strongly. We were quite disaffected. My

memory is we were constantly harassed by the cops in our local
station ... So the ideas coming in through poetry like [Gary] Snyder's
were giving me the questions I needed to ask, and they were also
giving me an alternative to what I was getting through the church, the
state, and the family. (Meehan 2009: 248)

The New Seeker Milieux

In a culture which was still very closed, those who later became
Buddhists rarely started out knowing what they were looking for or
where to find it. Between feeling a need to change and developing
commitment to Buddhism or some other alternative religion, a
mediating context where like-minded individuals could be met and
different possibilities explored – a seeker milieu – was very helpful.
Such milieux were generated as part of the broader 'anti-systemic
movements' (Arrighi et al., 1989) of the 1960s, particularly those
elements questioning everyday culture and social routines. One
participant noted:

Buddhism/eastern philosophy was "in the air" in the late sixties/
early seventies. There was a bookshop upstairs above a health food
shop called Green Acres in Great Strand Street (off Capel Street)
which was a good place for books on Buddhism, Taoism and so on.
Eason's was also a good place for books. Another parallel conduit was
the Macrobiotic food movement with its oriental concepts of Yin &
Yang. There was at least one shortlived Macrobiotic restaurant located
somewhere like Fitzwilliam Square where diners sat on the floor and
ate with chopsticks! In a more mainstream context there were books
like *Zen and the art of motorcycle maintenance* and Hesse's *Siddartha* and
even popular TV programs like *Kung-Fu*. (pers. comm. E)

As with the Theosophical Household, there were vegetarian
restaurants, insider literature and a broader presence in popular
culture. Another, less purely macrobiotic restaurant, the Golden
Dawn, opened in 1976–7 on Crowe Street as:

A place where people could learn about all aspects of alternative
living. There was a shop, restaurant and an area that people could
rent to give tai-chi classes, yoga, shiatsu massage, etc. (Fitzmaurice
et al., 2004)

A 'Good Karma' vegetarian restaurant had also opened in 1973,
perhaps associated with the Divine Light Mission (Mulholland
2009: 5), while Comerford's (1975) discussion of vegetarianism in
Dublin referenced the Buddha.

Mulholland identifies a rise of 'incipient seekers' in the 1960s and
1970s, with media attention given to folk healing, occultism, UFOs,
tarot cards and groups such as the Jesus Movement, Jehovah's
Witnesses and the Mormons. The period saw the foundation or
revival of the Irish Society of Water Diviners (1958, revived 1976), the
School of Philosophy and Economic Science (1960s), Eckankar (by
1974), the Unification Church (by 1977) and the Farrar's witchcraft
group (1977). Particularly successful groups were Transcendental
Meditation (from 1964), Tony Quinn's yoga chain (by the 1970s),
the Divine Light Mission (by the 1970s) and ISKCON (by 1972)
(Mulholland 2009: 4–5). In such contexts, a range of alternatives
could be explored:

> My best mate at the time would have had somewhat similar interests,
> but his interest was mainly in the martial arts, and also he was into
> Krishnamurti … And some of my mates at school with Guru Maharaj
> Ji, that was another thing in the background … So it's just part of the
> consciousness, this idea of the meditation and the martial arts … In
> the seventies. So that's kind of the background. I didn't do an actual
> Buddhist retreat until it was January '79. (interview D)

Belfast-born Van Morrison described a similar early 1960s context
in his 1982 'Cleaning Windows', name checking blues musicians,
Jack Kerouac's *The dharma bums* and 'my Christmas Humphreys
book on Zen'. Maura O'Halloran's mother observed:

> Her interest in meditation … was not an uncommon interest among
> her peers in the 1970s. In our Dublin home in those days one often came
> upon her in some corner, sitting in the lotus position, calmly centered
> within herself, oblivious to phone, TV, and family. (O'Halloran 1992)

There was substantial continuity in this general counter cultural
picture over three decades. Growing up in the 1980s, participating
in and researching the counter-culture (Cox 2011), I encountered a
largely similar world: macrobiotic restaurants had been replaced by
the ISKCON café Golden Avatar, while bookshops played a larger
role, whether more occult or more New Age in focus. Linked to the
musical end of the drugs culture, those sufficiently motivated to
track down the books pursued consciousness-expanding literature
from the American 1960s, including D.T. Suzuki as much as
Carlos Castañeda. Outside Ireland, contemporary reference points
included British New Age Travellers and the Rainbow Family.

As common heritage for dropouts as much as professionals, Celtic legend and earlier archaeology were available to anyone who had visited museums or entered a library – but awareness of paganism as contemporary was largely absent until the later 1990s. However, if yoga and transcendental meditation were widespread (along with tarot reading and ouija), the idea that Buddhism was something you could *do*, not only read about, was absent in my circles. I recall with the force of revelation hearing a 1992 talk which presented the Buddhist meditation I had encountered in books as something that could be taught and learnt, in Dublin. In this period Buddhism existed only in a handful of semi-public groups, and it took a certain effort to find it beyond the pages of books – or even to find the books:

> [Buddhism] came from the counterculture that I was floating in when I was a young teenager, from West Coast literature, from books that were passed around like the Holy Grail on street corners in Finglas. (Meehan 2009: 247)

Seeking and Connecting

Within these explorations and experiments, particular interests slowly crystallised out. One participant recalled:

> Many people in the 1960s and early 1970s were caught up with the interest in Eastern religions at the time. Some students and fellow travellers were reading books such as *Dharma bums* by Jack Kerouac, *The way of Zen* by Alan Watts, books on Zen by Suzuki, and *The Tibetan book of the dead*. Perhaps it would be true to say that, generally, an interest in Zen preceded one in Tibetan Buddhism? (pers. comm. F)

These memories show how interest could lead to engagement: interested as a student in the late 1960s, this participant read a range of Buddhist books, attended teachings in Dublin in the late 1970s and early 1980s, and travelled to India, Nepal and Sri Lanka in 1980–1, making a range of Buddhist connections and returning to attend retreats in Ireland.

Similarly, for Graham Shepherd (2011) a 1977 Gestalt Therapy weekend in Louth led to an encounter with the American Buddhist couple who owned the venue, attending an introductory talk in Dublin by Michael Kohn of Trungpa's European sangha and travel to India in 1979 to meet the Karmapa.

As might be expected, the counter-cultural scene included a wide range of artists and intellectuals, many of whom drew on Buddhism in various ways.[4] Thus, for example, Tim Goulding, painter and member of seminal folk-rock group Dr Strangely Strange, spent time in the Scottish Samye Ling centre, where he was married. His recent *Floating world* collection referenced,

> his awareness of Japanese philosophy and art and also ... a non-attached or ethereal state. (Campbell 2008: 1)

Douglas Hyde Gallery director John Hutchinson studied Sanskrit and Pali at Oxford and ran an exhibition on the theme of the Hungry Ghost (Ryan 1988). Poet Paula Meehan, strongly influenced by Gary Snyder's eco-Buddhism (Kirkpatrick 2009) has published collections such as *Dharmakaya* (2000).

Other writers – including Ciaran Carson, Michael Longley and Paddy Bushe – draw on Buddhist themes in various ways (Murphy 2011: 95; Ohno 2002; McAuley 2005). More recently, folk-rock group Kíla have brought out both a 2002 *Monkey!* Soundtrack and a 2010 *Soisín* album named after Maureen O'Halloran.

Out of early versions of such engagements, the first Irish Buddhist organisation for forty years appeared in the 1971 *Irish Times* thus:

> The following notice, pregnant with dramatic possibilities, appeared last week in the New University at Coleraine: *Buddhist Society: Meeting cancelled because of Trojan Women.*[5]

A university setting is of course where we would expect to find organised Buddhist activity appearing. In 1971 in Northern Ireland, it is unlikely that it survived long.

Journey to the East

Michael Hall, a few years later, was prompted by death threats to his cross-denominational relationship to leave the North emotionally and then physically:

> among young people in the 1970s another journey was often talked about – the inward journey – and like many of my contemporaries I delved into Zen, meditation, yoga, and, most potent of all, experimentation with the "mind-expanding" drug LSD ... [W]hen you combined

---

4. Thanks are due to Julian Campbell for pointers to some of the material below.
5. Feb 17 1971: 15.

a desire to travel with the search for inner knowledge, it automatically
pointed in one direction – a journey to the East. (2007: 12–13)

Travelling across Asia in 1976–7, he and his partner visited
Buddhist sites in Pakistan, India, Sri Lanka, Burma and Thailand.
Although they 'experienced few esoteric musings and no preoccu-
pation with developing our inner-awareness' (2007: 145), they had
a far clearer grasp of the realities of Buddhist Asia than did Fennell
two decades previously.

Similarly, if Dervla Murphy started her work with Tibetan
refugees in India knowing 'no more about Tibet and her people
than does the average European newspaper reader' (1966: 1), she
could nevertheless draw on Hugh Richardson, Walpola Rahula
and Evans-Wentz to write up her experiences, which are free from
romanticism. Although sceptical of an eastern response to the crisis
of western religion, Murphy nevertheless engaged with 'Southern
criticisms of Northern Buddhism', enthused over the possibility of
female bodhisattvas, and wrote of Tibetan women:

> They may *know* very little about their religion, yet unless they *felt* it as
> a significant force in their lives they could never render these hymns
> as they do. (1966: 39–40)

Her own reactions changed, blowing an ant off her arm rather
than squashing it:

> I've not consciously acquired any new principles about preserving life
> so it must simply be the effect of living in such a highly concentrated
> Buddhist atmosphere. (1966: 85)[6]

Murphy and Hall are exceptional people by any standards, but
their interest and knowledge was shared by a far wider spectrum,
whose final responses were equally varied, from Hall's secular
left activism via Murphy's lifelong travelling to the foundation of
Buddhist organisations.

Even for those whose journey East was in uniform rather than
hippy clothes, personal contact with Buddhists could have transfor-
mational results:

> I wasn't reading about [Buddhism], I was observing it. This is the
> lovely thing about it, is the nature of these people … I can lapse into
> [bliss] very quickly. (interview B)

---

6. In Ladakh three years previously, Jivaka had taken on board his lama's
injunction against killing lice (1962: 134–5).

Unlike defectors of an earlier generation, many (not all) journeyers to the East returned,[7] and found new allies, including 'blow-ins' from other counter-cultures, themselves making the journey to another society, and eventually Asian teachers. The counter-culture, with its international connections, was one place where such alliances were possible:

> If I can give you an anecdote, one of the people that was a regular attendant at our meditations at the Priory Road in Harold's Cross was Polish, and at that time that was really exotic. (interview D)

In an alternative Orientalism, participants could understand the relationship between war and refugees, counter-culture and the availability of Buddhist teachers:

> When the Chinese invaded Tibet through the fifties, and then in 1959 when the Dalai Lama finally fled from Tibet and so many of the Tibetans left, and then there was just this really interesting meeting between the Tibetans and the hippies in northern India ... So I think that time at the end of the 70s was very rich, particularly the Tibetans; they'd started coming to Nepal and India and they'd started to get invited west. (Interview A)

Such links were sometimes directly political: one group of Japanese Buddhist monks visited on a peace pilgrimage in the early 1980s, and took part in protests against plans to mine uranium in Donegal.[8]

Coming Out of The Closet

In the 1960s and 1970s, Irish Catholicism was in the first phase of unofficial change, which preceded both political change – contraception was legalised for married couples in 1979 and others in 1986, homosexuality in 1993 and divorce in 1997 – and changing church practice.

One interviewee 'came from a very strict Irish Catholic family. So they wouldn't have had any interest but they're very tolerant; there wasn't any difficulty.' (Interview C). Another found the Christian Brothers anything other than tolerant, but he and his classmates nevertheless explored Krishnamurti, the Maharaj-ji and

---

7. In Jim O'Hanlon's 2003 play *The Buddhist of Castleknock*, it is the Buddhist's *return* to the family Christmas that catalyses domestic crisis.

8. http://revpatrickcomerford.blogspot.com/2010_02_27_archive.html

Zen Buddhism (interview D). Responses to such explorations were uneven: in 1965 the *Anglo-Celt* could unproblematically headline an article 'Buddhists and Moslems hinder Church's work', referring to South Vietnam and Ceylon.[9] More soberly, a letter from Rev. Eugene McDermott to the *Meath Chronicle*, discussing changes in religious vocations, noted 'No doubt, too, other religions such as Buddhism need to reassess their recruitment structures.'[10]

By the early 1970s Irish Buddhists started to come out of the closet, appearing in the newspapers for the first time *a hundred years* after appearing in the census. Following the 1971 Coleraine Buddhists, DA Marks of Blackrock wrote to the *Irish Times* in 1972 on religion in the constitution and on contraception and abortion. One letter stressed 'that I am Irish by birth and upbringing, and that I am a Buddhist', before quoting Asoka on religious tolerance.[11] A second stated from a Buddhist point of view that contraception and abortion were matters for one's own conscience.[12]

The Dalai Lama's 1973 visit included a TV interview 'with the High Lama of Tibetan Buddhism in which he discusses his belief and his daily life', picked out by the *Sunday Independent* as a TV highlight.[13] By 1974, barrister Desmond Boal told Sunday newspapers that he was off to practise meditation in a Himalayan Buddhist monastery (Mulholland 2009: 3).

An anecdote about the first Karma Kagyu centre, in a respectable working-class Dublin suburb in the late 1970s, illustrates the changing atmosphere:

> The guy that sold the house [to the centre] came back and apologized to the neighbours for selling it to the Buddhists, and the neighbours said "It's fine, they're the best neighbours we've ever had." There were sort of jokes around that time, because it was very new. (Interview A)

A limited tolerance was starting to weaken sectarian identities:

> When I still lived in Inchicore, an elderly lady came up ... on the street, you know, "are you a Protestant or a Catholic?" – "Well, actually, I'm a Buddhist." And she said "Ooh, it's alright dear, so long as you're a Christian." (Interview A)

9. Feb 27: 2.
10. Feb 22 1969: 12.
11. Jun 5: 11.
12. Aug 25: 9.
13. Nov 13: 2.

Graham Shepherd's experience was different. Having been involved in the student Campaign for Nuclear Disarmament in 1961 and 'outed' as a member of the Irish-USSR Friendship Society the following year, his view when visiting the Irish embassy in Delhi in 1979 was still that:

> In Ireland an interest in Buddhism was akin at that time to being a card-carrying communist, a vegetarian or coming out as a homosexual. You had to be weird. (2011: no pagination)

Popular referenda removed Catholicism's special place in the constitution in 1973, but introduced a constitutional ban on abortion in 1986. It was only in the 1990s that divorce and abortion referenda showed consistent majorities unwilling to enshrine Catholic teaching in the constitution. In 1996 a Presbyterian minister wrote:

> [I]n some rural areas, local Buddhist groups can be looked upon slightly askance as members of a strange religious sect, but this would seem to be the result of lack of understanding rather than the presence of ill-will or animosity ... (Ryan 1996: 127-8)

The reality was perhaps less quaint; as Cosgrove (2012) notes, MacGréil's surveys in 1972-3, 1988-9 and 2007-8 found consistent levels of hostility to minority religions, and her own research shows that discrimination on these grounds continues to the present day (chapter seven).[14]

The First Irish Sangha

The first organised Buddhist communities only had loose links with earlier practitioners:

> There would have been some individuals [in the early 1970s] who would have followed their own version of the Buddhist way for decades ... they're probably dead now. There wasn't any organisation or sense of community ...
>
> I remember one man ... [who] would have regarded himself as a Buddhist for decades. So there was a few like that. And there would have been members of the Buddhist Society ... (interview C)

14. Importantly, she notes that discrimination does not vary significantly depending on *which* new religions are involved; while Russell et al., (2008) show that discrimination against religious minorities is statistically significant even when ethnicity is controlled for. Cosgrove's new religions are primarily constituted of Irish converts, making their situation particularly relevant.

We were fortunate enough to secure interviews and communications from people who were involved in this foundational period, so that this is more certain territory. One had spent five or six months at Samye Ling monastery in Scotland and then visited:

> Some of the pilgrimage places in India, monasteries and Tibetan refugee centres in Nepal ... the tradition was very strong there and very unselfconscious. (interview C)

Another trained for ordination in the Soto Zen monasteries at Throssel Hole (UK) and Shasta Abbey (US). Both, however, returned to Ireland rather than complete their training; those who were ordained tended to remain abroad. Such people helped create or run institutions like Samyedzong in Inchicore, Ireland's first Buddhist organisation, the roughly contemporary Zen Meditation Group in Tallaght, and slightly later retreat centres like Jampa Ling in Cavan and Dzogchen Beara in west Cork.

The move to institution-building was not an obvious one, particularly in light of the isolation of Irish Buddhists before the 1970s:

Fig. 6.2 Building the Dzogchen Beara centre in the 1980s. Permission granted by Matt Padwick.

It is possible to practise Buddhism in a solitary way: you don't need any kind of congregation or community or centre. And some of the best practitioners would be hermits living in the Himalayas. It's quite OK, but it's desirable to have contact with good teachers, and the idea of sangha – for community in a way to knock off the corners, to have some kind of abrasion almost, so that one doesn't go off just following one's own ideas. If you're interested in the tradition then it can be very easy to tailor it to yourself (interview C)

– as earlier western Buddhists had often done. Such individual practice, in this period, might mean

some kind of regular meditation but very simple and not overdone, just trying to live, and I also became vegetarian. (interview C)

Organisation, of course, also met other needs:

Our group in Harold's Cross did other things together. We did hiking and some of us went on holidays together ... Outside of [that] people formed friendships. (interview D)

In practice this generation mixed individual paths with inter-connections. Linked by personal networks, people chose divergent paths:

[one person's] interest was in the Theravada, [another's] interest was in Sogyal Rinpoche's tradition and [a third] was interested in Akong Rinpoche's, so at a certain point everyone went and did their own thing. (interview C)

So far, so much like the Theosophists, but less contentiously:

I was familiar with what was happening in Dzogchen Beara, and then there's another centre [Jampa Ling] now in Cavan which has been there for at least fifteen years and I had been there a few times, and we've very good relationships, you know. The smaller groups around the country, some of them appear and disappear. But the Cork one, the Cavan one, and ourselves in Dublin, and Rigpa then would have a few small ones, would be the main stable places. (interview C)

Another interviewee similarly mentioned early links between the Zen Meditation Group, Samyedzong and Jampa Ling, and a pan-Buddhist Wesak celebration at Dzogchen Beara in the late 1980s (interview D). Such links have continued to the present day:

I went to this restaurant ... and a whole lot of other people came in and they were people from about five different Buddhist groups from Dublin, and it was just "Oh hi!" and "How are you?" People you'd

Fig. 6.3 Ireland's first Buddhist centre: Samyedzong at its original (Inchicore) site, c.1981. Visit by Tai Situpa Rinpoche (centre) with others from Samyedzong and the Zen Meditation Group, including Fr. Philip McShane (at back, with beard and glasses), Ann Graham (right front) and Donal Creedon (far left). Copyright Eugene Kelly; permission also granted by Philip McShane.

known for years, but their particular path was more in this group or that group ... (interview A)

In this early context of small numbers of intensely interested people, cooperation and networking were obvious:

My connection was always with [one teacher], but I just worked with [another group], it was ridiculous not to. There was about twenty people, it was getting bigger, but there was really no point in setting up other Buddhist groups. There was some Zen Buddhists practising out in a monastery in Churchtown, and [one woman] would have been involved in that. And [her partner] would have been involved in Theravadin Buddhism ... I used to go to anyone who was practising. There was an aikido group who also brought over a teacher called Master Hogan. Anne Hyland was one of the people who was involved, in that she also set up a centre in Kerry. It's not there any more ... (interview A)

Later intra-Buddhist sectarianism is perhaps the luxury of a better-developed situation:

> When I started the problem was finding a Buddhist group; now the
> problem is choosing between all the different Buddhists groups that
> there are. (interview A)

From a broad interest in 'something different', via counter-
culture and the hippie trail, a more specifically Buddhist network
crystallised by the late 1970s and early 1980s, and organised groups
formed within this. These 'import Buddhist' groups, Irish people
who invited teachers from abroad, were followed from the 1990s by
the 'export Buddhism' of missionaries from other western countries.
The 'baggage Buddhism' of Asian migrants, finally, existed in low
numbers from the late 1970s and grew exponentially from the
late 1990s.

Irish Buddhism Seen Through the Counter Culture

Irish Buddhism's relationship to the counter-culture can be neatly
traced through the *Alternative Ireland Directory*, associated with
Cork's wholefood Quay Co-op (Davies 1982, Sheehan 1990, Boyd
1993). The *Directory* covered everything from the new shapes
of traditional social movements (Irish language, Third World
solidarity, community organising) via 'new social movements'
(ecology, the women's movement, gay rights) to categories such as
organic gardening, homebirth and 'growth and counselling', the
heading under which Buddhism appeared in 1982.

'Growth and counselling' included mainstream counselling and
psychotherapy as well as EST, human potential and bioenergy;
various yoga and Hindu groups (Brahma Kumaris, ISKCON, Ram
Das) and other groups such as the Grail Movement, Eckankar,
Quakers or Anthroposophy. Three Buddhist groups appeared in
a subsection on meditation, along with Shree Rajneesh, 'New Age
Centres', the East West Centre and a Krishnamurti discussion group.

By 1990, the relevant category was 'Communities and spirituality',
including the Celtic Christian Aisling Arann, the eclectic *Network*
magazine, the neo-pagan Fellowship of Isis and the Alchemist's
Head bookshop. Organic farmer Anthony Kaye wrote an essay
setting community-building in a political and social context and
arguing against closure:

> For many individuals, the times we live in are not easy; loneliness and
> competitiveness wear down one's sense of security. Community can
> offer a refuge or, alternatively, a loss of independence ...

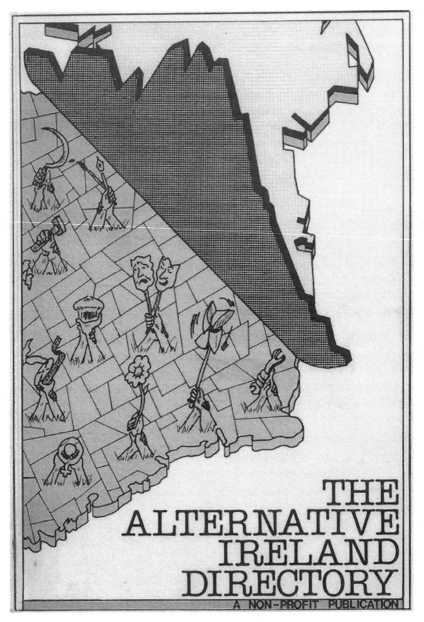

Fig. 6.4 Cover of *Alternative Ireland Directory* from 1982. Thanks to Arthur Leahy. Permission granted by Quay Co-op.

[The former] can easily become standardised and set in its ways – "we have found *it!*" An outward looking group is active in its searching for identity, it never "arrives" at a set of rules but, if it does, it soon changes them again … (Sheehan 1990: 73–4).

The eleven Buddhist groups now had their own sub-category, commented thus:

The different groups vary in both size and approach, some with their own premises and full or part-time staff. Other groups are more nomadic in nature, operating from living rooms and kitchen tables. So the choice is yours. (1990: 79)

Irish Buddhism, then, could be seen as part of a broader counter-culture in ways that parallel British analyses (Vishvapani 1994, Cush 1996). An important aspect of this was that – like other counter cultural projects of the period – it was done on a shoestring, or a kitchen table:

When we started we had nothing. Not a penny, and then slowly, slowly, it has taken a long time, as there's no outside input. Because if you're dealing with the Tibetan tradition they're exiled, so there's no oil money [as with some mosques] or anything. And with the other traditions they're mostly coming from fairly poor Asian countries, there's no sponsorship or anything, so everything has to be produced by the people who are interested. (interview C)

For material reasons, groups which lack funding or wealthy members find themselves using fundamentally the same kinds of infrastructure: borrowing or renting the same rooms, putting up notices in the same cafés or health-food shops, writing for the same magazines and recruiting in the same networks. Groups seeking respectability may then actively seek to 'mainstream' themselves and abandon these contexts – often unsuccessfully, unless they have the financial resources and cultural acceptability to compete successfully on terrain already occupied by commercial projects and established institutions. Irish Buddhism's eventual successful move from counter-culture to respectability was not a foregone conclusion, and could not have been achieved before the collapse of Catholic institutional power.

The 'Brezhnev Years' of Catholic Ireland

In this foundational period, Ireland was still dominated by religious practice and belief to an extent that has since declined massively, and the changing Catholic responses to Buddhism conditioned some of its early development.[15] The image of a 'Brezhnev era' may be useful: following a brief period of openness and self-criticism, an institution turning back to internal certainties and organisational routine, relying on increasingly greying cadres to sustain itself.

The impact of Vatican II (1962–5) and the brief Irish growth of the 1960s were rapidly curtailed in the face of the 1970s recession, with real unemployment rates around 20% and massive emigration and war in the North. For the church, the period of opening had meant a loss of control over public discussion, as it was replaced by the media as the central locus of debate (Inglis 1998b) and the bishops were replaced as political actors by right-wing lay movements from the 1980s onward.

A similar narrative – of opening followed by closure – can be told of Catholic responses to Buddhism. The sporadic interest visible from the Maynooth library up to 1960 was followed by a new burst of acquisitions from 1967 onward. Some showed a desire to challenge Buddhism on theological grounds, with titles like *Buddhism and the claims of Christ* (1967) or *Buddhism and the death of God* (1970). Others, such as acquisitions of the *Digha Nikaya* and *Dialogues of the Buddha* in 1975 or Max Müller's *Sacred books of the East* in 1975, suggest a more academic interest, perhaps tied to course development.

Alongside these polemical and pedagogical purposes came texts reflecting Buddhist-Christian dialogue and the appropriation of Buddhism by sympathetic Catholics in the 1970s, following the injunctions of Vatican II:

> Buddhism in its multiple forms acknowledges the radical insuffi-ciency of this shifting world …
>
> [P]rudently and lovingly, through dialogue and collaboration with the followers of other religions, and in witness of Christian faith and life, acknowledge, preserve, and promote the spiritual and moral goods found among these men (cited in Sutin 2006: 283–4).

Works from this ecumenical period include Dom Aelred Graham's 1968 *Conversations Christian and Buddhist*, Étienne Lamotte's 1970 *Towards the meeting with Buddhism*, Hugo Enomiya-Lassalle's 1973 *Méditation Zen et prière chrétienne* and Heinrich Dumoulin's 1974 *Christianity meets Buddhism*.

15. I have not come across much by way of *Protestant* responses; attention in the North was presumably focused elsewhere.

The library also holds nine books by Trappist Thomas Merton, famous for his dialogues with Zen (dates from 1954 to 1989); three by now-anathemised Indian Jesuit and Buddhist sympathiser Anthony de Mello from the 1990s; and five by Irish Jesuit missionary to Japan William Johnston (from 1967 to 1998). Johnston, professor of religion at Sophia University, Tokyo, emphasises Zen and the recovery of the Christian contemplative tradition, writing as recently as 2000:

> Dialogue with the mystical tradition of Asia is surely the way of theology in the twenty-first century (cited in Sutin 2006: 284–5)

Johnston represents a rare glimpse into alternative modes of missionary engagement with Buddhism. Maynooth holdings of his work include *Silent music: the science of meditation* (1974), *The still point: reflections on Zen and Christian mysticism* (1977) and *Christian Zen* (1979). We can also mention Cork-born Joseph O'Leary, another Catholic theologian in Japan, who has engaged substantially with Buddhist-Christian dialogue (O'Leary 1999).

Such connections have ripples in Ireland: Colum Kenny, author of a book on St Molaise of Holy Island, notes that it was Merton's *Asian journal* which alerted him to Lama Yeshe and Samye Ling, who now use the island for Buddhist retreats.[16]

In the late 1970s, Dominican priest Philip McShane set up the Zen Meditation Group in Tallaght after a visit to Japan (interview C). In its early days,

> a significant number of them would have considered themselves Catholics who were using a very useful practice, as opposed to being Buddhist. (Interview D)

When Sogyal Rinpoche gave a talk in Dublin in 1979,

> there was a Jesuit or ex-Jesuit there who Sogyal Rinpoche had questioned. He had said to Sogyal Rinpoche that he was very interested in Buddhism ... but that he had found the visualisations that had to be done of Indian deities with several arms and legs rather challenging and was it alright to visualise Jesus? And I remember Sogyal Rinpoche saying "it's absolutely fine to visualise him, but next time you do it imagine that he has four arms and four legs." I remember that so well: he turned it round, he wasn't getting at him or anything. (interview A)

16. *The Well*, 1998 (vol. 4/1–3): 7.

Also in this period, Jesuit Peter McVerry's sympathetic account of his time in a Buddhist monastery influenced one Irishwoman to synthesise Buddhism and Christianity. One of her supporters in defending Buddhism against orthodox Catholic attacks was involved in:

> the Christian meditation which John Main, OSB, started. This was as a result of him coming under the influence of a Buddhist master while travelling in the east. (pers. comm. G)

Such experiences, of mixed routes to Buddhism, are probably frequent among Irish people who are 'not-just-Buddhist'. As this example highlights, though, they have increasingly taken place under the shadow of Vatican disapproval.

Changing Winds from Rome

As noted in chapter three, we found it hard to research beyond public records in this area, perhaps because of this earlier history of sympathetic interest and later condemnation. This also means, of course, that Irish Catholics who *do* adopt Buddhist practices or understandings are less likely to state the fact plainly and more likely to present their position as indigenous to Catholic tradition.

The then-Cardinal Ratzinger, as head of the Congregation for the Doctrine of the Faith, declared the incompatibility of Eastern spirituality with Catholicism with a 1989 ban on Eastern-inspired meditation practices; a 1996 address to Latin American bishops; a 1997 condemnation of western Buddhism as 'autoerotic spirituality' and de Mello's condemnation in 1998 (Kemp 2003: 137). Anything that smacked of syncretism was to be avoided at all costs. Under such circumstances, Irish religious who were once sympathetic to Buddhism may be wary of suffering the fate of those once associated with liberation theology.

The backlash in Ireland started in 1983, with a warning from the hierarchy about 'cults and non-denominational Christian groups' and an anti-cult book by Fr Martin Tierney in 1985 from the church publisher Veritas (Mulholland 2009: 9). In 1994, the Irish Theological Commission issued a condemnation of the New Age, including western Buddhism. Kemp (2003: 136) rightly describes this as sensationalist: like de Harlez in 1890, it is worried about global conspiracies and treats as literal reality 'NAM [New Age Movement] missionary policy':

What is afoot is the reconstruction of a new World Order, carried out by a group of high Initiates who are experts in every field. The New Age social structures will come from these people ...

[T]he three main channels through which the New World religion will accomplish its plans are the Church, the Masonic Fraternity, and the field of education ... resistence [sic] will be crushed ...

those [New Age adherents] interested in politics work together; those interested in education collaborate, just as they do in health, social and religious matters. They contact each other through an international computer-based system called "Peacenet" which acts as an information pool.

NAM is targetting the schools ... The infiltration of education began in the 1960s with the introduction of "humanistic" elements ... Children are taught "right brain" activities such as meditation, Yoga, guided imagery, chanting, and fantasy role-playing games (Irish Theological Commission 1994: 50-4)

The document had little tolerance for the earlier Catholic exploration of Buddhism:

Zen Buddhism has had great influence [on the New Age], with its emphasis on the higher consciousness, or the true self, and seeking enlightenment ...

Many of these groups abuse prayer techniques such as "centreing". They also use relaxation techniques, or mind control techniques in order to achieve "peace" or quiet in mind and body. The centre is the self, not God, therefore there is no prayer. (1994: 25, 47-8)

The concern was apparently to prevent Catholics from exploring such activities (1994: 56) and target unorthodox Christians, but overall the document is very poorly informed, and Ireland is barely mentioned. As Kemp (2003: 135) notes, its main source of information is US evangelicals, and it is unclear whether it responded to Vatican policy, US moral panics or developments in Ireland. Clearly, however, the goal was to prevent exploration, creolisation and tolerance, whether understood as already present or to be feared. Buddhism appears as one part of a more general, and global threat; as in 1875, it seems probable that the real target was liberal Catholics as much as the handful of actual converts.

Under such circumstances, more sympathetic Catholics had to keep their wits about them. Dominican Louis Hughes, then chaplain at Tallaght Regional Technical College, was one example, albeit in relation to Hinduism and yoga. His *Yoga: a path to God?* put the

Theological Commission to shame in its understanding of different forms of Hinduism and NRMs, varieties of yoga and meditation, and the relationship of all of these to Catholic practice (e.g. 1997: 127, 130-1). The book was defensive with respect to Ratzinger's 1989 critique, and argued for the continued legitimacy of yoga and meditation in Catholic contexts:

> At the time of its publication a number of Catholic commentators expressed disappointment at what they felt to be the negative tone of the Ratzinger document. However, bearing in mind that the role of the Congregation for the Doctrine of the Faith is that of "goal-keeper" among the Church's departments, cautionary language was to be expected. (Hughes 1997: 103)

Writers less certain of their institutional future (Hughes was 55 at time of writing) may well have decided that it was not worth the effort to protest their orthodoxy and continue such explorations publicly. Joseph O'Leary commented of his own prize-winning *Religious pluralism and Christian truth*

> If I were paranoid I could see [the silencing of allied theologian Jacques Dupuis] as a sinister indirect response to my book! ... It is not surprising that much of the reaction to [religious pluralism] takes the form of denial, phobia and panic. (1999: 240-1)

As we shall see, contemporary liberal strategies are now more likely to come from Catholic laity and draw on the language of 'Celticity' (Gierek 2011) and ecumenical relations. Interfaith dialogue continues, exemplified by figures such as John D'Arcy May in Trinity, but often restricted in scope; a formal inter-religious forum, with two Buddhist representatives, was not constituted in the South until 2010.[17]

Irish Buddhism, Social Movements and the End of Catholic Hegemony

In social movement studies, it is widely understood that the existence of (for example) feminist or pacifist movements pre-World War I does not mean that their contemporary counterparts are a simple continuation of the past. Unless effective submerged networks emerge after periods of repression or public indifference, new organisations largely have to start from scratch.

17. *Irish Times*, Dec 12 2010.

Contemporary Irish Buddhism is a similar case. It is not a simple continuation of earlier explorations, but is shaped by its new world-systems context of post-colonial societies, the rise of neo-liberal globalisation and the 'anti-systemic movements' of the late 1960s and early 1970s (Arrighi et al., 1989, Katsiaficas 1988, Horn 2008). These movements had different outcomes in different contexts (Cox 2002, 2011): in continental western Europe their dominant (self-) understanding was political, leading to ghettoisation for some and co-option for others. In the Anglo-American world cultural frames were more powerful, leading to the fragmentation of 'identity politics'. In post-colonial settings like Ireland, the failure of direct confrontation with the state led to broader forms of community-based organising.

Although schematic, this analysis may offer some starting-points (Cox 2007b). For example, it explains the particular success of convert Buddhism in Anglophone countries since the 1960s and their counter-cultural tone – widely seen as characteristic of 'western Buddhism' as a whole. Until recently, West German and Italian alternative milieus were far more suspicious of mysticism and esotericism, not least for historical reasons. It also explains the relatively marginal character of Irish Buddhism as we have just surveyed its (new) beginnings.

Fig. 6.5 FWBO retreat with bodhráns and green cloaks, Cavan, 1990s. Permission granted by Dh. Vajrashura.

This period saw massive popular mobilisation around contraception, divorce, gay rights and abortion; opposition to nuclear power and nuclear weapons; and defence of the remains of Viking Dublin. The scale of these represented not counter-cultural strength but connection to broader issues of gender, nationalism, opposition to new capitalist modes of development and so on. As Little writes, of 1992–3:

> In those days a lot of the questions people had were related to the social dimension of Buddhism. There were questions like "why do Buddhists sit around when there are people all over the world suffering?" (1998: 3)

Similarly, while developing her interest in Buddhism O'Halloran did volunteer work with drug addicts and inner-city communities, joined college protests and a union in her workplace, together with anti-nuclear activity and Steiner/Waldorf education (1995: 3–4). Even after two years in Japan, she wrote:

> I must go deeper and deeper [in zazen] and work hard, no longer for me but for everyone I can help. And still I can't save everyone. They must work themselves, and not everyone will. Thus I should also work politically, work to make people's surroundings that much more tolerable, work for a society that fosters more spiritual, more human, values. A society for people, not profits. What better way to instil the Bodhisattvic spirit in people? But they should work for each other, not for personal gain, and they shouldn't have to worry about economic muck. (1995: 233)

Irish Buddhism was nourished by these wider social movements. Indeed the counter-culture as a whole in this period remained structured by broader popular movements, in contrast to core countries where the New Left 'made the running' in the aftermath of 1968 (Fraser 1988, Hamon and Rotman 1988 etc.)

Ethnicity, Gender and Class

This period was also that of political and military confrontation on the streets of Derry and Belfast (McCann 1993), and later in working-class Dublin, where republican organisations were key to community organising of various kinds, notably against drugs (Lyder 2005) and socialist debates revolved around the North. This context had particular effects on Irish Buddhism.

Sectarianism survived and intensified in Northern Ireland even as it softened in the Republic, so that Buddhism in the North has been 'little and late' by comparison, and Northern Buddhists have been even more likely than Southern ones to emigrate. Conversely, as in the late nineteenth century, Buddhism's identification with peace and tolerance has made it particularly attractive to many people. Northern Irish essayist Chris Arthur, for example, uses Buddhist perspectives to 'renounce our small-scale herdings which follow merely sectarian senses of order' (Gray 2011). This theme also plays a role in contemporary Irish Buddhism's tendency to creolisation and diffidence about distinguishing itself from other religions. The 'shadow of the gunman' looms over the Irish meditator – in particular the thoughtful and sincere meditator who is seeking 'religion, but not as we know it'.

The other key movement of these decades was feminism. The effects of the women's movement on western Buddhism are still poorly understood (Gross 1993, Dresser 1996, Simmer-Brown 2002). In Ireland, feminism played a crucial role in breaking up Catholic hegemony in the South (Connolly 2003), and Buddhism could connect with this:

> [Buddhism] did give me a powerful support system at a time when I couldn't have had any kind of a spiritual life within Catholicism. It was just so septic, the whole patriarchy, the priesthood, the role in our culture, the way I saw my mother's generation churning out children because they were denied access to contraception. (Meehan 2009: 249)

However religion also split the women's movement (Coulter 1993), separating an academic feminism whose activists could afford the social costs of dissociation from the church, its institutions such as schools and life-course rituals, from working-class women's community organising, where community membership was crucial politically and personally, so that other ways of being Catholic as social and ethnic identity were sought.

For those who could do so, Irish Buddhism offered an alternative religious identity which could avoid at least some of the patriarchal issues of Irish Catholicism, and not reproduce participants' childhood experience of religion. For those who could not, it was drawn on piecemeal, part of a 'night-stand Buddhism' bricolage supporting lives, for example as community activist, geared to social change in communities still structured by Catholic rituals (baptism, school, communion, confirmation, marriage, funerals) if not belief.

Hence self-identified feminists were and are probably more likely to be found in formal and explicitly Buddhist groups, while working-class women are more likely to draw on Buddhist meditation techniques without a wider identification, or to be loosely syncretistic. The large-scale cottage industry of 'women's Catholicism', like that of Catholic Christianity, articulated not a feminist but a 'strong women's' position that could legitimate continued participation in the church to those affected by the women's movement.

Maura O'Halloran, from a mixed Irish-American family, recorded her own awareness of gender issues in Ireland and Japan during her Zen training (1979–92). On the one hand, there was relief to discover

> The monks are not at all sexist. I'm totally "one of the lads" in dress, behaviour and treatment (1995: 17)

and concern over a Japanese woman's situation:

> I wonder sometimes about Kobai-san's relationship to her own sexuality. She is staying with us until a husband can be found for her. She's apparently not worried about her future as the servant of a total stranger and has no idea at all of marrying for love ... She seemed to know nothing about Zen but talked incessantly about how hard it would be to marry someone without any hair. (1995: 110)

Much of the book chronicles her own culture shock at proposals of marriage arranged to enable her continuation within the family-structured world of Zen temples:

> You recall my telling you the plan for [Go Roshi's] daughter, Mariko-san, to marry a priest from Kyushu and then inherit this temple by way of dowry ... [When she refused] Go Roshi stripped her of the dowry and in dokusan suddenly floors me by saying that if I marry a good Zen man, he'll give me the temple as a wedding present with which to build an international Zen dojo. I was very touched by his offer, once I got over my shock, but had to turn him down. (1995: 175)

The relationship between the agendas which converts brought to Buddhism, what they found, and what they did with it was not a straightforward one, and Irish Buddhism is in a sense the product of these negotiations.

Fig. 6.6 Marjó Oosterhoff with Burmese sayalay Daw Sasanasingi. Permission granted by Marjó Oosterhoff.

Escape from Carceral Catholicism?

More work remains to be done, in Buddhist studies generally, on feminism and ordinary practitioners. Certainly the Irish church has been unusual even among Catholicisms in how much sexual morality and gender relations defined its practical social meanings; recent revelations of systematic abuse highlight the continuing centrality of gender and the body to the politics of religion in Ireland.

These have shown how a 'carceral Catholicism' – the combination of Magdalen asylums (e.g. Finnegan 2004), industrial schools (e.g. Raftery and O'Sullivan 1999) and institutionally-protected abusers (e.g. Commission to Inquire into Child Abuse 2009, Commission of Investigation into the Catholic Archdiocese of Dublin 2009) – entailed the systematic targeting of the most vulnerable children as part of the maintenance of a particular regime of 'biopower', geared in particular to the reproduction of property-owning families.

Widespread collusion in these horrors and in informal abuse, sanctified by religion and family, shaped many lives, and spiritual

searches. As with the attempt to escape from sectarianism, there
is a search for Buddhisms which could be 'religion, but not as we
know it' – not focused on sexual morality and the rhetoric of bodily
purity, but enabling different experiences of embodiment. Rowen
(2011: 21) cites one of her interviewees as saying

> [In Catholicism, you're] cutting yourself off, to some extent, from
> nature … it is very "anti the body" … The place of nature in my
> practice now is far more richer and meaningful than anything I had in
> previous religious groups.

Conclusion

The period from the late 1960s to the early 1990s laid the foundations
for contemporary Buddhism in Ireland. Irish religion being primarily
a matter of ethnic identity, community membership and political
orientation, Irish Buddhism was shaped by this: part of counter-
cultural formations in the 1960s as in the 1890s, it was shaped by
anti-colonial nationalisms, resistance to capitalist modernisation
and challenges to taken-for-granted gender relations. Individual
participants risked the loss of secure career paths and stepped
outside safe family structures.

This rejection of the existing order was real, and spoke for
genuine needs which would become more powerfully voiced in
later decades, but had its limits. Irish Buddhists did not play major
roles in the movements of the day; 'closet' Buddhism continued
and organisation in any form was weak. By the end of this foundational period, in 1991, alongside 'blow-ins' from other western
countries and Asian immigrants, only 264 Irish nationals registered
as 'Buddhist' in the southern census. Resistance to exclusive and
sectarian religion was never likely to produce mass conversion.

Conversely, and for similar reasons, Buddhism provided a
(distant) point of reference in wider struggles over the direction of
Irish society. As in earlier centuries, it stood as a symbol of another
culture at least equal to local ones in age and sophistication. From an
Irish perspective, it stood as a symbol of tolerance and pacifism: an
elsewhere which held up the here-and-now to radical questioning.

The point, of course, is not whether Buddhism or indeed
Christianity *is* essentially this. It is how participants *experienced*
'actually-existing Christianity' in their own lives, and what they
looked for in Buddhism. These questions cannot be answered
separately from the social relationships in which participants

encountered both: Catholic and Protestant as ethnic and sectarian identities related to class power and career expectations, and structuring gender, sexuality and embodiment. The search for a new religion is at the same time a struggle to find an adequate language to express what had previously been unsayable.

Chapter Seven

Cultivating Buddhism in Ireland:
Choices For the Future

Three Historical Trajectories

Chapter six discussed the emergence of publicly organised Buddhism in Ireland. Chapter seven explores how that Buddhism has developed. Here I follow Nattier's (1998) framework, which distinguishes between the 'baggage Buddhism' brought by immigrants; the 'export Buddhism' led by missionaries from other countries; and the 'import Buddhism' sought out by groups originating within the country.

This distinction has been contested within the US (Numrich 2003); in Ireland, the three trajectories certainly exist, but differently. Unlike America, where migrant Buddhism is well over a century old, in Ireland it dates back to the 1970s and has expanded largely since the late 1990s; unusually, immigrants from any one Buddhist country rarely have the numbers to develop institutions of their own.

Similarly, while export Buddhism in the US began with South and East Asian missionaries in the late nineteenth and early twentieth centuries, those who 'exported' Buddhism to Ireland from the late 1980s on were typically west European teachers in organisations founded by earlier waves of exporters.

Lastly, while Nattier's importers were well-educated Americans who sought formal training in Asia in the 1960s and 1970s before establishing centres, and traditions, in the west, Irish 'importer Buddhists' in the 1970s were mostly lay rather than monastic, and there is also substantial use of 'Mind-Body-Spirit' publishing circuits to construct informal Buddhisms in private contexts.

This chapter also discusses the growing interest in, and respectability of, Buddhism in Ireland from the 1990s on, as well as issues of hybridity, creolisation and refusal of identification, which are constitutive of Irish Buddhism. It also asks about the needs it expresses and whether it is now becoming 'affirmative' rather than 'critical' (Williams 1989). Firstly, though, the history needs to be understood. I will discuss import and export Buddhism first.

Irish Buddhism as Dependent Development

Perhaps the relative youth of the Irish sangha explains the persistence of institutional differences between import, export and baggage traditions. Another interpretation is that in a peripheral country the key relationships are not *internal* ones. Like the Irish economy, Irish Buddhism is 'dependent' – on international Buddhist organisations, on the 'Mind-Body-Spirit' publishing industry and on Asian diaspora networks. If so, Nattier's categories are useful precisely because they are not *national* ones, but mark different relationships to global contexts.

This double sense of being isolated locally but connected globally was already felt in the 1970s:

> One person had put up a notice in what was called the "East West Centre" … saying that they were interested in Buddhism, and was there anyone else in Dublin who was? And after that, I guess about ten or fifteen people came together, and all of those people at that time had thought that they were the only Buddhists in Ireland. (interview A)

Far more than in core societies, Irish Buddhism's key relationships have pointed outwards, and most formal organisations are subsidiaries of international groups. The friendship networks of the first generation of importers have only had limited results in pan-Buddhist communication within Ireland, so that organisational loyalty and reliance on second-hand images of other traditions are commonplace, as they are in export groups. Inter-Buddhist organisation has been historically limited and is only now starting to develop in response to the state's need to engage with immigrant groups around health, education and justice.

In this sense, Buddhism remains a reaching outside of the existing society rather than a conscious attempt to change it – an important element of continuity with earlier generations.

Importing Buddhism: Two Histories

From the 1960s, the new Buddhist-sympathetic counter-culture often led to travel abroad, bringing back literature unavailable in Ireland,

and into Buddhist retreats abroad, particularly in Britain where by 1966 the Buddhist Society's *Middle Way* felt at least twenty-two UK groups were 'worthy of the name' of Buddhist. The next years in Britain saw the foundation of the Friends of the Western Buddhist Order (FWBO) and Kagyu Samye Ling in 1967, Throssel Hole Priory in 1972, the Samatha Trust in 1973, the Manjushri Institute in 1976 and Ven Sumedho's arrival at the Hampstead Vihara in 1978 (Bluck 2006). Ireland's oldest surviving organisation, the (Kagyupa) Samye Dzong in Dublin, came out of this experience abroad:

> Quite frequently I would go over to London or to Samye Ling in Scotland, and a few other places to hear teachers speak. And I went to some courses, and as time went on there might be groups of people going off to different courses ... [W]e thought maybe it would be cheaper to pay for one teacher to come over than everybody going over somewhere else, so we got together and we did organise many visits with monks and nuns ... There wouldn't have been many [of us] and it didn't take many to do it, you just need to have two or three people, reasonably good organisers. (Interview C)

Founded in 1977, Samye Dzong has Akong Rinpoche as its spiritual director and is affiliated with Samye Ling. It started with hired rooms above the 'East West Café' and elsewhere before taking out a mortgage around 1980. It organised 100–150 visits by teachers in its early years, mostly Tibetans but also some western Theravadin-trained teachers (Ani Tsondru, pers. comm.)

Insofar as Ireland ever had an *elite* import Buddhism of the kind Nattier describes for the US, this was it. Rather than being strongly committed to a single path, however, it was 'very certainly multi-denominational, not even that, but just a bunch of people who were meeting with an interest in Buddhism' (interview A) – or, from another perspective, despite being founded in the Tibetan tradition its practitioners 'had influences from other traditions (Zen, Theravadin etc.)' (Ani Tsondru pers. comm.)

A comparable situation holds for the Zen Meditation Group (now Insight Meditation Group). Founded by Dominican Philip McShane in Tallaght, it always contained Buddhists and non-Buddhists. In early years, it invited Soto Zen teachers from Throssel Hole[1] while in the later 1980s, having moved from the church building, it redescribed itself as an insight meditation group, inviting

1. Its first retreat was led by a female Zen monk, Rev. Hogetsu, in 1979.

Fig. 7.1 Ajahn Sucitto and Anagarika Jonathan (now Ajahn Jutindharo) on O'Connell St, 1989. Copyright Eugene Kelly; permission also granted by Sucitto and Jutindharo.

Theravadin teachers from the Birmingham Buddhist Vihara and Amaravati (Kelly 1990):

> We became more independent. There was something around the whole Throssel Hole tradition which I and some of us were uncomfortable with. And our connection with them weakened but we kept going as a group, but we were a little bit directionless, in terms of getting outside direction …
>
> [After meeting a Sri Lankan monk] I would have had the view that they were less enlightened because they were more conservative and less interested in compassion as a mechanism for development. That would be the view you'd get from Zen and probably from Tibetans as well. And I found myself in a situation where here I am with somebody who is part of an uncompassionate tradition and he's very compassionate …
>
> [When] I was back home I did a retreat the following year in the Theravadin tradition in Birmingham. And again I was very impressed and I got an English Theravadin monk then … to come over two months later to give a retreat in Tallaght … (Interview D)

It is hard to imagine such a shift taking place in an export centre whose subordinate relationship to an external organisation is more fundamental. Of course, this may overstate the extent to which participants share organisers' sense of affiliation in the first place:

> The group now leans more to this tradition for inspiration and guidance on the path but many continue to call it the Zen Meditation Group regardless! (Kelly 1990)

For organisers, however, *some* institutional connection is important:

> We had sort of been freewheeling for a while, so now we had monks of a lineage of a tradition who were willing to come and give retreats. So we felt better supported externally and some of us went away and did retreats in various places abroad and found that valuable. (Interview D)

A third case is that of the initial contacts with Sogyal Rinpoche in Ireland:

> He was invited to Galway first by a man called John Stanley who actually lives in Galway even now and runs a Buddhist group called the Prajna community ... He knew Patrick Gaffney, one of Rinpoche's closest and oldest students, and they invited Sogyal Rinpoche and he went to Galway sometime in the spring of 1978.
>
> And subsequently he was invited to talk in Dublin and I think it was late May or early June in '78, and Sogyal Rinpoche gave a public talk in the Golden Dawn, probably early June, and that was the first time I met Sogyal Rinpoche ... I think he came again in 1979 and gave another course in the Golden Dawn ... (Interview A)

Here the boundaries between 'import' and 'export' – or the need to have both committed local organisers and experienced teachers – perhaps breaks down. One reason for this is that unlike American 'importers' the Irish participants had not engaged in long-term training in Asia aiming at certification to teach at home – a situation which also builds commitment to a single approach. Early Irish 'importers' had sometimes started, but abandoned, such training; those who completed it abroad rarely returned to Ireland. These early import foundations, run by lay practitioners, had considerable control over the direction of their own centres and the choice of teachers, and could change allegiance relatively easily.

Informal Importers

Samye Dzong and the Zen/Insight group, well-organised institutions with over thirty years' history grounded in a thoughtful and hard-working core, represent one, early face of import Buddhism in Ireland. Most import groups, however, are structured quite differently. UK and US publishing circuits, long-distance travel, retreats abroad and the Internet mean that imported knowledge is as important in Ireland as it has ever been. As Wendy Jermyn's (unfortunately unpublished) research shows, it has given rise to a proliferation of informal, essentially private, groups of practitioners: for example, one group meets weekly in a private house, listens to CDs of Thich Nhat Hanh and meditates together. Many Irish people also 'practise with' teachers abroad, visiting e.g. Thich Nhat Hanh's Plum Village, Pema Chödron's Gampo Abbey or centres in Asia without any affiliated organisation in Ireland.

At a rough estimate, based on the activity levels of *public* groups and the numbers of non-Asian Buddhists in Ireland, these informal groups, together with more isolated 'night-stand Buddhists' (Tweed 2002), account for a third or more of those identifying as Buddhist in Ireland. They also provide an important bridge to the broader penumbra of those who are Buddhist by practice or theory but do not formally or exclusively identify as such.

This new import Buddhism has its origins in the counter-culture and Christian appropriation of Buddhist meditation and ideas, but is now as in Britain more nourished by the 'New Age' (Cush 1993: 195–6), which Vishvapani (1994: 21) describes as 'where people start looking when they want an alternative to conventional society', and by the 'Mind-Body-Spirit' industry (Puttick 2005). With the shift from counter culture to New Age, informal importers and night-stand Buddhists are less likely to be Nattier's educated elite (1998: 189). Anecdotally, they are less educated, more dependent on commercial distribution, and more likely to be women than Buddhists involved in 'export' groups. As one earlier 'importer' notes:

> I walk into any bookshop now, there's almost too much information, too many books, you don't know where to start. And, eh, they're not all of the same quality, let's say. (Interview C)

By contrast, the stronger organisational hierarchies of export groups, necessitated by relationships to organisations based elsewhere, and their tighter approaches to doctrine and practice, give greater scope to a particular kind of 'spiritual career', modelled on service-class professions, and to men.

Both the earlier and later import models depend on Buddhism's prior arrival in more powerful core countries, from which it can now be diffused in Ireland – whether by adding Irish centres to Asian teachers' touring schedules, through teachers trained in Britain or Europe moving to Ireland, or through the broader publishing market.

Missionaries and Blow-ins

The one known attempt at a direct foundation by Asian teachers was both early and unsuccessful. In 1969 a group of Tibetan monks including Chögyam Trungpa and Chime Rinpoche aimed to set up a centre, with Sonya Kelly's help, at Cloona near Westport. After two years' renovation the government ultimately refused permission. Accounts differ as to whether the monks ever visited, and whether the refusal concerned asylum, work or residence permits (interviews A, D, Cloona n.d., Anon n.d. [e]).

Successful export foundations would not arrive for another two decades. Driven by teachers from other European countries, this was a second generation of western Buddhist foundations often dependent on the new organisations of the 1960s and 1970s. Thus Soto Zen monk Taishen Deshimaru arrived in France in the 1960s to found the Association Zen Internationale (AZI). One of his original disciples, Alain Liebmann, came to Ireland in 1991 and set up the Galway Zen Centre (James Moynes, pers. comm.) Similarly, Sangharakshita, founder of the FWBO (now Triratna), arrived in Britain in the 1960s; one of his students, Dharmachari Sanghapala, came to Ireland in 1990 to set up the Dublin Meditation Centre (now Dublin Buddhist Centre). Vipassana also arrived in this period; the New Kadampa Tradition (NKT) was present by 1996.

Independent teachers also came, such as Marjó Oosterhoff from the Netherlands, who arrived in 1990. Trained by Thai and Burmese monks in the vipassana tradition, she has led retreats at Passaddhi meditation centre and elsewhere from 1995 (Marjó Oosterhoff, pers. comm.).

More commonly, though, the traditions which arrived in this period had bases closer to hand and represented relationships already developed with core western European countries. Nattier (1998: 189) predicts correctly that such groups will be evangelical in orientation (although this often lessens over time), but her expectation of greater ethnic diversity only holds in the sense that a higher-than-normal proportion of participants are also 'blow-ins' from other parts of the global North.

The role of 'blow-ins' in the Irish counter-culture ranges from the New Age (Kuhling 2004) to organic farming (Moore 2003). Up to the 1990s, leeway in lifestyles was granted far more readily to foreigners engaged in counter-cultural activities than to Irish people. Other barriers continue: in Rowen's (2011: 33) research, one rural retreat centre expresses concern about the lack of overlap between the local community and its international visitors and consequent 'misunderstanding about what we do here'.

Study Abroad and Irish Teachers

One traditional definition of the establishment of Buddhism in a country highlights the ordination of locals by locals. In these terms Irish Buddhism is still in its infancy, and Ireland is definitely 'border country', where a smaller quorum would be needed for *vinaya* ordinations (Cox and Griffin 2009). Relatively few ordinations have happened in Ireland: monk and nun ordinations in the AZI since the 1990s, and bodhisattva ordinations in the AZI and Black

Fig. 7.2 Ten-day ordination of Buddhist nuns at Passaddhi for May 2011. Thanks to Marjó Oosterhoff.

Mountain Zen Centre (Eilis Ward, pers. comm),[2] while in 2011 eight women took temporary nun ordinations in the Burmese tradition for a Passaddhi retreat (Marjó Oosterhoff, pers. comm).

Export groups normally seek local sustainability, and Buddhist teachers in (say) the UK, US or France are likely to have done much of their training at home (depending on tradition), with only some having been trained in Thailand, Japan or the Tibetan world. In Ireland, most training and ordinations happen in Britain, despite the dramatic differences between one of the world's most secular countries and one of Europe's most religious.[3]

Many or most export organisations also send students abroad for retreats; Irish students use Samye Ling's Holy Isle, the Goenka/Vipassana 10-day retreats abroad, the NKT or Triratna retreat centres in the UK. In this sense, Baumann's (2002) concept of 'global Buddhism' is true at the simplest level – to practise in Ireland past a certain point is impossible, by contrast with many other countries:

> Even just in Scotland there's a facility for people to go on year-long retreats; there are many of these facilities in Europe. And I don't know if there are any of the European universities that have degree courses, but certainly in America and I think in Australia they do. (Interview C)

Irish *import* groups, too, rely on teachers trained abroad, as do immigrant groups such as Thais; more broadly, the proportion of non-resident teachers in Ireland is higher than the usual circuits of celebrity and senior teachers in any western country.

All of this has implications for who becomes a Buddhist teacher in Ireland. In Dzogchen Beara, senior Irish students act as 'Presenters', leading groups and presenting videos, but 'are not really teachers in their own right' (Matt Padwick, pers. comm). The Tibetan context – where it will presumably take decades for Irish people to be recognised as incarnations and hence full teachers – is an extreme case of a more general situation.

It takes time to train up local teachers, although Samye Dzong had its first two Irish teachers in the 1980s and 1990s respectively. More typical is the then Dublin Meditation Centre (FWBO), which developed after a 1988 visit from Britain. The first Irish-born teacher

2. The Black Mountain ordinations involve 90-day retreats.

3. Special mention should be made of Samyedzong's six-year Tara Rokpa Therapy training; in the 1990s this provided one of four residential modules each year in Ireland (*The Well*, vol. 2/3, autumn 1996: 6).

(trained in Britain) arrived in 1993; the first Irish-based teacher was ordained in Britain in 1998 and left for Latin America; and the first Irish-based teacher to stay and teach was as late as 2001. By 1996, however, Drogheda-born nun Kelsang Drolkar was running NKT courses in Belfast (Ryan 1996: 125); a decade later she was teaching together with Paul Haller from West Belfast (first ordained in Thailand, now abbot of San Francisco Zen Centre) who visits regularly from the US (Breen 2007).

This contrasts sharply with the large number of Irish Buddhist teachers who trained abroad and did not return. Thus Anglo-Irish Mary Weinberg, one of the first women ordained in the UK (1979), now teaches in South Africa and California; Maura O'Halloran received Dharma transmission in Japan shortly before her death in 1982; Finian Airton (Dublin) was ordained at Throssel Hole around 1984; Jinpa Tarchin (Dublin) was at Samye Ling in the 1990s; Kevin Breen was ordained a Zen priest in the late 1990s (Little 1998: 10); Dharmachari Ratnaghosa (Kildare) was chair of the London Buddhist Centre from 1994–2003 (Ratnaghosa n.d.); Irish-born Kelsang Dekyong is General Spiritual Director of the NKT. Examples could be multiplied: during the 2007 protests in Burma, concern was raised over an Irishwoman who had become a Buddhist nun.

In O'Halloran's journal, Ireland represented family expectations, marriage and further study, while Zen practice and teaching were identified with Japan until the very end of her stay (e.g. 1995: 289–90). Other Buddhists experienced similar tensions:

> There was no opportunity to practise training in Ireland. It just wasn't here … I spent about three months [at an American monastery] and I found it very valuable but I decided you know it wasn't for me. Number one not at that stage, and not in that position. So I came back to Ireland and I had to recreate my career and things like that … (Interview D)

Return to Ireland and paid work were closely associated, while training or life as a full-time Buddhist teacher were associated with living abroad. These choices paralleled those made by counter cultural participants (Cox 2011), where the choice often seemed to be between an Irish 'normality' of family, career and so on and an 'alternative' career (politically, spiritually, sexually, economically etc.) abroad. Ní Laoire (2007) similarly found that returned migrants saw Ireland as a place to 'settle down' and live conventionally after exploring greater freedoms abroad.

Like gay and lesbian people, who still sometimes have to separate their relationships abroad from Irish families, so too returning Buddhists sometimes separate their 'Buddhist' lives abroad from family life in Ireland. As one of our interviewees, who had spent his entire working life abroad, commented:

> [My sister] doesn't know where I've been, she won't stop and listen. (Interview B)

Under these circumstances, it is only very recently that working as a Buddhist teacher *in Ireland* has come to seem a real option for Irish people:

> one of the things I think that is different actually, if I can be specific, some of the people who would have been involved in the group over the years have moved somewhat into a teaching role. Not overnight, believe me ... (Interview D)

This change is also related to the difficulties faced by other western sanghas in training and retaining *monastic* teachers, and an increased interest in developing lay teacher models (Wetzel 2002).

Thus until recently, becoming a teacher usually meant going abroad; an extreme case of the difficulties of being Irish, Buddhist, and in Ireland (only 264 such people appeared in the 1991 southern census; by 2006 this had increased to 2175 and by 2011 it was about 3300). Conversely, it has always been attractive to practise Buddhism elsewhere. This situation – where most teachers are trained abroad, and a high proportion of Irish teachers do not return – offered benefits in terms of perceived authenticity (and organisational control) but could create tensions between the specific needs Irish people bring to Buddhist practice and the content of training abroad, especially in relation to Irish people's earlier religious socialisation.

Import or Export?

So far I have presented import groups as being relatively free to choose their teachers, and export groups as more closely tied to their 'home' bases. However, the relationship between two Tibetan lamas and various Irish Buddhist centres suggests nuances.

In the 1980s and 1990s, two American followers of Chögyam Trungpa ran the Netterville Centre, once a 'widows' and orphans' home' near Dowth in Co. Meath, as Dao Shonu. The centre was still in use in 1996 with around thirty practitioners (Ryan 1996: 120–1), but now seems to be defunct (interview A). Although Trungpa ran a substantial organisation in the US, Dao Shonu was not the exporting of a franchise but the result of local initiative.

The role of local agency is even clearer for Dzogchen Beara. This began as the home of Peter and Harriet Cornish (Cornish 2007), who arrived from Britain in the early 1970s as practitioners in Trungpa's tradition:

> Trungpa Rinpoche had gone to America so they decided they would just come and live here and quietly practise Buddhism and meditation themselves. And they came, they bought the farm and they just started building houses here, and having their kids and living their lives here ...
>
> [On Sogyal Rinpoche's visit in 1986] they asked him to become spiritual director ... but there was an incredible generosity, they gave their home away, their whole place. (Interview A)

As with the Zen Meditation Group, then, local Buddhists felt free to change affiliations.[4] Furthermore, international Buddhist organisations' capacity to sustain international links has varied. In 1969, Trungpa had failed to get a visa; by 1981, however, he was able to visit Dao Shonu and ratify the relationship with its founders (Shepherd 2011).

Tibetan lamas, of course, have a peculiar situation, sometimes being at once refugees, prominent diapora figures, active authors and celebrity teachers on an international Buddhist circuit:

> Some of the Tibetan lamas, they live out of suitcases and kind of never stop moving. (Interview C)

Similarly with Sogyal Rinpoche's organisation,

> I believe that someone at that point invited Sogyal Rinpoche to come and be the director of [the Kilmainham group] and that he said "no, it's too soon", and "just see how you go along". And then maybe a year after that some of the people of that group went to Samye Ling ... Somewhere within the next year or so they invited Akong Rinpoche to be the director of the group and Akong Rinpoche said yes. (Interview A)

4. Relatively few centres are owned outright in Ireland, one factor that can prevent a shift of allegiance.

A decade later, as we have seen, he felt able to accept the Allihies centre. The different processes of organisation-building, then, could be tackled differently by different 'exporters', depending on their own capacity and what was already existing on the ground.[5]

Similar issues are endemic in social movement organising in Ireland – both the export of British or American organisations to Ireland and that of Dublin-based organisations to other areas – in everything from left parties via anti-capitalist activism to alternative education. At times there are conscious choices made – 'export' models offer more support but also more control, with 'import' offering greater autonomy and engagement with local realities but less prestige and fewer resources. At other times, it is more a question of two or three organisers with time and commitment, negotiating relationships with an international body.

Organising Irish Buddhism

The practical challenges were considerable. So far the emphasis has been on teachers, but printed resources too came from abroad. In the 1970s,

> there was next to nothing, but then going into the 80s things began to trickle through …. But it would be a case of just going over to London and go through the bookshops and pick up what you wanted …
>
> There were some specialised bookshops in London. They're probably all gone now, but around the British Museum. (Interview C)

Still in the mid-1980s, tapes ordered by mail or brought from abroad could form the basis for a group (as CDs still do for some informal groups):

> I think the group had been running a little bit before I actually found out about it. We used to meet on Sunday nights. I think it was called the Golden Harvest. It was at the top of Harcourt St. It belonged to the Divine Light people, and we used to meet there on Sunday nights and listen to tapes of Sangharakshita. (Interview A)

With the main orientation overseas, there was relatively little sense of wanting to convert others or to do much beyond supporting each other's practice:

---

5. An extreme case is the Diamond Way, present in Ireland since 1976 but with a public centre only since 2007 (http://www.diamondway-buddhism.ie/groups.htm).

We didn't do much to advertise it. You know, largely word of mouth ... We were letting it grow organically or not, whatever the case may be, but we certainly didn't try to rope in people ... We would put up notices when we were running retreats, but I don't think we advertised the group at all. (Interview D)

Even so, the effort of sustaining a centre was immense:

I must have been involved in ... at least 100 visits [by teachers], maybe 150. Because we would be having visiting teachers every two months some years, you know. And it was a lot of commitment for people because there everybody had to put themselves out. They had to take days off and if something had to be done it was the same handful of people to do it. (Interview C)

For the more evangelical Dublin Meditation Centre in 1993, one of its founders recalls –

The atmosphere really was one of creative energy and life. Sanghapala talked as if war had just broken out and the four of us became inspired to brainstorm our way to Enlightenment. We printed our first programme, we photocopied our first posters, we put on our first round of talks, we did interviews on the radio, we made contact with lots of people and lots of people made contact with us ... Sanghapala had dreamed up an intense schedule of courses and classes which stretched us just about to our limits. (Little 1998: 7)

The results of organising were typically seen over decades rather than years:

when I came here first in 1986, we would run retreats and maybe three people would come. [Now] we run a New Year retreat without any special teachers, and we get about 100 people. And our summer retreat ... we got about 300 people and that limits us: any more people and [we'd have] no space. So it's really taken off. (Interview A)

Organising effort itself could come to be central to practice:

For a lot of us who work here we'd probably prefer to be having more time to practise ... So working here is our practice ...

We don't always remember that and [laughs] that would be our perspective, because you get busy and there's things between people. It's not all plain sailing when you come to a Buddhist centre and everyone's just full of rainbows and light. And people work very, very hard here. A lot of people work voluntarily and have done during the years ...

> But also over the years the generosity of so many people who've
> worked here for little or nothing way beyond normal hours. People
> just come here and get inspired and then give and give and give …
> (Interview A)

The reverse of this effort is the ease with which groups could
fail. Public centres require a lot of (usually volunteer) labour and
financial supporters, and achieving organisational sustainability
usually takes decades. More informal groups typically depend on
one or two key people, and can easily fall apart.

We have already seen the failed attempt to found a Tibetan centre
in Westport; a now defunct centre in Co. Kerry; a vanished Dublin
group listening to tapes of Sangharakshita; and Dao Shonu in Meath
which seems to have disappeared. Examples could be multiplied.

In smaller towns, where neither urban centres nor rural retreats
are likely to be viable, it can be hard to trace the growth and decline
of individual groups. Samye Dzong, for example, organised events
in Bray, Galway and Waterford in its first two decades (Ryan 1996:
111). An FWBO Mullingar existed half a decade before the Dublin
Centre (Dharmachari Akshobin, pers. comm.) Rigpa groups have
come and gone since the 1970s. Skuce (2006: 111) counted centres in
Athlone, Cork, Dublin, Galway, Killarney, Limerick and Delgany;
only five years on, the Rigpa site had lost its Galway and Delgany
groups and gained a Waterford one. Other early groups existed in
Limerick and Cork; and so on.

Thus the impression of longer-established centres needs to be
balanced with an awareness that far more groups flourished for a
while and then vanished. A group may even have been founded and
refounded more than once in a particular town, without necessarily
leaving a trace for researchers.

Growth and Networking

As we have seen, Samye Dzong and the Zen/Insight Meditation
Group both date to the late 1970s. In 1982, the *Alternative Ireland
Directory* also listed another Zen group in Dublin and an English
address for Goenka vipassana, implying an early export strategy.
By 1990,

> The last ten years has seen buddhism [sic] in its various forms take
> root on Irish soil … Two of the four schools of Tibetan buddhism
> are represented and Japanese buddhism in the form of the Soto Zen
> and Nichiren Shoshu schools have also aroused interest. Finally the

vipassana meditation of the Theravadin schools of South-East Asia is
practised by an increasing number of people. (Sheehan 1990: 79)

At this point, the *Directory* listed Samye Dzong (now offering its
psychotherapy programme), Rigpa at Dzogchen Beara and Dublin
(the latter with beginners meditation, meditation practice and
Tibetan chanting on different weeknights), Trungpa's Vajradhatu/
Shambhala in Dublin and Cork (weekly meditation, individual
instruction and dharma classes), a Maitreya Zen Group based at
a yoga centre in Co. Wexford, Cork Zen Group (in Crosshaven),
Nichiren Shoshu (Dublin and Cork), a Dublin Theravadin Group
and a Cork-based Vipassana group. Most had classes on weekday
evenings; where prices were quoted they were low (£2–2.50; for
comparison, the directory cost £4.95). Retreats at Dzogchen Beara
cost more at £10 per night, but cheaper, hostel-style accommodation
would soon be available (1990: 79–80).

The 1993 *Directory* (Boyd 1993) was substantially similar but with
more Rigpa groups; Ryan (1996) found ten Tibetan groups (including
NKT in Dublin and Belfast) together with two Theravadin, one
Zen, one western and two unclassifiable.[6] Not identified by these

Fig. 7.3 Irish Buddhists in 1991, including Peter Cornish, Marjorie Cross, Paddy Boyle
and Catherine Sutton. Copyright Eugene Kelly.

6. The proportions of different traditions probably reflect snowball sampling.

surveys are immigrant groups, though the Vietnamese temple in Dublin was open around this period. Nichiren Shoshu (up to 1991 including Soka Gakkai (SGI)), with perhaps more Japanese representation, once had a public centre in Dublin.

This general diversity has continued into the present: Skuce counted twenty-four groups in 2006 across all traditions (2006: 111), while in 2008, Dharmachari Akshobin studied active websites to identify fourteen public groups, of which five were broadly Theravadin (including vipassana), three Mahayana, five Tibetan and one western (pers. comm.).[7] Buddhist Network Ireland's 2009 calculations of 'mainstream' Buddhist communities in Ireland (see below) was roughly comparable: three Theravadin, three Zen and five Tibetan groups.[8] Most of these represent urban Dharma centres or groups affiliated to major traditions which hold public events in private houses. There are also a handful of retreat centres in rural areas popular with the 1960s–1980s generation of urban-rural alternative migrants such as Leitrim, Clare and west Cork.

With increasing numbers, the late 1980s saw a pan-Buddhist gathering for Wesak in Dzogchen Beara. One participant noted,

> I would have been a bit naïve, not being very politically minded, and I would have wanted just a single Buddhist community …
>
> So we had no teachers, it was just us, we got together and we had the meditations and the thoughts and things together, but I was trying to encourage unity at the time and I felt there was still people wanted to belong to their groups. And that is the way it's turned out. And that's fine …
>
> At a certain point I gave up trying to have a unified approach. I just felt "let people follow whatever road they want to go." We might have needed more resources or to have something like the Buddhist Society in England … So we largely just went our own ways I think. (Interview D)

Annual gatherings did continue on a reduced scale for at least eight years.[9]

---

7. It is often asked whether Irish Buddhists' past as Catholics or Protestants affects their approach to Buddhism. This seems likely, but hardly in linear ways. One person brought up in old-style Irish Catholicism, for example, may react sharply against ritualism and seek a 'low church' Buddhism, while another may respond positively to those same elements in a more performance-oriented school of Buddhism.

8. www.buddha.ie, accessed 23.8.2009.

9. *The Well*, vol. 1/1 (Spring 1995): 4–5.

At present a 'Buddhist Network Ireland' (BNI) is attempting to bring together what it describes as 'mainstream groups'. A 2009 version of its website polemically described itself as excluding 'groups who don't come from an authentic lineage or those who create disharmony between Buddhist communities'. This – not entirely harmonious – language was dropped by 2011. Definitions of 'authentic' and 'mainstream' are of course inherently open to argument; the BNI's definitions apparently exclude some of the largest and most active Buddhist groups in the country, such as the Diamond Way, Triratna, NKT, SGI and Goenka vipassana, from its 2008 foundation[10] on.

More substantially, Buddhism is starting to acquire elements of the public face (in particular interaction with the state) which typically spur intra-Buddhist organising: engagement with curriculum development, prison visits, hospital practices, funerals and so on. This situation makes it more urgent for Buddhist institutions to consider how they relate to one another and to become aware of their common historical framework.

Making Converts

Starting from the rejection of strident sectarian religion and strong identifications, many Buddhists (including in formal organisations) have been reluctant to advertise their existence. In the 1960s and 1970s,

> No one was trying to make you a Buddhist, no one was on the streets ... get you to belong or become a member. It was largely auto-generated.

Later,

> Well, we didn't do much to advertise. You know, largely word of mouth ... The FWBO were more pushy. We would see that we were letting it grow organically or not, whatever the case may be. And we certainly didn't try to rope in people. And we would put up notices when we were running retreats but I don't think we advertised the group at all.

Recruits were nevertheless made:

> And so our mailing list, we probably would have had upwards of a hundred people, maybe even more. (Interview D)

10. http://buddhistnetworkireland.blogspot.com/2008/08/annual-council-meeting-of-bni.html, accessed 20.6.2011.

Fig. 7.4 Dh. Pavara in Pantheon gallery window, Dawson Street, for Dublin Meditation Week 1994. Permission granted by Dh. Pavara.

Of course groups which do not rely on childhood socialisation must find some way to let people know of their existence and survive (even if by word of mouth rather than posters, or advertising retreats rather than courses). Most public groups today do this with websites advertising retreats, talks and classes of various kinds and in some cases promotional DVDs. Some, too, benefit from bookshops stocking their teachers' publications. In this respect, little of substance has changed since the days of Col. Olcott.

There were particular tensions in the UK, where the culturally conservative Buddhist Society had been outflanked in the 1960s and 1970s by the organising efforts of the new 'export' groups, following the directions of their Asian spiritual leaders, to construct urban and retreat centres, give talks and run courses and generally publicise their own existence. By the 1990s tensions divided the once-new generation (Vishvapani 2001), between groups which saw themselves as orthodox traditionalists and those which were seen as 'movement' Buddhisms (at the time NKT, the FWBO and SGI).

Some part of these tensions were imported to Ireland: fingers were being pointed at export and 'movement' Buddhisms when Ryan's informants told him:

> As a community, the Buddhists of Ireland would be concerned with preserving and maintaining the quality of contemplative learning and experience which they are gradually inheriting from the East and creating the necessary supports for this, rather than attempting to create a movement for its own sake (1996: 127–8).

Later still, in 2009, the BNI (n.d.) warned darkly against groups which 'appear to advertise heavily for new members'.

Of course, these feelings may also reflect well-established organisations' suspicion of 'new kids on the block' and their supporters' enthusiasm, or indeed a concern not to be seen as contentious and to achieve respectability through avoiding overt recruitment. There is nothing unusual about such divergences: in a crowded Buddhist 'marketplace', difference is necessarily a selling point, whether the difference is public accessibility – or the claim not to proselytise.

The Wider Picture

If export groups form the bulk of publicly visible Buddhism in Ireland, they need to be set alongside informal import groups, family practice in immigrant communities, isolated practitioners with connections abroad and creolising 'night-stand Buddhists'.

In 1991, there were 986 *self-identified* Buddhists in the Republic, about 0.025% of the population.[11] By 2002 the figure had risen to 3,894 (0.1%); it was 6,516 (0.15%) in 2006 and increased to 8,703 (0.19%) in 2011, with perhaps another 1,000 in the North.[12]

The proportions of women and men changed gradually between 1991 (only 75% as many women as men), 2002 (90%), 2006 (108%) and 2011 (120%). The relationship between ethnic and convert Buddhists fluctuated: converts made up roughly 45% of Buddhists in 1991, 57% in 2002 and 45% in 2006, with a rise over time in the proportion of Irish nationals among converts (from 26% via 39% to 33%, and 38% in 2011).[13] These proportions are similar to Baumann's (2001) figures for countries like the Netherlands or South Africa with no recent colonial history in Buddhist Asia. Of the 779 immigrant Buddhists from other EU countries in 2006, nearly half were British, followed by German and French (Central Statistics Office 2008: 93).

In 1991, 71% of Buddhists were in Leinster (including Dublin), with the vast bulk of the rest in Munster (including Cork). This picture (paralleled by other new religions) did not change hugely in 2002 and 2006 with 64% and 67% respectively in Leinster, 25% and 22% in Munster.[14]

If we compare the 2002 proportion of 0.1% to Baumann's European estimates for the late 1990s, Ireland fell towards the lower end of the European spectrum, on a par with Italy, Denmark and Hungary.

However, in 1996 Samye Dzong estimated that there were between 300 and 400 people with some commitment to their tradition alone, and Jampa Ling made similar estimates (Ryan 1996: 111, 122). Even allowing for some exaggeration and overlap, there were several other very active groups at the time (the figure seems plausible for the Dublin Meditation Centre, for example), and many Buddhists not associated with public centres (Wendy Jermyn, pers. comm.) Thus census figures have to be seen as an absolute minimum.[15]

11. The census breakdowns here and later in this chapter were kindly generated by Central Statistics Office officials.

12. As yet only limited information is available for Buddhists in the 2011 census.

13. These figures are based on the 'Asian and other' (non-EU) category which in 2002 and 2006 had around 90% Asian membership, hence few US, Australian etc. converts. 'Converts' probably only includes a small proportion of children of convert parents. Most Irish Buddhists seem not to bring their children up Buddhist.

14. In 2006 Leinster made up 54% of the Republic's population and Munster 28%.

15. Many Irish people treat census questions on religious affiliation as being about their *ethnic* community (Macourt 2011).

Based on physical space and organising capacity, there might at present be 3,000 or 4,000 people, mostly converts, in the Republic for whom a Buddhist practice or worldview is primary and who are linked to a specific centre for classes, retreats, festivals, visiting teachers etc. As Skuce (2006: 111) notes, such centres operate 'more as teaching and meditation centres than places of worship for a faith community'. Twice or three times this number might have a private, family or informal group practice or worldview as primary;[16] many of these being 'born Buddhists'. We should also note, impossible though it is to quantify, the wider diffusion of Buddhism within Irish society:

> arguably Buddhism is the non-Christian religion that is making the most impact on the nominally Christian traditional Irish population. Irish are visiting Buddhist centres, taking courses, buying books, practising meditation and exploring what Buddhism is about. (Skuce 2006: 129)

Resisting Classification

This figure also misses out those who refuse identification on principle[17] as well as hybrid and mixed identities (particularly those who are largely Buddhist in practice or worldview but retain links with the church of their birth for family, ethnic or social reasons).[18] Macourt asks,

> How do those persons who have some involvement with a "new religious movement" or who have a new way of being respond to the religion question? Should that involvement become their response? "Yes" may be too simple an answer in an island with a long history of religious and tribal identification. (2011: 47–8)

In this vein Allihies artist Tim Goulding now

> admits to having no spiritual beliefs or to treading no spiritual path, quoting the Buddhist saying "The path exists but not the traveller on it." (Campbell 2008: 2)

16. As Scharbrodt (2011) observes, the Christian assumption of exclusive identification with a single church and denomination is not one that can easily be transferred to other religions.

17. In 2006 over 45,000 people objected to *both* the questions on religion and ethnicity (Macourt 2011: 39).

18. See Macourt 2011 for the difficulties of using Irish census data on small religions.

This refusal of categorisation exists on a spectrum from religious universalism to a heartfelt religious humanism:

> I met great people. I met heroes amongst us, of all faiths and religions and persuasions, all with a great belief in God. It doesn't really matter what banner they carry. (Interview B)

From a more intellectual view,

> I had this debate with myself at one stage about calling myself a Buddhist or not, because it's almost unBuddhist to call yourself Buddhist, particularly because they're labelling and they're categorising ... But then I decided at some point for conventional communication I would use the label. (Interview D)

And again,

> I'm always reluctant to say I'm a Buddhist. When they send the census forms around you put in Buddhist maybe, but it's not a mark of identity because again from the Buddhist point of view all identities are transient ... (Interview C)

Fieldwork in the 1990s counter culture identified autonomy and reflexivity in all areas of life as key themes (Cox 2011); refusing categorisation is a related response shaped strongly by the religious past. MacGréil (MacGréil and Rhatigan 2009: 85) notes that in 1972-3, 71% of respondents in the Republic (comparable to 72% in the Northern Ireland of 1968) saw it as 'very important' (1 on a scale of 5) that children be brought up with the same religious views as their parents; but in 1988-9 the figure for the Republic was 52.5% and by 2007-8 only 33%. By this latter point, only 65.5% of the population saw handing on their religious views as important in any way (58% in Dublin), with 'let them make up their own minds' at 23.6% and 30% respectively.[19]

In other words, the last thing many Irish people want to do is to repeat their own experience of sectarian upbringing, and this is no doubt particularly true of Buddhist converts: interest in ideas like a Buddhist school, for example, has been practically zero. In these terms, Irish Buddhism has been successful in escaping the context of its birth.

19. As a Jesuit, MacGréil is bitterly hostile to this position, which he attributes to an *'ideology of individualism'* hostile to *'loyalty'* and denying 'the *social nature* of human beings' (2009: 86; emphases in original). He goes on to call for 'effective efforts ... to persuade [parents] of the importance of 'handing on their faith', i.e., religious affiliation, to the young' (2009: 89).

Buddhism and Northern Ireland

There is a complex relationship between Irish sectarianism, interest in Buddhism either as a religion of 'tolerance and peace' or as a way of stepping outside the conflict, and people's ability or desire to remain in Ireland. Until the mid-1990s this applied to Ireland as a whole; continuing sectarian identification in the North (and sanctioning of those who breach boundaries) perpetuates a once-general situation:

> Belfast is where Dublin was twenty years ago (cited in Rowen 2011: 35).

As late as 1996 Ryan, based in Northern Ireland, could identify only three Buddhist groups there: the Theravadin Asanga institute in Belfast (founded 1979); Tashi Khyil centre in a private home in Crossgar, Co. Down (founded 1990 and linked to Jampa Ling); and Kelsang Drolkar's evening classes in the People's College in Belfast (1996: 110, 124–5).

Census results support this picture of divergence: in 2011 there were 1,046 Buddhists in the North (pop. 1.8 million) but 8,703 in the Republic (pop. 4.58 million); in 2001 there had been 533 Northern Buddhists and 3,894 in the Republic and in 1991 270 (Macourt 2011: 46) to 986. [20] Haller notes that not being 'a religion' is particularly attractive in the North:

> Those groups in Northern Ireland that strongly and simply align themselves with Soto Zen do so because they see it as a method of meditation …
>
> They don't see themselves as adhering to a church or religion …
> (Okado-Gough 2009)

This affects census figures *at the same time* as Buddhist teachers present Buddhism as a direct response to sectarianism, and for the same reasons. Such a presentation is most visible in Haller's Black Mountain Zen Centre (Okado-Gough 2009).[21] The Centre started in the late 1990s with a foundation in cross-community work and found a permanent Belfast location in 2002 with a board including a former Sinn Féin activist and a member of the Progressive Unionist Party (Clarke 2002). Many participants are practising Protestants

20. Skuce (2006: 112) suggests that these figures are too high for the scale of organised Buddhism and should be read as jokes. As this chapter argues, however, organised Buddhists represent only a small proportion of those identifying as Buddhist.

21. Thanks to John L. Murphy for references.

or Catholics (Rowen 2011: 39). Such stories are the exception that proves the rule: Northern Ireland is stony soil today as it was for Olcott in 1889.

'Baggage Buddhism' in Ireland

The methodological problems of studying Ireland's immigrant Buddhists – whether born in Asia or Ireland – are daunting. Most Buddhist immigration is very recent, and from many different countries, so that an adequate study would be a book in itself and require a team of ethnographers fluent in over a dozen languages.[22]

Ireland does not possess the array of ethnic Buddhist temples common to the New World and Oceania, with their 150-year history of labour migration from the Far East, or to European colonial powers, which have large groups of immigrants from specific countries. In fact there are few if any continuous or public immigrant Buddhist organisations in Ireland (excepting perhaps Internet fora). Even more than convert Buddhism, then, ethnic Buddhism is private or familial in nature. No doubt as elsewhere it provides a mechanism for group solidarity and in some cases long-distance politics.

Nevertheless, there are some available data which can be used in connection with experiences of migrant Buddhism elsewhere to draw moderately robust conclusions. Until the late 1990s most immigration from Buddhist countries consisted of small and specific categories: Vietnamese 'boat people', Chinese restaurant families, Malaysian medical students etc. The Celtic Tiger brought a recent growth, but still in relatively small categories. In 1991, 60% of Buddhists in the Republic held 'Asian or other' non-EU nationality (596 individuals); in 2002 the figure was 1,897 (49%) and in 2006 it was 3,562 (55%). Only a handful of these were converts: the 2002 and 2006 breakdowns show that Asians make up about 90%.

In 2006, the largest total migrant groups from those Asian populations with significant Buddhist populations were as follows:
Over 10,000 people – China.
Over 1,000 – Malaysia (and Bangladesh, India, Philippines, Russia).
Over 200 – Japan, Mongolia, Sri Lanka, Vietnam, Nepal.
Over 50 – Burma, Indonesia, Taiwan, South Korea.

22. Ryan 1996, Maguire 2004 and O'Leary and Li 2007 are the best published sources to date.

By contrast, the populations from Cambodia, Laos and Bhutan were all under 50.

The implication is that perhaps half of Asian Buddhists are Chinese in the broad sense (PRC, Taiwan, Malaysia), with the next most significant populations being Japanese, Vietnamese and Mongolian.[23]

Chinese Buddhists

In 2006, 6% of PRC nationals in Ireland described themselves as Buddhist, with 80% giving 'no religion' (Central Statistics Office 2008: 50), suggesting around 670 *mainland* Chinese Buddhists among the 3,562 Asians. O'Leary and Li (2007: 1) found a quarter of PRC students describing themselves as religious, over half of whom saw themselves as Buddhists.[24] Whatever the exact figure, it is clear that the Chinese population is central – but also that temples are unlikely to displace food shops as ethnic centres (Ryan 1996: 93).

In all there were another 1,026 Malaysians of Chinese background and 336 other Chinese diaspora Asians (Central Statistics Office 2007b: 24). A total of 2,159 ethnically Chinese people were of 'other' religions (2007b: 25), though not all will see themselves as Buddhist (rather than Confucian, Taoist, traditionalists etc.); multiple religious affiliations are common. Malaysian Chinese, some of whom are Theravadin, are perhaps most likely to identify as Buddhist.[25]

Anecdotally, it seems that the experience of *individual* emigration can lead some Chinese people to rediscover Buddhism as an aspect of identity which is recognisable abroad. Nevertheless language and generational barriers, together with high turnover among Malaysian and PRC students, limit institutional formation even among those who identify as Buddhist, although informal groups such as study circles have developed. The only visible Chinese group is Falun Dafa/Falun Gong, which is well represented in Ireland, with a free newspaper available in local supermarkets and frequent public demonstrations. Participants occasionally claim Falun Dafa as Buddhist or as including Buddhism, a claim which most other Buddhists might contest.

23. Tamils are overrepresented in the Sri Lankan diaspora; while few Nepalis are Buddhist.
24. Some of these may have been Falun Gong converts.
25. Historically most Malaysian Chinese in Ireland have been students.

Ethnic Buddhist Organisations

The oldest Buddhist ethnic community in Ireland is that of Vietnamese 'quota refugees' who arrived in the late 1970s and early 1980s. Some of the 803 people who arrived up to 2000 were Catholics, but many were Buddhist; others again identified as Chinese (Maguire 2004). For a time, this community operated a temple in a Dublin suburban house.

Soka Gakkai's Irish beginnings were uncharacteristic for that movement, with Máirín ni Bhriain learning the practice through Hiro Yoshii, a Japanese member of her English language class, in 1978. Reliant mostly on Irish members in its early years, it was boosted by Japanese immigrants in the 1990s, several of whom now hold leadership positions (Sinéad Lynch, pers. comm.). In Ireland as elsewhere, SGI blurs the ethnic/convert distinction more than most Buddhist groups.

The Thai community, for its part, has organised annual Wesak celebrations since 2005 with the support of the Thai consulate in London, and in 2011 opened the Rattanapadipa centre, also in suburban Dublin.[26]

Finally, Mongolian Buddhists follow the Tibetan Gelugpa tradition, and Otrul Rinpoche, spiritual director of Jampa Ling, is closely involved with the revival of Buddhism in Mongolia.

Considerations

Without ethnographic research, it is hard to say much about the specific character of these different Buddhisms, their traditionalist or modernist character (Baumann 2001: 3), although a number feature the 'engaged' elements characteristic of modernist Buddhism (discussed below). Certainly the experience of many immigrant groups in Ireland has been that of compromise around internal diversity in attempts to organise on an ethnic basis – a basis often forced in the case of Buddhism by language barriers and sectarian differences.

However, since numbers of most Buddhist ethnicities are very small, and most immigrants are recent, the development of formal institutions is a daunting proposition, not least in a recession. It is perhaps more likely that some will turn to existing convert Buddhist

26. http://rattanapadipa.org

centres, at least where there is sufficient common ground. This was not a feature of earlier Buddhist immigration (Ryan 1996: 111), but anecdotal evidence suggests that tentative moves are being made in this direction. If so, we may see a reversal of the common situation, elsewhere in the west, where immigrant temples have often made space for convert practitioners.

The Lotus and the Shamrock: Creolisation and Celticity[27]

> I have always been aware that my interest in Buddhism may be rather superficial, and I am not a good or committed practitioner! However, I remain a sympathiser and an admirer, often reading Buddhist literature. But I haven't attended Buddhist teachings in recent years. Moreover, I retain a certain Christian faith, and have an interest in some of the teachings of Islam. (pers. comm. F)

The linguistic metaphor of creolisation has been widely used to discuss the adoption of new religions. Prothero's discussion of Olcott's modernist Buddhism describes it as 'a Buddhist lexicon informed by a Protestant grammar and spoken with a theosophical accent' (2010: 69). Rocha's (2006) analysis of Brazilian Buddhism similarly uses the concept along with broader categories of multiple affiliation, such as Tweed's (2002: 28–9) Buddhist sympathisers, night-stand Buddhists, Dharma-hoppers, lukewarm Buddhists and not-just-Buddhists.

Most convert Buddhism in Ireland takes place outside the organised, public groups which can be easily studied, and in a context which is particularly conducive to DIY religion of this sort. The practical meaning is often that, as one teacher observed, 'we have Irish Catholic Buddhists, Irish Catholic pagans, Irish Catholic atheists ...' who use a Buddhist (etc.) vocabulary within a grammar drawn from their earlier religious socialisation.

Creolisation co-exists with other strategies, such as resisting categorisation, practising dual religions, and religious universalism. From a Buddhist point of view, these are not necessarily bad things:

> I think Buddhism will never be really big in the West. It may be big in influencing generalised western culture, which it has already to some degree in various ways. (Interview C)

27. Many thanks to John O'Neill and Ani Tsondru for copies of the *Well* drawn on in this section.

Such a perception is often built into Buddhist organisations:

> we have an awful lot of people come here and it isn't our purpose
> that they all become Buddhist. It's our purpose that they maybe learn
> meditation or hear some of the Buddhist views on things. That helps
> them in their life ... People will practise at their level. (Interview A)

This approach leads to a committed and more or less Buddhist-
identified core with dedicated activities (such as longer retreats,
dharma study, training abroad etc.), along with broader programmes
that do not entail Buddhist identification (courses in meditation,
yoga etc.; public rituals and festivals; shorter retreats and general
'night-stand' literature). As in Asia, the notion of exclusive identification is less than helpful in understanding Buddhist groups in
Ireland: whether or not they are interested in 'conversion', they are
routinely interested in including newcomers without requiring any
Buddhist commitment.

While rhetorical gestures of the 'all faiths are one' variety are
widespread, and some Buddhist teachers proclaim this, more
sophisticated syncretic philosophies are no longer as significant as
in Theosophy's heyday. One reason, of course, is the greater availability of Buddhist texts, enabling theological dialogue but making
it hard to sustain any easy equivalence at any level of intellectual
seriousness. Another is the general downturn in *cognitive* and
philosophical approaches to religion. Finally, as discussed above,
the Vatican's hostility to what it sees as syncretism discourages
overt statements which are liable to lead to silencing or excommu-
nication. If creolisation avoids these difficulties, it is by the same
token slippery and harder to research.

This section discusses creolisation and how those influenced by
Buddhism relate it to their own socialisation. The easy aspects to
research are those connected with the institutional Catholic church;
but these are the visible sides of a more complex relationship,
affected by concerns for conventional respectability, but also by the
practical aspects of ethnic Irish religion, and the changing nature of
religious consumer culture.[28]

28. Here I draw on personal observation through teaching in Buddhist contexts
and third-level institutions and as an organiser in alternative education and other
political contexts, as well as my own research on the Irish counter culture and
conversation with Wendy Jermyn.

'Institutional Religionism'

Religious affiliation is central, formally and otherwise, to many aspects of daily life in Ireland. Schools and hospitals have with few exceptions an overtly religious ethos; marriages and funerals are typically religious; baptisms, first communions and confirmations are major events; and so on. As Coulter (1993) observed for the women's movement, all of this exerts major pressures on Irish people's ability to 'be Buddhist' if it means leaving or confronting these institutions. Thus southern Irish Buddhists often give their children Christian religious rites and have church marriages 'for the sake of the family', without this being seen as contradictory.

Cosgrove's (2012) findings show that 68% of respondents in minority religions had experienced discrimination, mostly in relation to work, access to services such as health and education (where religious discrimination is institutionalised) as well as financial services and local groups of various kinds. 72% feared discrimination, either based on experience or the reaction of others to religious minorities.

A 2008 Equality Authority report found levels of religious discrimination slightly higher than those based on sexual orientation and only slightly lower than those based on membership of the travelling community. While racism plays a role, non-Catholics are more vulnerable to religious discrimination even when nationality and ethnicity are controlled for (Russell et al., 2008: 47).

We have seen previously that 70% of Cosgrove's respondents conceal or have concealed their membership in minority religions, in order to adapt to what she describes as the 'institutional religionism' of Irish society. Creolisation can also mean this: the attempt to 'fit in', to adopt Buddhist ideas and practices without incurring the perceived costs from leaving the dominant fold, and to participate in the religiously-structured activities of family, school and rites of passage. Such pressures also lead to denial of difference between Buddhism and Christianity, as we shall see.

Buddhism as Religion?

One effect of 'Mind-Body-Spirit' publishing on the wider reception of Buddhism in Ireland is that, largely produced in the US, it is marked by the exceptionally high levels of religious practice and identification in that country and the unusual character of its religious settlement. While the growth of Irish Buddhism is taking place in the midst of a crisis of established religion, and its institutions are largely based in secularised countries such as Britain and France, what Irish Buddhists *read* is shaped by American agendas such as the need to play down Buddhism's lack of theistic elements, and presenting all 'faiths' as fundamentally similar.[29] In this way Buddhism's *difference* from orthodox Christianity – its key attractions for conscious converts – are downplayed in popular reception.

More broadly, if religion in the Irish sense is part of the problem to which Irish Buddhism has responded, the re-definition of the 'Buddhist solution' as itself a religion brings new questions. The traditions of Irish Christianity – which have not been famous for their reflective and questioning approach – do not, perhaps, help when translated into an anti-intellectual form of 'Buddhism as wished for'. As one more thoughtful Buddhist puts it,

> I think Buddhism ought to be rigorously studied and the cultural accumulations weeded out or recognised for what they are. And study of the history and study of the philosophy, very critically ... And Buddhist teachers themselves, almost all of them, would applaud this ... (Interview C)

The Politics of Celticity

> At this point I'm not very interested anymore in being in Asian culture ... what I would find of interest now would be more a marriage of the best of European culture with the best of Buddhist insight. (Interview C)

As early as the 1980s it was clear that Irish Buddhism could mean different things:

> An anthropologist ... wrote a paper way back, when the Randalls were offering this place in Netterville to [Trungpa] and there was this "wow, what is this going to become here?" He wrote a paper called "Neither a shamrock nor a lotus" ... it was a little bit of a discussion of "how would Buddhism be in Ireland?" (Interview A)

This question can be tackled in various ways. Folk history may provide elements of an answer: if many Buddhist groups have

---

29. While nineteenth-century sympathisers were often concerned by the doctrine of *anatta* and the question of morality, twenty-first century concerns have more to do with whether all religions can be seen as 'the search for the divine'. See also Schmidt (2007).

no sense of Buddhism in Ireland before their founder's arrival, others referenced Yeats and AE, the BSGBI, Lobsang Rampa and suggestions of an early twentieth century visit by a Buddhist monk. Beyond their historical value, these comments serve as answers to the question 'What is Buddhism doing in Ireland?'

Something similar is true for claims of Buddhist connections to 'Celtic' Ireland, discussed by Murphy (2011), a variant on the long tradition of antiquarian pseudohistories which linked Ireland to Asia (Lennon 2004). Such stories – be it the spurious quote from Origen noted in chapter two linking Druids and Buddhists or the identification of cross-legged figures in Iron Age art with Buddhist meditators – serve to legitimate Buddhism in Ireland.

They are one form of religious creolisation; attachment to pre-Christian myths and archaeological sites is widespread in Ireland, thanks both to the Romantic movement and to cultural nationalisms including those of Yeats and AE, and it would be surprising if *Irish* Buddhists did not seek to find ways to connect the two – as we have already seen for the 'Irish Gael', combining personal experience of fairy folk with Buddhist practice.

'Celtic' identities, however, are notoriously fluid: the archaeo-logical, historical and other evidence for pre-Christian and early medieval 'Celticity' is fragmentary, complex and ambiguous (Chapman 1992, Collis 2003), so that modern accounts are necessarily constructs which often serve present-day purposes. As Piggott (1968: 3) neatly put it, we cannot know 'Druids-in-themselves' and all too often see 'Druids-as-wished-for' rather than 'Druids-as-known'. The same is true for Celts in general, and nowhere more so than in the sphere of religion (Hutton 2007).

In particular, 'Celtic' can have at least two meanings – one as pagan and one as Christian (Butler 2011, Gierek 2011) – and these different myths can be seen in the different meanings deployed by different Buddhist groups in Ireland.

Celticity as Pagan

One mode of Celticity has been developed within the UK FWBO, which is sympathetic to presenting Buddhism in forms appropriate to local culture and folklore. In the 1990s, their Dublin centre used a 'local puja book', using imagery and lettering from the Book of Kells, an Irish-language translation of the Heart Sutra, and a liturgy stressing the Irish countryside.

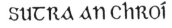

SUTRA AN CHROÍ

honaic boohisattva na taise
agus é ag machnamh go domhain,
foilmhe na gcúig scunda
agus bhris na ceangail a thug dó fulaingt.

anseo mar sin,
ní tada cruth ach foilmhe,
tada foilmhe ach cruth.
níl i gcruth ach foilmhe,
i bhfoilmhe níl ach cruth.

is mar a chéile leis seo
mochúchán, smaoineamh agus rogha,
anmheabhraíocht féin.

is ionann gach ní agus an folúntas cianaosta,
nach mbeirtear ná nach milltear í,
nach bhfuil smálta ná glan,
nach líonann ná nach dtránn.

Fig. 7.5 Prajnaparamita Heart Sutra in Irish (tr Lorcan MacMenamin) from FWBO Ireland puja book. Thanks to Dh. Sanghapala.

The text was prefaced by a 1993 talk noting,

> Because of the basic healthy pagan nature of Buddhist ritual, it can help to heal. It can help to heal the pain of the disconnection from our archetypal basic "natural self" which predates sin and guilt and unworthiness …
>
> The suppression of these rites over the last few hundred years and their replacement by the rule of law and a creed of shoulds and oughts is a tragic loss. This disconnection from humanity's fundamentally natural and psychologically healthy native roots, and the consequent dislocation and fragmentation of our spiritual heritage, might alone be a major factor in the genesis of an increasingly alienated and spiritually desolate modern west … (Sanghapala 1993: 3–4)

The analysis drew on anti-clerical discourses to oppose 'Celtic' to 'Roman' and 'pagan' to 'Christian', in a counter-cultural mode. In particular, the identification of sexual policing with morality (Inglis 1998a) and the nineteenth-century attack on folk religion were addressed. The liturgy retranslated elements of the *Bodhicaryavatara* without the references to sin, fear, worship etc., in the standard Triratna translation, producing a less authoritarian religious tone. As with Dhammaloka's emphasis on free thought or Jivaka's on conscious living, the effect was to stress Buddhism as different from Irish Christianity.

In this kind of Buddhist Celticism, paganism was a tool for liberation:

> Unfortunately, people can often feel a sort of unresourceful kind of reaction to ritual because of past association. Their emotions have perhaps in the past been hijacked by such and such a group. Our practices might remind them of what they encountered in the Masonic Lodge or in the Communist Party. Or perhaps ... one's parents were followers of a religion? ...
>
> Buddhist ritual practice owes nothing to creeds or beliefs, one is not asked to accept outlandish tales as facts and there is no chanting of religious dogma. (Sanghapala 1993: 4–5)

In the 1990s FWBO retreats sometimes featured subsidiary shrines to nature spirits, and a snakeskin was ritually buried at the Hill of Tara, symbolically reversing the St Patrick myth of the eviction of paganism from Ireland.[30] More recently, the 'Song of Amergin' from the *Lebor Gabála Éirinn* has been used to set Buddhism against a pagan backdrop.

This approach responds to the fact that until recently the single most salient fact about Buddhism in Ireland has been its character as 'new religion', a way out of the old. Speaking of the 1970s,

> I was coming at it from almost an intellectual point of view ... and I didn't know about the cultural accretions of Buddhism really. And in fact when I did my first retreat, that was a shock. I felt a reaction against it: "God, this is like the church", you know. The fear there was a ritualistic element. And my first retreat was a Zen retreat now! (Interview D)

As in previous generations (such as chapter five's 'Irish Gael'), what many Irish people want from Buddhism is something *different* from their inherited religion, and thus *pagan* Celtic connections become important.

---

30. In similar mode, the NKT Potala Kadampa Centre in Belfast held an 'Irish Dharma celebration' centred around Green Tara (Rowen 2011: 12).

Celticity and Catholicism

An alternative Celtic ideology is to see 'Celtic Christianity' or 'simple country faith' as a vehicle for pre-Christian spirituality in Catholic garb. In mainstream Irish religion, this often serves the purpose of allowing continued self-identification as Catholic while quietly rewriting practice and doctrine (Gierek 2011) – a co-optation of contemporary paganism. In the 1990s, Samye Dzong situated itself in this context.

Thus a 1996 issue of its *Well*[31] featured as its cover picture an Iron Age wheel from the National Museum and an Irish-language translation of the four *brahma-viharas* in Celtic lettering. An article in the same issue drew links between folk etymology in Irish and Tibetan monasticism, noting that

> English becomes more and more dominant as a world language bringing with it the inherent danger of monoculturalism and the elision of conceptual differences embedded in linguistic diversity (1996: 4–5).

The article related the Sanskrit *sukha* and *duhkha* (pleasure and pain) to the Irish phrase *sochar agus dochar an tsaoil* (ups and downs of life):

> This is one instance where the Celtic linguistic inheritance in these islands can be used in the most beneficial way possible, as an important spiritual resource.[32]

These fit within a broader exploration of Celticity. Chronicling the search for the medieval well after which Kilmainham Well House is named:

> On being told a little of Kilmainham's holy spring, which last emerged not far from where the centre stands, Akong Rinpoche asked for some wire. A pair of dowsing rods were duly fashioned, and he methodically paced the rear garden, locating a "strong but deep" current emerging from a specific point and flowing in a particular direction … This place which, providentially, is framed by a screen of young wild ash (a tree often associated with Irish holy wells), has now been marked in a permanent manner and will be a focal point for future garden design.[33]

31. Vol. 2/3 (autumn): 1.
32. In fact Sanskrit's position as the language of power, forbidden to lower castes on pain of death, was more comparable to English or Latin than to Irish.
33. *The Well*, spring 1995 (vol. 1/1): 6.

Later issues made links with a medieval church bell found locally and with the Irish site of St Molaise (of Samye Dzong's Scottish retreat site on Holy Isle): an article on bells in religion connected 'ancient Celtic bells', Buddhist symbolism, Druids and followers of Isis (Nic Dhiarmada 1997). As in Lennon's (2004) antiquarian mode, 'Irish' was identified with 'Asian' in ways that superimpose 'Catholic' and 'Celtic'.[34]

This superimposition is relatively recent. In turn-of-the-century Ireland, Theosophists identified with folk religion *against* the modernising church which sought to abolish it, and newspapers were highly critical of 'superstition', including in Buddhism. The most frequent example was the Kandy tooth, which Protestants used as a stick to beat Catholics with, while Catholic ridicule of Buddhists represented an attempt to modernise and rationalise folk religion towards continental respectability.

By the 1990s, however, folk religion was unquestionably good. Reporting on a Carlow well associated with Molaise, *The Well* reported

> The continual stream of individuals to the well through the days, the numbers (400+) of all ages lingering there on a cold, damp evening … indicate a lively and unselfconscious Irish rememberance [sic] of and faith in Molaise, whose name in Scotland is inseparable from that of Holy Island.[35]

Here folk Christianity legitimates Buddhist practice in historically Irish contexts, gaining further credence from pre-Christian links. Holy Island, an early Irish monastic site in SW Scotland, was purchased by Samye Ling in 1991 for retreats. Jinpa Tarchin's account is entitled 'An Irish monk on Holy Island':

> There is an atmosphere of magic, but with a certain raw quality which can be almost overwhelming at times. H.E. Tai Situ Rinpoche … said of Holy Island: "It has lots of 'living kind of something' – it's not just a flat dead place, it is alive …" The island's history as a place of spirituality or retreat from pre-Christian times through to Saint Molaise and the monastic settlement in mediaeval times, testifies to the living quality of this "holy island". (Tarchin 1995: 2)

34. See Kemp 2007: 108–11 for a comparable origin myth involving Tibetan lamas, an Australian Buddhist nun and a leading figure of the Maori renaissance.
35. Spring 1996 (vol. 2/1): 10.

Moving from personal experience via Tibetan interpretation to Celticising history, the passage comes, powerfully, to rest in nature:

> [W]e made our way up the hill under a clear, starry sky. Reaching the top of a south-facing cliff, we sat down. In front of us the sea stretched wide under a bright, full moon ... Below us on the rocks, the black seals began to sing, deep and haunting songs. Their calls echoed out over the still sea ...

Such links legitimate the presence of Buddhism in Ireland not by reference to pagan Celts *against* later Christianity but rather in terms of a generic 'Irish spirituality', supposedly found equally in pre-Christian religion and the medieval church.[36]

These contrasting 1990s explorations illustrate different possible myths of 'Buddhism and Ireland.' As with the Theosophists, musings about Buddhism and Celtic religion also represent attempts to position oneself within the field of contemporary Irish religious politics – now not in terms of the conflict between Protestant Ascendancy and Catholic nationalism but rather of the conflict between the increasingly widespread critique of religion as such and religio-ethnic identification.

Celtic Buddhism

Since 1989, a conscious 'Celtic Buddhism' lineage has explored these topics (Murphy 2011). Developed by Chögyam Trungpa's disciple Seonaidh Perks, the group's main centre is in Vermont, but several members spent 2006 in Ireland on retreat with the Irish College of Druids, and other attempts have been made to develop Irish connections. Along with ecological themes, the group has a strong aesthetic element, exploring various aspects of 'Celtic' music. Artist Bill Burns has taken the attempt to develop a Celtic Buddhist imagery further than the FWBO and Samye Dzong artwork mentioned above, with dramatic large-scale paintings placing Buddhist deities in frameworks suggested by illuminated manuscripts.[37]

If on the one hand this group tends more towards an under-standing of Buddhism, Celtic paganism and Celtic Christianity as

---

36. I plead guilty to a variant of this: organising open-air retreats in pagan settings a few years later, I used early Christian nature poetry as the most suitably indigenous readings.

37. See www.celticbuddhism.org for examples.

38. www.celticbuddhism.org

Fig. 7.6 Close-up of Prajnaparamita deity in 'Celtic Mandala' by Bill Burns, 2004. Images available from www.celticbuddhism.org. Thanks to Bill Burns.

not mutually exclusive, this is on the basis of a refusal to identify Celtic Buddhism as a religion (although it is a 'complete path').[38] One member highlights his own 'skepticism as a Celtic Christian chaplain who trained as a Buddhist' (Murphy 2011: 89), while Celtic Buddhist priest Peers, an ex-Trappist with a background in monastic religious dialogue, writes that his

> Order of the Longing Look has grown out of this path through the three great vehicles (yanas) of Buddhism, whilst not abandoning the spiritual roots of the Christian and pre-Christian West.

Perks says:

> It's still a big question mark as to what Celtic Buddhism is going to evolve into. It's important to make the question mark very big, so that it remains a big open question. Not only about oneself, but the society in which one lives. Celtic Buddhism could be viewed as an open exploratory adventure with no conclusion.[39]

In this formulation, freedom from dogma is used not to legitimate mainstream Christianity but to avoid religious identification as far as possible, in ways that show some continuity with earlier Irish Buddhisms.

Engaging Buddhism in the World

Another aspect of 'localising' Buddhism is to ask about its relationship with wider society. This has of course long been central to Asian Buddhism, and this spills over into western organisations which legitimate themselves through their Asian links. By some margin, Ireland's most visible 'engaged Buddhists' are Falun Dafa supporters, via public protests against the treatment of their devotees and its widely distributed *Epoch Times*, which relentlessly criticises the Chinese government. The 'Tibetan Community in Ireland' group and the associated 'Tibet Support Group – Ireland' have organised regular protests in the context of popular unrest and Chinese repression in Tibet; while predominantly secular this has naturally included Buddhist aspects.

There have been small Buddhist elements to protests against the war in Afghanistan (FWBO) and in solidarity with Catholic Workers on trial for sabotaging US warplanes at Shannon (Rev. Gyosei

39. http://wisdomquarterly.blogspot.com/2008/10/celtic-buddhism.html

Fig. 7.7 Rev. Gyosei Handa (Milton Keynes Peace Pagoda) supporting the Dublin Catholic Workers at their first (2005) trial for damaging a US war plane at Shannon airport. Thanks to Ciaron O'Reilly, Dublin Catholic Worker.

Handa of the Milton Keynes peace pagoda).[40] During solidarity events with the Burmese democracy movement, the *Metta sutta* was recited, although much of the Irish Burmese population are Christian Karens. Most recently, a Network of Engaged Buddhists has been initiated.

In less overtly political ways, a number of convert groups support Asian organisations of various kinds. For example, in 1995 Samye Dzong trust recorded donations to support a teacher and students at a Tibetan monastery; in 1996 it sought volunteers to collect for Rokpa activities in Dublin shopping centres; and in 1998 it secured an Irish Aid grant for medical projects in Tibet. In the same period the Dublin Meditation Centre was involved in support for *dalit* Buddhists in India via its fair trade co-operative shop. Examples could be multiplied.

Dzogchen Beara's Buddhist hospice is another, local form of engagement paralleled by Rigpa's training courses for working with

40. See http://www.indymedia.ie/article/83925?author_name=robbie&condense_comments=false, accessed 18.1.12. Thanks to Ciaron O'Reilly.

the sick and dying and Triratna projects around pain management courses and work with those recovering from depression. Prison visits are carried out by several groups, while Black Mountain Zen Centre in Belfast does cross-community work.

In Ireland, as elsewhere in the west, engaged Buddhism is sporadic and only rarely contentious.[41] 'Engaged Buddhism' in Asia is arguably a majority position in many countries, and in one sense simply recognises that as a key national institution Buddhism is necessarily concerned with politics and with development. This is particularly visible for oppressed populations such as Tibetans, Indian *dalits* or, differently, Burmese, but is important elsewhere (Queen and King 1996).

Convert Buddhism in Ireland is probably *less* politicised than in the past, whether the 1900s or the 1960s. Its institutions are more established, and becoming Buddhist now involves far less personal courage and effort than it once did. Irish Buddhists today are better-off and less radical, often more interested in Inglis' (1998a) personalised ethics for professionals than in any sense that an alternative consciousness might entail social transformation.

Certainly few Irish Buddhists today express O'Halloran's view that Buddhism and socialism go hand in hand; it is more common to hear clichés opposing 'changing the world' to 'changing yourself' or that social change is simply the product of individual transformations. This change between the 1970s and 1990s is reminiscent of what E.P. Thompson wrote of the 1830s:

> [Handloom weavers] fought, not the machine, but the exploitive and oppressive relationships intrinsic to industrial capitalism. In these same years, the great Romantic criticism of Utilitarianism was running its parallel but altogether separate course. After William Blake, no mind was at home in both cultures, nor had the genius to interpret the two traditions to each other …. Hence these years appear at times to display, not a revolutionary challenge, but a resistance movement, in which both the Romantics and the Radical craftsmen opposed the annunciation of Acquisitive Man [sic]. In the failure of the two traditions to come to a point of junction, something was lost. How much we cannot be sure, for we are among the losers. (1968: 915)

In Ireland, perhaps, service-class romanticism has paid too little attention to changing social relationships (Cox 2007a), while

41. See e.g. Rothberg 2006, Jones 2003, Kraft 1999, Glassman 1998, Snyder 1990 etc.

the struggles of the poor have remained caught within ethnic and religious community structures (Coulter 1993). Contemporary Irish Buddhism, with its unwillingness to challenge either, shares these limitations. Nonetheless some Irish Buddhists continue to argue that

> There is a future for an Irish form of Buddhism and it will probably have to be an engaged form of Buddhism. I think it will have to have a strong social dimension … (cited in Rowen 2011: 32)

Conclusion: Irish Buddhism's Alternative Futures

The Turn of the Millennium: Why Buddhism Became Respectable

This book has highlighted the difficulties of being Irish, and Buddhist, and in Ireland; most 'Irish Buddhists' from the 1870s until the 1990s were immigrants, emigrants or closet Buddhists. This was just starting to change in 1991, when only 2% of the population of the Republic claimed to be 'without religion', and over 70% claimed to be *practising* Catholics; the less than 1,000 self-identified Buddhists made up 0.025% of the population, and only 27% (264 people) had been born in the country.

In 2002, there were 1,510 Irish nationals; by 2006, this had risen to 2,175 and by 2011 to around 3,300. Buddhism is alternately Ireland's third or fourth religion, after Christianity and Islam (and sometimes Hinduism). Somewhere around the turn of the millennium, then, a change in its acceptability to 'ordinary' Irish people and society began and a 'normalisation' to rates comparable with other European societies.

The few Irish Buddhists of the early 1990s could still be described thus:

> A lot of us were on the dole, graduates or students of life. We had lots of time to hang out and think, without having to worry too much about paying mortgages or bills. Some of us were bored with life. Some of us were just getting into altered states of consciousness. Some of us, fed up with Christianity, were looking for the big unifying meaning to it all. (Little 1998: 9)

This picture, which parallels my own fieldwork (Cox 2011), is sharply different from that only ten years later, at the height of the neoliberal boom, with relentless pressure for workplace productivity. Now Buddhism increasingly distanced itself not just from criticism of dominant religion or 'altered states of consciousness' but more generally from the grungy, plebeian image of earlier generations of seekers. Signs of change had been present from the mid-1990s:

> The number of requests for visits to and from schools and other insti-
> tutions continues to increase, perhaps reflecting a growing awareness
> of the magnitude and vibrancy of the Buddhist tradition. There seems
> to be room for improvement in the coverage of Buddhism in some
> school textbooks ...[42]

This is gentle; still today teachers of 'world religions' are almost all products of confessional teacher-training, and accurate knowledge is rare. Along with this normalisation came a steady stream of Buddhist involvement, first in 'ecumenical' and then in 'inter-faith' gatherings from the mid-1990s.[43] Mary McAleese's Samye Dzong speech came in the context of what was 'probably the first visit by a European Head of State to a Buddhist centre in Europe'.[44] Somewhat trumping her previous taking of Anglican communion, she joined the assembly in a Padmasambhava liturgy.

Parallel to this upward mobility and establishment acceptance came the gradual withdrawal of Buddhist organisations from what remains of the counter culture. There are still occasional posters for meditation events in health food shops or vegetarian cafes, but Buddhists no longer advertise (for example) their courses or centres in *Network Ireland*, the main listings magazine for all things 'holistic' and 'healing', or in other consciously 'alternative' contexts such as Indymedia.

By comparison with earlier decades, at least, Buddhism has achieved respectability. Though the Dublin Buddhist Centre has recently been the target of attacks by an 'anti-cult' group, the only direct negative response to our research came in the form of an anonymously posted evangelical tract.[45]

It seems, on the face of it, possible to be 'Irish', in Ireland, and Buddhist, without the previous tensions. This is in large part the

42. *The Well*, spring 1996 (vol. 2/1): 10.

43. In 1995, for example, a conference at the Irish School of Ecumenics was opened and closed by two Tibetan nuns from Samye Ling playing the gyaling (*The Well*, winter 1995–6, vol. 1/4: 1–2).

44. *The Well*, 1998 (vol. 4/1): 4.

45. On a similarly trivial note, a recent *Church of Ireland Gazette* included in its 'Buy this book' rubric Edward Vaughan's *Why I gave up Buddhism* (online at http://gazette.ireland.anglican.org/208/120908/index120908.htm; accessed 31.10.08).

result of wider changes: the women's movement's disruption of institutional Catholicism, the shift from an inheritance-based petite bourgeoisie to one based on credentialism, and globalisation.[46] It is also, however, the result of the hard effort of earlier generations of Buddhists:

> In the 50s, 60s and 70s I suppose they had a pioneering interest. But now people interested in Buddhism, most of them look up the Internet, they see "Buddhist centre", they come along and in a way it's all there, provided for them. So I suppose that has changed quite a lot. It still depends on their own efforts, [but] in a way it's on a plate. If you're interested now it's there, easy access. (Interview C)

At the same time, Cosgrove's research on discrimination shows the need to nuance this: members of minority religions continue to experience discrimination, and Buddhist attempts to 'blend in' through baptising and confirming their children, holding church weddings and so on are of a piece with the attempts at 'passing' as Catholic which she chronicles. There is an anxious tone to some statements about how accepted Buddhism is – and to attempts to demonstrate this – suggesting doubts as to how deep the acceptance goes.

Buddhism and Cultural Modernisation

> We [the 1968 generation] have thoroughly civilised this German society. (Green politician Antje Vollmer, 1990)

Beyond religion, Buddhism has been part of a general transformation of Irish culture:

> we have been exposed since [the 1970s] to a lot more cultural variation, just a lot more different ways of being and doing things ... And a lot of Buddhist concepts or practices, somewhat detached from their origin, are being used in more mainstream practices, the like of psychology and medicine and things like that. (Interview D)

Meditation, often minus the 'Buddhism', has become a frequent element of evening courses in adult education: thus the trade union People's College offers 'Mindfulness, meditation and relaxation', including 'the relief of worry, stress and pain' (2009: 15), while a school in working-class Ballymun offers 'Meditation for beginners', giving 'an inner poise which ultimately percolates into your daily

46. See Cosgrove et al., (2011) for a broader study of new religions in Ireland.

life' (Trinity Comprehensive 2009: 7). 'Secular Buddhist' practices such as mindfulness-based cognitive therapy are widely used in mainstream health contexts, and routinely recommended in the media.

A book could be written on the spread of meditation into various aspects of western life, and the historical origins of the various techniques employed; here I want simply to note the sheer ordinariness that now appears, by contrast with the hysteria of, say, the Irish Theological Commission in 1994.

The same could be said for Buddhist art. The 1925 'dancing lamas' were sheer entertainment; by 1978, when Switzers department store used four Thai dancers to open a Thai crafts section, the performance included explanations of the Buddhist context.[47] By 1990, Tibetan Buddhist organisations were occasionally hosting performances of 'Tibetan sacred music and dance'.[48] In 1994 Trinity's Douglas Hyde Gallery hosted the creation of a Kalachakra sand mandala with support from Samye Dzong and a visit from President Robinson.[49] In 1996, Tibetan thangkas were exhibited in Dublin's RHA and Belfast's Ormeau Baths galleries;

> The Dublin exhibition was opened with a flourish by the *Spirit of Tibet* group, comprising monks from Gyume Tantric University and a lay troupe ... from Kalimpong.[50]

If there are elements of continuity, with Buddhist monks presenting art in a secular context, there is also increasing respect for the event's Buddhist nature. No doubt for many Buddhists of the 1960s and 1970s generation – as more generally for many older feminists, gays and lesbians, ecologists and members of the counter culture – the experience of being somewhat accepted within a somewhat modified Irish society was achieved with a sense of relief and, perhaps, the abandonment of what remain as unfinished agendas for younger generations.

Buddhism in the Celtic Tiger: Critical Modernism and Downshifting

Buddhism's increasing respectability might be said to parallel Zukin's (1989) two-stage analysis of urban gentrification, in which

47. *Irish Times*, Feb 10 1978: 11.
48. *The Well*, autumn 1995 (vol. 1/3): 1.
49. *The Well*, spring 1995 (vol. 1/1): 4.
50. *The Well*, summer 1996 (vol. 2/2): 7.

a first generation of consciously counter-cultural pioneers creates space for a second generation of mainstream urban professionals to reap the benefits of a congenial environment. But just as most of those in Irish city-centre apartments are not gentrifiers but Eastern European or majority world immigrants, so too most Buddhists in Ireland are not Irish urban professionals, who are merely its most visible face. Buddhism in Ireland has not become, as Rocha (2006) suggests for Zen in Brazil, a form of upper middle-class cultural capital: 'elite Buddhism' remains marginal, and the vast majority of Irish Buddhists are not intellectuals.

A better parallel than Zukin's might be Williams' (1989) contrast between the radical modernism of late nineteenth and early twentieth century artistic movements and the conservative redeployment of similar forms in the postwar period. If so, the *critical* modernisms of feminism, the anti-nuclear movement, community organising etc., of Buddhism's 1970s and 1980s context can be contrasted to the *affirmative* modernisms of the new private-sector service class, shielded by class and generation from the most damaging effects of past sectarianism and, perhaps, without a broader agenda.

However, Höllinger's (2006) substantial research across Northern countries nuances this, finding two divergent trends within New Age activities, including 'Oriental spiritual methods' and meditation. One subgroup was committed to self-development along with alternative medicine and psychotherapy, with work, money and professional success significantly less important than for the population as a whole. Others, interested in dreams, divination and psychic healing, were not distinctive in their life priorities.

For New Agers as a whole, even including the latter group, partic-ipation in protest, grassroots activism, political parties, solidarity campaigns and charitable activities was substantially higher than for the rest of the population. More generally, the self-developers were more liberal on gender, sexuality, ethnic and religious difference:

> In spite of its commercialisation and integration into mainstream society, the New Age movement has, to a certain degree, maintained its counter-cultural character to the present time. By "counter-cultural" I mean in this context the ideals of the anti-authoritarian, grassroots democracy, and libertarian social movements emerging in the last decades of the twentieth century … (2006: 82)

If this is true for Irish Buddhism, its striving towards respect-ability is not a feature of all Irish Buddhists, but an *organisational* choice, geared towards institutional goals of acceptance and recognition, visible without being representative of non-affiliated and informal Buddhists or of Asian Buddhists. Recession and crisis may well mean yet another shift in meaning for Irish Buddhism, returning to a 'downshifting' critique of consumerist ways of life, as in Andrew Peers' formulation:

> Counter to the current flow of society, where the demand to manufacture and market a self is getting louder, [Longing Look] serves as a reminder to look at the way we live life ... [it] is about the discovery of the inherent richness in each person, irrespective of whether one is materially wealthy or not, whether the times are hard or not ... The increasing materialism of the times, even in spiritual matters, asks for an appropriate response.[51]

Creolisation and The Second Generation

Recent creolisation between Buddhism and Christianity is histori-cally conditioned by the fact that most contemporary Irish converts were brought up within western Europe's most religious country. This situation is unstable, whether church scandals lead to deeper secularisation or a successful backlash is mounted. The equation 'Irish = Catholic', and the particular meanings given to 'Catholic', *assume* what are in fact central objects of contention in Irish cultural politics, and Buddhism and other new religions play a part in this.

History has not stopped, and as in other European countries coming generations of Irish Buddhists will relate differently to Buddhism than do present ones. It would be unwise to project continued Catholic hegemony, and Buddhism's continued existence as tolerated and timid challenger, into the indefinite future. One way of thinking through this problem may be Gramsci's observation that most people

> have two theoretical consciousnesses (or one contradictory consciousness): one implicit in their activity and which truly unites them with their collaborators in the practical transformation of reality; and one which is superficially explicit or verbal, which they have inherited from the past and have accepted without criticism. Nevertheless, this 'verbal' consciousness is not without consequences:

51. www.longinglook.org

it connects them to a given social group and influences them in their moral conduct and in the direction of their will, in more or less energetic ways, which can lead to a point in which the contradictory nature of their consciousness does not permit any action, any decision or any choice, and produces a situation of moral and political passivity. (1991: 13)

This is not a bad way of describing a situation in which some people borrow meditation techniques from Buddhism to enable them to remain Christians, while others become Buddhists but insist that they are fundamentally in agreement with the religion they have left.

Such situations are likely to be resolved either in favour of a re-establishment of hegemonic religion, or a more definitive disruption of that hegemony. As in previous generations, outcomes may differ in different classes, as between men and women, or south and north of the border.

Choices for The Future

Organised Buddhism is only thirty years old, thirty-two. That's nothing. So if you came back and interviewed me in another few hundred years – if we have another hundred years – then there might be a story or it might be clear. (Interview D)

Ireland's relationship with Buddhism has always been determined by global processes: the circuits of medieval Christian knowledge, the publishing of early modern travellers' tales, involvement with British and Catholic empires or opposition to them, the role of Anglophone publishing in the 1960s and 1970s, 'blow-ins' from the counter culture and immigration from Buddhist Asia. This book is not a separate and self-contained 'history of Buddhism in Ireland' but rather a series of contrasting histories and encounters, created and ending as broader world-systemic relationships have risen and fallen. In recent centuries, the most central feature of 'Irish culture' in relation to Buddhism was the existence of two warring cultures in a conflict which squeezed out most alternative religious options. In very recent years this has changed, particularly in the Republic, leaving Buddhism more 'respectable' than it has ever been. Is this the end of history?

At one level, *any* successful new religion exists in contentious dialogue with established religions. It needs to offer something

Fig. 7.8 Stupa at Dzogchen Beara (c. 2011). Photo courtesy of Chinch Gryniewicz. Permission granted by Dzogchen Beara.

different, to those seeking escape; and it needs to do so in a way which is locally recognisable as an answer to those problems. Buddhism, as it now exists in Ireland, highlights needs which have not been met under either the residual authoritarian-Christian alliances or the dominant modernist-consumerist formations: it has the potential to mark a rejection *both* of 'moral monopoly' and of 'consumption as a way of life'.

Those Irish people in the 1970s and 1980s who found in Buddhism a recognition of respect for other cultures, nonviolence as a question of principle, spiritual *practice* rather than professions of faith and ritual observance, solidarity with majority world countries and 'working to live rather than living to work', were arguably anticipating in their lives and through these choices directions which would become articulate for other people later and less consciously, within mainstream structures which attempt 'to change everything in order to keep everything the same'. In this sense, Buddhism – with its relative prestige and its remarkable resources in terms of technique and doctrine – can most effectively help Irish people (Buddhist and otherwise) by being most clearly and uncompromisingly itself, rather than by attempting to minimise difference.

Another way of putting this is to say that when Buddhists encounter what is by now a widespread scepticism to religion, the *least* helpful response is to throw their weight on the side of religion (or 'spirituality') in general, and use Buddhism's relative innocence of Irish religious history to legitimise the institutions which produced that scepticism. Rather, we should recognise that this hostility – whether driven by plebeian anticlericalism, feminist opposition to patriarchal religion, liberal or counter cultural emancipation from oppressive religious upbringings or the experience of religiously sanctioned abuse – is amply justified by people's experience.

Buddhism, in this view, should find its first point of contact with those who seek an end of suffering in the world, not with those who share a self-definition as 'spiritual'. This does not exclude dialogue with other religions, but such dialogue should not start from the assumption that membership of the church of one's birth is *per se* a good thing. To do so is to ignore the needs which push people out of such churches, and their often traumatic experience. Buddhism's role in interfaith dialogue is surely rather to speak for those needs – and to support Christians who are actively struggling to change their own churches in an emancipatory direction – rather than to engage in mutual recognition pacts with conservative leaderships.

Agendas for Change

If organised Buddhism in the West now often lacks a political vision of social change and accepts the given social order – in contrast to much of its own history and many Asian counterparts – it is not completely self-centred. 'Prosperity Buddhism' is almost entirely absent in Ireland and there is a continuing concern with hospice work, mental health, global solidarity, peace or ecology. Irish Buddhism is individualistic but not self-centred.

Buddhism is increasingly associated in popular culture with the language of the simple life, downshifting, and 'opting out' of late capitalist productivity. Returning to Dublin after a rural retreat,

> I felt genuinely different, inspired and uplifted. I felt fresh. A whole bunch of us walked down the quays from O'Connell Bridge with our sleeping bags and backpacks discussing how Ireland would become the Tibet of western Europe! (Little 1998: 5)

Another important area is gender, and the widespread search for forms of religious expression which do not represent forms of 'moral' control of bodies and emotions in particular: feminism, GLBTQ liberation and the revelations of physical and sexual abuse in religious institutions make this an immensely important area. As Mulholland (2006) argues, this particularly affects those who were not protected by class privilege from the coercion of earlier decades, but also lacked the resources to stand outside their churches. Forms of spiritual practice which restore people's own relationship to their bodies are significant far beyond the individual in this context.

Thirdly, Asian Buddhism in Ireland has yet to find its own voice. In recession, where immigrants who decide not to return home often recognise that their stay is more permanent than originally intended, religion often becomes a more important source of support. Racism is also rising, and it is not yet clear either how this will affect Asian Buddhists or westerners' willingness to explore Asian religion.

Until Asian Buddhists in Ireland can bridge the gap to English-language Buddhist organisations, and vice versa, they are likely to remain the poor relations of Buddhists in Britain or Asia. Similarly, import Buddhists will remain dependent on the various circuits of global publishing, touring celebrities, Internet ordering and so on;

while the Irish franchises of international organisations will remain so, as training and ordination resources remain beyond the reach of all but the largest groups.

The most significant effects of Buddhism in Ireland, however, are probably not through the small minority of those organised in formal structures, or the slightly larger minority who identify as Buddhists, but the much greater numbers of those who draw on Buddhism as resources for personal and social change, outside of institutional parameters, and can use Buddhism creatively in contemporary movements for global justice (Cox 2006, Cox and Nilsen 2007, Cox 2010a) – whether this means solidarity with movements in Asia, peace activism, community organising or intensifying ecological effort.

And Lastly ...

The future of Buddhism in Ireland, and the direction of alternative religions in western countries generally, is not pre-determined, but nor do debates over its direction take place on a blank canvas. 'Buddhism' is neither essentially one thing nor an empty signifier. Rather, its meaning to many people comes from its identification with meaningful ways of life and spiritual practice, which are shaped in relation to people's cultures of origin (Buddhist, Christian and atheist) and through local and global relationships with other people.

These possibilities are created by the rise and fall of world-systems on a large scale; and on a smaller scale by the shift from, say, high imperialism to decolonisation, or as now from neo-liberalism to whatever comes next. Buddhism in the west has a future if, against this changing background, it can offer significant numbers of people ways of 'doing Buddhism' which make sense in terms of their own lives and struggles.

This does not mean that normative or theoretical works on the topic (Kraft 1999, Jones 2003, Rothberg 2006) are pointless; people need to be convinced of the value, the *Buddhist* character, and the possibility of particular choices. But those proposing directions also need to think about *who* is likely to find a choice attractive and for what purposes, and to see the kinds of problems to which 'Buddhism' appears as a solution. This book is intended as a small contribution to that process.

Afterword:
The Global Politics of Irish Buddhism

Historian Marco Revelli writes 'The centre is blind; truth can be seen from the margins'.[1] If Ireland is marginal to Buddhism and Buddhism to Ireland, nevertheless the story sheds light on two things. One is the third, global expansion of Buddhism in the last two centuries, after its initial Indian development and its secondary extension to much of Southern, Eastern and Central Asia. The other, in the west, is how we can understand 'elsewhere' as a counter-weight to 'here' in formulating alternatives, utopias, counter-cultures and social movements. I have argued that these potentially liberating developments – in the Buddhist and the political sense – have been massively marked by the global structures of power, economics and knowledge which made the encounter possible.

Chapter one outlined a western Marxist approach to western Buddhism; this sees popular religion as collective agency that can be analysed in terms of the needs it expresses, the visions it articulates, and the limits to the action it enables. Chapter two explored 'Buddhism and the west' in the world-systems context of shifting social and political relationships across Eurasia, and used textual reception in particular to explore this history to 1850.

Chapter three located the first development of Irish Buddhism in the context of Irish involvement in the British Empire in Asia and the Catholic 'spiritual empire'. Chapter four explored the politics of Irish Theosophy as a counter-cultural response to the crisis of the Anglo-Irish imperial service class, seeking new roles in Irish or Indian politics. Chapter five discussed the first Irish Buddhists as 'going native' in Asia, in alliance with the anti-colonial cultural nationalisms of the Buddhist Revival.

---

1. *Il manifesto*, Jul 1 2011.

Chapter six discussed the first Buddhist defectors from Ireland's new Catholic national service class in the post-1960s crisis of *Catholic* hegemony and the development of mass social movements from below. Chapter seven mapped the development of present-day Buddhism and its multiple connections – as Irish-led 'import', missionary-driven 'export' and immigrant 'baggage' – and noted the recent respectability of Buddhism in Ireland.

It is a rather recent cliché that 'changing the world' and 'changing yourself' are mutually exclusive. I hope this book may convince some Irish Buddhists to move away from isolated individualism towards a broader sense of human beings as interconnected, and that it may persuade some Irish activists that spirituality need not be conservative. Both, of course, imply a more reflective, engaged and critical Buddhism – one genuinely dedicated to 'the liberation of all sentient beings'.

Bibliography

'Aesop' (1881, orig. date unknown). *Aesop's Fables*. Trans. George Townsend; New York: McLoughlin.

'A Veteran Diplomat' (1913). 'English Peer, Once a Prospector Here, Turns Muslim'. *The New York Times*, November 23.

Acharya, S. (D.M. Murdock) (2004). *Suns of God*. Kempton, IL: Adventures Unlimited.

Acheson, Nicholas (2004). *Two Paths, One Purpose*. Dublin: Institute of Public Administration.

Aiken, Charles (1900). *The Dhamma of Gotama the Buddha and the Gospel of Jesus the Christ*. Boston, MA: Marlier.

Akai, Toshio (2007). 'The Theosophical Accounts in Japanese Buddhist Publications Issued in the Late Nineteenth Century', 55–79, in *Hira Kinza and the Globalization of Japanese Buddhism of Meiji era*. Available at: http://www.maizuruct.ac.jp/human/yosinaga/hirai_kaken_report_16520060.pdf

Akenson, Donald (1991). *Small Differences*. Montreal: McGill-Queen's.

Alldritt, Keith (1997). *W.B. Yeats*. London: John Murray.

Allen, Charles (2003). *The Buddha and the Sahibs*. London: John Murray.

— (2009). *The Buddha and Dr Führer*. London: Haus.

Allen, Nicholas (2003). *George Russell (AE) and the New Ireland*. Dublin: Four Courts.

Allen, Robert and Tara Jones (1990). *Guests of the Nation*. London: Earthscan.

Almond, Philip (1988). *The British Discovery of Buddhism*. Cambridge: Cambridge University Press.

Ames, M.M. (1967). 'The Impact of Western Education on Religion and Society in Ceylon'. *Pacific Affairs*, vol. 40, No. 1/2, 19–42.

'An Irish Gael' (1928). 'How I Found Buddhism', *The British Buddhist*, May, 6–8.

Anderson, R.A. (1935). *With Sir Horace Plunkett in Ireland*. London: Macmillan.

Anonymous (1961), *All Hallows Annual* vol. 37 (1959–61). Dublin: Hely's.

Anonymous (1991), *The Noble Path*. Dublin: Trustees of the Chester Beatty Library.

Anonymous (2004). 'Simon Gevers'. Catalogue of *Galerie Düsseldorf* exhibition. Available at: http://www.galeriedusseldorf.com.au/GDArtists/Gevers/SGExh04/SGExhCat04.pdf

Anonymous (no date) (a). 'Rev. William Hayes'. Available at: http://mysite.wanadoo-members.co.uk/unitarian/chatham/Historyrevised.htm

Anonymous (no date) (b). 'Thomas Watters'. Available at: http://www.takaoclub.com/personalities/watters/index.htm

Bibliography 383

Anonymous (no date) (c). 'Early History and Founders'. Available at: http://
www.theosophical-society.org.uk/html/ttsie_early_history.html

Anonymous (no date) (d). *All Hallows College, Drumcondra, Dublin.*

Anonymous (no date) (e). 'Cloona Health Centre'. Available at: http://www.
whatsonwhen.com/sisp/index.htm?fx=event&event_id=45419

Anonymous (no date) (f). Centenary Souvenir 1860–1960 of the Brother Schools,
Burma.

Anthony, Dick and Thomas Robbins (2004). 'Conversion and 'Brainwashing'
in New Religious Movements', 243–97, in James Lewis (ed.) *The Oxford
Handbook of New Religious Movements.* Oxford: Oxford University Press.

Arrighi, Giovanni (1994). *The Long Twentieth Century.* London: Verso.

Arrighi, Giovanni, Terence Hopkins and Immanuel Wallerstein (1989).
Anti-systemic Movements. London: Verso.

Atmaprana, Pravrajika (1991). *The Story of Sister Nivedita.* 7th edn, Bourne End,
Bucks: Ramakrishna Vedanta Centre.

Barger, Jorn, (no date). 'The Household'. Available at: www.robotwisdom.
com/jaj/household.html

Barker, Eileen (1984). *The Making of a Moonie.* Oxford: Blackwell.

Barnard, Toby (1999). 'Reading in Eighteenth-century Ireland', 60–77, in
Bernadette Cunningham and Máire Kennedy (eds), *The Experience of Reading.*
Dublin: Rare Books Group/Economic and Social History Society of Ireland.

Barrett, William (1967). *The Red Lacquered Gate.* New York: Sheed and Ward.

Barrow, Logie (1986). *Independent Spirits.* London: History Workshop/Routledge
and Kegan Paul.

Barrows, J.H. (ed.) (1893). *The World's Parliament of Religions*, vol. 1. Chicago,
IL: Parliament.

Barry, William Francis (published anonymously) (1875). 'Modern Society and
the Sacred Heart'. *Dublin Review,* vol. 25 (July): 3–38.

Bartlett, Thomas (1997). 'The Irish Soldier in India', 12–28, in Michael Holmes
and Denis Holmes (eds), *Ireland and India.* Dublin: Folens.

Bately, Janet (1970). 'King Alfred and the Old English Translation of Orosius'.
Anglia 88: 433–60.

Bateman, Fiona (2006). 'An Irish Missionary in India', 117–30, in Tadhg Foley
and Maureen O'Connor (eds), *Ireland and India.* Dublin/Portland: Irish
Academic Press, 2006.

Baumann, Martin (2001). 'Global Buddhism'. *Journal of Global Buddhism* 2: 1–43.

— (2002). 'Buddhism in Europe'. 85–105, in Charles Prebish and Martin Baumann
(eds), *Westward Dharma.* Berkeley/LA: University of California Press.

Bayly, C.A. (2000). 'Ireland, India and Empire'. *Transactions of the Royal Historical
Society*, sixth series, vol. 10: 377–97.

Beinorius, Audrius (2005). 'Buddhism in the Early European Imagination'. *Acta
Orientalia Vilnensia* 6.2: 7–22.

Bellonci, Maria (1990). 'Nota introduttiva', 37–42, in Marco Polo, *Il milione.*
Roma: Mondadori.

Bennett, Allan (Ananda Metteyya, 1923). *The Wisdom of the Aryas.* London: Paul,
Trench, Trübner.

Benson, Charles (2010). *The Irish in India.* Dublin: Trinity College Dublin.

Berman, Marshall (1982). *All That is Solid Melts into Air.* London: Penguin.

Berry, Thomas (1891). *Christianity and Buddhism*. London: SPCK.

Besant, Annie (1907). 'Colonel Henry Steel Olcott'. *The Theosophist*, vol. 27 (March): Available at: http://theosophical.org/resources/articles/ColonelHenryOlcott.pdf

Bharati, Agehananda (1974). 'Fictitious Tibet'. *Tibet Society Bulletin*, vol. 7. Available at: http://www.serendipity.li/baba/rampa.html

Black, John (1881). *Young Japan (vol. 2)*. London: Trubner & Co.

Blackburn, Anne (2010). *Locations of Buddhism*. Chicago, IL: University of Chicago Press.

Blavatsky, Helena (1877). *Isis Unveiled (vol. 2)*. New York: Bouton.

— (2003). *The Secret Doctrine (vol. 1)*. Whitefish, MT: Kessinger.

Bluck, Robert (2006). *British Buddhism*. Abingdon: Routledge.

Bocking, Brian (2010). 'A Man of Work and Few Words'? *Contemporary Buddhism*, 11/2: 229–80.

— (2011). 'Dhammaloka's Irish Connections'. Paper to *Dhammaloka Day* Conference, University College Cork (February).

— (2012). 'The First Irish Buddhist Missionary?' Paper to ISASR Conference, Cork (May).

— (2013). 'Flagging up Buddhism'. *Contemporary Buddhism*, 14/1.

Bocking, Brian, Laurence Cox and Yoshinaga Shin'ichi (2013). 'Rewriting the History of UK Buddhism'. Paper presented at the 2nd ISASR Annual Conference, Dublin (May).

Boland, Rosita (2005). *A Secret Map of Ireland*. Dublin: New Island.

Bolger, Patrick (1977). *The Irish Co-operative Movement*. Dublin: Institute of Public Administration.

Bonwick, James (1894). *Irish Druids and Old Irish Religions*. London: Griffith, Farran.

Bourdieu, Pierre and Jean-Claude Passeron (1990). *Reproduction in Education, Society and Culture*. New York: SAGE.

Boyd, Stephen (ed.) (1993). *Alternative Ireland Directory*. 6th edn, Cork: Quay Co-op.

Bradney, Anthony (1999). 'NRMs: the Legal Dimension', 81–99, in Bryan Wilson and Jamie Cresswell, *New Religious Movements*. London: Routledge.

Breen, Richard, Damian Hannan, David Rottman and Christopher Whelan (1990). *Understanding Contemporary Ireland*. Basingstoke: Gill and Macmillan.

Breen, Suzanne (2007). 'Buddhist Teacher to Create Zen in the North'. *Sunday Tribune* 19 August, p. 8.

Bromley, David (2004). 'Leaving the Fold', 298–314, in James Lewis (ed.), *The Oxford Handbook of New Religious Movements*. Oxford: Oxford University Press.

Brown, Barbara (1987). 'Three Centuries of Journals in Ireland', 11–28, in Barbara Hayley and Enda McKay (eds), *Three Hundred Years of Irish Periodicals*. Dublin/Mullingar: Association of Irish Learned Journals/Lilliput.

Brown, Michael, Charles McGrath and Thomas Power (eds) (2005). 'Introduction', 11–34, in Brown, McGrath and Power (eds), *Converts and Conversion in Ireland 1650–1850*. Dublin: Four Courts.

Brown, Stephen (1941). 'John Howley 1866–1941'. *Studies* 30/120: 601–604.

Brown, Terence (2001). *The Life of W.B. Yeats*. Dublin: Gill and Macmillan.

Bryson, Mary (1977). 'Metaphors for Freedom'. *Canadian Journal of Irish Studies* 3/1: 32–40.

Bubb, Alexander (2012). 'The Life of the Irish Soldier in India'. *Modern Asian Studies* 46/4: 769–813.

Buddhist Network Ireland (no date). 'Disclaimer'. Available at: www.buddha.ie

Burleigh, David (ed.) (2005). *Helen Waddell's Writings from Japan*. Dublin/ Portland: Irish Academic Press.

Bushell, S.W. (1904–1905). 'Thomas Watters', viii–x, in Thomas Watters, *On Yuan Chwang's Travels in India*. London: Royal Asiatic Society.

Butler, Jenny (2011). 'Irish Paganism', 111–30, in Olivia Cosgrove, Laurence Cox, Carmen Kuhling and Peter Mulholland (eds), *Ireland's New Religious Movements*. Newcastle: Cambridge Scholars.

Campbell, Julian (2008). 'Introduction', 1–8, in Tim Goulding, *Floating World*. Dublin: Taylor Galleries.

Canny, Nicholas (2004). 'Foreword', ix–xviii, in Kevin Kenny (ed.), *Ireland and the British Empire*. Oxford: Oxford University Press.

Carrithers, Michael (1983). *The Buddha*. Oxford: Oxford University Press.

Cary, George (1956). *The Mediaeval Alexander*. Cambridge: Cambridge University Press.

Central Statistics Office (2007). *Census 2006, vol. 13*. Dublin: Stationery Office.

Central Statistics Office (2007b). *Census 2006, vol. 5*. Dublin: Stationery Office.

Central Statistics Office (2008). *Non-Irish Nationals Living in Ireland*. Dublin: Stationery Office.

Chambers, Liam (2001). 'A Displaced Intelligentsia', 157–74, in Thomas O'Connor, *The Irish in Europe, 1580–1815*. Dublin: Four Courts Press.

Chang, Maria (2004). *Falun Gong*. New Haven, CT: Yale University Press.

Chapman, Malcolm (1992). *The Celts*. Basingstoke: Macmillan.

Choompolpaisal, Phibul (2012). '20th Century Thai Buddhism and Politics'. Paper to ISASR Conference, Cork (May).

Clarke, J.J. (1997). *Oriental Enlightenment*. London: Routledge.

Clarke, Liam (2002). 'Zen in Belfast'. *The Sunday Times*, 11 March 2002.

Clarkson, L., and Margaret Crawford (2001). *Feast and Famine*. Oxford: Oxford University Press.

Cloona Health Retreat (no date). 'Introduction'. Available at:www.cloona.ie/ index.html

Cohen, Richard (2006). *Beyond Enlightenment*. Abingdon: Routledge.

Colinet, Philippe (1890). 'Recent Works on Primitive Buddhism'. *Dublin Review*, 3rd series, vol. 23: 256–85.

Colles, Ramsay (1911). *In Castle and Court House*. London: T. Werner Laurie.

Collins, Neil (2009). *The Splendid Cause*. Dublin: Columba Press.

Collis, John (2003). *The Celts*. Stroud: Tempus.

Collis, Maurice (1943). *The Land of the Great Image*. New York: New Directions.

— (1947). *Lord of the Three Worlds*. London: Faber and Faber.

Collis, Maurice (1953). *Into Hidden Burma*. London: Faber and Faber.

Comerford, Patrick (1975). 'The Whole Vegetarian Thing'. *The Irish Times*, 30 July 1975: 12.

Comerford, Patrick and Richard O'Leary (2009). 'Heroism and Zeal', 73–87, in Jerusha McCormack (ed.), *China and the Irish*. Dublin: New Island.

Commission to Inquire into Child Abuse (2009). 'Executive Summary'. Available at: http://www.childabusecommission.com/rpt/pdfs/CICA-Executive%20Summary.pdf

Commission of Investigation into the Catholic Archdiocese of Dublin (2009). *Report of Commission of Investigation into Catholic Archdiocese of Dublin*. Dublin: Department of Justice, Equality and Law Reform.

Connell, Bob (2001). *The Men and the Boys*. Berkeley, CA: University of California Press.

Connolly, James (1967, orig. 1910). *Labour in Irish History*. Dublin: New Books.

Connolly, Linda (2003). *The Irish Women's Movement*. Dublin: Lilliput.

Cook, Scott (1987). 'The Irish Raj'. *Journal of Social History* 20/3: 507–29.

Cornish, Peter (2007). *In Memory of Harriet*. Dzogchen Beara: Allihies, West Cork.

Cornwell, Paul (2004). *Only by Failure*. Cambridge: Salt Publishing.Cosgrove, Olivia, Cox, Laurence, Kuhling, Carmel and Peter Mulholland (eds) (2011). *Ireland's New Religious Movements*. Newcastle: Cambridge Scholars.

Cosgrove, Olivia (2012). 'Religious Discrimination in Ireland'. Paper to ISASR Conference, Cork (May).

Cott, Jonathan (1991). *Wandering Ghost*. New York: Knopf.

Coulter, Carol (1993). *The Hidden Tradition*. Cork: Cork University Press.

Coulter, Colin (1999a). *Contemporary Northern Irish Society*. London: Pluto.

— (1999b). 'The Absence of Class Politics in Northern Ireland'. *Capital and Class* 69 (autumn): 77–100.

Count Me Out (2009). *Count Me Out* (website). www.countmeout.ie

Cousins, James (1940). *Collected Poems (1894–1940)*. Adyar: Kalakshetra.

Cousins, Wendy (2008). 'Annie Besant in Ireland'. *Psypioneer* (4/8): 186–89.

Cox, Laurence (2002). 'Globalisation from Below?' Anthropology/Sociology Seminar Paper, National University of Ireland, Maynooth.

— (2006). 'News from Nowhere', 210–29, in Linda Connolly and Niamh Hourigan (eds), *Social Movements and Ireland*. Manchester: Manchester University Press.

— (2007a). 'Building Utopias Here and Now?' *Ecopolitics Online*, vol. 1 no. 1: 123–32.

— (ed.) (2007b). *Everyday Creativity, Counter Cultures and Social Change* (Symposium Proceedings, Department of Sociology, 13 October 2007). Maynooth: unpublished.

— (2009a). 'How Do We Keep Going?' Paper to 14th *Alternative Futures and Popular Protest* Conference, Manchester.

— (2009b). 'Lawrence O'Rourke/U Dhammaloka'. *Journal of Global Buddhism*, vol. 10: 135–44.

— (2010a). 'Plebeian Freethought and the Politics of Anti-colonial Solidarity', in Colin Barker and Mike Tyldesley (eds) *Fifteenth International Conference on Alternative Futures and Popular Protest*. Manchester: Manchester Metropolitan University (CD-ROM).

— (2010b). 'The Politics of Buddhist Revival'. *Contemporary Buddhism* (11/2): 173–227.

— (2011). *Building Counter Cultures*. Helsinki: into-ebooks. Available at: http://www.into-ebooks.com/book/building_counter_culture/

— (forthcoming). 'Buddhist Communities in Ireland', in Patricia Kieran (ed.) *Handbook of World Religions in Ireland*. Dublin: Veritas.

— (2013). Rethinking Early Western Buddhists: Beachcombers, 'Going Native' and Dissident Orientalism. *Contemporary Buddhism* 14/1.

Cox, Laurence and Nilsen, Alf (2007). Social Movements Research and the 'Movement of Movements'. *Sociological Compass* 1: 424–42.

Cox, Laurence and Maria Griffin (2009). Border Country Dharma. *Journal of Global Buddhism*, vol. 10: 93–125.

Cox, Richard (2009). *This Father I Never Knew*. Dublin: Original Writing.

Crone, G.R., and Skelton, R.A. (1946). 'English Collections of Voyages and Travels, 1625–1846', 63–140, in Edward Lynam (ed), *Richard Hakluyt and His Successors*. London: Hakluyt Society.

Croker, Bithia (1917). *The Road to Mandalay*. London: Cassell Cronin, Nessa (2006). 'Monstrous Hybridity', 131–39 in Tadhg Foley and Maureen O'Connor (eds), *Ireland and India*. Dublin/Portland: Irish Academic Press.

Crooke, Elizabeth (2004). 'Revivalist Archaeology and Museum Politics During the Irish Revival', 83–93 in Betsey FitzSimon and James Murphy (eds), *The Irish Revival Reappraised*. Dublin: Four Courts Press.

Crosbie, Barry (2012). *Irish Imperial Networks*. Cambridge: Cambridge University Press.

Croucher, Paul (1989). *A History of Buddhism in Australia*. Sydney: University of New South Wales.

Cullen, L.M. (2006). 'Apotheosis and Crisis', 6–31, in Thomas O'Connor and Mary Lyons (eds), *Irish Communities in Early-modern Europe*. Dublin: Four Courts Press.

Cunliffe, Barry (2002). *The Extraordinary Voyage of Pytheas the Greek*. 2nd edn, London: Penguin.

Curriculum Development Unit (1978). *Viking Settlement to Medieval Dublin*. Dublin: O'Brien Press.

Cush, Denise (1996). 'British Buddhism and the New Age'. *Journal of Contemporary Religion*, 11/2: 195–208.

Dalrymple, William (2000). 'When Albion's Sons Went Native'. *Biblio* vi (7–8): 11–12.

Daly, J. Bowles (1890a). 'The Situation in Ceylon'. *The Theosophist* (May–Sept): 465–70.

— (1890b). 'Clairvoyance'. *The Theosophist* (May–Sept): 701–11.

— (1896). *Indian Sketches and Rambles*. Calcutta: Patrick Press.

Davies, Sean (ed.) (1982). *Alternative Ireland Directory*. 2nd edn, Cork: Quay Co-op.

Davies, Stevie (1998). *Unbridled Spirits*. London: Women's Press.

Davis, Wade (2012). *Into the Silence*. New York: Vintage.

Dawson, Carl (1992). *Lafcadio Hearn and the Vision of Japan*. Baltimore, MD: Johns Hopkins University Press.

de Harlez, Charles (1889). 'The Buddhistic Schools'. *Dublin Review*, vol. 43: 47–71.

de Harlez, Charles (1890). 'Buddhist Propaganda in Christian Countries'. *Dublin Review 3* July series, vol. 23: 54–73.

de la Vallée Poussin, Louis (1910). *Buddhism*. London: Catholic Truth Society.

de Rachewiltz, Igor (1998). 'Marco Polo Went to China'. *Zentralasiatische Studien* 27: 34–92.

Deegan, Gordon (2008). 'Steiner School Plan Meets 52 Objections.' *Irish Times*, 4 April 2008.

Della Valle, Valeria (1990). 'Introduzione', 7–15, in Marco Polo, *Il milione*. Roma: Mondadori.

De la Vallée Poussin (1910). *Buddhism*. London: Catholic Truth Society.

Dennis, James (1897). *Christian Missions and Social Progress*. New York: Fleming H. Revell.

Denny, Kevin, Colm Harmon, Doreen McMahon and Sandra Redmond (1999). 'Literacy and Education in Ireland'. *Economic and Social Review*, vol. 30 no. 3: 215–26.

Denson, Alan (ed.) (1961). *Letters from AE*. London: Abelard-Schuman.

Derné, Steve and Lisa Jadwin (2006). 'Living with Empire'. In Tadhg Foley and Maureen O'Connor (eds), *Ireland and India*. Dublin: Irish Academic Press.

U Dhammaloka (1910). 'A Wicked Proclamation …' in Anon., *The Teachings of Jesus Not Adapted for Modern Civilization*. Rangoon: Buddhist Tract Society.

Dharmadasa, K.N.O. (1992). *Language, Religion and Ethnicity*. Ann Arbor, MI: University of Michigan Press.

Digby, Margaret (1949). *Horace Plunkett*. Oxford: Blackwell.

Dillon, Charles (2006). 'Irish Translation in Continental Europe, 1630–60', 383–94, in Thomas O'Connor and Mary Lyons (eds), *Irish Communities in Early-modern Europe*. Dublin: Four Courts Press.

Dillon, Michael (Lobzang Jivaka) (1946). *Self*. London: Heinemann.

Doherty, Gerald (1983). 'The World that Shines and Sounds'. *Irish Renaissance Annual*, vol. 4: 57–75.

Doods, E.R. (2007) (orig. 1936). *Journal and Letters of Stephen MacKenna*. New York: Ballou.

Doyle, Arthur Conan (1981). *The Penguin Complete Sherlock Holmes*. Harmondsworth: Penguin.

Dresser, Marianne (1996). *Buddhist Women on the Edge*. Berkeley, CA: North Atlantic.

Dunne, Aidan (1986). 'Barrie Cooke', 23 in Catalogue of Exhibition at Douglas Hyde Gallery.

Lord Dunsany (Horace Plunkett) (1970). *At the Edge of the World*. New York: Ballantine.

Eagleton, Terry (1995). *Heathcliff and the Great Hunger*. London: Verso.

Edwards, Nancy (2007). *The Archaeology of Early Mediaeval Ireland*. London: Routledge.

Ellis, F.S. (1900) (orig. 1483), *The Golden Legend or Lives of the Saints*. London: Temple Classics.

Ellis, Havelock (1967) (orig. 1939). *My Life*. London: Spearman.

Eperjesi, John (2001). 'The American Asiatic Association and the Imperial Imaginary of the American Pacific'. *Boundary 2* (28/1): 195–219.

Matthew Errey (ed.) (no date). 'Bits and Pieces'. Available at: www.weiwuwei.8k.com/bits.html

Faul, Denis (1992). Review of Edmund Hogan, *The Irish Missionary Movement*, in *Seanchas Ardmhacha*, vol. 15/1: 313.

Fennell, Desmond (1959). *Mainly in Wonder*. London: Hutchinson.

Ferguson, John (1991). *Clement of Alexandria*. Washington DC: Catholic University of America Press.

Fields, Rick (1992). *How the Swans Came to the Lake*. 3rd edn, Boston, MA: Shambhala.

Findly, Ellison Banks (2000). *Women's Buddhism, Buddhism's Women*. Boston, MA: Wisdom.

Finnegan, Frances (2004). *Do Penance or Perish*. Oxford: Oxford University Press.

Fitzmaurice, E.B., and A.G. Little (eds) (1920). Materials for the History of the Franciscan Province of Ireland, AD 1230–1450. Manchester: Manchester University Press.

Fitzmaurice, Lorraine, Joe Fitzmaurice and Pamela Fitzmaurice (2004). *The Blazing Salads Cookbook*. Dublin: Gill and Macmillan.

Foley, Tadhg (2012). 'Max Arthur Macauliffe and the Sikh Religion'. Keynote Lecture, ISASR Conference, Cork (May).

Foley, Tadhg and Maureen O'Connor (eds) (2006), *Ireland and India*. Dublin: Irish Academic Press.

Foley, Tadhg and Sean Rider (1998). *Ideology and Ireland in the Nineteenth Century*. Dublin: Four Courts.

Foster, Roy (1997). *W.B. Yeats* (vol. 1). Oxford: Oxford University Press.

— (2011). *Words Alone*. Oxford: Oxford University Press.

Foster, William (1946). 'Samuel Purchas', 47–62, in Edward Lynam (ed.), *Richard Hakluyt and His Successors*. London: Hakluyt Society.

Foucault, Michel (1981). *The History of Sexuality, vol. 1*. Harmondsworth: Penguin.

Franck, Harry A. (1910). *A Vagabond Journey Around the World*. New York: Century.

Franklin, J. Jeffrey (2008). *The Lotus and the Lion*. Ithaca, NY: Cornell University Press.

Frasch, Tilman (2004). 'A Preliminary Survey of Burmese Manuscripts in Great Britain and Ireland'. *SOAS Bulletin of Burma Research* 2/1 (spring).

Fraser, Ronald (1988). *1968*. London: Chatto & Windus.

Fremantle, W.H., G. Lewis and W.G. Martley (eds) (1997, orig. 1892) 'Against Jovinianus'. 750–825, in *The Principal Works of St Jerome*, in P. Schaff and H. Wace, *The Nicene and Post-Nicene Fathers*. Albany, OR: SAGE Digital Library.

Galambos, Imre (2008). 'The Story of the Chinese Seals Found in Ireland.' *Journal of the Royal Asiatic Society of Great Britain and Ireland* (third series, vol. 18): 465–79.

Gandhi, Leela (2006). *Affective Communities*. Durham, NC: Duke University Press.

Garbe, Richard (1914). 'Buddhist Influence in the Gospels.' *The Monist* (vol. 24/4): 481–92.

Geras, Norman (1983). *Marx and Human Nature*. London: New Left Books/ Verso.

Gibbs, Laura (2002). *Aesop's Fables*. Oxford: Oxford University Press.

Gierek, Bozena (2011). 'Celtic Spirituality in Contemporary Ireland', 301–16, in Olivia Cosgrove, Laurence Cox, Carmen Kuhling and Peter Mulholland (eds), *Ireland's New Religious Movements*. Newcastle: Cambridge Scholars.

Gillespie, Raymond (2005). *Reading Ireland*. Manchester: Manchester University Press.

Gilmour, David (2002). *The Long Recessional*. London: John Murray.

Glassman, Bernie (1998). *Bearing Witness*. New York: Bell Tower.

Gombrich, Richard (1971). *Precept and Practice*. Oxford: Clarendon.

Gordon-Finlayson, Alasdair and Michael Daniels (2008). 'Westerners Converting to Buddhism'. *Transpersonal Psychology Review* (vol. 12/1): 100–18.

Gott, Richard (2011). *Britain's Empire*. London: Verso.

Gottlieb, Roger (1989). *An Anthology of Western Marxism*. Oxford: Oxford University Press.

Grace, Pierce (2010). 'The Amritsar Massacre, 1919'. *History Ireland* (July/August): 24–25.

Graf, Susan (2003). 'Heterodox Religions in Ireland'. *Irish Studies Review* 11/1: 51–59.

Gramsci, Antonio (1971). *Selections from Prison Notebooks*. London: Lawrence and Wishart.

— (1978). *Selections from Political Writings 1921–1926*. London: Lawrence and Wishart.

— (1991). *Il materialismo storico e la filosofia di Benedetto Croce*. Roma: Riuniti.

— (1997). *La religione come senso comune*. Milano: Nuova Pratiche Editrice.

Graves, Robert (1961). *The White Goddess*. London: Faber and Faber.

Gray, Billy (2011). 'Less Like Marching, More Like Meditation', in Hedda Friberg-Harnesk, Gerald Porter and Joakim Wrethed (eds), *Beyond Ireland*. Oxford: Peter Lang.

Gross, Rita (1993). *Buddhism After Patriarchy*. Albany, NY: State University of New York Press.

Guinness, Selina (2003). 'Protestant Magic Reappraised.' *Irish University Review* 33/1 (spring–summer): 14–27.

— (2004). 'Ireland Through the Stereoscope', 19–33, in Betsey FitzSimon and James Murphy (eds), *The Irish Revival Reappraised*. Dublin: Four Courts.

— (2006). 'James Cousins and His Nation of Free Slaves', 68–80, in Tadhg Foley and Maureen O'Connor (eds), *Ireland and India*. Dublin/Portland: Irish Academic Press.

Gunder Frank, André (1971). *Capitalism and Underdevelopment in Latin America*. 2nd edn, Harmondsworth: Penguin.

Gurney, Edmund, Frederic Myers and Frank Podmore (1886). *Phantasms of the Living*. London: Society for Psychical Research.

Guruge, Ananda (ed.) (1965). *Return to Righteousness*. Colombo: Ministry of Education and Cultural Affairs.

Gwynn, Stephen (1911). *The Case for Home Rule*. Dublin: Maunsel.

Hadot, Pierre (1995). *Philosophy As a Way of Life*. Oxford: Blackwell.

Hall, Michael (2007). *Remembering the Hippie Trail*. Belfast: Island.

Hall, Stuart (1980). 'Encoding/Decoding', 128–38, in Centre for Contemporary Cultural Studies (ed), *Culture, Media, Language*. London: Hutchinson.

Hall, Thomas (2000). 'World-systems Analysis', 3–28 in Hall (ed), *A World-systems Reader*. Boulder, CO: Rowman and Littlefield.

Hall, Wayne (2000). *Dialogues in the Margin*. Gerrards Cross: Colin Smythe.

Hamon, Hervé and Patrick Rotman (1988). *Génération* (2 vols). Paris: Seuil.

Hannay, James (1903). *The Spirit and Origin of Christian Monasticism*. London: Methuen.

Hansen, Peter (1996). 'The Dancing Lamas of Everest'. *American Historical Review*, vol. 101, no. 3 (June): 712–74.

Harding, Timothy (2011). 'From Michael Collins to Aung San'. Unpublished manuscript.

Harper, George (1974). *Yeats' Golden Dawn*. London: Macmillan.

Harris, Elizabeth (2006). *Theravada Buddhism and the British Encounter*. London: Routledge.

— (2007, orig. 1998). *Ananda Metteyya*. Kandy: Buddhist Publication Society.

Hawkes, Charles (1973). *The Prehistoric Foundations of Europe*. London: Taylor and Francis.

Hayes, Maurice (2010). 'Dedicated to Indian Nationalism'. *History Ireland* (July/August): 66.

Hayley, Elizabeth (1987). 'A Reading and Thinking Nation', 29–48, in Barbara Hayley and Enda McKay (eds), *Three Hundred Years of Irish Periodicals*. Dublin/Mullingar: Association of Irish Learned Journals/Lilliput.

Hearn, Lafcadio (1992). Louis Allen and Jean Wilson (eds), *Lafcadio Hearn*. Folkestone: Japan Library.

Hechter, Michael (1975). *Internal Colonialism*. London: Routledge and Kegan Paul.

Van Hecken, Joseph (1963). *The Catholic Church in Japan Since 1859*. Tokyo: Herder.

Heckett, E. Wincott (1997). 'Textiles, Cordage, Basketry and Raw Fibre', 743–60, in Maurice Hurley and Orla Scully (eds), *Late Viking Age and Medieval Waterford*. Waterford: Waterford Corporation.

Heelas, Paul (1996). *The New Age Movement*. Oxford: Blackwell.

— (2008). *Spiritualities of Life*. Oxford: Blackwell.

Heelas, Paul, Scott Lash and Paul Morris (1996). *Detraditionalization*. New York: Wiley-Blackwell.

Helmstadter, Richard (1989). 'The Nonconformist Conscience', 61–95, in Gerald Parsons and James Moore (eds), *Religion in Victorian Britain*. Manchester: Manchester University Press.

Herren, Michael (2005). 'Biblical and Church Fathers Scholarship', 39–41, in Seán Duffy, Ailbhe MacShamhráin and James Moynes (eds), *Mediaeval Ireland*. London: CRC Press.

Hill, Christopher (1975). *The World Turned Upside Down*. Harmondsworth: Penguin.

Hilton, James (1933). *Lost Horizon*. London: Macmillan.

Hodgkinson, Liz (1989). *Michael Née Laura*. London: Columbus.

Hoey, William (1997, orig. 1882). 'Translator's Preface', iii–iv, in Hermann Oldenberg, *Buddha*. Delhi: Motilal Banarsidass.

Hogan, Edmund (1990). *The Irish Missionary Movement*. Dublin/Washington: Gill and Macmillan/Catholic University of America.

Holland, C.H. (ed.) (1991). *Trinity College Dublin and the Idea of a University*. Dublin: Trinity College Dublin.

Holmes, Michael and Denis (eds) (1997), *Ireland and India*. Dublin: Folens.

Holstun, James (2002). *Ehud's Dagger*. London: Verso.

Horn, Gerd-Rainer (2008). *The Spirit of '68*. Oxford: Oxford University Press.

Höllinger, Franz (2006). 'Does the Counter-cultural Character of New Age Persist?' *Journal of Alternative Spiritualities and New Age Studies* 2: 63–89.

Hopkins, Frank (2002). *Rare Old Dublin*. Cork: Mercier.

House of Commons (1836). *Selection of Reports and Papers of the House of Commons*, vol. 2. London: House of Commons.

Howley, John (1920). *Psychology and Mystical Experience*. London: Kegan, Paul.

— (1935). Untitled Review: 141–43, in *Studies* 24/93.

Huber, Emily (no date). 'Alexander the Great'. Available at: http://www. library.rochester.edu/camelot/Alexander/alexengbib.htm

Hughes, Kathleen (2005). 'The Church in Irish Society, 400–800', 301–30, in Dáibhí Ó Cróinín (ed), *A New History of Ireland*. Oxford: Oxford University Press.

Hughes, Louis (1997). *Yoga: a Path to God?* Cork: Mercier.

Humphreys, Christmas (1935). *Concentration and Meditation*. London: Buddhist Society.

— (1937). *The Development of Buddhism in England*. London: Buddhist Lodge.

— (1968). *Sixty Years of Buddhism in England (1907–1967)*. London: Buddhist Society.

Hutton, Ronald (1995). *The Triumph of the Moon*. Oxford: Oxford University Press.

— (2001). *Shamanism*. London: Hambledon.

— (2007). *The Druids*. London: Hambledon.

Huxley, Andrew (2001). 'Positivists and Buddhists'. *Law and Social Inquiry* 26/1: 113–42.

Inglis, Tom (1998a). *Moral Monopoly*. 2nd edn, Dublin: Gill and Macmillan.

— (1998b). *Lessons in Irish Sexuality*. Dublin: University College Dublin Press.

Introvigne, Massimo (2004). 'Something Peculiar About France', 206–20, in James Lewis (ed.), *The Oxford Handbook of New Religious Movements*. Oxford: Oxford University Press.

Ito, Eishiro (2003). 'Mediterranean Joyce Meditates on Buddha'. *Language and Culture* 5. Available at: http://ci.nii.ac.jp/lognavi?name=nels&lang=en&type=pdf&id=ART0007415345 and http://p-www.iwate-pu.ac.jp/~acro-ito/Joycean_Essays/MJMonBuddha.html

— (2004). 'How Did Buddhism Influence James Joyce and Kenji Miyazawa?' *Language and Culture* 6: 11–23.

Irish Theological Commission (1994). *A New Age of the Spirit?* Dublin: Veritas.

Iyer, Raghavan and Nandini Iyer (1988). *The Descent of the Gods*. Gerrards Cross: Colin Smythe.

Jacobs, Joseph (1901–1906). 'Aesop's Fables Among the Jews'. *The Jewish Encyclopedia*.

Janz, Robert (2007). *Robert Janz*. Catalogue of Exhibition at Peppercanister Gallery. Dublin.

Jinarajadasa, C. (1951). 'The Services of Col. Olcott for Buddhism'. *Theosophist Magazine* (Feb–Oct): 385–93.

Jivaka, Lobzang (Michael Dillon) (1962), *Imji Getsul*. London: Routledge Paul.

— (Michael Dillon) (1994, orig. 1962). *The Life of Milarepa*. Felinfach: Llanerch.

Jivaka, Sramanera (Michael Dillon) (1960). *Growing Up into Buddhism*. Calcutta: Maha Bodhi Society.

Johnson, Richard Colles (1983). 'Richard William (Ramsay) Colles'. *Notes and Queries* (30/4): 317.

Joinville, John of (2008), 'The Life of St Louis', 137–335, in John of Joinville and Geoffrey of Villehardouin, *Chronicles of the Crusades*. London: Penguin.

Jones, Ken (2003). *The New Social Face of Buddhism*. Wisdom.

Jones, Robin (2006). 'An Englishman Abroad'. *Apollo*, November 1.

Jordanus (1863). *Mirabilia Descripta*. London: Hakluyt Society.

Joyce, James (1960). *Ulysses*. Harmondsworth: Penguin.

— (2003). *Portrait of the Artist as a Young Man*. London: Penguin.

Katsiaficas, George (1988). *The Imagination of the New Left*. Boston, MA: South End.

Kearney, Richard (1997). *Postnationalist Ireland*. London: Routledge.

Keating, H.R.F. (1963). *Zen There Was Murder*. Harmondsworth: Penguin.

Kelly, Eugene (1990). 'The Priory Road (Harold's Cross) Zen Meditation Group'. Available at: http://insightmeditationdublin.com/doc/ZENGRP_HST.doc

Kemp, Darren (2003). *New Age*. Edinburgh: Edinburgh University Press.

Kemp, Hugh (2007). 'How the Dharma Landed'. *Journal of Global Buddhism* 8: 107–31.

Kennedy, J. (1902). 'Buddhist Gnosticism'. *Journal of the Royal Asiatic Society of Great Britain and Ireland* (1902): 377–415; Available at: http://ccbs.ntu.edu.tw/FULLTEXT/JR-ENG/kenn.htm

Kennedy, Máire (1999). 'Women and Reading in Eighteenth-century Ireland', 78–98, in Bernadette Cunningham and Máire Kennedy (eds), *The Experience of Reading*. Dublin: Rare Books Group/Economic and Social History Society of Ireland.

— (2001). *French Books in Eighteenth-century Ireland*. Oxford: Voltaire Foundation.

Kennedy, Pagan (2007). *The First Man-made Man*. New York: Bloomsbury.

Keogh, Dermot (1999). *Jews in Twentieth-century Ireland*. Cork: Cork University Press.

Kinnard, Jacob (1998), 'When Is the Buddha Not the Buddha?'. *Journal of the American Academy of Religion* 66/4: 817–39.

Kingston, Phil (Dharmachari Lalitavira) (2006). *Dr Dillon and Ms Georgia*. Unpublished play.

Kipling, Rudyard (1908). *Kim*. Edinburgh: R&R Clark.

Kirkpatrick, Kathryn (2008a). 'Introduction', Vii–xviii, in Sydney Owenson, *The Wild Irish Girl*. Oxford: Oxford University Press.

— (2008b). 'Note on the Text', Vii–xviii, in Sydney Owenson, *The Wild Irish Girl*. Oxford: Oxford University Press.

— (2009). 'A Murmuration of Starlings in a Rowan Tree', 195–207, in *An Sionnach* 5: (1–2).

Kirthisinghe, B.P. and M.P. Amarasuriya (2007, orig. 1981). *Colonel Olcott*. Kandy: Buddhist Publication Society.

Klein, Stacy and Mary Swan (2004). 'Old English'. *The Year's Work in English Studies* 83: 109–44.

Kolakowski, Leszek (1978). *Main Currents of Marxism*. Oxford: Clarendon.

Komroff, Manuel (1929). *Contemporaries of Marco Polo.* London: Travellers' Library.

Koné, Alione (2001). 'Zen in Europe: a Survey of the Territory'. *Journal of Global Buddhism* 2: 139–61.

Kraft, Kenneth (1999). *The Wheel of Engaged Buddhism.* Trumbull, CT: Weatherhill. Kshirasagara, Ramacandra (1994). *Dalit Movement in India and Its Leaders, 1857–1956.* New Delhi: MD Publications.

Kuch, Peter (1986). *Yeats and AE.* Totowa, NJ: Barnes & Noble.

Kuhling, Carmen (2004). *The New Age Ethic and the Spirit of Postmodernity.* Cresskill, NJ: Hampton.

Kwon, Young Hee (2007). 'The Buddhist Subtext and the Imperial Soul-making in *Kim'. Victorian Newsletter* (Spring). Available at: http://www. thefreelibrary.com/The+Buddhist+sub-text+and+the+imperial+soul-making+in+Kim-a0162920314

Lamb, Christopher (1999). 'Conversion as a Process Leading to Enlightenment', 75–88, in Christopher Lamb and M. Darrol Bryant (eds), *Religious Conversion.* London: Cassell.

Lapidge, Michael et al (eds) (2001). *The Blackwell Encyclopedia of Anglo-Saxon England.* Oxford: Wiley-Blackwell.

Lebowitz, Michael (1991). *Beyond Capital.* New York: St Martin's.

Legg, Marie-Louise (1999). 'The Kilkenny Circulating-Library Society and the Growth of Reading Rooms in Nineteenth-century Ireland', 109–23, in Bernadette Cunningham and Máire Kennedy (eds), *The Experience of Reading.* Dublin: Rare Books Group/Economic and Social History Society of Ireland.

Lenihan, Eddie with Carolyn Green (2003). *Meeting the Other Crowd.* Dublin: Gill and Macmillan.

Lennon, Joseph (2004). *Irish Orientalism.* Syracuse: Syracuse University Press.

Lennon, Joseph (2009). 'Irish Orientalism'. Paper to 'Asian Art and Ireland' Conference, National Museum of Ireland (November).

Lewis, Uncle Dave (no date). 'Stephen Adams (Michael Maybrick)'. Available at: http://www.allmusic.com/cg/amg.dll?p=amg&sql=41:25~T1

Lewis, James (ed.) (2004). *The Oxford Handbook of New Religious Movements.* Oxford: Oxford University Press.

Lillie, Arthur (1981, orig. 1909). *India in Primitive Christianity.* N.P.: Forgotten Books.

Ling, Trevor (1966). *Buddha, Marx and God.* London: Macmillan.

Link, Arthur (1959). Review of Brooks Wright, *Interpreter of Buddhism to the West. Journal of Asian Studies,* vol 18 no. 2: 304–305.

Lipset, Seymour and Stein Rokkan (1967). 'Cleavage Structures, Party Systems and Voter Alignments', 1–64, in Lipset and Rokkan (eds), *Party Systems and Voter Alignments.* New York: Free Press.

Little, Stephen (Dharmachari Manjupriya) (1998). *The Early Days of the Dublin Meditation Centre.* Dublin: Dublin Buddhist Centre.

Loeber, Rolf and Magda Stouthamer-Loeber (1999). 'Fiction Available to and Written for Cottagers and Their Children', 124–72, in Bernadette Cunningham and Máire Kennedy (eds), *The Experience of Reading.* Dublin: Rare Books Group/Economic and Social History Society of Ireland.

Lofland, J., and N. Skonovd (1981). 'Conversion Motifs'. *Journal for the Scientific Study of Religion*, 20: 371–85.

Lopéz, Donald (ed.) (1995). *Curators of the Buddha*. Chicago, IL: UC Press

Lopéz, Donald (1998). *Prisoners of Shangri-la*. Chicago, IL: University of Chicago Press.

— (2002). *Modern Buddhism*. London: Penguin.

Lyder, André (2005). *Pushers Out*. Bloomington, IN: Trafford.

Lynch, Brendan (1988). 'Irish Patrons and Collectors of Indian Art'. *GPA Irish Arts Review Book*: 169–84.

Lyons, Mary and Thomas O'Connor (2008). *Strangers to Citizens*. Dublin: National Library of Ireland.

MacCorristine, Shane (2011). 'William Fletcher Barrett, Spiritualism, and Psychical Research in Edwardian Dublin'. *Estudios Irlandeses*, 6: 39–53.

Mackenzie, Donald (1928). *Buddhism in Pre-Christian Britain*. London: Blackie and Son.

MacLiammóir, Micheál (1947). *All for Hecuba*. 2nd edn, London: Methuen.

Macmillan, M. (1904). 'The Oriental Congress at Hanoi'. *Journal of the Asiatic Society of Bombay* (21): 501–502.

Macourt, Malcolm (2011). Mapping the 'New Religious Landscape' and the 'New Irish', 28–49, in Olivia Cosgrove, Laurence Cox, Carmen Kuhling and Peter Mulholland (eds), *Ireland's New Religious Movements*. Newcastle: Cambridge Scholars.

— (2012). 'What Use Can Data From the Question on Religion in the Census of the Population Be to Students of Religion?' Paper to ISASR Conference, Cork (May).

MacQuitty, William (1991). *A Life to Remember*. London: Quartet.

Maguire, Mark (2004). *Differently Irish*. Dublin: Woodfield.

Mahlmann, John (1918). *Reminiscences of An Ancient Mariner*. Yokohama: Japan Gazette.

Mahony, Capt. William (1801). 'On Singhala, or Ceylon, and the Doctrines of Bhoodha from the Books of the Singhalais'. *Asiatick Researches*, 7: 32–56.

Ananda Maitreya Thero (1956). *The Dawn and Spread of Buddhism*. Available at: http://web.ukonline.co.uk/buddhism/anandam1.htm

Malalgoda, Kitsiri (1976). *Buddhism in Sinhalese Society 1750–1900*. Berkeley, CA: University of California Press.

'Mandeville, John' (pseudonym, 2006). *The Travels of Sir John Mandeville*. Dover: New York.

Mansoor, Menahem (1944). *The Story of Irish Orientalism*. Dublin: Hodges, Figgis and Co.

Marquez, Luiz (1963). 'An Irish Buddhist'. *Kilkenny Magazine*, issues 10–15: 18–27.

Marx, Karl (1859). *Preface to A contribution to the Critique of Political Economy*. Available at: http://www.marxists.org/archive/marx/works/1859/critique-pol-economy/preface.htm

— (1977, orig. 1852). *The Eighteenth Brumaire of Louis Bonaparte*. Moscow: Progress.

Marx, Karl and Friedrich Engels (1967, orig. 1848). *The Communist Manifesto*. Harmondsworth: Penguin.

— (1970, orig. 1846). *The German Ideology, Part I*. London: Lawrence and Wishart.

Matthews, Bruce (2002). 'Buddhism in Canada', 120–38, in Charles Prebish and Martin Baumann (eds), *Westward Dharma*. Berkeley, CA: University of California Press.

Mayo, Peter (1999). *Gramsci, Freire and Adult Education*. London: Zed.

McAuley, James (2005). 'Found in Translation'. *Irish Times* 12 February 2005.

McCann, Eamonn (1993). *War and An Irish Town*. 3rd edn, London: Pluto.

McCormack, Jerusha (ed.) (2009), *China and the Irish*. Dublin: New Island.

McCourt, Frank (1998). *Angela's Ashes*. New York: Simon & Schuster.

McCullagh, Francis (1929). 'Notes on Linguistic Studies in Paris', 111–23, in *Studies* (18/69).

McDowell, R.B., and D.A. Webb (2004). *Trinity College Dublin 1592–1952*. Dublin: Trinity College Dublin.

McEvansoneya, Philip (2009). 'Sir William Gregory and the National Museum of Ceylon.' Paper to 'Asian Art and Ireland' Conference, National Museum of Ireland (November).

McFate, Patricia (1979). *The Writings of James Stephens*. London: Macmillan.

McGlade, Joseph (1967). *The Missions*. Dublin: Gill and Son.

McGrath, Charles (2005). 'The Provisions for Conversion in the Penal Laws, 1695–1750, 35–59 in Michael Brown, Charles McGrath and Thomas Power (eds), *Converts and Conversion in Ireland 1650–1850*. Dublin: Four Courts.

MacGréil, Micheál and Fergal Rhatigan (2009). *The Challenge of Indifference*. Maynooth: Survey and Research Unit.

McKay, Alex (2005). 'The Birth of a Clinic'?' *Medical History* 49/2 (April): 135–54.

— (2007). *Their Footprints Remain*. Amsterdam: International Institute for Asian Studies/Amsterdam University Press.

McLeod, Hugh (1997). *Religion and the People of Western Europe 1789–1989*. 2nd edn, Oxford: Opus.

McLoughlin, Barry (2007). *Left to the Wolves*. Dublin: Irish Academic Press.

McMahan, David (2008). *The Making of Buddhist Modernism*. Oxford: Oxford University Press.

McMahon, Deirdre (2010). 'The 1947 Partition of India'. *History Ireland* (July/August): 40–43.

McManus, Antonia (2002). *The Irish Hedge School and Its Books, 1695–1831*. Dublin: Four Courts.

McRedmond, Louis (1991). *To the Greater Glory*. Dublin: Gill and Macmillan.

McVeigh, Robbie (1995). 'Cherishing the Children of the Nation Unequally', 620–51, in Patrick Clancy et al., (eds), *Irish Society*. Dublin: Institute of Public Administration.

Mayeda, Y. (1893). *An Outline of the True Sect of Buddhism*. Tokyo: Buddhist Propagation Society.

Meehan, Paula (2009). 'The Body Politic', 239–71, in *An Sionnach*, 5/1–2.

Melton, J. Gordon (2004). 'An Introduction to New Religions', 16–38, in James Lewis (ed.), *The Oxford Handbook of New Religious Movements*. Oxford: Oxford University Press.

Melucci, Alberto (1989). *Nomads of the Present*. London: Hutchinson.

Meserve, Margaret (2006). 'Introduction', v–xiv, in 'John Mandeville', *The Travels of Sir John Mandeville*. New York: Dover.

Ananda Metteyya (Allan Bennett) (1923). *The Wisdom of the Aryas*. London: Paul, Trench, Trubner.

Meyer, Robert (1949). 'The Sources of the Middle Irish *Alexander*.' *Modern Philology* (47/1): 1–7.

Meyer, T.H. (1992). *D.N. Dunlop: a Man of Our Times*. London: Temple Lodge.

Millar, Ashley (2009). 'Authority and Parenthood.' *Graduate Journal of Social Science* 6/2: 7–33.

Miller, John (2002). *Beads and Prayers*. New York: Continuum.

Mills, Lennox (1964). *Ceylon Under British Rule 1795–1832*. London: Routledge.

Møllgaard, Eske (2008). 'Slavoj Žižek's Critique of Western Buddhism'. *Contemporary Buddhism* (9/2): 167–80.

Moore, Oliver (2003). 'Spirituality, Self-sufficiency, Selling and the Split'. Paper to European Society for Rural Sociology Conference, Sligo (August).

Morgan, David (2007). *The Mongols*. 2nd edn, Oxford: Wiley-Blackwell.

Moriya, Tomoe (2005). 'Social Ethics of 'New Buddhists' At the Turn of the Twentieth Century'. *Japanese Journal of Religious Studies*, 32/2: 283–304.

Morrisson, Mark (2008). 'The Periodical Culture of the Occult Revival'. *Journal of Modern Literature* 31/1: 1–22.

Mulholland, Peter (2006). *The New Age Movement in Ireland*. Unpublished PhD Thesis, Department of Anthropology, National University of Ireland, Maynooth.

— (2009). 'New Religious Movements in Modern Ireland'. Paper to *Alternative Spiritualities, the New Age and New Religious Movements in Ireland* Conference, Maynooth (October).

Murphy, Dervla (1966). *Tibetan Foothold*. London: John Murray, 1966.

— (2006). *Silverland*. London: John Murray.

Murphy, John L. (2009). 'Inventing the Concept of Celtic Buddhism', in Olivia Cosgrove and Laurence Cox (eds), *Alternative Spiritualities, the New Age and New Religious Movements in Ireland: Conference Proceedings*. Limerick: Irish Research Network on Alternative Religions and Spiritualities (CD-ROM).

— (2011). 'Inventing the Concept of Celtic Buddhism', 74–95, in Olivia Cosgrove, Laurence Cox, Carmen Kuhling and Peter Mulholland (eds.), *Ireland's New Religious Movements*. Newcastle: Cambridge Scholars.

Murray, Alfonso (1935). *The World's Handbook of Dairying*. Wells, Somerset: Clare's.

Murray, Paul (1993). *A Fantastic Journey*. Folkestone: Japan Library/Curzon.

Murry, Colin Middleton (1975). *One Hand Clapping*. London: Gollancz.

Mutton, Karen (no date) *Lobsang Rampa*. NP: Lulu.com

Nagai, Kaori (2006). *Empire of Analogies*. Cork: Cork University Press.

Nairn, Tom (1982). 'Antonu su Gobbu', 159–79, in Anne Sassoon, *Approaches to Gramsci*. London: Writers and Readers Co-op.

Nattier, Jan (1998). 'Who Is a Buddhist?' 183–95 in Charles Prebish and Kenneth Tanaka (eds), *The Faces of Buddhism in America*. Berkeley, CA: University of California Press.

Neal, Patrick (1988). *Sectarian Violence*. Manchester: Manchester University Press.

Nevin, Donal (2005). *James Connolly*. Dublin: Gill and Macmillan.

Newsinger, John (2006). *The Blood Never Dried*. London: Bookmarks.

Nic Dhiarmada, Bríona (1996). 'Sukha-duhkha, Sochar-dochar'. *The Well*, vol. 2/3 (autumn): 4–5.

— (1997). 'Bells ...' *The Well*, vol. 2/4 and 3/1 (winter/spring 1996/7): 12–13.

Nic Ghiolla Phádraig, Máire (1995). 'The Power of the Catholic Church in the Republic of Ireland', 593–619, in Patrick Clancy, Sheelagh Drudy, Kathleen Lynch and Liam O'Dowd (eds), *Irish Society*. Dublin: Institute for Public Administration.

Ní Laoire, Caitríona (2007). 'Reflections on Narratives of Migration and Return Project'. Paper to Sociological Association of Ireland Conference, Limerick (May).

Norman, Alexander (2008). *Holder of the White Lotus*. New York: Little, Brown.

Nottingham, Chris (1999). *The Pursuit of Serenity*. Amsterdam: Amsterdam University Press.

Numrich, Paul (2003). 'Two Buddhisms Further Considered'. *Contemporary Buddhism* 4/1: 55–78.

Ó Ciosáin, Niall (2010) *Print and Popular Culture in Ireland*. Dublin: Lilliput.

O'Connor, Elizabeth (Mrs T.P.) (2009, orig. 1913). *Herself – Ireland*. Charleston, SC: BiblioBazaar.

O'Connor, Thomas (ed.) (2001). *The Irish in Europe, 1580–1815*. Dublin: Four Courts Press.

O'Connor, Thomas and Mary Lyons (eds) (2006). *Irish Communities in Early-modern Europe*. Dublin: Four Courts Press.

O'Connor, T.P. (1913). 'Sir Thomas Lipton'. *Boston Daily Globe*, 4 May, 50.

O'Connor, Yvonne Altman (2009). 'The Bender Family and the Jewish Community of Dublin.' Paper to 'Asian Art and Ireland' Conference, National Museum of Ireland (November).

Ó Cróinín, Dáibhi (2005). 'Hiberno-Latin Literature to 1169', 371–404 in Dáibhí Ó Cróinín (ed), *A New History of Ireland*. Oxford: Oxford University Press.

Ó Dúshláine, Tadhg (2001). 'Devout Humanism Irish-style', 79–92, in Thomas O'Connor, *The Irish in Europe, 1580–1815*. Dublin: Four Courts Press.

O'Halloran, Ruth (1992). 'In Twenty-seven Short Years', 11–15, in *Commonweal* 14.

O'Halloran, Maura (1995). *Pure Heart, Enlightened Mind*. London: Thorsons.

O'Leary, Joseph (1999). 'Religious Pluralism and Christian Truth', 239–41, in *Buddhist-Christian Studies* (19/1).

O'Leary, Richard (2009). 'An Irish Mandarin', 26–39, in Jerusha McCormack (ed.), *China and the Irish*. Dublin: New Island.

O'Leary, Richard and Lan Li (2007). 'Executive Summary in English'. Dublin: Dublin University Far Eastern Mission.

O'Malley, Kate (2008). *Ireland, India and Empire*. Manchester: Manchester University Press.

— (2010). 'Learning the Tricks of the Imperial Secession Trade'. *History Ireland* (July/August): 32–35.

Ó Néill, Pádraig (2005). 'Anglo-Saxon Literature, Influence of', 19–20, in Seán Duffy, Ailbhe MacShamhráin and James Moynes (eds), *Mediaeval Ireland*. London: CRC Press.

O'Toole, Fintan (1998). *The Lie of the Land*. Dublin: New Island.

— (2009). 'From Patsy O'Wang to Fu Manchu', 40–50, in Jerusha McCormack (ed.), *China and the Irish*. Dublin: New Island.

Offermans, Jürgen (2005). 'Debates on Atheism, Quietism and Sodomy'. *Journal of Global Buddhism*, 6: 16–35.

Oderberg, Israel (1995–6). 'H.P. Blavatsky's Cultural Impact', in *Sunrise*, December 1995/January 1996 and February–March 1996; Available at: http://www.theosociety.org/pasadena/sunrise/45-95-6/th-imo.htm

Ohlmeyer, Jane (2006). 'Seventeenth-century Ireland and Scotland and Their Wider Worlds', 457–84, in Thomas O'Connor and Mary Lyons (eds), *Irish Communities in Early-modern Europe*. Dublin: Four Courts Press.

Ohno, Mitsuko (2002). 'Hokusai, Basho, Zen and More', 15–31, in *Journal of Irish Studies* 17.

Okado-Gough, Damien (2009). 'Zen Buddhist Monk Aids Peace Effort in Native Belfast'. *Japan Times*, 27 June 2009.

Olcott, Henry (1889a). *Old Diary Leaves (Fourth Series), Chapter X*. Available at: http://www.theosophy.ph/onlinebooks/odl/odl410.html

— (1889b). *Old Diary Leaves (Fourth Series), Chapter XI*. Available at: http://www.theosophy.ph/onlinebooks/odl/odl411.html

— (2003). *Old Diary Leaves (Fourth Series)*. Whitefish, MT: Kessinger.

Oldenberg, Hermann (trans. William Hoey) (1882). *Buddha*. London: Williams and Norgate.

Ontario Department of Agriculture and Food (1907). *Report of the Minister of Agriculture and Food*. Toronto: Department of Agriculture and Food.

Owenson, Sydney (Lady Morgan) (2008). *The Wild Irish Girl*. Oxford: Oxford University Press.

Parmentier, Jan (2006). 'The Ray Dynasty', 367–82, in Thomas O'Connor and Mary Lyons (eds), *Irish Communities in Early-modern Europe*. Dublin: Four Courts Press.

Parsons, Brendan (2009). 'Transplanting China to Ireland', 62–72, in Jerusha McCormack (ed.), *China and the Irish*. Dublin: New Island.

Payne, Charles (1995). *I've Got the Light of Freedom*. Berkeley, CA: University of California Press.

People's College (2009). *Syllabus 2009–2010*. Dublin: People's College.

Perera, H.R. (2006, orig. 1988). *Buddhism in Sri Lanka*. Kandy: Buddhist Publication Society. Available at: www.accesstoinsight.org/lib/authors/perera/wheel100.html

Pettipiece, Timothy (2009). 'The Buddha in Early Christian Literature', 133–44, in Wolfram Brandes, Alexander Demandt, Helmut Krasser, Hartmut Leppin and Peter von Möllendorff (eds), *Millennium Jahrbuch*. Berlin & New York: De Gruyter.

Pfoundes, Capt. Charles (1875). *Fu-so Mimi Bukuro*. Yokohama: Japan Mail.

— (1882). 'Notes on the History of Eastern Adventure, Exploration, and Discovery, and Foreign Intercourse with Japan'. *Transactions of the Royal Historical Society* (10): 82–92.

— (1883). 'On Some Rites and Customs of Old Japan'. *Journal of the Royal Anthropological Institute of Great Britain and Ireland* (12): 222–27.

— (1888). 'Divyatchakchus'. *Theosophical Siftings* (1/6): 9–15.

— (1890a). 'The Religions of Japan', 101–107, in Edward Clodd, *Religious Systems of the World*. London: Swan Sonnenschein.

— (1890b). 'Japanese Spiritualism'. *The Two Worlds* (March).

— (1895a). 'Religion in Japan'. *Open Court,* vol. IX/4 no. 387 (24 January): 4372–74.

— (1895b). 'Religion in Japan'. *Open Court,* vol. IX/5 no. 388 (31 January 1895): 4377–79.

— (1895c). 'Why Buddhism?' *Open Court,* vol. IX/32 no. 415 (8 August 1895): 4594–97.

— (1905). 'The Fire Ordeal'. *East of Asia Magazine* (IV): 310–17.

Pfoundes, Capt. C, Charles Johnston and T.B. Harbottle (1888). *Re-incarnation.* London: Theosophical Publication Society.

Pierce, Peter (1996). 'Dunn, Maxwell Walter Dumont'. *Australian Dictionary of Biography,* vol. 14. Melbourne: Melbourne University Press. Available at: http://adb.anu.edu.au/biography/dunn-maxwell-walter-dumont-10071

Piggott, Stuart (1968). *The Druids*. London: Thames and Hudson.

Polo, Marco (1990). *Il Milione*. Roma: Mondadori.

Prebish, Charles (2002). 'Studying the Spread and Histories of Buddhism in the West', 66–82, in Charles Prebish and Martin Baumann (eds), *Westward Dharma*. Berkeley, LA: University of California Press.

Prothero, Stephen (2010). *The White Buddhist*. Bloomington, IN: Indiana University Press.

Puttick, Elizabeth (2005). 'The Rise of Mind-body-spirit Publishing'. *Journal of Alternative Spiritualities and New Age Studies,* 1: 129–50.

Pyle, Hilary (1965). *James Stephens*. London: Routledge and Kegan Paul.

— (1998). *Red-headed Rebel*. Dublin: Woodfield.

Quane, Michael (1950). 'Pococke School, Kilkenny'. *Journal of the Royal Society of Antiquaries of Ireland* (80/1): 36–72.

Queen, Christopher (2004). 'Ambedkar's Dhamma', 132–50, in Surendra Jondhale and Johannes Beltz (eds), *Reconstructing the World*. New Delhi: Oxford University Press.

Queen, Christopher and Sallie King (1996). *Engaged Buddhism*. Albany, NY: State University of New York Press.

Raftery, Barry (1994). *Pagan Celtic Ireland*. London: Thames and Hudson.

Raftery, Mary and Eoin O'Sullivan (1999). *Suffer the Little Children*. Dublin: New Island.

Rambo, Lewis and Charles Farhadian (1999). 'Converting', 23–34, in Christopher Lamb and M. Darrol Bryant (eds), *Religious Conversion*. London: Cassell.

Rampa, T. Lobsang (1960). *The Rampa Story*. London: Souvenir.

Ratcliffe, S.K. (1913). 'Margaret Noble', vii–xxx, in Sister Nivedita, *Studies From an Eastern Home*. London: Longmans, Gree. Available at: www.sacred-texts.com/hin/seh/seh03.htm

Ratnaghosha, Dharmachari (n.d.) 'My Early Life'. Available at: http://www.angelfire.com/wizard2/ratnaghosha/lifestory1.html

Ray, Reginald (1999). *Buddhist Saints in India*. Oxford: Oxford University Press.

Rexroth, Kenneth (ed.) (1977). *The Buddhist Writings of Lafcadio Hearn*. Santa Barbara, CA: Ross-Erikson.

Rhys Davids, T.W. (1904–1905). 'Preface', v–vii, in Thomas Watters, *On Yuan Chwang's Travels in India*. London: Royal Asiatic Society.

Robbins, Thomas (1988). *Cults, Converts and Charisma*. London: SAGE/ International Sociological Association.

Roberts, Alexander and James Donaldson (1869). *Clement of Alexandria II*. Edinburgh: Clark.

Roberts, Courtney (2009). 'Astrology in Ireland'. Paper to 'Alternative Spiritualities, New Religious Movements and the New Age in Ireland' Conference. National University of Ireland Maynooth.

Robinson, Jane (1990). *Wayward Women*. Oxford: Oxford University Press.

Rocha, Christina (2006). *Zen in Brazil*. Honolulu: University of Hawaii Press.

Rockhill, William (1900). *The Journey of William of Rubruck*. London: Hakluyt Society.

Ronan, Sean (ed.) (1997). *Irish Writing on Lafcadio Hearn and Japan*. Folkestone: Global Oriental.

Rosemary Presbyterian Church (2009). *Order of Service 15 March*. Available at: www.rosemarypresbyterianchurch.org/oos_150309.htm

Rothberg, Donald (2006). *The Engaged Spiritual Life*. Beacon.

Rothstein, Andrew (1983). *A House on Clerkenwell Green*. 2nd edn, London: Marx Memorial Library.

Rothsten, Mikael (1996). 'Patterns of Diffusion and Religious Globalization'. *Temenos* 32: 195–220.

Rouse, Sheelagh ('Buttercup') (no date). *Grace: the World of Rampa*. Available at: www.lobsangrampa.org/buttercup.html

Rouse, William (1895). E.B. Cowell (ed.) *The Jataka, or Story of the Buddha's Former Births, vol. 2*. Cambridge: University Press.

Rowen, Elizabeth (2011). 'The Buddha and the Cross'. Richter Research Abroad Student Scholarship Report. Available at: http://scholar.oxy.edu/ rrap_student/4/

Ruane, Joseph and Jennifer Todd (1991). 'Why Can't You Get Along With One Another?' 27–43, in Eamonn Hughes (ed). *Culture and Politics in Northern Ireland*. Milton Keynes: The Open University.

Russell, George (1978). *Selections From the Contributions to the* Irish Homestead. London: C. Smythe.

Russell, Helen, Emma Quinn, Rebecca King O'Riain and Frances McGinnity, (2008). *The Experience of Discrimination in Ireland*. Dublin: Equality Authority.

Ruxton, Ian (ed.) (2008). *Sir Ernest Satow's Private Letters to W.G. Aston and F.V. Dickins*. N.P.: Lulu.com

Ryan, Maurice (1996). *Another Ireland*. Belfast: Stranmillis College.

Ryan, Orla (1988). 'Hungry Ghost'. *Variant*, vol. 2 no. 6: 4. Available at: http:// www.variant.randomstate.org/pdfs/issue6/ghosts.pdf

Ryder, Sean (2006). 'India, Ireland and Popular Nationalism in the Early Nineteenth Century', 12–25, in Tadhg Foley and Maureen O'Connor (eds), *Ireland and India*. Dublin/Portland: Irish Academic Press.

Said, Edward (2003). *Orientalism*. 2nd edn, London: Penguin.

Saliba, John (2004). 'Psychology and the New Religious Movements', 317–32, in James Lewis (ed.), *The Oxford Handbook of New Religious Movements*. Oxford: Oxford University Press.

Sanghapala, Dharmachari (1993). *An FWBO Puja Book*. Dublin: Dublin Meditation Centre.

Sangharakshita (1979). 'Question and Answer Evening in Auckland'. Available at: www.freebuddhistaudio.com/texts/seminartexts/SEM051_Auckland_Questions_and_Answers_-_May_1979.pdf

Sangharakshita, Bhikkhu (2007a, orig. 1952). *Anagarika Dharmapala*. Kandy: Buddhist Publication Society. Available at: http://www.bps.lk/wheels_library/wheels_pdf/wh_070_072.pdf

— (2007b). *Precious Teachers*. Birmingham: Windhorse.

Sarkisyanz, Manuel (1961). 'On the Place of U Nu's Buddhist Socialism in Burma's History of Ideas'. *Studies on Asia,* Series 1 vol. 2: 53–62.

Satlow, Michael (2008). 'Theophrastus' Jewish Philosophers'. *Journal of Jewish Studies,* LIX/1: 1–20.

Scharbrodt, Oliver (2011). 'Islam in Ireland', 319–37, in Olivia Cosgrove, Laurence Cox, Carmen Kuhling and Peter Mulholland (eds), *Ireland's New Religious Movements*. Newcastle: Cambridge Scholars.

— (2012). 'Islam in the Census.' Paper to ISASR Conference, Cork (May).

Schmidt, Leigh (2007). 'The Aspiring Side of Religion', 89–92, in *Spiritus* 7/1.

Schmidt-Leukel, Perry (2006). *Buddhism, Christianity and the Question of Creation*. Farnham: Ashgate.

Schopen, Gregory (1997). *Bones, Stones and Buddhist Monks*. Honolulu: University of Hawaii Press.

Scott, David (1992). 'Conversion and Demonism'. *Comparative Studies in Society and History,* vol. 34 no. 2 (April): 331–65.

Scott, Derek (1997). 'Orientalism and Musical Style'. *Critical Musicology* online journal. Available at: http://www.leeds.ac.uk/music/Info/critmus/articles/1997/02/01.html

Scott, James (1990). *Domination and The Arts of Resistance*. New Haven, CT: Yale University Press.

Seager, Richard (2002). 'American Buddhism in the Making', 106–19, in Charles Prebish and Martin Baumann (eds), *Westward Dharma*. Berkeley, CA: University of California Press.

Sen, Malcolm (2003). 'India and Ireland'. Lecture to Chester Beatty Library, Dublin (October).

Shan, Yuwu (2012). 'The Pioneer of the Irish Mission to China.' Paper to ISASR Conference, Cork (May).

Share, Perry, Hilary Tovey and Mary Corcoran (2007). *A Sociology of Ireland*. 3rd edn, Dublin: Gill and Macmillan.

Sharf, Robert (1995). 'Buddhist Modernism and the Rhetoric of Meditative Experience.' *Numen,* 42/3: 228–83.

Sheerin, Bill (2003). 'The Irish Astrological Society'. Available at: http://www.radical-astrology.com/irish/ias/IAS.html

Sheehan, Donal (ed.) (1990). *Alternative Ireland Directory*. 4th edn, Cork: Quay Co-op.

Shepherd, Graham (2011). *Travels With a Monkey Mind*. Witchford: E-Books.

Sherwood, Patricia (2001). 'Buddhist Contribution to Social Welfare in Australia'. *Journal of Buddhist Ethics,* 8: 61–74.

Shiels, John (1998). *Ecumenical Buddhism*. Unpublished Thesis, Trinity College Dublin.

Shiro, Naito (1972). 'Yeats and Zen Buddhism'. *The Eastern Buddhist*, 5/2: 171–78.

Silvestri, Michael (2009). *Ireland and Empire*. Cambridge: Cambridge University Press.

Simmer-Brown, Judith (2002). 'The Roar of the Lioness', 309–23, in Charles Prebish and Martin Baumann (eds), *Westward Dharma*. Berkeley, CA: University of California Press.

Singh, Maina (2006). 'Political Activism and the Politics of Spirituality', 39–57, in Tadhg Foley and Maureen O'Connor (eds), *Ireland and India*. Dublin/ Portland: Irish Academic Press.

Sirisena, Mihirini and Laurence Cox (2013). 'What Buddhism?' Paper to 2nd ISASR Annual Conference, Dublin (May).

Skeggs, Beverley (1997). *Formations of Class and Gender*. London: SAGE.

Skuce, Stephen (2006), *The Faiths of Ireland*. Blackrock: Columba Press.

Smith, Caroline (2008). 'Introduction', xi–xl, in John of Joinville and Geoffrey of Villehardouin, *Chronicles of The Crusades*. London: Penguin.

Snyder, Gary (1990). *The Practice of The Wild: Essays*. San Francisco, CA: North Point.

Sproule, John (1854). *The Irish Industrial Exhibition of 1853*. Dublin: McGlashan.

Spuler, Michelle (2002). 'The Development of Buddhism in Australia and New Zealand', 139–51, in Charles Prebish and Martin Baumann (eds), *Westward Dharma*. Berkeley, CA: University of California Press.

Stark, Rodney (1987). 'How New Religions Succeed', 11–29, in David Bromley and Philip Hammond (eds), *The Future of New Religious Movements*. Macon, GA: Mercer University Press.

Stark, Rodney and William Bainbridge (1985). *The Future of Religion: Secularization, Revival and Cult Formation*. Berkeley, CA: University of California Press.

Starr, Ruth (2009). 'Japanese Art and Design in Ireland'. Paper to 'Asian Art and Ireland' Conference, National Museum of Ireland (November).

Stoneman, Richard (ed.) (1991). *The Greek Alexander Romance*. London: Penguin.

Stoneman, Richard (1995). 'Naked Philosophers'. *Journal of Hellenic Studies*, 115: 99–114.

Sutcliffe, Steven (2004). 'The Dynamics of Alternative Spirituality', 466–90, in James Lewis (ed.), *The Oxford Handbook of New Religious Movements*. Oxford: Oxford University Press.

Sutin, Lawrence (2006). *All Is Change*. New York: Little, Brown.

Suzuki, Daisetz (1969). *The Field of Zen*. London: Buddhist Society.

Tarchin, Jinpa (1995–6). 'An Irish Monk on Holy Island'. *The Well*, vol. 1 issue 4 (winter): 2–7.

Taylor, Donald (1999). 'Conversion', 35–50, in Christopher Lamb and M. Darrol Bryant (eds), *Religious Conversion*. London: Cassell.

Taylor, Lawrence (1995). *Occasions of Faith*. Dublin: Lilliput.

Teltscher, Kate (2006). *The High Road to China*. London: Bloomsbury.

Thelle, Notto (1987). *Buddhism and Christianity in Japan*. Honolulu: University of Hawaii Press.

Thompson, E.P. (1968). *The Making of the English Working Class*. 2nd edn, Harmondsworth: Penguin.

— (1978). *The Poverty of Theory and Other Essays*. London: Merlin.

— (1993). *Witness Against the Beast*. Cambridge: Cambridge University Press.

Thundy, Zacharias (1993). *Buddha and Christ*. Amsterdam: Brill.

Tierney, J.J. (1967). *Dicuil: liber de mensura orbis terrae*. Dublin: Institute for Advanced Studies.

Tonkinson, Carole (ed.) (1995). *Big Sky Mind*. New York: Putnam's.

Trinity Comprehensive School (2009). *Adult Education Programme for Autumn 2009*. Dublin: Trinity Comprehensive.

Trumbull, Robert (1956). *As I See India*. New York: W. Sloane.

Turner, Alicia (2009). *Buddhism, Colonialism and the Boundaries of Religion*. Unpublished PhD Dissertation, University of Chicago Faculty of Divinity, Chicago, USA.

— (2010). 'The Irish Pongyi in Colonial Burma'. *Contemporary Buddhism* (11/2): 149-71.

— (2011). 'Buddhism Across Colonial Contexts With an Irish Ally'. Paper to American Association for Asian Studies/International Convention of Asia Scholars Conference (April).

Turner, Alicia, Laurence Cox and Brian Bocking (2010). 'Beachcombing, Going Native and Freethinking'. *Contemporary Buddhism* (11/2): 125-47.

Tweed, Thomas (2000). The American Encounter with Buddhism 1844-1912. Chapel Hill, NC: University of North Carolina Press.

— (2002). 'Who Is a Buddhist?', 17-33, in Charles Prebish and Martin Baumann (eds), *Westward Dharma*. Berkeley & Los Angeles, CA: University of California Press.

— (2006). *Crossing and Dwelling*. Cambridge, MA: Harvard University Press.

— (2010). 'Towards the Study of Vernacular Intellectualism'. *Contemporary Buddhism* (11/2): 281-86.

— (2011). 'Theory and Method in the Study of Buddhism'. *Journal of Global Buddhism* 12: 17-32.

Urquhart, Diane (2000). *Women in Ulster Politics 1890-1940*. Dublin: Irish Academic Press.

Victoria, Brian (2006). *Zen at War*. 2nd edn, Lanham, MD: Rowman and Littlefeld.

Vishvapani, Dharmachari (1994). 'Buddhism and the New Age'. *Western Buddhist Review*, 1: 9-22.

— (2001). 'Perceptions of the FWBO in British Buddhism'. *Western Buddhist Review*, 3; Available at: http://www.westernbuddhistreview.com/vol3/Perceptions.htm

Viswanathan, Gauri (1998). *Outside the Fold*. Princeton, NJ: Princeton University Press.

von Siebold, Alexander (1984). *Acta Sieboldiana, vol. 9*. Wiesbaden: Otto Harrassowitz.

Wainwright, Hilary (1994). *Arguments For a New Left*. Oxford: Blackwell.

Wallace, Pat (2009). 'Welcome and Opening Remarks'. Paper to 'Asian Art and Ireland' Conference, National Museum of Ireland (November).

Wallerstein, Immanuel (1988). 'World-systems Analysis', 309-24, in Anthony Giddens and Jonathan Turner (eds), *Social Theory Today*. Cambridge: Polity.

Walsh, Ed (2011). 'Educating Irish People to Live and Work Successfully'. *Irish Times*, November 25.

Walshe, Maurice (1980). *Buddhism and Christianity*. Kandy: Buddhist Publication Society (Wheel 275–76).

Watt, James (2006). 'Goldsmith's Cosmopolitanism', 56–75, in *Eighteenth-century Life* 30/1.

Watters, Thomas (1904–1905). T.W. Rhys Davids and S.W. Bushnell (eds), *On Yuan Chwang's Travels in India, 629–45 AD*. London: Royal Asiatic Society.

Weatherford, Jack (2004). *Genghis Khan and the Making of the Modern World*. New York: Crown.

Weber, Max (1922). *Wirtschaft und Gesellschaft*. Tübingen: Mohr.

— (1967). *The Religion of India*. New York: Free Press.

— (1978). *Economy and Society* (2 vols.) Berkeley, CA: University of California Press.

Wei Wu Wei (1970). *All Else is Bondage*. Hong Kong: Hong Kong University Press.

Welch, Christina (2007). 'Complicating Spiritual Appropriation'. *Journal of Alternative Spiritualities and New Age Studies*, 3: 97–117.

Welch, Robert and Bruce Stewart (1996). *The Oxford Companion to Irish Literature*. Oxford: Oxford University Press.

Westlake, John (1911). *The Prose Life of Alexander*. London: Kegan Paul.

Wetzel, Sylvia (2002). 'Neither Monk Nor Nun', 275–84, in Charles Prebish and Martin Baumann (eds), *Westward Dharma*. Berkeley, CA: University of California Press.

Whitty, Audrey (2009). 'The Albert Bender Collection of Chinese, Japanese, and Tibetan Buddhist Art in the NMI in Art-historical Context.' Paper to 'Asian Art and Ireland' Conference, National Museum of Ireland (November).

— (2011). The Albert Bender Collection of Asian Art in the National Museum of Ireland. Bray: Wordwell.

Wickremeratne, L.A. (1982). 'An American Bodhisattva and An Irish Karmayogin'. *Journal of the American Academy of Religion*, vol. 50 no. 2 (June): 237–54.

Williams, Duncan and Christopher Queen (eds) (1999). *American Buddhism*. Richmond: Curzon.

Williams, Raymond (1981). *Culture*. London: Fontana.

— (1982). *Problems in Materialism and Culture*. London: Verso.

— (1989). *The Politics of Modernism*. London: Verso.

— (1999). 'Culture is Ordinary' (orig. 1958), 10–24 in John Higgins (ed.), *The Raymond Williams Reader*. Oxford: Wiley-Blackwell.

Williamson, J.A. (1946). 'Richard Hakluyt', 9–46, in Edward Lynam (ed.), *Richard Hakluyt and His Successors*. London: Hakluyt Society.

Wilson, Joseph (2009). 'The Life of the Saint and the Animal'. *Journal for the Study of Religion, Nature and Culture* 3/2: 169–94.

Wise, Thomas, (1884) *History of Paganism in Caledonia*. London: Trübner.

Wood, Frances (1998). *Did Marco Polo Go to China?* Boulder, CO: Westview.

Wright, Julia (2007). *Ireland, India and Nationalism in Nineteenth-century Literature*. Cambridge: Cambridge University Press.

Yeates, Padraig (2000). *Lockout*. Dublin: Gill and Macmillan.

Yeats, William Butler (1926a). *Autobiographies*. London: Macmillan.
— (1926b). *Late Poems*. London: Macmillan.
— (1986). *Collected Letters, vol. 1*. Oxford: Clarendon.
Yeshe, Lama (1998).'The Refuge Tree'. *The Well*, vol. 4/1–3: 3–20.
Young, Ella (1945). *Flowering Dusk*. London: Longman's, Green and Co.
Yoshinaga, Shin'ichi (2007). 'Japanese Buddhism and the Theosophical Movement', 80–86, in Yoshinaga Shin'ichi, Akai Toshio, Hashimoto Yorimitsu and Jeff Shore, *Hirai Kinza and the Globalization of Japanese Buddhism of Meiji Era*. Available at: http://www.maizuru-ct.ac.jp/human/yosinaga/hirai_kaken_report_16520060.pdf
Yule, Henry and Henri Cordier (eds) (1903). *The Book of Ser Marco Polo, the Venetian*. 3rd edn, London: Murray.
Žižek, Slavoj (2001). 'From Western Marxism to Western Buddhism'. *Cabinet Magazine Online* Issue 2 (spring): 1–4. Available at: http://www.cabinet-magazine.org/issues/2/western.php
Zukin, Sharon (1989). *Loft Living*. New Brunswick, NJ: Rutgers University Press.

Index